ACCOUNTS AND RECORDS OF THE MANOR OF MOTE IN IDEN

1442–1551, 1673

Illustration of an idealized moated manor house and park in the initial capital of the licence to crenellate the dwelling-place of The Mote granted to Sir Edmund de Pashley in 1318 (ESRO ACC 7001)

ACCOUNTS AND RECORDS OF THE MANOR OF MOTE IN IDEN

1442–1551, 1673

EDITED BY

MARK GARDINER AND CHRISTOPHER WHITTICK

SUSSEX RECORD SOCIETY
VOLUME 92

Issued to members of the Society for the year 2008

Published 2011 by
Sussex Record Society
Barbican House,
High Street,
Lewes,
East Sussex, BN7 1YE.

ISBN 978 0 85445 074 9

Printed by Hobbs the Printers Ltd., Totton, Hampshire.

SUSSEX RECORD SOCIETY

VOLUMES ISSUED BY THE SOCIETY

Volumes marked with an asterisk can be obtained from the Hon. Secretary, Sussex Record Society, Barbican House, Lewes, East Sussex, BN7 1YE.

CONTENTS

TABLES

ILLUSTRATIONS

ACKNOWLEDGEMENTS

This volume consists of records preserved at the East Sussex Record Office and our thanks are due to the County Archivist for encouraging their publication.

We have received valued assistance from Sir John Baker, John Blair, Lesley Boatwright, Martin Brown, Bruce Campbell, Michael Carter, Margot Charlton, Pam Combes, James Davies, John Dines, David Grummitt, Diana Hansen, Paul Harvey, Roy Hunnisett, Susanne Jenks, Casper Johnson, Gwen Jones, John Langdon, Tim McCann, Darryl Major, Libby Mulqueeny, Vicky Pannell, Jason Peacey, Nigel Saul, Henry Summerson, Chris Thornton, Pamela Tudor-Craig, Martin Watts and Chris Woolgar regarding specific points of information, and are particularly grateful to the History of Parliament Trust for making available the draft texts of entries in the section covering 1422-1509.

Anne Drewery checked the text against the original documents on several occasions, and made many helpful suggestions regarding the introduction. Special thanks are due to David and Barbara Martin for drawing attention to the importance of the archive, for making available to us their plans of the manorial tenements, and for constant encouragement and assistance. It is our particular pleasure to dedicate this volume to them.

We owe final thanks to Chris Leighton, whose meticulous indexing has saved us from many errors and inconsistencies, to John Barnes for his careful and thorough work in finalising the text and to Peter Wilkinson, whose indefatigable patience and optimism over a long period has encouraged us to see the work through to completion.

March 2011

Mark Gardiner
Christopher Whittick

This volume is dedicated to David and Barbara Martin, who first introduced the editors to the documents which form the basis of this volume, and whose own work and assistance has been an invaluable element in its production.

INTRODUCTION

This volume consists of an edition, in translation, of four groups of documents held at East Sussex Record Office, Lewes, relating to the manor of Mote in Iden, and dating from 1442 to 1673. They are manorial accounts, dating from 1464 to 1484 (ESRO NOR 15/103-121); a court roll of the manor, 1442-1551 (NOR 15/1); a rental of the manor, compiled in 1478 (NOR 15/13); and a survey of 1673 (NOR 15/92). It has been edited and indexed in accordance with the principles set out by R. F. Hunnisett in 1972 and 1977.[1]

The text of the records themselves is preceded by an introduction which sets out their historical context. It examines the descent of the manor, its purchase by Sir John Scott, his career and character and the management of his demesne and household at Mote. The later descent of the manor, the history of the archive and the diplomatic of the documents are then discussed. The final part of the introduction considers the use of stock-deeds and the nature of manorial tenure in the Weald of Sussex, and sets out the editorial conventions used in the text. Appendices provide examples of stock-deeds in calendar form, a prosopography of the leading individuals mentioned in the accounts, identify the location of the tenements of Mote manor and provide a glossary of archaic or obscure words. For the sake of brevity the accounts are referred to in the introduction by harvest year, whereby the account which (ostensibly) runs from Michaelmas 1476 to Michaelmas 1477 appears as 1477.

Historians must distil from their sources a clear understanding of motivation, experience and character. The more strictly the format of the source is dictated by convention, the more difficult it is to discern the human actors behind the record in question. The Mote manorial accounts, the central record printed in this volume, adhere only loosely to the prescribed form of such records. They cover the usual matter of demesne accounts – the income from rents and sales and the expenditure on the business of agriculture and on buildings – but also the sort of entries which might otherwise have been placed in household accounts and in building records.[2] All the financial transactions which took place at Mote have been forced into the conventional structure of the manorial account, and the resulting record is consequently of the utmost interest. It is the breadth of information in a single series of records, together with the detail provided to justify the expenditure to the auditor, which makes them so informative about this late fifteenth-century estate on the border of Kent and Sussex.

---

[1] R. F. Hunnisett, *Indexing for Editors* (British Records Association, Archives and the User Series 2. London, 1972); R. F. Hunnisett, *Editing Records for Publication* (British Records Association, Archives and the User Series 4. London, 1977).

[2] For such records, see *Household Accounts from Medieval England* (Records of Social and Economic History, new series XVII, XVIII. Oxford, 1993), ed. C. M. Woolgar; E. M. Myatt-Price, 'Examples of techniques in medieval building accounts', *Abacus* 2 (1966), 41-48.

Manorial accounts survive mainly from the two centuries or less in the late Middle Ages when lords directly cultivated their own demesne lands, using the customary labour of their tenants. Before and after the thirteenth and fourteenth centuries most lords found it more profitable, and certainly less onerous, to lease their demesnes to others who would cultivate them and make what profit they could, while paying the lord a fixed rent or 'farm'. When estates were run directly by their lords, the accounts prepared by the manorial reeves were highly informative. Once direct management had been abandoned, as was increasingly the case after 1400, demesne accounts, if they survive at all, are much less informative. The lessee or farmer did not have to account for live or dead stock and might record only the allowable expenses, typically those involving repairs to buildings.[3] In Norfolk, a county possessing a relative abundance of medieval records, the number of accounts declines from the 1380s, and from 1450 onwards only an insignificant number survive. So for reasons which owe more to accounting conventions than to changes in farming practice, the almost complete cessation of the direct management of demesnes marks the effective end of the most valuable source of information on the operation of agriculture in medieval England.[4]

For that reason alone, any series of accounts from the 1460s, 70s and 80s would be of interest. The accounts of the manor of Mote, however, have a much wider significance. In 1471 Scott decided to take the management of the manor back into his own hands. As a result, the documents edited here allow us to observe the process of transition from a leasehold regime to one of demesne agriculture. We expect manorial accounts to shed light on the agrarian economy and the Mote accounts do not disappoint us. It is, perhaps, more surprising to find records of the expenditure of the household among them. The Norfolk lord, John Paston, wrote to his wife in 1465 instructing her not to include any household expenses and foreign payments within the manorial accounts, but that doctrine was ignored by the accountants at Mote.[5] These accounts, therefore, reach beyond the farmyard and fields to reveal the life of the manor house and its occupants. They provide an insight into the activities of a gentry family and the management of their estate in a time of considerable political upheaval. It is possible to follow the comings and goings of Sir John Scott's officials and the arrival of the lord and his lady at Mote, and to pick up an echo of the tumultuous events of 1470, the re-appearance of Henry VI and the return the following year of Edward IV.

---

[3] P. D. A. Harvey, *Manorial Records* (British Records Association, Archives and the User Series 5, revised edn. London, 1999), 35-37.

[4] B. M. S. Campbell, *English Seigniorial Agriculture 1250-1450* (Cambridge, 2000), fig. 2.01 shows the steep decline in surviving Norfolk accounts. Norfolk is an exceptionally well documented county, but reflects the pattern of evidence more generally. For farming out of lands, see J .L. Bolton, *The Medieval English Economy, 1150-1500* (London, 1980), 220.

[5] C. Richmond, *John Hopton. A Fifteenth Century Suffolk Gentleman* (Cambridge, 1981), 50; *Paston Letters and Papers of the Fifteenth Century*, ed. N. Davis (Early English Text Society, supplementary series 20), 1, 142.

Mote lay at the edge of Sir John Scott's estate, which had its centre in the eastern Weald of Kent. Nevertheless, in 1466 Scott cast aside his initial decision merely to extend the manor house at Mote and determined to construct a grand building more appropriate to his status. The accounts provide, like the near-contemporary records for Tattershall Castle and Kirby Muxloe, detailed information about the building process, the labourers and craftsmen and the supply of building materials.[6] We can learn about the way in which the building was planned and the works undertaken, and form a reliable estimate of the costs of construction.

Finally, the accounts also allow us to examine the patterns of sales and purchases of commodities in a period for which relatively little information about the operation of markets survives: these records provide a window through which to examine the nature of commercial activity in the closing decades of the fifteenth century. Many of the transactions made outside any market – the sales which Christopher Dyer has referred to as the 'hidden trade' – are revealed, at least in part, in these accounts.[7] They also shed light on another aspect of fifteenth-century trade in south-east England: the exchange of goods with Calais. Sir John Scott, as Marshal of Calais from 1472, was particularly aware of the market for produce in the English territories in France. Animals were butchered at Mote and sealed into barrels for sale on the other side of the Channel, and he also dispatched firewood to Calais in enormous quantities. Equally, he was able to obtain goods for his estate, including millstones and glass from continental Europe.

Today the site of all this activity and endeavour is a deserted rectangular platform in an idyllic landscape of water and reeds. The buildings on which Sir John Scott lavished such attention and treasure have entirely disappeared. The documents edited here bring this landscape and the men and women who worked there vividly alive, and with it shine light on the political, social and economic life of the eastern end of Sussex in the second half of the fifteenth century.

THE DESCENT OF THE LORDSHIP OF MOTE TO THE DEATH OF SIR JOHN SCOTT IN 1485

The origins of the manor of Mote and the Pashley family

The Mote is first mentioned in 1318, when Sir Edmund de Pashley, lord of the manor of Leigh in Iden, obtained a licence to crenellate his dwelling-place of The

---

[6] *The Building Accounts of Tattershall Castle, 1434-1472* (Lincoln Record Society 55 (1960)), ed. W. D. Simpson; A. Hamilton Thompson, 'The building accounts of Kirby Muxloe Castle, 1480--1484', *Transactions of the Leicestershire Architectural and Archaeological Society* 11 (1913--1920), 193-345.

[7] C. C. Dyer, *Everyday Life in Medieval England* (London, 1994), 283-303.

Mote (Frontispiece).[8] Whether the site of Mote represents the ancient *curia* of the manor is uncertain; by the sixteenth century, when Leigh and Mote had become distinct entities, Barons Grange in Iden was the manor house of Leigh.

Sir Edmund's father Robert, the son of Ralph de Alderstead of Merstham in Surrey, probably assumed the surname Pashley only on his marriage to Sarah, the heiress of an estate centred on Pashley in Ticehurst, in about 1265.[9] He and his son Edmund Pashley purchased the manor of Leigh in 1289 from Hamo de Crevequer, whose ancestors had held it from before 1166. Hamo reserved a sizeable rent of £23 a year for his life, and in 1298 his widow Alice secured a pension of £3 6s 8d in lieu of her dower rights in the manor. In the same year Edmund obtained a grant of free warren in Leigh. Alice seems to have maintained an interest in the manor – in 1306 Edmund Pashley paid a further £100 to Bartholomew de Setfontain and his wife Alice, possibly Hamo's widow, to extinguish their claim to Leigh.

Edmund probably received a university education in Roman law (possibly at Oxford), but pursued a career in the common law. His first known employment was as steward of the rape of Hastings (in 1298), and he later served as steward of the liberty of the archbishop of Canterbury between 1298 and 1302. He was appointed a justice of the London eyre of 1321 soon after it opened, and seems to have been knighted shortly before he took his seat on the bench. He sat as a Baron of the Exchequer from the beginning of Michaelmas term 1323 to the end of Michaelmas term 1326.

Leigh was probably acquired as part of Edmund's settlement on his first wife Maud, the daughter and heir of John de Kitchenour, to whom he was married by 1288.

Maud was dead by 1318, and thereafter Sir Edmund's matrimonial history becomes confused. It seems that he had married Joan, a member of the Greyly family, with whom he acquired the manors of Crimsham in Pagham and Evegate in Kent,[10] but by November 1318 he and his wife Margaret, the widow of William de Basing, were granted a market and fair at Empingham in Rutland, a manor that had belonged to her father Thomas de Normanville. By June 1319 they had a son Edmund, and at least three more children followed. The story of Margaret's successful attempt to promote her children's interests, which probably involved the poisoning of her husband in 1327 and the murder in the following year of two of his sons, her predecessor Maud Kitchenour's children, has been ably told by Nigel Saul.[11] Maud's surviving son John de Pashley pursued his

---

[8] For an account of the descent of the manors of Leigh and Mote, see *VCH Sx* 9 153-54; the licence to crenellate survives as ESRO ACC 7001 (see frontispiece).

[9] P. Brand, 'Passele, Sir Edmund (*b*. in or before 1267, *d.* 1327)', *Oxford Dictionary of National Biography* (Oxford, 2004).

[10] *VCH Sx* 4, 230; N. H. MacMichael 'The descent of the manor of Evegate in Smeeth', *AC* 74 (1960), 1-47.

[11] N. Saul, *Scenes from Provincial Life* (Oxford, 1986) 85-87; N. Saul, 'Murder and justice, medieval style'; *History Today* 34 (1984), 30-35; MacMichael, 'Descent of the manor of Evegate'.

stepmother and her Pashley sons through the courts for more than ten years, but seems to have recovered nothing. He was able to retain only his mother's manor of Kitchenour, and Crimsham; Mote, Pashley in Ticehurst and his father's other manors in Sussex and Surrey all descended to the offspring of Margaret de Basing. The beginning of Sir Edmund Pashley's relationship with Margaret can be dated to 1317 or 1318, and it is perhaps no coincidence that on 10 December 1318 he obtained a licence to crenellate 'his dwelling-place (*mansum*) of The Mote'. Perhaps Margaret had no desire to live in the houses of her predecessors, and required a newly-built home on land with a clear title. The surviving licence (Frontispiece) incorporates an elaborate depiction of the building, including a chapel complete with chantry priest, and in 1320 Sir Edmund transferred to the new house the chapel of Leigh, which he had founded and generously endowed in 1304. The relocation was accompanied by a further grant of lands in Sussex, and the advowson of Fairlight; the writ *ad quod damnum* of May 1320 to permit the endowment describes Mote as newly built, and the resulting inquisition was convened there in September. A further tranche of land in Romney Marsh was added in 1326, and the tempting conclusion is that Sir Edmund, having spent almost a decade ignoring the advice of his confessors to abandon Margaret and return to his lawful wife, was nevertheless concerned for the health of his immortal soul.[12]

By 1389 Mote and Leigh were two distinct manors, but it is unclear when and by what means the division had taken place.[13] It may even have occurred before the purchase of 'Leigh' by Robert and Edmund Pashley in 1289. The previous year Leigh's owner Hamo de Crevequer had come to an agreement with John Blundel to partition Hamo's rents in Leigh, Northiam, Iden and Peasmarsh – among the rents which John acquired, eighteen shillings were paid by William son of Richard de Leigh for a tenement in Iden, whose homage and service Hamo retained. In 1351 Thomas Pashley was entitled to the wardship and marriage of the heir of Leigh, and by 1478 the manor of Leigh was deemed to be held of Mote by a quitrent of a halfpenny.[14] Since Leigh seems to have had no tenements and no manorial jurisdiction, it is possible that its separate existence was the result of Hamo de Crevequer's alienation of the rent from Leigh immediately before he sold the rest of his rights to the Pashleys. What they acquired became the manor of Mote, and its entitlement to the halfpenny quitrent was the surviving evidence of the right to the homage of Leigh, which Crevequer had retained and presumably sold to the Pashleys.[15]

---

[12] TNA PRO C143/50 no 7; *CPR 1324-27*, 299; MacMichael, quoting TNA PRO SC 8/266/3293.

[13] John Salerne, a Rye merchant, mayor and MP for the town, was lord of Leigh by 1389, when he attempted to obtain a papal bull for a chaplain at his manor house there; for an account of him, see *The House of Commons 1386-1421* 4, 286-87.

[14] ESRO NOR 15/60; NOR 15/13.

[15] *An Abstract of Feet of Fines for the County of Sussex from 34 Henry III to 35 Edward I (SRS* 7 (1903)), ed. L. F. Salzman, 1027, 1038; the descent of the two manors in *VCH Sx* 9 is unsatisfactory, and confused by the tendency of contemporary documents to use the term Leigh to refer to the manor of Mote.

On the death of Margaret de Basing in 1341 the manor of Mote passed to her sons Thomas, Edmund and Robert in turn, and from Robert to his great-grandson Sir John Pashley, who died in 1453.[16] Throughout this period, the family's interests lay chiefly in Kent.

Sir John Pashley (1398-1453) served in France from before 1422, and in 1426 left Poole with his own force of thirty men-at-arms and ninety archers.[17] Despite inheriting a large estate in Cornwall and Oxfordshire from his mother Philippa Cergeaux and a marriage into the powerful Woodville family of Northamptonshire, Sir John mismanaged his affairs, and left a muddled inheritance. The evidence points to a chronic shortage of funds, but whether as a result of the need for a ransom, the costs of campaigning or simple financial ineptitude is unclear: on at least one occasion Sir John's illiteracy, increasingly rare in a man of his class, led to his being defrauded by his lawyer. His first wife, Elizabeth Woodville, died in the 1430s, and at some date after 1443 he married Alice, the widow of William Ryman of Appledram, a lawyer retained by the Earl of Arundel; her first husband, John Beaufitz of Gillingham in Kent, had died in 1433. Rated at over £13 a year, Mote was the most valuable of Sir John's six Sussex manors at his death in 1453, although it was overshadowed by his principal residence, Evegate in Kent, assessed at over £20.[18] Following litigation in Chancery, on 20 October 1454 Sir John's feoffees vested his remaining manors in Sussex and Kent in his son John Pashley (c1432-68).[19] The deeds, sealed at Evegate, were witnessed by John Scott and Robert Horne, and the feoffees appointed John Tregoff, the town clerk of Rye, to deliver seisin. John Pashley had been a freeman of the port since 1452, and sat as its MP in 1455.

Like his father, John Pashley seems to have been in chronic need of money. As well as inherited debts, and involvement in the financial liabilities of his brother-in-law Richard Gower, it is possible that John, in a fruitless attempt to keep up with his Woodville cousins, simply lived beyond his means: his elegant heraldic seal, with a counterseal showing a barking mastiff with the legend *Passhle*, suggests a man who liked to cut a dash.[20] Pashley continued the practice of his ancestors by raising money from the manor of Mote by creating new freehold tenures: two were granted at The Mote on 17 April 1455; the necessary deeds were written by John Tregoff, whom Pashley described as his servant.[21] Pashley seems to have antagonized the tenants of his manor. In 1456 he was the object of a claim for damages by Thomas Fowle whose livestock and household

---

[16] The descent is set out in a case in Common Pleas in 1433: TNA PRO CP 40/690, m. 125, and by MacMichael, 'The descent of the manor of Evegate'.

[17] TNA PRO E101/71/2, no. 822.

[18] TNA PRO C139/149/26.

[19] History of Parliament Trust, London, unpublished article on John Pashley for 1422-1509 section by Linda Clark, 2003; we are grateful to the Trust for allowing us to see this article in draft.

[20] For fine examples of this seal, see CKS U455/T122/7 and BL Add MS 16156.

[21] CKS U455 T121/4, T123/5 (Tufton Place in Northiam), printed as Appendix 1 number 5; T122/7-8 (two crofts in Northiam), printed as Appendix 1 number 6; in 1646, Nathaniel Powell had the counterpart of the first grant: NOR 15/60, p. 23.

goods had been seized by Pashley, described as of Rye, and a group of six local men. Pashley's defence was that Fowle was his bondman, and indeed he can probably be identified with the Thomas Fowle who in 1478 held a large estate at Flackley Ash in Peasmarsh, including eight tenements of the manor of Mote. To be in dispute with a manorial tenant is understandable; to reach the stage of being sued by one of them in the court of Common Pleas reveals a failure of good lordship.

In the course of 1458 John Pashley made a feoffment of the manor of Mote to Nicholas Sharp, Thomas Sharp and John Grene, who enfeoffed Sir John Cheyne of Kent, William Beaufitz, citizen of London, John Scott, esquire, and John Methlay, gentleman, to whom Pashley quitclaimed the manor on 6 December 1458. On 12 June the following year Pashley granted the patronage and advowson of the chapel 'belonging to the manor of old called The Legh, now The Mote' to the same group of men. This transaction may have begun as a mortgage, but in the autumn of 1460 the manor of Mote was definitively conveyed to John Scott by a final concord.[22]

The Pashleys and their Woodville relatives were adherents of the house of Lancaster, and John Scott was at the centre of the Yorkist lords' project to place Edward Earl of March on the throne. It is tempting to associate Scott's final acquisition of Mote with the Yorkist victory at Northampton in July 1460, but there were less momentous reasons why Pashley might have turned to Scott to raise funds. John Scott and the Pashleys were no strangers. Their estates in Brabourne were intertwined, and the Pashley manor there would pass by marriage to Scott's grandson John Scott in the first decade of the sixteenth century. As early as 1445 John Scott, his stepfather Gervase Clifton and Sir John Pashley had witnessed the deed by which the manor of Brabourne was settled on Joan Lewknor, and almost a decade later John Scott and his ally Robert Horne were present when Sir John's feoffees vested the Pashley estates, including Mote, in his son John Pashley.[23] But the most important factor was probably the family relationship between the Pashleys and the Scotts. Pashley's stepmother Alice was first married to John Beaufitz, the elder brother of Scott's father-in-law William Beaufitz. The two years during which Mote was transferred to John Scott most probably encompass the occasion of his marriage to Agnes Beaufitz – their first son William Scott was born in 1459 – and it is tempting to see the acquisition of Mote as part of a marriage settlement, brokered in part by William Beaufitz.

The life and career of Sir John Scott

When John Scott acquired the manor of Mote at the end of the 1450s he was already a force to be reckoned with in Kentish politics and society, but had not

---

22 BL Add Ms 16156, 16325.
23 CKS U1115 T13/3, *CPR 1454-1461*, 44.

yet come to the national eminence he was to achieve with the Yorkist ascent to the throne in 1461.

John Scott (1423-1485) was the son of William Scott of Scots Hall in Smeeth near Brabourne, Kent, and his second wife Isabel, daughter of Vincent Finch of Netherfield in Battle (Illus. 1). To a greater degree than his father, John Scott was to develop interests in both counties, but although by the accident of archival survival we are able to know far more about his activities in Sussex, we should not forget that Kent was always the centre of the family's concerns. The Scotts were long established in Brabourne and lord of a manor or two, but William Scott enhanced the family's standing and his own wealth by serving as a lawyer for not only Robert, Lord Poynings, but also the prelate John Kemp, to whom he was related.[24] It was probably Kemp's influence which secured him the offices of escheator of Kent and Middlesex, sheriff of Kent and a justice of the peace. In 1420 he began to build a mansion at Smeeth; completed by 1429, it was to become known as Scots Hall.[25] One of the wealthiest men in Kent, Scott died on 5 February 1434, leaving six under-age children. By the end of the year John Kemp, now archbishop of York (where he was rarely seen), had arranged a marriage between his protégé Gervase Clifton and Scott's widow, who consented only on condition that she should be allowed control over the thousand marks bequeathed to her to carry out the provisions of William Scott's will.[26]

The evidence demonstrates that the relationship between Clifton and his stepson John Scott was close, and on several occasions after 1461 Scott would intervene to rescue Clifton from the ultimately fatal consequences of his recidivist support for the house of Lancaster. Clifton's pattern of office-holding, in Kent, Calais, the Cinque Ports and the royal household, foreshadows that of his stepson, but from the perspective of Scott's activities as a builder, it was Clifton's service as a feoffee of Ralph, Lord Cromwell, and eventual marriage to his co-heiress, which was to have the most tangible results.

Clifton's influence determined the early career of his stepson. John Scott may have attended an inn of Chancery to obtain a preliminary legal education, and began to appear on Kentish commissions in 1450.[27] In June that year Scott, Robert Horne and John Fogge were ordered by the council to resist Cade's rebels in Kent, and they and Clifton received a reward of £100 in August, and a customs

---

[24] He acted for Kemp as custodian of the temporalities of his dioceses of Rochester and Chichester.

[25] History of Parliament Trust, London, unpublished article on William Scott for 1422-1509 section by David Grummitt. We are grateful to the History of Parliament Trust for allowing us to see this article in draft; Peter Fleming, 'Scott family (*per. c.*1400–*c.*1525)', *Oxford Dictionary of National Biography* (Oxford, 2004).

[26] History of Parliament Trust, London, unpublished article on Sir Gervase Clifton for 1422-1509 section by David Grummitt. We are grateful to the History of Parliament Trust for allowing us to see this article in draft.

[27] He and John Fogge were retained as counsel by Archbishop Bourgchier in 1479-80 (F. R. H. Du Boulay, *The Lordship of Canterbury: An Essay on Medieval Society* (London, 1966), 275-76), but although the first-named arbitrator in a case concerning John Pympe, Scott was not one of the two described as a 'learned man': CKS U1115 E1.

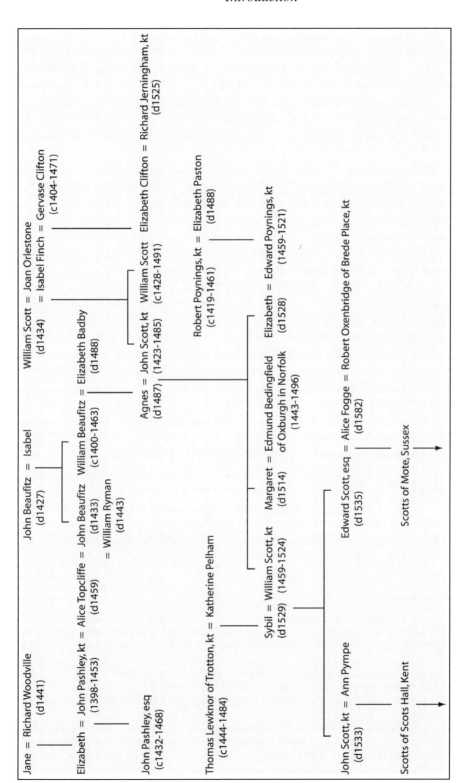

Illus. 1   Pedigree of the Scott family of Kent and Sussex

exemption to recoup the five hundred marks they had borrowed to finance their campaign. In June 1452 Clifton and Scott were among the grantees of the temporalities of the lordship of Canterbury pending John Kemp's translation from York. Clifton and possibly Scott had met Richard, Duke of York in France in 1441, but there is no evidence that they or any of the group were attracted to him politically in the 1450s; rather the reverse. Scott was a king's esquire by 1456, was involved in military exercises in Kent and joined the county bench in 1458.

Perhaps with the death of Scott's mother on 20 December 1457, Clifton's influence on his stepson began to wane. Scott may have married at about this time: on 26 January 1458 his father-in-law William Beaufitz made a grant of all his goods, chattels and debts to a group of men headed by Ralph Butler, but including John Scott of Smeeth.[28]

The turning-point of Scott's life was his decision, in the summer of 1460, finally to abandon his mentor Clifton and support the landing of the Yorkist lords, an invasion which Clifton, as sheriff of Kent, had been prominent in resisting. William Beaufitz seems to have lost favour with the crown towards the end of the 1450s, and Scott's change of heart may suggest the increasing influence of his father-in-law.[29] Warwick, Salisbury and March landed at Sandwich on 26 June. Although they had been involved in every recent array and muster and had been ordered to resist the lords, Scott, Fogge and Horne opened the gates of Canterbury (already posted with Yorkist propaganda), joined their forces and marched with them to London.[30] On 2 July they entered the capital and when, at the end of the month, Sir Thomas Brown was among the defenders of the Tower executed at Tyburn, John Scott was appointed sheriff of Kent in his place. Although on the winning side, Horne was killed at the Battle of Towton on 29 March. On 27 June 1461, the day before Edward IV's coronation, Scott and Fogge were knighted, and emerged as two of the closest servants of Edward IV, and the leaders of political society in Kent. Scott was appointed controller of the royal household and lieutenant of Dover Castle; he sat as MP for Kent in the 1460s, was rewarded with numerous custodies, keeperships and commissions and

---

[28] *CCR 1454-61*, 271; another of the group, John Goldwell, citizen and mercer of London, was later to be bound with John Scott in connection with his acquisition of Chilham Castle: *CCR 1461--68*, 227.

[29] His brother, William Scott, seems to have remained loyal to the crown and his stepfather Clifton: History of Parliament Trust, London, unpublished article on William Scott for 1422-1509 section by David Grummitt. We are grateful to the History of Parliament Trust for allowing us to see this article in draft.

[30] History of Parliament Trust, London, unpublished article on Robert Horne for 1422-1509 section by David Grummitt. We are grateful to the History of Parliament Trust for allowing us to see this article in draft; for the text of a macaronic ballad 'set on the gates of Canterbury', see R. H. Robbins, *Historical Poems of the Fourteenth and Fifteenth Centuries* (New York, 1959), 207-20.

was frequently employed on diplomatic missions of both commercial and dynastic consequence.[31]

Although there is some evidence that Lady Scott may have spent longer periods there when her husband was abroad on diplomatic business, it is clear from the accounts that the Scott household was at Mote only occasionally. Indeed Scott's motivation in investing in the property is open to question. He may have intended to establish a junior, Sussex branch of the family there, as was in fact to happen after the death of his son Sir William Scott in 1524. But military considerations, and in particular Mote's proximity to Rye, at this time supplanting its neighbour Winchelsea as the leading western Cinque Port, may have played their part. When Scott was building a defensible tower at Mote in the second half of the 1460s, few contemporaries would have imagined that the civil wars had run their course; and so it proved. From May 1469 to February 1470, a period for which no accounts survive, Sir John was conducting trade negotiations in Flanders. It was perhaps this absence, rather than any difference in policy, which in 1469 saved Scott from the rebels' denunciation of those, including Sir John Fogge, 'whose covetous rule and guiding' had brought the king and his realm to poverty and misery.[32]

In May 1470, perhaps as suspicion of the Earl of Warwick mounted, Scott was sent by the council to hold Dover Castle. The account for 1470-71 – a year in which building-works at Mote ceased, no courts could be held and few rents collected *propter inquietudinem mundi* – records the purchase of oil for cleaning Scott's armour. The manor was stocked with meat and wheat, perhaps in the expectation of a siege, but it is clear from the accounts that Lady Agnes Scott was left in charge at Mote while Sir John left the country, probably joining Edward IV in his brief exile at The Hague.

The king's triumphant return, and the death of the Earl of Warwick on 14 April 1471, mark another turning-point in the career of Sir John Scott and of the management of the manor of Mote. He immediately succeeded Warwick as lieutenant of the Cinque Ports and by March 1472, as deputy to the lieutenant Lord Hastings, was Marshal of Calais, where he took up residence at Warwick's former house in Pickering Street.[33] Edward IV had suffered from Warwick's ability to use Calais as a rival power-base, and to command the Channel by the additional possession of Dover. In allowing him to hold the two offices, the king at once demonstrated his complete confidence in Sir John Scott, and his

[31] See Fleming, 'Scott family'; J. C. Wedgwood, *History of Parliament: Biographies of the Members of the Commons House, 1439-1509* (London, 1936), 750-52.

[32] R. Horrox, 'Fogge, Sir John (*b.* in or before 1417, *d.* 1490)', *Oxford Dictionary of National Biography* (Oxford, 2004).

[33] TNA PRO C76/172 includes two grants of the property, 'late the Earl of Warwick in which Sir John Scott lately dwelt', and of a plot called The Vines in Castle Street, to Humphrey Talbot, kt, marshal of Calais, who was rebuilding them; 7 March and 14 August 1488.

determination not to allow Hastings to repeat Warwick's exploitation of the simultaneous lieutenancy of the Ports and Calais.[34]

From Calais Scott was sent on diplomatic missions to Burgundy, Utrecht and Bruges.[35] On one these embassies, Duke Charles presented Scott with 'a standing cup gilt with a greyhound in the bottom' and his duchess, Margaret of York, gave 'a little gilt standing cup' to Lady Agnes.[36] Once he had departed for Calais, Scott terminated the lease of Mote's demesne lands and took them back into his own hands. He bought a stock of seed-corn and livestock; thereafter a proportion of Mote's produce was regularly shipped to Calais to provision his household. Firewood was in short supply in Flanders, and Scott took advantage of its abundance in the Sussex Weald to establish a lucrative trade with Calais, a business in which members of Scott's family, Rye merchants and even the vicar of Iden had shares. Scott held annual wood-sales at Orlestone in Kent, and made careful provision in his will for their continuance by his wife, specifying that no timber was to be felled other than for repairs. In or before 1479 Scott constructed a float or dock near Saltcote in Playden, which soon became known as Scott's Float. Over 600,000 billets of wood were shipped from the float between 1481 and 1483; many, if not most of the purchasers were based at Calais or had connections there.

In February 1473 Scott was appointed one of the councillors and tutors to the Prince of Wales. He sat for Appleby in Westmorland in the parliament of 1472-75 and possibly in 1483, perhaps to free the Kent seat for a royal nominee. Evidence for the Scott family's loyalty to Richard III is contradictory. Sir John Scott retained his place on all the Kent commissions and his duties as an ambassador throughout the reign. On 13 June 1484 he obtained a confirmation from Richard of his life pension of fifty marks a year, granted by Edward IV in 1461. In November 1483 his son William Scott was among the Kent and Sussex men commissioned to besiege Sir Thomas Lewknor and other adherents of the Duke of Buckingham, who were holding out at Lewknor's castle at Bodiam. William Scott was a commissioner of array in Sussex and Essex in 1484, was pardoned by Henry VII and in November 1489, when he was knighted with Prince Arthur, was controller of the household and a member of the council. He was twice to serve as sheriff of Kent in Henry's reign. Neither William Scott nor his father was included in the act of attainder of Buckingham's adherents passed in the parliament of January 1484.[37] On the other hand John Stow, who had access to contemporary records now lost, includes 'Scott' among the rebels with

---

[34] For an excellent discussion of the role of Calais in the 1460s and 70s see D. Grummitt, 'William, Lord Hastings and the defence of Calais, 1471-83', in T. Thornton (ed), *Social Attitudes and Political Structures* (Stroud, 2000), 150-67.

[35] Listed by Grummitt, 'Lord Hastings', 157.

[36] In 1487 Agnes Scott bequeathed these treasures to her daughters Elizabeth Poynings and Margaret Bedingfield: TNA PRO PROB 11/8, f. 123.

[37] Fleming, 'Scott family'; *CPR 1476-1485*, 433, 370; A. E. Conway, 'The Maidstone sector of Buckingham's rebellion' *AC* 37 (1925), 97-120.

Fogge and Haute.[38] It is certainly the case that Sir John Scott was required to enter into a recognizance of £1000 in March 1485 to appear before the king and council in September.[39] Richard had good grounds to be wary of the Scotts' loyalty. William Scott was both Sir Thomas Lewknor's son-in-law, and brother-in-law to Edward Poynings, husband of his sister Elizabeth. His inclusion on the commission to reduce Bodiam may have been a test of his allegiance; Sir Thomas's uncle Sir Richard Lewknor of Brambletye was also called to attend.[40]

What can be discerned of Sir John Scott's character, personality and attitudes? For any major landowner and administrator to have survived in the middle years of the fifteenth century was an achievement; to have thrived as he did, leaving major estates in two counties and a son established in a third, with an honourable record of royal service, was something of a triumph. He was clearly not a fighting man – of the three 'captains' who suppressed Cade's rebels in 1450, Robert Horne was the soldier; Scott and Fogge were administrators and accountants. On the accession of Edward IV, Fogge became treasurer of the royal household and Scott its controller, and his close familiarity with accounts is evidenced by his frequent autograph interventions in the margins of the Mote rolls in both English and Latin, and for his personal accounts which he seems to have written himself (Illus. 2).[41] His characteristic hand can be recognized in a Chancery answer of 1483, and his readiness to draw such a document himself may, as has been suggested, indicate that he had received a preliminary legal education at one of the Inns of Chancery.[42] His frequent employment on diplomatic missions, some involving the personal alliances of the royal family, shows that he was trusted by his sovereign. Like his father, who created Scots Hall in Smeeth, Sir John was a builder, and capable of controlling several projects, both official and personal, simultaneously and remotely. Perhaps the traditional makeup of the Mote accounts, compiled when detailed records of income and expenditure were becoming rare in such a format, suggests a conservative outlook, and his readiness to annotate the accounts a precise and controlling nature. He negotiated good marriages for his three children, two of whom found spouses – Sybil Lewknor and Edward Poynings – from families whose interests, like those of the Scotts, straddled Sussex and Kent. Poynings, his brother and Richard Sackville (c1460-1524) all spent some time in the Scott household, which was clearly an establishment to which gentry families

---

[38] J. Stow, *The Annales of England* (London, 1592), 465; only surnames are used. Stow had access to the indictments against the Londoners who attempted to rescue the sons of Edward IV from the Tower, and probably based his account of the Kentish sector of the rising on similar documents: R. Horrox, *Richard III: A Study in Service* (Cambridge, 1989) 149, 155-56.

[39] *CCR 1476-1485*, 1408.

[40] *CPR 1476-1485*, 370; in Oxfordshire, Sir Richard Harcourt was commissioned to arrest rebels, including his nephew John Harcourt: L. Gill, *Richard III and Buckingham's Rebellion* (Stroud, 1999) 27-28.

[41] J. R. Scott, 'Receipts and expenditure of Sir John Scott, in the reign of Edward IV', *AC* 10 (1876), 250-58.

[42] TNA PRO C1/67/332.

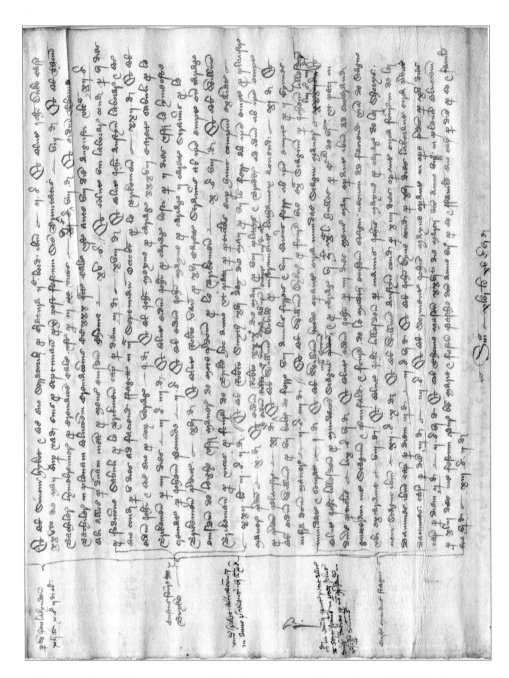

Illus. 2   Part of the account roll for the manor of Mote for 1466-67 listing
Repairs to the manor and the *Costs of making 'Bryke'*. Sir John Scott's
annotations appear in the left-hand margin.

were happy to entrust their children. Scott was on good terms with his sons-in-law at the time of his death, when he expressed his trust in Poynings 'to be the great comfort, cheer and aider' of his widow Agnes.[43]

Scott's religious attitude, at least during the years of his prime, can only be guessed at. Although the advowson of 'the chapel of The Leigh otherwise The Mote' had been included in John Pashley's quitclaim of the manor to Scott's feoffees on 6 December 1458, within a year he was careful to obtain from Pashley a less ambiguous grant of 'the patronage and advowson of the chapel or chantry belonging to the manor of old called The Legh, now The Mote'.[44] With the advowson ran a considerable acreage in Beckley, Peasmarsh and Northiam, and the advowson and tithes of Fairlight.[45] In November 1467, at the height of the building works, Scott petitioned the pope to be allowed to rebuild the ancient chapel, dedicated to the Virgin and standing on the gate of the manor house, on a smaller site.[46] Paul II instructed the bishop of Chichester to grant a faculty on certain conditions, but it appears that John Arundel, who came to Chichester in 1458, had been one of Henry VI's physicians and was a devoted Lancastrian, succeeded in thwarting this aspect of Scott's project. Although rebuilding the chapel had been on the agenda in September 1467 when the works were planned, it was not until after the bishop's death on 18 October 1477 that the new chapel was fitted out, the tiled floor laid and the timber benches, desks and *sedilia* installed.[47] But the challenge to Scott's plans had more to do with politics than piety, as did his establishment in 1462, with John Fogge, of a chantry to pray for the souls of Robert Horne, Sir Thomas Kyriell and the other victims of the battles of Northampton, St Albans and Towton.[48]

---

[43] TNA PRO PROB 11/7, f. 116; he was clearly unaware of the imminent breakup of the marriage: see p. xxvii.

[44] BL Add Ch 16156, 16325, of 12 June 1459.

[45] For the inquisitions *ad quod damnum* permitting Sir Edmund Pashley to alienate land to the chapel, 1304-1320, see TNA PRO C143/50/7, C143/101/12, and C143/144/15.

[46] *Calendar of Papal Letters* 12, 608.

[47] The entries for expenditure on the chapel occur in the account which was opened on 1 March 1478. For Arundel, who was implicated in Fauconberg's rising of May 1471, see C. H. C. Whittick, 'Arundell, John (*c.*1400–1477)', *Oxford Dictionary of National Biography* (Oxford, 2004). His successor, Edward Story, was the queen's confessor and a trusted member of the court: see R. J. Schoeck, 'Story, Edward (*d.* 1503)', *Oxford Dictionary of National Biography* (Oxford, 2004). The contention of *VCH Sx* 9 that the chantry's new location was in Peasmarsh, on a site which remained in the hands of the Crown until 1818, seems unsupported by the evidence. This site was clearly the 'land joining to the Old Chantry, called Chantry Lands, lying to Hatchis ward' [Hatches in Peasmarsh], which had to be pointed out to Sir John Scott by 'Old Watell' (TNA PRO PROB 11/7. f. 115v.), scarcely necessary if Scott had been responsible for its relocation. The site in Peasmarsh, shown as a building on a map of 1689 and a moated enclosure in 1808, seems more likely to have been the original chapel of Leigh, which Sir Edmund Pashley moved to The Mote in 1320. The land at Peasmarsh remained part of the chantry's endowment when it was dissolved in 1549 (ESRO ACC 2806/1/9/5; TNA PRO LRRO 1/2838 (MPE 1/221); *VCH Sx* 9,156-57; J. R. Daniel-Tyssen, 'The Parliamentary surveys of the county of Sussex, Anno Dom. 1649-1653', *SAC* 23 (1871), 277-80; *Sussex Chantry Records* (*SRS* 36 (1931)), ed. J. E. Ray, 9, 29).

[48] Wedgwood, *History of Parliament,* 340.

When moved by imminent death to make his will on 'the feast of St Luke the Evangelist' 1485, Scott's piety was evidently stronger than average. He bequeathed his soul not only to God and the Virgin, but also to seventeen named saints.[49] As well as singing masses, his priest John Bonbassall was to complete the writing of two 'legends', books of readings or lessons for use at divine service, containing passages from scripture and the lives of saints, which Scott bequeathed to the churches at Brabourne and Smeeth; for this task he was to be allowed £6 over three years. A third volume, 'my old legend', was bequeathed to the chapel of The Mote, along with a chalice, vestments 'and all other ornaments belonging to a priest'. Brabourne and Orlestone churches were to receive the remnants of his silk gowns 'to be made to the worship of God'. Dover Priory received Scott's lands in Calais and its vicinity, some during the term of a sixty-year Crown grant, to fund the rebuilding of their house; the only obligation was to pray for the souls of his parents, parents-in-law, his aunt Denise Finch and William Langham, and to pay an annuity of £13 6s 8d to Agnes Scott.[50] Sir John provided for his domestic chaplain William to be sent to Rome for three months. Once there, he was to say three masses at Santa Maria in Scala Coeli, whose particularly effective indulgence, giving instant relief from purgatory, had become popular in the royal household after a visit to Rome by Anthony Woodville, Lord Rivers, in 1476.[51] William was also 'to worship with prayer and offerings the chains of St Peter'. On his return from the holy city and until he obtained a better benefice, William was to become the chantry priest at The Mote.

Scott's will includes extremely generous bequests to his servants, both current and retired, including an annuity of forty shillings to 'Henry Turnour mine old servant', who had taken over as accountant at Mote on the departure of William Harlakenden in 1471. The payments were charged on Scots Float in Sussex and were to be paid by William Scott, further evidence of his establishment at Mote in the closing years of his father's life. Two of the payments amounted to pensions, to be paid to the recipient 'when he falleth from his labour into age', and five more old servants were to be kept by Agnes Scott until their legacies could be paid. Sir John gave his wife the residue of all his goods and chattels 'to do therewith her own free will', and, rather than appoint a second executor with her, gave her the option, which she seems not to have taken, to select 'another special friend that it shall please her to have with her as an executor if she will'.

---

[49] L. Boatwright, M. Habberjam and P. Hammond (eds), *The Logge Register of PCC Wills, 1479 to 1486* (Knaphill, 2008), 2, 16; the saints invoked by Scott were Mary the Virgin, John the Baptist, Michael, John the Evangelist, Dennis, Erasmus, Christopher, Giles, George, Anthony, Blaise, Katherine, Mary Magdalen, Margaret, Martha, Winifred, Barbara and Susanne.

[50] The bequest was to little effect: in 1511 many parts of the priory were said to be in ruins: *VCH Kt* 2, 133-37.

[51] For the indulgence, the powers of which had been transferred to a chapel in Westminster Palace in 1476, see N. Morgan, 'The Scala Coeli indulgence and the royal chapels', in B. Thompson (ed), *The Reign of Henry VII* (Stamford, 1985), 82-97.

Scott's financial generosity was matched by a capacity to forgive. On several occasions, it can only have been his influence which saved his stepfather Sir Gervase Clifton from forfeiture and execution. Despite having fought against Edward IV at the battles of Wakefield and Towton and having been exempted from the general pardon of 4 March 1461, almost four months later he received a specific pardon, and thus escaped the Act of Attainder passed in Edward's first parliament.[52] In 1465 Scott stood surety for Clifton in a thousand marks to secure a pardon for treason, and in 1468, although among a group indicted for treason before a special commission, Clifton's name was dropped from the charge before trial. On 10 January 1470 he was again pardoned, but having been proclaimed one of 'our open and notorious traitors, rebels and enemies' after the battle of Barnet, Clifton fought at Tewkesbury and was among those executed after the battle, having sought sanctuary in the abbey church on 6 May 1471. There was nothing even Scott could do to save him.

Sir John Scott died on 18 October 1485, the feast of St Luke on which he had made his will. His son William Scott, with whom he held Mote jointly, was aged 26 and more.[53] Sir John's widow Agnes Scott survived her husband by less than two years – her will, written on 25 March 1487, was proved on 4 July.[54] It is clear from its bequests that the marriage of her daughter Elizabeth and Edward Poynings, in whom Sir John had expressed so much confidence, had failed – perhaps the couple had been unwilling to risk her father's wrath by separating during his lifetime. By the time of her mother's death Elizabeth was living with her at Scots Hall, and most likely running the farm – Agnes left her 'four working oxen with all manner husbandry as well wains, carts, wheels, ploughs [and] harness thereto belonging which she occupieth at Hall'. The only child of her marriage, John Poynings, was dead, but by the time of his own death in 1521 Edward Poynings was the father of seven illegitimate children. Elizabeth seems to have remained at Brabourne where she was buried, beneath a commemorative brass, in August 1528.[55]

THE SCOTT ESTATE

The inquisition *post mortem* taken after his death suggests that Sir John Scott held a modest estate comprising the manors of Hall (in Smeeth), *Mead*, Capel (in Warehorne), Orlestone and Hayton (in Stanford), all within the same area of

---

[52] Grummitt, 'Clifton'.

[53] *CIPM Henry VII* (1) 110, 134, 138; during the previous month Sir John had sold a 'place', either in London or Calais, to the stockfish-monger and former Stonor intimate Thomas Betson, a merchant of the Calais Staple: L. Boatwright, *et al.*, *The Logge Register of PCC Wills, 1479 to 1486*, 2, 331.

[54] TNA PRO PROB 11/8, f. 123.

[55] TNA PRO PROB 11/8, f. 123; S. G. Ellis, 'Poynings, Sir Edward (1459–1521)', *Oxford Dictionary of National Biography* (Oxford, 2004).

Kent, and the manor of St Cleres in East and West Tilbury, Essex.[56] However, this gives little idea of the full extent of the lands he had held during his life. Scott's role in the events of 1460 was amply rewarded by Edward IV who in the succeeding years showered him with the property of attainted Lancastrians. In 1462 he was granted custody of the lands of the Earl of Oxford, the farm for three years of the lands of Robert Hungerford, lord Moleyns and the reversion of the castle and honour of Chilham, a short distance to the north of his main manor at Smeeth. The following year he was also given two-thirds of the Worcestershire manors of Old Swinford and Snodsbury and the reversion of the remainder, held by Margaret, widow of Fulk Stafford.[57] He was granted the farm of the manor of Huntingfield (in Eastling) in 1465, formerly held by the Lancastrian knight Thomas Browne. In 1467 he was given custody of fourteen manors in Kent which had been held by Sir Robert Poynings. As well as freehold property in Calais and its environs, Scott was the beneficiary of a sixty-year lease of crown lands in the English enclave. His son Sir William Scott cleared over £32 a year from the leasehold after the payment of the £9 18s 0d rent reserved by the grant.[58] Despite its spread, Scott's estate retained a strong focus in the eastern Weald of Kent, which was extended into the adjoining area of Sussex by the purchase of Mote.

The tenements of the manor of Mote lay in a broad band to the south of the River Rother extending from Walland Marsh in the east to Ewhurst in the west, with a small area at Hollington near Hastings and an outlier in Ninfield (Illus. 3). The pattern was similar to other manors in the north-east of Sussex. The rental of 1478 describes the bounds of each tenement, but these are insufficient to locate all of them exactly. Work by David and Barbara Martin has identified the location of most of the tenements listed in the survey of 1673, which is also published here. The relationship between the lists of 1478 and 1673 is not entirely straightforward. We might hope that the descriptions of land and the stability of quit-rents would make it a simple matter to reconcile tenements in the later record with those in the earlier, but that is not the case. A concordance is provided here (Appendix 3), but not every fifteenth-century tenement can be recognized in the later record. Memory of the extent of tenements and their payments had been forgotten or confused in the intervening period, and it is no simple matter to match one with the other.

The administration of this dispersed lordship inevitably caused difficulties for Scott's officials. By the 1440s Mote manor court, like others in Wealden Sussex, served as little more than a registry for sales and the inheritance of land. The problem for the manorial officials was to maintain adequate records to allow the collection of quitrents, and payments of heriots and relief. The compilation of two successive rentals in 1473 and 1478 (see below) suggests that

---

[56] *CIPM Henry VII*, 1, nos 134, 138.

[57] *CPR 1461-67*, 178, 229; *CPR 1476-85*, 5, 281.

[58] *CFR 1461-71*, 151; *CPR 1461-67*, 544; Boatwright *et al.*, *The Logge Register of PCC Wills*, 2, 16; TNA PRO E101/ 207/7.

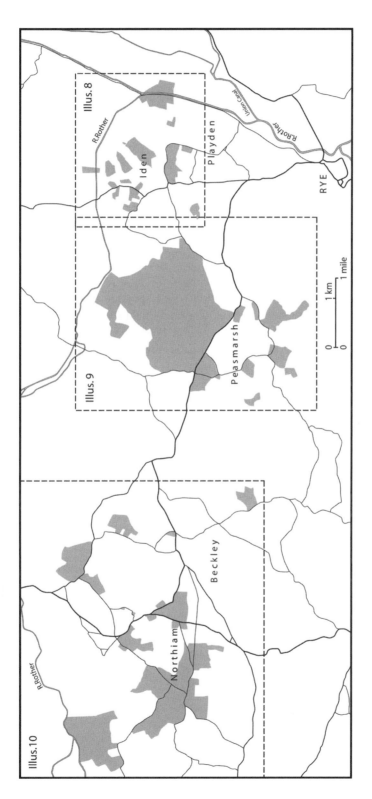

Illus. 3 The extent of the manor of Mote in East Sussex in the parishes of Ewhurst, Northiam, Beckley, Peasmarsh, Iden and Playden. Outlying tenements in Ninfield, Hollington and Playden are not shown.

considerable efforts were being made to maintain up-to-date records in order to preserve rents and minimize arrears. The 1478 rental contains records of earlier deeds which clarified the rent owed. In spite of these efforts, a number of tenements had been lost to the manor between the 1440s and the compilation of the new rental in 1478, either because they could no longer be traced, no tenants could be found to take the land or because the holders simply refused pay. It was evidently impractical or unpolitic to distrain Lord Dacre, the heirs of Sir Thomas Kyriell or the abbot of Robertsbridge to pay their rents, and these went uncollected.[59] Further small allowances were made for the rents due for collection in 1476, reflecting the continuing problems for collectors in obtaining what was due. In spite of these difficulties, or perhaps because of the assiduity of Scott's officials, arrears and evasions remained relatively few by comparison with manors elsewhere at this period.

In 1460 the demesne at Mote was described in a final concord as 203 acres of land, two hundred acres of meadow, two hundred acres of pasture, two hundred acres of wood and two hundred acres of heath. Although hardly a precise statement, it does give the impression of the character of the land.[60] We can assume that, broadly speaking, the woodland and heath would have been situated towards the top of the ridge, near the present Peasmarsh village, the meadow in the Rother valley and the arable between. Some of the demesne in the Rother valley was very marshy, and this provided reeds which were sold for thatching.

Amongst the lands held in demesne was an area on the west of Walland Marsh adjoining the broad estuary of the River Rother (Illus. 4). In 1476 Sir John Scott and William Cheyney, his neighbour at Leigh, exchanged land. Scott granted Cheyney an area of sixty acres, later known as Scots Marsh on the east of the River Rother, in return for a yearly payment of twelve shillings and another tract of land nearby. The accounts for 1477 mention the expenses of William, Sir John's son, who was sent to take seisin of this land. As a result of this exchange, the area on which scots or marsh payments were made was reduced from 142 to 112 acres.[61]

---

[59] The payment of 10s 7d owed by Lord Dacre continues to be listed in the account of 1470, but was not included in the sums to be collected from Ewhurst. The 1472 account contains an allowance for the rent of 'John' Kyriel 'until it can be levied'. The rent owed by the abbot of Robertsbridge for the manor of Methersham in 1443 simply disappears from the record. We can compare the policy at Mote with that of John Hopton, a Suffolk lord, who similarly pardoned the prior of Blythburgh the arrears of rents he owed (Richmond, *John Hopton*, 47). In Warwickshire a similar pragmatic approach was taken to the payment of amercements; C. Carpenter, *Locality and Polity: A Study of Warwickshire Landed Society, 1401-1499* (Cambridge, 1992), 173.

[60] *An Abstract of Feet of Fines for the County of Sussex vol. 3: 1308-1509* (SRS 23 (1916)), ed. L. F. Salzman, no. 3151.

[61] W. Dugdale, *The History of Imbanking and Drayning of Diverse Fens and Marshes* (London, 1662), 101; CCA DCc Charta Antiqua F35. Scots Marsh was subsequently the subject of prolonged dispute: TNA PRO C1/405/24; C1/770/38; MPA 1/61; Lambeth Palace Library, CM III/14; see also, M. F. Gardiner, The late medieval 'antediluvian' landscape of Walland Marsh, in A. Long, S. Hipkin and H. Clarke (eds), *Romney Marsh: Coastal and Landscape Change through the Ages* (Oxford, 2002), 104.

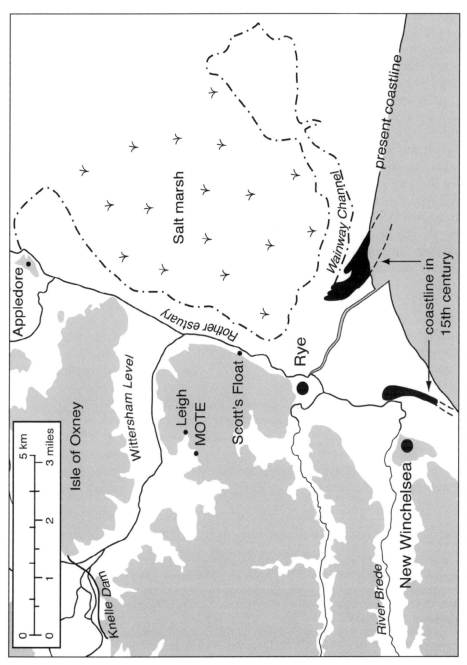

Illus. 4   The lower Rother Valley and Walland Marsh in the late fifteenth century.

THE AGRARIAN ECONOMY OF MOTE AND PROVISIONING THE HOUSEHOLD

The fifteenth century was a difficult time for lords and the period between 1420 and 1470 was particularly challenging, as the falling prices of grain and wool combined to reduce manorial revenues. It was hard to secure farmers for the demesne and to induce tenants to pay rents, so that substantial arrears accumulated on many manors. Grain prices began to pick up in the late 1460s, but fell away again in the early 1470s, although overall there was an upward trend from the low point reached in the 1440s.[62] It was in these unpromising conditions that in 1471 Scott decided to take the demesne at Mote in hand.

It was common practice in the fifteenth century to establish a home farm to supply the household with grain, meat and dairy products on those manors where the lord was resident.[63] This reduced the costs of transport and also the impact of price fluctuations in the years of bad harvest. The resumption of the demesne was therefore part of the wider policy of establishing Mote as a second centre for the Scott family. It is doubtful whether taking the demesne in hand yielded any immediate economic benefit. The loss of the rent of £13 which had been received from the farmer, John Mayne, was partly offset by letting a few of the fields on an annual basis. Grazing was also sold and this brought in £3 18s 10d in 1475. But these small sums were exceeded by the very considerable investment in the lands and buildings made in the decade following the resumption of the demesne. In the short term there were also the expenses in stocking the farm at Mote and establishing direct management, only some of which are valued in the accounts. The livestock transferred from Smeeth and later from Orlestone, for example, was not recorded as an expense.

There was sustained investment in the farmland at Mote throughout the 1470s. An average of £3 2s 0d was spent each year on the work of 'ridding' or uprooting stumps to create new fields. This allowed the clearance of about seven acres every year. The work was undertaken by contract. The plots of land were measured and payment was agreed with the contractors at a rate of about nine shillings an acre, implying over a month's labour.[64] The cumulative result over a

---

[62] J. M. W. Bean, 'Landlords', in E. Miller (ed.), *Agrarian History of England and Wales, III: 1348-1500* (Cambridge, 1991), 582-84; C. C. Dyer, *Lords and Peasants in a Changing Society: The Estates of the Bishop of Worcester 680-1540* (Cambridge, 1980), 188-89; A. J. Pollard, 'Estate management in the late Middle Ages: the Talbots and Whitchurch, 1383-1525', *Economic History Review*, second ser., 25 (1972), 563-65; Du Boulay, *The Lordship of Canterbury*, 225-26; D. L. Farmer, 'Prices and wages', in E. Miller (ed.), *Agrarian History of England and Wales: 1348-1500* (Cambridge, 1991), 504-05.

[63] A. Watkins, 'Landowners and their estates in the Forest of Arden in the fifteenth century', *Agricultural History Review* 45 (1997), 20; Carpenter, *Locality and Polity*, 176-78.

[64] Based on a wage-rate of about four pence a day, which seems to have been common in this area in the later fifteenth century: M. E. Mate, 'Tenant farming and farmers', in E. Miller (ed.), *Agrarian History of England and Wales, III: 1348-1500* (Cambridge, 1991), 693-96; M. E. Mate, *Trade and Economic Developments 1450-1550: The Experience of Kent, Surrey, and Sussex* (2006), 145.

decade was a substantial increase in the size of the area of farmland with new fields carved out at *Calvenlese, Kereslond, Brikoast, Skeryslond* and *Dornettgrove*, as well as the extension of *Presonfeld*. Once the land had been cleared of stumps, it had to be hedged and ditched. In the accounts for 1475 Scott noted carefully the costs of ridding the fourteen-acre field of *Calvenlese* and then 'earing' or ploughing it up in preparation for sowing with wheat. There were further costs both in that year and in 1478 for hedging it. Similar work can be followed in the accounts in the establishment of another field at *Kereslond*, where further expenses were later incurred in marling and manuring.

Corn mills were another source from which enterprising lords might seek to maximize their revenue. The number of mills in England had declined throughout the first half of the fifteenth century, though they began to increase in the second half as lords started to invest in what were by then often derelict or decaying structures.[65] The condition of the mill at Mote before it was rebuilt is unclear, but it was evidently unusable as corn had to be sent to Appledore to be ground. The lower reaches of the River Rother did not provide suitable conditions for water power, and the mill at Appledore was driven by wind. Animals provided an alternative source of power. Horsemills were not common in medieval England, though their numbers did grow slightly in the fifteenth century.[66] It was perhaps owing to lack of local expertise that Scott sent to Flanders for millwrights. Work proceeded rapidly during 1478 and within the year the timber-framed millhouse was constructed, roofed with tile, the French millstones were installed and two horses purchased to drive them. Accounts for the following year record the construction of a chamber beside the mill for preparing malt. They also make reference to an old millhouse at Mote, which seems to have been renovated, albeit for a different use. The total costs of construction of the mill came to a little over £10, though there were further expenses in purchasing and subsequently in feeding a gelding to work it. The tolls in 1479 amounted to £2 10s 0d, though they were not so great in later years.

Arable did not occupy a very significant part of the demesne. The greatest area under plough during the period of the surviving accounts was 48 acres sown in 1480, and corn was grown almost entirely for feeding the household and livestock rather than for the market. Even some of the sales may, in fact, have been exchanges for goods or labour, rather than market transactions. John Twyk, who bought two quarters of wheat in 1478, was a smith supplying ironwork for the manor, while Cornelius Mason who had ten quarters of wheat in the same year was probably the Cornelius Ducheman who was hired to lay the paving-tiles in the chapel. Wheat and oats were the main crops grown, though small quantities of barley and beans were occasionally sown. Wheat was baked

---

[65] J. Langdon, *Mills in the Medieval Economy: England 1300-1540* (Oxford, 2004), 28-30; Watkins, 'Landowners and their estates', 28; Dyer, *Lords and Peasants,* 173; D. Youngs, 'Estate management, investment and the gentleman landlord in later medieval England', *Historical Research* 73 (2000), 133-34.

[66] Langdon, *Mills in the Medieval Economy*, 35, 38-39.

into bread and consumed by the household, while oats were used for a variety of purposes. They were milled for oatmeal, malted for ale (though the resulting drink was considered by contemporaries to be very poor),[67] fed to poultry, geese and doves, and to horses, and unthreshed oats were fed to cattle to fatten them. The quantities of corn grown were sometimes insufficient for the household's needs and small quantities were bought, particularly malt for producing beer or ale.

Harvest year	Wheat	Barley	Oats
1472	-	-	5
1475	3	-	4
1477	2.7	4.7	5.1
1478	3	3.4	5
1479	2.9	6	5.1
1480	3	-	5

Table 1
Seeding Rates on the Mote Demesne (bushels/acre)

The seeding rates at Mote for wheat and oats were fairly consistent (Table 1), though they varied more widely on the small areas sown with barley. All the figures suggest that the fields at Mote were densely sown.[68] The yield figures show much greater variation (Table 2). These, following Campbell's practice, have been presented per seed, net of tithe and gross of seed, the assumption being that a tenth of the yield was removed in the field by the tithe-owner. The yield of wheat in 1477 is particularly notable, though this was a good year for oats too. The wheat was planted in a newly cleared field, *Kereslond*, which since it was hedged and ditched the same year, was probably being cultivated for the first time. The quite remarkable yield may, therefore, reflect the stored fertility of the land. However, if we compare the yields overall with those from the Battle Abbey manor of Alciston, it is evident that the Mote was achieving consistently a greater harvest in every single year and in every grain.[69]

---

[67] H. S. A. Fox, 'Farming practice and technique: Devon and Cornwall', in E. Miller (ed.), *Agricultural History of Engand and Wales, III: 1348-1500* (Cambridge, 1991), 304.
[68] Campbell, *English Seigniorial Agriculture*, 310.
[69] We are grateful to Professor Bruce Campbell for making available to us his figures for Alciston.

Harvest year	*Wheat*	*Barley*	*Oats*
1475	-	-	3.8
1477	9.5	-	6.2
1478	7.4	3.4	4.5
1479	4.3	-	2.5
1480	8.2	4.3	4.2

Table 2
Yield of Grain on the Mote Demesne
(net of tithe and gross of seed)

The greater part of the demesne was used for pasture. The economy of Mote was overwhelmingly devoted to cattle-fattening and to a lesser extent to pig-farming, although there were also a few horses and a very small number of sheep. Cattle were bred at Mote, though the number born each year varied. The greater number of beasts were bought as one- or two-year-old animals and then fattened for beef. Many of the mature cattle were sent for sale in Calais or to Hall for sale elsewhere. Cattle destined for shipment were driven to Dover and then taken across to Calais, or might be butchered at Mote and the meat sent to Calais in barrels.[70] Calais evidently provided a good market, but the later accounts suggest that there may have been a change in the pattern of commerce with a shift towards sales in the locality. In 1480 twenty-six oxen were sold from Mote and the following year another ten.

Both agriculture and grazing at Mote was very largely directed towards the supply of the household, with only cattle-raising undertaken with a view to sale. Medieval lords, no less than their tenants, aimed at self-sufficiency wherever possible, though the mobile households of great lords tended to buy in more food because they were not able to establish the routines necessary for its preparation.[71]

Nevertheless a proportion of the cattle raised at Mote were slaughtered for feeding the household. The few geese and sheep kept on the manor were also raised solely for consumption. When Agnes Scott was there in September 1475 two oxen, one calf and two ewes and two lambs were slaughtered and eaten, but when the lord and lady were not present the household would have subsisted upon a less carnivorous diet. A breeding-stock of pigs was kept at Mote, and these too were raised mainly for consumption by the household, though a few were sent for sale both in Calais and locally.

---

[70] Calais provided a useful market for livestock from south-east Kent and the adjoining area of Sussex: M. E. Mate, 'Pastoral farming in south-east England in the fifteenth century', *Economic History Review* second series, 40 (1987), 533-34.

[71] C. C. Dyer, *An Age of Transition?: Economy and Society in England in the Later Middle Ages* (Oxford, 2005), 99-102, 179; K. Mertes, *The English Noble Household 1250-1600* (Oxford, 1988), 101.

The servants at Mote undertook much of the work of processing the food. They malted grain and subsequently brewed ale and beer, and baked bread. They made candles from tallow and prepared cheese in the dairy. In 1477 new nets were made for fishing and for catching foxes and rabbits, and the old ones repaired. The following year a small boat was purchased, perhaps to be used for fishing in the moat, the pond in the orchard, or on the Rother. Details of the fish caught, apples grown in the orchard, and the doves and pheasants raised around the manor buildings are not entered in the accounts because all were consumed by the household at Mote. Equally, there is an entry for the purchase of hemp seed, perhaps for the garden, but not for the hemp which was grown. The produce of the garden remains largely hidden from us.

The accounts suggest that the most profitable aspects of the demesne were not anticipated when the land was taken in hand, but emerged over the years. The future importance of the production of firewood, for example, is not evident from the account of 1473 when small parcels of wood were sold, producing an income of only 8s 4d. Wood continued to be sold standing – that is, as it grew and ready to cut – throughout the mid-1470s. The market for wood was, no doubt, particularly competitive in the Weald where there was a very considerable supply.[72] The turning-point came in 1479 when billet wood was bought in and sent to Sir John Scott for sale at Calais. The following year labourers were employed to prepare billets from his own woods, and firewood was sold in this form and sent to the dock at Scots Float for shipment across the Channel. Having appreciated the market for firewood in Calais, Scott moved rapidly to invest in its production and transport. The site of the float on the Rother was purchased in 1478 or 1479 and work began shortly after to create a yard and dock at which billet wood might be loaded for shipment. Wood was a high-bulk and low-value cargo which would yield a profit only if it could be moved cheaply by water.[73] Within a few years Scott was dealing in firewood, both his own and others, on a vast scale.

A similar alertness to market opportunities is suggested by the growth in the production of reed for roofing and the sale of livestock at Calais. Relatively little corn was grown at the east end of Sussex and reed was used for thatching instead of straw. Reed was cut from 1473, not only for use on the farm at Mote, but also for sale. Within a few years of taking the demesne in hand the quantity of reed being mown had almost trebled to 10,900 sheaves, the majority of which was sold.

Once the demesne had been taken in hand, the household at Mote grew and consumed much of its own food, but no estate in late medieval England was

---

[72] J. Hatcher, 'The great slump of the mid-fifteenth century', in R. Britnell and J. Hatcher (eds), *Progress and Problems in Medieval England* (Cambridge, 1996), 254-55.

[73] J. Galloway, D. Keene and M. Murphy, 'Fuelling the city: production and distribution of firewood and fuel in London's region, 1290-1400', *Economic History Review* second series, 49 (1996), 447-72; M. F. Gardiner, 'Medieval farming and flooding in the Brede Valley', in J. Eddison (ed.), *Romney Marsh: The Debatable Ground* (Oxford, 1995), 131.

entirely self-supporting. Some food had to be bought since it was not possible to predict the yields from crops which fluctuated considerably at this time. Equally, excess produce prepared by the household might be sold, though it is possible that some of the sales recorded in the accounts were, in fact, the exchange of goods for labour. The problems caused by a shortage of coinage in early fifteenth-century England are well documented and although the situation may have eased a little by the 1470s, it could still be difficult to get enough coins to pay debts. The Paston Letters suggest that coins were used to make payments almost as soon as they had been received.[74] The problems in acquiring cash were matched by those in obtaining credit, which was not readily given when the chances of repayment were diminished by the paucity of coins in circulation.[75] It has already been suggested that some of the sales of grain were in fact payments in kind for works, and scrutiny of the accounts suggests a number of other possible examples. Amongst these are the 'sale' in 1479 of a quarter ox and two barrels of beer to William Hammez. He was being fed at the lord's expense and these victuals may have been part payment for his work in clearing woodland. Equally, the parcel of wood sold to Thomas Rider in 1472, but not charged until the following year, may have been an exchange for his work in mowing and binding reeds. Further examples of possible payments in the form of goods may be found, but one certain instance is revealed through a duplication of entries in the accounts of 1470-71. They record an apparent payment of £13 by John Mayne for the farm of the demesne, but other entries show that only £2 of it was in cash, and the remainder was paid in oxen to the value of £10 and billet wood worth £1 5s 0d.

The pattern of food-purchasing at the manor can be divided into three periods. From 1465 until 1467 there were very few servants normally resident at Mote and the expenditure on food was low. Particular expenses were incurred when Sir John or Lady Agnes Scott visited and when their officials were also present. Building workers labouring on the manor were boarded out at the rate of ten pence a week, or sometime stayed with John German, the bailiff, who was paid a similar amount for their accommodation. The second period began in 1468. As the number of labourers increased, it became more economic to accommodate them on the manor and provide them with food at the lord's expense. The costs of the household increased correspondingly and a weekly record of expenses was kept, with larger purchases noted separately. When the demesne lands were taken in hand, less food had to be purchased, but there were a number of resident servants to be fed.[76] This marked the third period of

---

[74] N. J. Mayhew, 'The Yorkist recoinage of 1464-1471', *British Numismatic Journal* 44 (1974), 71-73.

[75] C. Briggs, 'The availability of credit in the English countryside, 1400-1480', *Agricultural History Review* 56 (2008), 3.

[76] On the question of resident household servants, see D. Youngs, 'Servants and labourers on a late medieval demesne: the case of Newton, Cheshire, 1498-1520', *Agricultural History Review* 47

household expenditure. In spite of the production of food on the manor farm, payments for victuals could be surprisingly high, rising to more than £16 for the fifteen months covered by the 1478 account, even though nothing was spent on buying grain that year. These exceptional costs may be attributable to the items of food bought in specially for Sir John and William Scott.

The purchasing patterns of individual households are not well understood, even though the operation of late medieval commerce in general has been much studied.[77] The Mote accounts allow some insight into this problem. The accounts often record the place of purchase of items. Most were made in the locality, though this is because the more costly items, at least some of which came from London (such as the saddles, armour, clothing and more expensive shoes mentioned in the notebooks of Sir John Scott) were recorded in such personal accounts rather than though the manorial system.[78] The only purchases from London noted in the manorial accounts were a bulk purchase of frieze cloth at St Batholomew's Fair, almost certainly for livery, and small quantities of russet for the Scotts themselves. The larger commercial centres near to Mote, the towns of Winchelsea and Rye to the south, and Appledore to the north supplied specialist goods. Winchelsea, though in decline, was still a substantial port and it was there that waterborne goods, including coal and lead could be obtained. Rye was an increasingly important source for the pitch, ochre, resin and oil used by the bricklayers in 1468, and also for other victuals for Mote. Appledore, though a smaller place, had a significant number of shops, including one selling paper. An inquiry held in 1430 recorded that sixty shops and stalls had been built there in 1394, though not all of these may have survived the recession of the middle years of the fifteenth century.[79] Many other smaller places supplied specialist products. The Scott household may have had a particular relationship with certain suppliers. The wheels bought at Rolvenden in 1466 and again in 1468 were perhaps the result of a connection with a specific wheelwright. The hops which came from Udimore on two occasions appear to have been part of a larger contract with the beerman there. So much ironmongery was purchased from Robert Smyth of Woodchurch that he was eventually employed by Scott for his building works and set up a smithy at Mote. Nails were also bought at Small Hythe, reflecting the concentration of metalworkers in that ship-building centre. Small Hythe also supplied a boat used at Mote.[80]

(1999), 151, and L. R. Poos, *A Rural Society after the Black Death: Essex 1350-1525* (Cambridge, 1991), 181-206.

[77] D. L. Farmer, 'Two Wiltshire manors and their markets', *Agricultural History Review* 37 (1989), 1-11; Dyer, *Everyday Life in Medieval England*, 257-81.

[78] Scott, 'Receipt and expenditure of Sir John Scott', 250-58.

[79] CCA Register C, verso of membrane after f. 270; M. E. Mate, 'The rise and fall of markets in southeast England', *Canadian Journal of History* 31 (1986), 67-73. For evidence for the continuing lease of shops in the 1470s, see CCA Register S, ff. 247, 252v., 414. On the market at Appledore, see Mate, 'Pastoral farming in south-east England', 534.

[80] P. S. Bellamy and G. Milne, 'An archaeological excavation of the medieval shipyard facilities at Small Hythe', *AC* 123 (2003), 353-82.

Such a pattern of purchasing very largely reflects the conclusions drawn by Dyer.[81] A considerable quantity of goods were bought directly from the producer, by-passing the market, and most items were obtained locally. Local contacts were important, if only because of the problems of finding sellers able to supply certain goods. Larger quantities were bought in the local towns, as references to food obtained from Rye, Winchelsea and Appledore suggest, and goods were also purchased at local fairs. The fairs at Bethersden in Kent and Ewhurst in Sussex are particularly note-worthy because they are otherwise unrecorded.[82] The Ewhurst fair, in particular, to judge from the number of purchases of cattle made there, seems to have been an important event. The purchase of sheep as far away as Seaford seems to be an exception to the general pattern of local purchases. Mote was situated in an area which was overwhelmingly given to cattle-raising, and sheep were evidently not readily available in the locality.

THE SCOTT HOUSEHOLD

The term 'servant' was applied by contemporaries to a wide spectrum of individuals, ranging from professional advisers to the likes of Simon the kitchen boy, whose surname seems to have remained unknown to successive accountants. The household at Mote was small, but it is difficult to determine its exact number. Some servants were employed elsewhere on the estate, but provided with livery at Mote while others, though working at Mote, are omitted from the accounts. The Mote accounts nevertheless reflect the complex and flexible nature of the fifteenth-century household. Sir John Scott, like his Norfolk contemporary John Paston, expected his servants to perform a number of different roles.[83] John Marener, for example, was not only expected to collect rents for Scott, but also serve in the house. Such wide responsibilities were perhaps inevitable for staff on gentry estates.

The senior members of Scott's administration were retained from the local professional classes. Some, such as the receiver William Harlakenden of Woodchurch, seem to have been in the sole service of the Scott household, while others, such as John Bookland of Battle, acted for Sir John amongst others. Harlakenden, who was receiver from before 1464 to 1470, himself possessed land at Woodchurch and Lydd. In 1460 he had acted as feoffee for Robert Horne

[81] Dyer, *Everyday Life in Medieval England*, 257-81.

[82] These markets are not identified in B. McClain, 'Factors in market establishment in medieval England: the evidence from Kent 1086-1350', *AC* 107 (1997), 83-103, or in J. Bleach and M. F. Gardiner, 'Medieval markets and ports, in K. Leslie and B. Short (eds), *An Historical Atlas of Sussex* (Chichester, 1999), 42-43, or in Centre for Metropolitan History, Gazetteer of Markets and Fairs in England and Wales to 1516 (http://www.history.ac.uk/cmh/gaz/gazweb2.html, accessed September 2009).

[83] R. H. Britnell, 'The Pastons and their Norfolk', *Agricultural History Review* 36 (1988), 135, quoting *Paston Letters and Papers*, 1, 127.

of Appledore, Sir John Scott's political ally, who appointed him executor of the will in the following year. Horne was killed at Towton in 1461, and by 1464 Harlakenden was in Scott's service.[84] In a pardon given after the Fauconberg Rising, Harlakenden was described as a gentleman, perhaps an indication of legal qualification. We should not necessarily assume that he had taken any part in the events of 1471, since, as in 1450, many of those given pardons appeared as representatives of their community.[85] The versatility of his service exemplifies the demands placed on the household servants. He held manorial court at Mote, treated with lawyers, organized building works and dealt with matters concerning the management of the household. He was, in effect, both a steward for Mote and receiver, tasks which on a bigger estate were divided.[86] While he served the Scotts, Harlakenden's house provided a convenient place to which goods could be delivered and a number of household purchases destined for Mote were initially carried to Woodchurch. His departure in 1471 left a significant gap in the Scott household. His attachment to the family did not cease with his leaving Scott's service – it was to Sir John that he turned in 1481 when appointing an overseer of his will.

Harlakenden's departure marks a new phase of accounting practice, doubtless the result of a redistribution of his workload. Only part of his duties were taken on by John German, the bailiff and rent-collector at Mote, who compiled the accounts from 1471 onwards. German's role, unlike the wider responsibilities of Harlakenden, was restricted to Mote, and he rarely ventured far beyond it. Although he returned the accounts, he is called the bailiff of husbandry, and separate payments were made by an accounting bailiff, a role fulfilled by Henry Turner. The position of steward of the household was taken over by Henry Finch, who also returned the Mote accounts for 1473 as receiver. He was not Scott's sole source of legal advice. On Harlakenden's departure, Scott seems to have bought in legal services as needed, turning to John Bookland of Battle, whose other employers included Richard Fiennes, Lord Dacre, and the abbots of Battle and Robertsbridge. In 1473 Bookland was provided with ale and wine while writing a new rental and engrossing the accounts, and by 1476 he was holding the Mote manorial court and writing charters on behalf of Sir John Scott. At about the same time, he and Henry Finch went to inspect the boundaries of a manorial tenement in Peasmarsh.

John Hale, who had acted as Harlakenden's assistant or servant, disappears from the Mote accounts in 1468, but is later mentioned as the

---

[84] TNA PRO C1/135/111; he acted as feoffee for some of Scott's lands in Kent in 1464: J. R. Scott, *Memorials of the Family of Scott, of Scott's Hall, Kent* (London, 1876), Appendix LIX.
[85] For William Harlakenden, see *Documents Illustrative of Medieval Kentish Society*, 251, and the documents cited in the prosopography; G. S. Steinman, 'Pedigree of Harlakenden, of Kent and Essex', *Topographer and Geneaologist* 1 (1846), 229; Richmond, 'Fauconberg's Kentish rising', 686-87; I. M. W. Harvey, *Jack Cade's Rebellion of 1450* (Oxford, 1991), 198.
[86] C. Rawcliffe, *The Staffords, Earls of Stafford and Dukes of Buckingham 1394-1521* (Cambridge, 1978), 46-50.

rent-collector of the manor of Icklesham; perhaps he had been poached by its lord – Henry's brother, Vincent Finch. The Finch brothers were Sir John Scott's first cousins: his mother Isabel was the sister of their father William Finch of Netherfield. Henry Finch is described as 'late surveyor' of Mote in the account for 1477, and evidently left Scott's service on inheriting the family estates that year. Vincent Finch of Gray's Inn and Sandhurst, another member of the family, also occasionally acted for Sir John, both in a legal capacity, and in more mundane affairs: in 1473 he went to Hawkhurst to obtain 150 apple trees for an orchard at Mote.[87]

The third phase of account-keeping begins after the death of John German in the same year, when Henry Turner took full responsibility for the accounts, although not for the collection of rent. That was dealt with first by John Marener and later by William Sharp, both of whom returned separate accounts. The role of receiver had been assumed by Christopher Gay, a lawyer of the Middle Temple and son of Thomas Gay of Elmsted in Kent.

None of the accounts before 1473 includes the servants' stipends, though they do include some expenses, including the cost of purchasing hose for Simon, the kitchen boy. Yet servants are very likely to have been present at Mote, not least when Sir John and his wife were staying there. Their wages must have been accounted for elsewhere. The situation is much clearer from 1473 onwards. Three ploughmen and one hand were generally employed on the farm under the direction of the bailiff, John German. Other labourers were employed as required at harvest time and to undertake specific tasks. There were two housemaids under the direction of Agnes at Wode, who was described as matron. A dairy-maid was employed in the summer when the cows were in milk to make cheese. Though the numbers varied slightly from year to year, the profile of staff at Mote remained more or less the same throughout the period of the accounts.

Most of the senior figures in the Scott household and some of its junior members were long-term servants, some even dying in post. It has already been noted that Sir John Scott granted Henry Turner an annuity of forty shillings to provide for his retirement, while John Adam, who acted as the purveyor from at least 1468, was to be given an annuity of twenty shillings when he retired. In the same way, the ploughman Pety John, who was buried at the lord's expense in 1479, may have been the John Heryng who had served as a labourer during the building works in 1471 and was subsequently employed as a ploughman, a role which included driving animals between manors and even crossing to Calais. Anthony Sellyng is first mentioned in the surviving accounts in 1471 and was still in Scott's employ in the last household account of 1481. Simon the kitchen boy, for whom hose was bought in 1472, is very probably the Simon who acted as a farm boy in 1479 and again in 1481.

---

[87] E. Hasted, *The History and Topographical Survey of the County of Kent* 6 (London, 1798), 112; 7, 159; Scott, 'Receipt and expenditure of Sir John Scott', 256-57; J. Greenstreet, 'Wills, and other records, relating to the family of Finch', *AC* 13 (1880), 323-26; *VCH Sx* 9, 107, 187.

It was a common expectation, even a requirement, that servants were single, but it was hardly a realistic demand for those employed for many years.[88] In Scott's household Henry Turner married Joan Gerard, a housemaid, and Alice, the wife of John German, was temporarily employed doing various jobs, including dairy and laundry work. The requirement of single status was more realistic for those servants such as William Amyot or John Lucas who worked for much shorter periods. These were 'life-cycle servants', adolescents or young adults who were acquiring experience and gaining capital before setting up their own households.[89]

It is possible to glimpse something of the close relationships that developed between servants and the Scott family. Sir John's daughter Elizabeth took her servant Elizabeth Turner with her after her marriage to Edward Poynings. In due course Elizabeth returned to Wittersham, and in 1487 was remembered in Agnes Scott's will. Another beneficiary was Margaret Bilborough who had been a housemaid at Mote until at least 1478, and seems to have found employment there for her daughter, Joan. Equally, Elizabeth German, who was evidently a relation of John German the bailiff, found work as a housemaid in the Scott household. Perhaps the clearest evidence of the close, long-term relationship between master and servant is the example of Agnes atte Wode, who became 'matron' at Mote, evidently in charge of household matters. When she fell ill in 1475, she was sent away to board with John Adam, another senior member of the household, and from 1477 was paid a stipend as the lord's bedeswoman, which seems to suggest she had become a pensioner. The accounts attribute to Lady Scott the decision to make payments on behalf of Agnes atte Wode.

It is not possible to read the accounts very long without becoming aware of the responsibilities exercised by Agnes Scott. She not only made payments and received money, but took an active role in the management of the estate. In March 1468 John Hale went to Hall to certify to her the good governance of the household and she sent him back to Mote with ropes and other goods which were required for the building-work there. Her role was greatly increased in 1470 while her husband was in exile and she was left to manage the estate, taking responsibility for the payment of the labourers at Mote. From thence forward she played a more prominent role in the management of affairs, in part, no doubt, because of the absence of John Scott at Calais and elsewhere. She purchased stock and grain for the estate and arranged the sale of wood. She travelled over to Calais in 1477 to join her husband, but even while there she paid attention to the estate, purchasing peas to be sent to Mote. In this role of estate manager, she was

---

[88] P. W. Fleming, 'Household servants of the Yorkist and early Tudor gentry', in D Williams (ed), *Early Tudor England: Proceedings of the 1987 Harlaxton Symposium* (1989, Woodbridge), 25-26; C. M. Woolgar, *The Great Household in Late Medieval England* (New Haven, 1999), 36.
[89] Fleming, 'Household servants', 22-26; Poos, *A Rural Society*, 188-92.

followed by her daughter Elizabeth who seems to have run the farm at Scots Hall after her separation from Edward Poynings.[90]

None of this should surprise us. Lady Agnes Scott was no different from her Norfolk contemporary Margaret Paston in the control she exercised over her estate in the absence of her husband. Margaret acted with the assistance of her council, trusted friends and servants who met weekly to take decisions on the running of the estate. Yet, even with the aid of such advisers, it is hard to imagine that a wife, or a widow, could step so readily into their husband's shoes without previous involvement in the day-to-day business of an estate. Margaret was ready to hold a manor court, if called on to do so by her husband. Although the best evidence for women as managers comes from periods when they acted in their husbands' absence, they must have performed this function to some extent at all times.[91] It is in this light that we should interpret the occasional references to payments made by Agnes Scott in the 1460s in the period before Sir John's appointment to Calais.

THE CONSTRUCTION OF THE NEW BUILDINGS AT MOTE

When Scott purchased the manor at the end of the 1450s, the buildings at Mote were almost 150 years old. Work began on providing larger and more impressive accommodation a few years later, and at the opening of the first surviving account in 1464 the construction of new stables, barn and kitchen was already in progress, along with work on the hall. These buildings were timber-framed, but activity was also taking place on unspecified masonry structures. Stone from the immediate vicinity of Mote was used for this initial work, apart from the jambs and quoins, which were brought from a quarry at Cranbrook. Local stone was not deemed suitable for the subsequent building, and John Mason was sent to look at quarries in the Hastings area, eventually selecting stone from Fairlight, which was used from 1465 onwards, and from Eastbourne, where digging began in 1468.

It is not clear whether these timber buildings were always meant to be temporary, or whether they were intended to be permanent and plans were subsequently changed. In mid-September 1466 Sir John Scott came down from Hall in Brabourne to confer with his feoffee Sir John Cheyney at Leigh and to discuss future work on the hall, chapel and chambers within the tower at Mote. The arrival of brickmakers, the preparatory work in ploughing up land, evidently in advance of clay-digging, fencing off an area to create a brickyard and the firing of initial loads of brick which had taken place earlier that year all suggest that a

---

[90] See above, p. xxvii.
[91] Britnell, 'The Pastons and their Norfolk', 135-36; R. E. Archer, '"How ladies... who live on their manors ought to manage their household and estates": women as landholders and administrators in the later Middle Ages', in P. J. P. Goldberg (ed.), *Women in Medieval English Society* (Stroud, 1997), 152-54.

decision had been made to embark upon a more ambitious scheme of building, and one which depended on the use of brick.

Brick was a prestigious and novel building material in the 1460s. Although it had been used for minor works and repairs – such as the construction of a wall near the Landgate in Rye and in the town wall – its use for the fabric of buildings was still uncommon. In choosing to use brick, Scott may well have been influenced by the moated castle not far away at Herstmonceux, built in the 1440s, and may also have admired other brick buildings in southern England, including the Manor of Moor and Rye House (both in Hertfordshire), Caister Castle in Norfolk, and Nether Hall and Faulkbourne Hall (both in Essex). Scott's familiarity with Calais and its vicinity may have provided a further impetus for his adoption of brick as a building material.[92] But perhaps the greatest influence was William Waynflete, bishop of Winchester, and Scott's own connections with the family of Ralph, Lord Cromwell, the builder of Tattershall Castle in Lincolnshire. In 1451 Scott and his stepfather Gervase Clifton had received the custody of three Cromwell manors in south-east Lincolnshire, and in 1454 Clifton became a feoffee of Cromwell's manor of Ampthill. Clifton's patron and Scott's relation Kemp had been a friend and supporter of Cromwell, and Waynflete, Cromwell's executor, had involved Clifton with the endowment of his foundation at Magdalen.[93] Waynflete took responsibility for the completion of Cromwell's college at Tattershall, and his influence as a promoter of brick in domestic architecture has been noted by his biographer.[94] As controller of the royal household, Sir John Scott may have known Waynflete, whom he had conceivably encountered during the bishop's involvement as a conciliator during the Cade revolt. Of all the buildings of the middle years of the fifteenth century, it is undoubtedly Tattershall which provides the closest parallel to Sir John Scott's brick tower at the manor of Mote.

Brick continued to be a material for the most important of buildings in the two decades after the work at Mote, being adopted, for example, for the tower at Buckden Palace in Huntingdonshire and by Sir John Scott's son-in-law Sir Edmund Bedingfield at Oxburgh Hall in Norfolk, for which a licence to crenellate was granted in 1482.[95] Its more general availability by the late fifteenth century is suggested by an undertaking made in Rye borough court in 1483 by

---

[92] M. Biddle, L. Barfield and A. Millard, 'The excavation of the Manor of the More, Rickmansworth, Hertfordshire', *Archaeological Journal* 106 (1949), 136-99; T. P. Smith, 'Rye House, Hertfordshire, and aspects of early brickwork in England', *Archaeological Journal* 132 (1976), 111-50; H. D. Barnes and W. D. Simpson, 'Caister Castle', *Antiquaries Journal* 32 (1952), 35-51; D. D. Andrews, 'Nether Hall. A fortified manor of the Wars of the Roses', *Essex Archaeology and History* 35 (2004), 78-97; R. Allen Brown, H. M. Colvin and A. J. Taylor, *History of the King's Works* (London, 1963), 1, 427, n. 4.

[93] Grummitt, 'Clifton'.

[94] V. Davis, 'Waynflete, William (c.1400–1486)', *Oxford Dictionary of National Biography* (Oxford, 2004).

[95] A. Emery, *Greater Medieval Houses of England and Wales, 1300-1500: II East Anglia, Central England, and Wales* (Cambridge, 2000), 138-40 (Oxburgh), 229-33 (Buckden).

William Belle to settle a debt of 8s 4d in 'brik stonys' or money. Locally made brick began to be used even for lesser buildings, including the new church at East Guldeford, begun in 1499, and a chimney built for John Shurley at Rye in 1504, although imported brick might still be preferred for external work.[96]

At the meeting in September 1466, Scott probably settled the details of the new work, and perhaps negotiated for the carriage of materials across Cheyney's land. Later that year or in 1467, John Cole came from Esher and 'Hunte of Westminster' from London to advise on the proposed works. Cole was almost certainly engaged on Waynflete's brick tower at Esher Palace, and must have been the 'brickmason' of the same name who was to work on the same prelate's tower at Farnham Castle in the early 1470s. The Mote rolls call him the 'surveyor of the work', though it is not apparent from the accounts that he was often on site. 'Hunte of Westminster', elsewhere called 'John Hunte', can probably be associated with the Thomas Hunt who served as Clerk of the King's Works between 1472 and 1485.[97]

There were two key individuals responsible for day-to-day decisions for the building project at Mote. Denis Lene, variously described as a bricklayer and mason, was paid more than his fellows at four shillings a week and, significantly, had a servant, Hugh White, who may have been an apprentice rather than a simple labourer. If Denis Lene's name indicates his origin, he may have hailed from King's Lynn where brick had been widely used since at least the middle of the fifteenth century.[98] The second individual was William Mason, who was in charge of the stone-cutters at Eastbourne. He was paid at a similar rate to Denis Lene and he too had an apprentice, William Squyer. Their rate of four shillings a week or eight pence a day was the same as that paid a decade later to the master mason and bricklayer at Kirby Muxloe (Leicestershire).[99]

Brick-making continued at Mote throughout 1467. Sand was dug to mix with the clay, wood was cut for the brick-kiln and straw purchased as bedding for the unfired bricks. No expenditure is recorded for digging clay, but the labour may have been hidden in the entries for other works. The following year the bricks were supplied at two rates. One third were charged at three pence a thousand, which can have covered the cost of the labour of William Brikeman only, and excluded the fuel and all materials which were supplied by Scott. The remainder, charged at 22 pence a thousand, may have been made elsewhere,

---

[96] ESRO RYE 33/5, 33/7, f. 159; D. Martin, B. Martin, J. Clubb and G. Draper, *Rye Rebuilt: Regeneration and Decline within a Susssex Port Town, 1350-1660* (Burgess Hill, 2009), 161.

[97] A. Emery, *Greater Medieval Houses of England and Wales, 1300-1500: III Southern England* (Cambridge, 2006) 336-39; M. W. Thompson, 'The date of "Fox's Tower," Farnham Castle, Surrey', *Surrey Archaeological Collections* 57 (1960), 88; *History of the King's Works* 1, 195, 1045.

[98] *The Making of King's Lynn: A Documentary Survey* (Records of Social and Economic History, new series, 9. London, 1984), ed. D. M. Owen, no. 197; T. P. Smith, *The Medieval Brickmaking Industry in England, 1400-1450* (Oxford, 1985), 36.

[99] Hamilton Thompson, 'The building accounts of Kirby Muxloe Castle', 199, 202.

possibly at the Wittersham brickyards, although even this rate was well below that charged at contemporary yards, and may reflect the scale of the order.[100]

In addition to the bricks, considerable quantities of stone were also required. During 1467 and 1468 the greensand quarries at Eastbourne provided most of the stone, which was shipped along the coast to a float or dock on the Rother. Lesser quantities of building stone continued to be obtained from Cranbrook, and chalk to make lime was also brought to Mote by sea. Work began in earnest in April 1468 with the arrival of the bricklayers. They continued throughout the summer until at least the end of October, after which there is a gap in the accounts. However, it is possible that building work went on throughout the winter of 1468-69 as John Mighell the mortar-maker continued working at Mote with his servants until March 1469. Nails, rope and hurdles were bought for the scaffolding; the 'stops' used by the masons were buckets presumably for wetting the lime, and the 'trays' obtained from Egerton in Kent were for carrying mortar.[101] Pitch, wax and resin, bought for the masons, were used instead of cement in very wet conditions. Resin, wax and 'glue' were used in limited quantities for the cement in similar work at Kirby Muxloe. The red ochre bought for their use is likely to have served, as at Farnham Castle, for colouring the mortar, although the modest quantities purchased for Mote suggest that it was used sparingly.[102] Eastland board (*estrichebord*) was bought to make moulds or patterns for stonework. These would have been prepared by the master mason at Mote and delivered to the masons at Eastbourne.[103]

Before 1468 most of the carpentry at Mote had been undertaken by John Duke and his two sons, but as the scale of work increased, more carpenters were employed. John Duke was a general carpenter able to build furniture as well as undertake larger building works, such as the construction of the solar in the kitchen.[104] However, if he can be identified with the person of the same name from Rolvenden who made his will in 1470, then John Duke must also have operated as a timber merchant and tanner. Most carpenters did not have the

---

[100] The Rye accounts mention the 'brickmen of Wittersham' suggesting that there may have been a semi-permanent kiln established there (ESRO RYE 60/3, f. 93v.). The kilns there evidently supplied the bricks transported from Knock House in Stone in 1464-65; Smith, *Medieval Brickmaking Industry*, 74-82. Bricks were being sold at Appledore in 1456 for 3s 8d a thousand (Lambeth Palace Library ED 1193A, m. 13v.)

[101] *OED*, sv *stop*, n¹, sense 1; *tray*, n², sense 1b. See also, H. D. Barnes and W. D. Simpson, 'The building accounts of Caister Castle A.D. 1432-1435', *Norfolk Archaeology*, 30-31, for *trayes* of lime.

[102] Hamilton Thompson, 'The building accounts of Kirby Muxloe', 270, 279; L. F. Salzman, *Building in England Down to 1540: A Documentary History* (Oxford, 1952), 153-54; Thompson, 'The date of "Fox's Tower"', 88.

[103] Salzman, *Building in England*, 20-21.

[104] For examples of solars within detached kitchens, see D. and B. Martin, 'Detached kitchens in eastern Sussex: a re-assessment of the evidence', *Vernacular Architecture* 28 (1997), 85-91.

resources to supply the timber for buildings works and few of them would have been as wealthy as Duke.[105]

The speed of building works was impressive. They were sufficiently well advanced by July 1468 that lead was obtained for the roof, though the costs of casting and laying it must have fallen in the subsequent year. However, James Plommer worked for twelve days on site in 1468. At least part of the large quantities of board which had been sawn that year were evidently intended for sarking – boarding laid under lead sheets. The tower itself was covered in lead, since a 'plumber' or lead-worker was subsequently employed in 1471 to sort out the defects. The four thousand tiles brought from Appledore must have served to cover only some of the outbuildings, since such a number would have been insufficient for any large roof.

The accounts for 1469 and 1470 are missing; by the time the record resumes, most of the construction seems to have been complete, although carpenters, masons and smiths were still retained, largely to fit out the buildings. The demand for ironwork for hinges, rides, nails and locks was such that it was worthwhile to employ smiths to work on the manor for a number of days, but for shorter periods than in 1468 when Robert Smith of Woodchurch had spent almost nine weeks at Mote to augment the ironmongery he had already supplied. Almost the last works undertaken in 1473 were the roofing of the lodgings and the landscaping of the area around the new buildings, although the five pence paid to John Gardener suggests that the new works were rather limited in scope, apart from a new apple orchard, the trees for which were purchased at Hawkhurst. The final work took place only in 1477 when glass was received from France and set into the windows.

The accounts provide only a slight impression of the finished buildings. In appearance, they may have resembled those at Nether Hall (Essex) and Esher (Surrey), which both employed stone surrounds for the windows, but were otherwise constructed in brick.[106] The meeting in September 1466 was said to have considered the erection of a hall, chambers within the tower and a chapel. A subsequent reference to 'the garden by the old hall' suggests that the new hall was constructed on a new site, and that the former building, which had only recently been re-roofed and re-floored, remained standing. The foundations for a larder and a withdrawing-room were dug in 1468. Many manorial brick buildings of the middle of the fifteenth century were tall structures or had large towers, including Fox's Tower at Farnham, the north-west tower of Caister Castle, Kirby Muxloe Castle and Tattershall Castle. Tall buildings in a novel material were evidently intended to impress visitors, as is still apparent from, for example, Fox's Tower which rises above the town of Farnham. The tower at Mote, like those in contemporary buildings, is unlikely to have been intended primarily for

---

[105] See Appendix 2 below; H. Swanson, *Building Craftsmen in Late Medieval York* (Borthwick paper, 63; 1983), 14-15.

[106] E. W. Holden, 'Sandstone extraction at Eastbourne', *SAC* 113 (1975), 187-89; Andrews, 'Nether Hall', 79; Emery, *Greater Medieval Houses: III Southern England*, 336-37.

defence, but would have offered comfortable accommodation and had stone chimneys to the north and south for heating the rooms. Sometime after its completion, Scott's coats of arms were added to the tower, just as the right-hand turret of the near-contemporary castle at Kirby Muxloe bears the arms of William, Lord Hastings. Probably due to the antagonism of the bishop of Chichester, work on the chapel lagged behind that on the house. The interior was not finished until 1478 when the floor was paved and *sedilia* and desks were installed.

The existing kitchen continued to serve the new hall. It was a timber-framed building, but was provided with a new chimney, most probably in brick, to replace either a central fireplace or an existing timber chimney. The kitchen had an upper floor and adjoining it was a malt-chamber which was floored in 1468 and subsequent provided with an oastcloth – a sheet on which grain was placed to allow it to sprout.

The surviving earthworks at Mote consist of an outer enclosure, which was crossed to reach the main moated island on which the manorial buildings stood (Illus. 5). A single timber wall of a barn still survives on the outer enclosure, now incorporated into modern farm buildings. The wall may date to the 1470s. The main island is trapezoidal in shape and has a rectangular projection on the west on which a gatehouse was sited. All that remains of this once substantial building are a fragment of masonry wall to the north and footings to the south. The mansion was probably dismantled in the 1660s to serve as a quarry for Ewhurst Place, which the owner of both properties was rebuilding. The buildings of Mote are depicted on small sketches on maps dating from 1633 and 1634 but the information which they contain cannot easily be reconciled (Illus 6, 7). The later, more diagrammatic, drawing, which agrees with the surviving evidence, is probably the more accurate. It shows a three-storeyed gate-tower, surmounted by crenellations and chimneys, which was approached over the moat and past a house. A further building is shown on the back (east) of the moat. It is possible that the gatehouse was the building whose construction was described in the surviving accounts. The layout of Mote would have resembled the fifteenth-century site at Caister Castle, and perhaps Kirby Muxloe, where little survives of the outer court. Certainly, Mote and Caister both had an outer court with farm and domestic buildings on one island. This was perhaps the 'lower court' mentioned in the Mote account of 1480. At both sites, the first island was crossed to gain access through a gatehouse to the main residential buildings on the larger island.[107]

The other major construction work recorded in these accounts was the building of a dock on the River Rother in a place still known as Scots Float.[108]

---

[107] Woolgar, *The Great Household*, 66-67; Barnes and Simpson, 'Caister Castle', 38-43.

[108] The location of the land by the Rother held by Scott is shown on a map drawn for the Commissioner of Sewers in 1633 (CKS S/RO/P1, ESRO ACC 2806/1/9/2). ESRO RYE 132/4 of 1594 shows a building in this position, presumably the watchman's house which was constructed here.

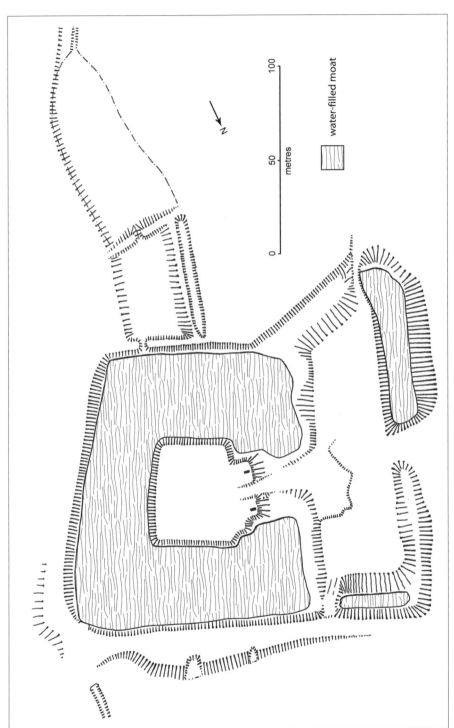

Illus. 5   The earthworks at the site of Mote manor in Iden parish (survey by David and Barbara Martin)

Land near Saltcot in Playden was purchased from Thomas Martham in or before 1479, when Robert a Broke was employed to construct a gut or drainage ditch. The bridge built at the same time is unlikely to have been over the river, since the costs of it were very modest, and it probably just crossed the ditch. A creek at the edge of the river was enlarged to make a dock, implying that the float was at right-angles to the river. Although the timber-framed building constructed alongside was perhaps intended for a watchman, 4200 billets of firewood were stolen in 1481 because there was no one there to guard them.

Illus. 6   Sketch illustration of the buildings at 'Motehouse' from a map of 1633 (CKS S/RO/P1).

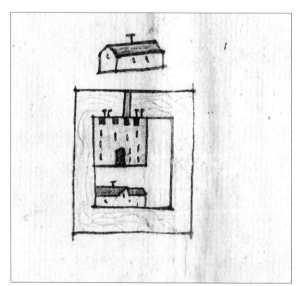

Illus. 7   Sketch illustration of the buildings at Mote depicted on a map of 1634 (ESRO NOR 17/2).

THE SUBSEQUENT HISTORY OF THE MANOR OF MOTE

The Scott family

Sir John Scott died on 18 October 1485 and was buried at Brabourne in Kent, under a large but relatively restrained tomb in the north wall of the chancel.[109] His son William Scott (1459-1524) succeeded to many of his father's offices, and to estates in twenty-three parishes in Kent (Illus. 1). By September 1480 William had married Sybil Lewknor, daughter of Sir Thomas Lewknor of Trotton, with whom he was to receive five hundred marks.[110] During the suppression of Buckingham's rebellion in the autumn of 1483, he was ordered to besiege his father-in-law at Bodiam castle, and was probably resident at Mote: Sir John's will of 1485 directs that his chaplain William, on his return from Rome, was to take over the chantry at Mote if he was 'pleasing [to] my son William Scott'. Despite his loyalty to Richard III and his family's Yorkist credentials, Scott was pardoned by Henry VII in 1488, when he was described as of Iden, suggesting that he continued to reside at Mote after his father's death. Scott served as sheriff of Kent in 1490, 1501 and 1516, and sat as MP for the county in 1495. In that year, on the death of Joan Lewknor, who had been widowed by the death of Sir John Lewknor at the battle of Tewkesbury, Scott inherited her family's manor of Brabourne, of which his father had purchased the reversion in 1465 in the (then improbable) event of the Lewknors dying without issue. According to the inscription on his tomb in Brabourne, Sir William Scott carried out extensive improvements at Iden church, including the addition of a chapel north of the chancel, known as the Mote or Scott Chapel; the tower bears the arms of Scott and Lewknor impaled, and was under construction in 1498.[111]

Sir William died on 24 August 1524. By his will of 1 August, he partitioned his estates between his sons Sir John and Edward Scott. Subject to the life estate of their mother Sybil, the core of the Kent estate was to descend to Sir John, and the 'manors of Leigh otherwise The Mote, River and Float', with extensive lands in Kent, were to pass to Edward, on whose impending marriage with Alice Fogge Sir William also settled the manor of East Tilbury in Essex.[112] The main branch of the family, seated at Scots Hall in Kent, conformed with the

---

[109] TNA PRO C142/1/139; Scott's feoffees of St Cleres were Sir Edward Poynings, [his brother] William Scott, John Digges, John Isaak and Ralph Cook esqs and John Aldy, Nicholas Burton, Thomas Blackham, Nicholas Condover, John Warner, Richard St Nicholas, Thomas Lawrence and John at Stock.

[110] The debate over Sybil's parentage is discussed by Malcolm Mercer in 'Driven to rebellion? Sir John Lewknor, dynastic loyalty and debt', *SAC* 137 (1999) 153-59, but is resolved by TNA PRO C1/1519/71, in which George Bainbridge, one of the defendants and a feoffee of the marriage settlement, names her as the daughter of Sir Thomas Lewknor.

[111] *VCH Sx* 9, 155-56; for Sir John Lewknor and a discussion of the agreement of 1465, see Mercer, 'Driven to rebellion?', 153-59.

[112] Brass at Brabourne, Kent; TNA PRO PROB 11/21, f. 229v.; Alice was the daughter of Thomas Fogge, sergeant-porter of Calais, and the grand-daughter of Sir John Scott's political ally Sir John Fogge of Ashford (Wedgwood, *History of Parliament*, 339-42).

religious changes and prospered; the Sussex branch, living at Mote in Iden, maintained the old religion and sank into obscurity and debt.[113]

1407-1453	Sir John Pashley
1453-1458	John Pashley, esq
1458-1485	Sir John Scott
1485-1524	Sir William Scott
1524-1535	Edward Scott
1535-1585	William Scott
1585-1589	William Scott
1589-1589+	William Scott
<1637	Edward Scott
<1637-1637	William Scott
1637-1646	Thomas Scott
1646-1675	Sir Nathaniel Powell

Table 3
Lords of the Manor of Mote, 1407-1675

In the Lay Subsidy returns of 1524 and 1525 it was Sir John Scott, perhaps as one of his father's feoffees, who was assessed at Iden, in both years for land valued at £40.[114] His mother Sybil Scott may have lived at Mote, where she had plate, household goods and livestock at her death in 1529.[115] Edward Scott of Iden made his will in April 1534, giving forty shillings towards the ceiling of Iden church and leaving his manor of Mote, River and Float to his wife for her life. By the time she proved the will on 19 November 1535, Alice was the wife of Sir Robert Oxenbridge of Brede Place, and she moved with him to Hurstbourne Priors in Hampshire to which, as a lifelong Catholic, he had retired on the accession of Elizabeth in 1558; she died in 1582.[116] Her son William Scott had continued in residence at Mote. In 1565 he participated in the settlement of an additional jointure on his mother, and in 1569 conveyed all his goods and lands to John Wybarne, Barnardine Fynche and Goddard Foster, gentlemen, in trust.

---

[113] For the careers of the Kent branch of the family see L. MacMahon, 'Scott, Sir John (*b.* in or before 1484, *d.* 1533)', *Oxford Dictionary of National Biography* (Oxford, 2004); L. A. Knafla, 'Scott, Sir Thomas (1534x6–1594)', *Oxford Dictionary of National Biography* (Oxford, 2004); for the Sussex branch, with useful references to their Catholicism, see J. E. Mousley, Sussex county gentry in the reign of Elizabeth (unpublished PhD thesis, University of London, 1955), 704-06.

[114] *The Lay Subsidy Rolls for the County of Sussex 1524-25* (SRS 56 (1957)), ed. J. Cornwall, 157-58.

[115] TNA PRO PROB 11/23 f32.

[116] S. T. Bindoff (ed.), *The House of Commons 1509-1558* (London, 1982), 3, 38; P. W. Hasler (ed.), *The House of Commons 1558-1603*, 3 (1981), 355-58; Oxenbridge had served as lieutenant and constable of the Tower of London under Queen Mary; SAC 8 (1856) 226-28; for Alice's will and probate papers, see Hampshire Record Office 1582/B67.

In the same year he refused to appear to take the oath of supremacy.[117] In December 1578 he was arrested by the efforts of Richard Fletcher, the town preacher of Rye, and one of the jurats,

> *with one which is thought to be a priest; and being brought to town, the people very desirous to see him and his masking apparel, for contentation of their minds, and to the end they might behold the vanity thereof, we were so bold to apparel him accordingly, and passing the streets was beheld both of young and old to no small number, whose acclamations and disliking of such vanities we refer to the report of the messenger.[118]*

His will, of Mote in Iden, was made in January 1584, and he died on 13 October 1585. He was not buried at Iden, and possibly died in prison; earlier in the same year Mote had been searched for arms. His eldest son William Scott was buried at Iden on 25 January 1589. The elder William's widow Mary lived until 1606, and in the meantime her son and grandson sustained themselves with ready money partly by selling timber. William Scott sold three hundred tons to Rye corporation in 1586, and in December 1588 had already been paid for another contract for timber on the manor of 'Pashley otherwise Mote', to be felled the following year, and for a further three hundred tons to be cut in a wood called The Grove at Mote.[119] However beleaguered, the Scotts of Mote were not poor: at his death on 22 January 1589, William Scott owned, albeit in reversion, the manors of Mote, River and The Float in Sussex and St Cleres in Essex, and two manors and other land in Kent in possession. His posthumous son William Scott, born on 29 May 1589, inherited his estates but probably died under age.[120] The child's uncle Edward Scott was confined in the Gatehouse prison at Westminster in the autumn of 1586 and subsequently ordered to live with his conformist kinsman Thomas Honeywood and made subject to a £300 bond, which he forfeited when he left Honeywood's custody and went into hiding.[121] Between 1588 and 1605 Edward Scott and his mother Mary were indicted as recusants as of Iden, although when excommunicated by the bishop of Chichester in 1601 they were living at Wootton in

---

[117] BL Add MS 41855; R. B. Manning, *Religion and Society in Elizabethan Sussex* (Leicester, 1969), 244.

[118] Rye Corporation to the Commissioners of Ecclesiastical Causes, 3 Dec 1578: ESRO RYE 47/20/3. Fletcher, father of the dramatist John Fletcher, was subsequently bishop of Bristol, Worcester and London: B. Usher, 'Fletcher, Richard (1544/5–1596)', *Oxford Dictionary of National Biography* (Oxford, 2004).

[119] *Sussex Inquisitions. Extracts from Rawlinson Ms B 433* (SRS 33 (1927)), ed. M. S. Holgate, 91; TNA PRO PROB 11/69, f. 166; ESRO RYE 46/7-8. Mary Scott, widow, was buried at Iden in 1606: PAR 402/1/1/1. She, as Mary Scott spinster, was subject to forfeiture for recusancy in 1593: *Recusant Roll no. 2, 1593-1594* (Catholic Record Society 57 (1964)), ed. H. Bowler, 175-78; TNA PRO PROB 11/73, f. 188.

[120] TNA PRO C142/225/43; PROB 11/73, f. 188.

[121] Revd J. H. Pollen (ed.), 'The official lists of Catholic prisoners during the reign of Queen Elizabeth, part II, 1581-1602', in *Miscellanea II* (Catholic Record Society 2 (1906)), 259, 262, 266 and 268; and J. J. N. McGurk, 'Lieutenancy and Catholic Recusants in Elizabethan Kent', *Recusant History* 12 (1974), 160.

Folkington as tenants of the equally recusant Shelleys of Michelgrove.[122] Edward's son William Scott, esq, was living at Mote in 1626, when John Padmore mentioned 'all my fellow servants at Mote' in his will.[123] As a child, William Scott's brother Nicholas served as a page in the household of the Spanish ambassador Count Gondomar, who sent him to study at St Omer. The record of his entry into the English College at Valladolid in 1621 describes his parents as 'noble and of the family of the Windsors, both Catholics, and suffered many things for the Catholic religion, especially they have lost virtually all their family estate, …, and spent long time in prison'. Nicholas left Spain in 1629 and returned to England as a priest, using the alias Newman.[124] William Scott was buried at Iden on 11 December 1637; letters of administration were granted to his son Thomas on the renunciation of his widow Elizabeth on 13 February 1638.[125]

By the time of his death, William Scott's financial affairs were in disarray. On 1 April 1638 an annuity of £80 was settled on his widow Elizabeth Scott, £24 on their younger children Edmund and Mary and portions provided for the daughters: by 1646, Katherine was the wife of Philip Bamfield and Mary of Mr Fagge. On 29 June 1640 Thomas Scott conveyed all his estates to Benjamin Wybarne, Thomas Threele and Thomas Houghton, in trust to pay his own debts and those of his father. Thomas died soon after, leaving a brother William Scott as his heir. The trustees sold their interest to Nathaniel Powell on 12 November 1646.[126]

Nathaniel Powell (c1600-1675) was the son of Meredith Powell (d1642) and his wife Alice Saffin, daughter of John Saffin of Cullompton in Devon, whom he married at Brompton Ralph in Somerset in 1597. In 1598, when only in deacon's orders, Meredith became vicar of the notoriously godly parish of Dedham in Essex, but amid accusations of simony returned to Somerset as rector of Brompton Ralph in 1603.[127] Nathaniel Powell was trained as a lawyer at Clifford's Inn, an inn of Chancery, and was in Sussex by 1623, when he witnessed deeds with Thomas Houghton of Mayfield, who was to prove a close associate of Powell's until his death.[128] Houghton (c1594-1669) was the son of William Houghton of Crebor in Tavistock, Devon and Elizabeth Comber of Shermanbury, and was perhaps a relative of Powell's mother Alice Saffin. He

---

[122]   *Recusant Documents from the Ellesmere Manuscripts* (Catholic Record Society 60 (1968)), ed. A. G. Petti, 118.

[123]   TNA PRO PROB 11/148, f. 29.

[124]   *The Registers of the English College at Valladolid, 1589-1862* (Catholic Record Society 30 (1930)), ed. E. Henson, 395; we owe this and other references to the Scott family to Tim McCann.

[125]   ESRO PAR 402/1/1/1; TNA PRO PROB 6/16, ff. 148, 154v.

[126]   ESRO NOR 17/4; Thomas Scott seems to have enjoyed part of the estate in possession as early as 1633: his name is marked on the land around Scots Float in a map drawn for the Commissioners of Sewers in 1633 (CKS S/RO/P1, ESRO ACC 2806/1/9/2).

[127]   Tom Webster, *Godly Clergy in Early Stuart England* (Cambridge, 1997), 190-91; *Conferences and Combination Lectures in the Elizabethan Church: Dedham and Bury St Edmunds 1582-1590* (Church of England Record Society 10, Woodbridge, 2003), ed. P. Collinson, J. Craig and B. Usher, lxxvi-vii, where Meredith is described as an 'unmitigated disaster'.

[128]   ESRO DUN 26/12; AMS 6086/34; Powell was recorded as of Clifford's Inn in 1632, 1633 and 1643: TNA PRO C54/2872/12, 2952/8; F. W. Weaver, *Somerset Incumbents* (Bristol, 1889), 320.

became principal of Clifford's Inn, where he had probably been Powell's contemporary.

In 1627 Powell married Sarah Muddle, the daughter of William Muddle, a Ewhurst landowner with an estate in Mayfield.[129] In 1635 he obtained a lease of Ewhurst Place and its demesne lands, and the right to hold Ewhurst Fair, and three years later, by a settlement of which Thomas Houghton was a trustee, obtained the residuary interest in his father-in-law's estate.[130] Marriage into the Muddle family and the move to Ewhurst put Powell in contact with the Tufton family, earls of Thanet, with whom his career would be linked for the rest of his life. The two were in partnership at Thanet's furnace in Northiam by 1636, and his energy as a commissioner of sewers can be interpreted as a means of protecting their business and landed interests. Powell can be seen speculating in land in Sussex and Kent from 1631 but in 1645, as part of a partnership with three London merchants, Powell purchased the manors of Bodiam and Broomham from John Tufton, the second Earl of Thanet, who the previous year had paid £9000 to release his estates from sequestration.[131] Within a year, Powell had recouped 90% of his outlay by sales, but retained Bodiam Castle and a tract of rich marshland conveniently located for his other property. At first sight an example of a Puritan taking advantage of the straightened circumstances of a beleaguered Royalist, Powell's purchase of Bodiam was clearly part of a plan to keep the Tufton estates viable through difficult times.

A similar pattern might be visible in his dealings with the Scott family of Mote. Nathaniel Powell's first foothold on the manor may have come in June 1640 when, probably on his deathbed, Thomas Scott conveyed all his estates to trustees for the payment of his debts and those of his late father. The first two trustees were Benjamin Wybarne and Thomas Threele of Leasam in Rye, both good Catholics; the third was Powell's partner Thomas Houghton.[132] In the Michaelmas term of 1640 Thomas's brothers William and Edmund Scott levied a fine of the manor to Thomas Gravett, Walter Oak and William Doble, and Powell's hand can also be seen in this transaction: Gravett was a trustee of the Earl of Thanet, Oak would be Powell's partner in the purchase of Bodiam in 1645 and Doble seems to have been Thomas Houghton's clerk.[133] On 12 November 1646 the Scott trustees assigned their interest to Nathaniel Powell, subject to whatever claim had been retained by William Scott. The first half-year's rental, amounting

[129] ESRO PAR 324/1/1/1; CHR 4/2/9; the Mayfield estate had been owned by William Muddle's grandfather: SAS/WH 247.

[130] HEH BA 71/4; TNA PRO C54/3168 m25.

[131] *Complete Peerage*, 12 (1), 692. Tufton subsequently co-operated with the state and served, albeit reluctantly, as sheriff of Kent in 1654.

[132] ESRO NOR 12/2, 17/4; T. J. McCann, 'Our "dear sister" Anne Threele and the Catholic recusancy of the Threeles of Leasam', *SAC* 125 (1987), 257-58.

[133] *Sussex Manors, Advowsons etc Recorded in the Feet of Fines: vol. 2* (SRS 20 (1915)), ed. E. H. W. Dunkin, 309; WSRO Wiston MS 3710 (Gravett); TNA PRO C54/3319, 3320 (Oak); ESRO DYK 539-40, 659, 691, AMS 1988, 5742/11, SAS/D 205, SAS/H 344, SAS/PN 517, PAR 422/35/3/1; WSRO Wiston 4762-3, Add MS 8740 (Doble).

to £125, included £6 10s 0d for *Perifield Farm*, £1 10s 0d for the smith's forge, £63 for the drowned lands in the Upper Levels and £54 from William Scott 'for the lands to him demised', suggesting that he continued to occupy the mansion and the bulk of the demesne lands as Powell's tenant. Two years later, Scott's annual rent had dropped to £30 and ten new tenants, paying rents amounting to almost £76, had made up the difference. Not content with the manorial rents and windfalls, Powell reaped additional profit from the sale of wood – the Commissioners of the Upper Levels paid £115 for 'walling stuff' for the work at Blackwall Bridge in 1647 and £310 for 'arming stuff' for work on the Rother in 1648. In March 1648 the moat at Mote was stocked with 237 carp and tench.[134] William Scott was buried at Battle in August 1653, and his widow Elizabeth obtained administration of his estate in January 1654. In 1668, Powell obtained a precautionary conveyance of Mote from a William Scott, gentleman, whose relationship to the family has not been determined.[135] Impoverished as the family had probably become, William Scott still merited the appellation 'esquire'.[136] Whether Powell had first acquired an interest and then purchased Mote as a means of protecting the Scotts is unclear, but a similar transaction in the same year, by which Powell acquired the Kent estate of the recusant Lord Teynham, strengthens the possibility.

    Powell's steward, Richard Kilburne of Fowlers in Hawkhurst and Staple Inn,[137] undertook a major analysis of the court rolls and other documents of Powell's manors; that for Bodiam is dated 1645, and the work on Mote was completed in 1648. The exercise involved the numbering of each membrane of the available court rolls, the examination of rentals and deeds and the establishment of customs. The methodology for these surveys was clearly Kilburne's: he had undertaken a similar exercise on the records of Thomas Foster's manor of Iden in 1643.

    Powell was nominated to the county bench in 1650, and he seems to have worked closely with Herbert Morley of Glynde, a religious and political radical who eventually became disillusioned with the Rump Parliament, Oliver Cromwell and the Protectorate, and became a focus for opposition. In 1651 Powell obtained a lease of Morley's forge at Hawksden in Mayfield, and supplied ordnance to the State. When in 1674 Powell brought an action in Chancery against Thomas Sackville for refusing to pay quitrent to the manor of Bodiam in respect of Brede High, Sackville admitted that he had paid the rent during the Civil War because he did not want to offend Powell, a JP and 'gunfounder to the state'. Powell had leased Sackville's ironworks at Brede, but refused to pay

---

[134] ESRO NOR 17/4.
[135] *Sussex Manors, Advowsons etc recorded in the Feet of Fines Henry VIII to William IV: vol. 2* (*SRS* 20 (1915)), ed. E. W. Dunkin, 309-10.
[136] ESRO PAR 236/1/1/1; TNA PRO PROB 6/29 f223v.
[137] For Kilburne, see J. Whyman, 'Kilburne, Richard (1605–1678)', *Oxford Dictionary of National Biography* (Oxford, 2004).

'pretending he blowed the stock for the state'.[138] It was probably Morley who recruited Powell as MP, bringing him in as member for Rye in 1654. Powell was still closely aligned with the Tufton family: he was removed from the bench in 1655, soon after Nicholas Tufton had been sent to the Tower on suspicion of plotting against Cromwell. In 1658 he was permitted to accompany the Earl of Thanet's children abroad, and there were sufficient doubts about his loyalties to require him to obtain a certificate from the Chief Baron of the Exchequer confirming that he was a Protestant.[139] His appointments to the livings of Ewhurst and Fairlight, the latter in respect of the manor of Mote, and the list of his library taken at his death, nevertheless show that his own personal views remained godly; he entered his heir, Nathaniel Powell, at the puritan Emmanuel College, Cambridge, in 1657. But he certainly had personal reasons to dislike the religious extremes of the Interregnum: in 1648 his brother-in-law John Hite, who had succeeded Meredith Powell as rector of Brompton Ralph in 1643, was ejected from the living for 'delinquency', to be restored only in 1660.[140] In June 1660 Powell issued a statement promising future loyalty, and within a month of the king's return his son had been knighted; Nathaniel was created a baronet on 10 May 1661.[141] He maintained close relations with the Thanets, retaining a chamber in Thanet House in Aldersgate Street, London. He had laid on piped water at Ewhurst Place in 1659 but by August 1662, although he retained rooms at Ewhurst, he had taken up residence at Wierton Place near Maidstone; an inventory of linen included napkins taken out of the drawers which stood in the hall chamber at Ewhurst. He described himself as of Wierton in his will, made in October 1674, but was brought back to Ewhurst for burial in the March of the following year.[142] Although the precise date cannot be determined, it was during Powell's ownership that the buildings at Mote were abandoned and dismantled. Powell enjoyed building – he entirely refashioned Ewhurst Place, and probably used the materials from the domestic ranges at Bodiam Castle to do so. He was ready to block up the chimneys at the new mansion to avoid the Hearth Tax, and to unblock them a year later, perhaps when the stratagem failed.[143] At the end of his life he specifically empowered his trustees to demolish and rebuild Wierton Place, and provided that his new school there should be built from local stone.[144]

---

[138] ESRO GLY 1229; DUN 27/3; AMS 5691/5/1.

[139] A note of the certificate was enrolled at the Quarter Sessions on 13 January 1659: ESRO QI 2, p. 36.

[140] A. G. Matthews, *Walker Revised* (Oxford, 1948), 314; John Hite of Taunton had married Frances Powell at Brompton Ralph on 10 May 1623.

[141] Most authorities apply the knighthood to Nathaniel Powell the elder, but see ESRO AMS 5404/4.

[142] HEH BA 71/6; ESRO NOR 17/4; TNA PRO PROB 11/348, f. 133; ESRO PAR 324/1/1/1; Powell's will provides for the foundation of a school at Boughton Monchelsea, and bequeaths his gold watch to the dowager Countess of Thanet 'as an acknowledgement of my gratitude for her ladyship's manifold favours conferred on me'.

[143] *Sussex Depicted: Views and Descriptions 1600-1800* (*SRS* 85 (2001)), ed. J. H. Farrant, 217.

[144] TNA PRO PROB 11/348, f. 133.

Mote was probably abandoned shortly after the last member of the Scott family had ceased to reside there, and its materials continued to be employed in various building works on the estate for many years: Forestall Farm in Iden was rebuilt entirely in stone, doubtless from Mote, in 1692.[145]

Nathaniel Powell was succeeded by his son Nathaniel Powell knight and baronet (1641-1707), who was educated at Emmanuel College, Cambridge, and the Inner Temple. In 1672 his father had settled his Sussex estates on Nathaniel, with remainder to his son Barnham Powell, and three years later had put Barnham in possession of the rents by his will. In 1686 when Barnham married Elizabeth Clitherow, daughter of James Clitherow of Boston House in Brentford, the manor of Mote, with Prawls in Ewhurst, the quitrents of Ewhurst manor and marshland in Bodiam were settled on Elizabeth as her jointure.[146] Barnham Powell died in October 1695, predeceasing his father; his eldest son Nathaniel Powell, having enjoyed the baronetcy for less than two years, bequeathed all his property to his mother and died in 1709.[147] He was succeeded by his brother Christopher Powell (c1690-1742), who had been educated at Queen's College, Oxford, and sat as MP for Kent between 1735 and 1741.[148] In 1720 he re-settled the estate, confirming his mother's life interest in the manor of Mote, and in 1723 they sold the manors of Bodiam and Ewhurst, including Ewhurst Place, the advowson of the church and over eight hundred acres of land, to Sir Thomas Webster of Battle Abbey for £8500.[149] Webster might have bought Mote as well had Sir John Scott's castle not been demolished – he seems to have had a liking for ruins.[150] In 1728 Sir Christopher married his first cousin Frances Newington (1690-1762).[151] Christopher Powell died on 25 June 1742, leaving his estate to his wife absolutely.[152] Their marriage had been childless and by her will of 1742, Frances appointed trustees for the sale of her assets, in order to raise large legacies and annuities for the benefit of her Clitherow relatives, including Sarah, who in 1761 would become the wife of the judge and legal writer Sir William Blackstone.[153] By 1746 Frances had been declared a lunatic, and the accounts of her trustees show that out of an average annual income of £800, the Sussex estates produced less than half, the majority from wood-sales.[154]

---

[145] ESRO HBR 1/268.
[146] J. Venn and J. A. Venn (eds), *Alumni Cantabrigienses*, Part 1 (3) (Cambridge, 1924), 388, 386; ESRO AMS 5904/4.
[147] TNA PRO PROB 11/510, f. 9; ESRO ACC 5164; monumental inscription at Boughton Monchelsea; he was of Queen's College, Oxford, and the Inner Temple.
[148] R. Sedgwick (ed.), *The House of Commons 1715-1754* (London, 1970) 2, 364.
[149] ESRO BAT 979.
[150] He purchased the Battle Abbey estate in 1721, Ewhurst and Bodiam in 1723 and the Robertsbridge Abbey estate in 1726.
[151] ESRO NOR 12/3, 6, 7; J. and J. B. Burke *A Genealogical and Heraldic History of the Extinct and Dormant Baronetcies of England, Ireland, and Scotland* (London, 1844); ESRO NOR 12/6.
[152] ESRO ACC 5164; TNA PRO PROB 11/719 (copy at ESRO NOR 12/4); monumental inscription at Boughton Monchelsea.
[153] TNA PRO PROB 11/876, f. 164v., 882, f. 358 (copy at ESRO NOR 12/5), ESRO NOR 12/7.
[154] CKS U1515 E1.

No maintenance was carried out on any of the buildings for over fifteen years, during which time Frances was under the care of the surgeon Thomas Bigg in Lincoln's Inn Fields.[155] She died on 26 January 1762, and on 26 April 1765 her trustees sold the manors of Mote and Broomham to Edward Curteis of Tenterden, gent, his son Jeremiah Curteis (1735-1806), an attorney at Rye, and Jeremiah Smith of Peasmarsh, gent, for £16,104 2s 0d, all of which was paid to the surviving beneficiaries of Frances Powell's will.[156] The partners had acquired the manors for the sake of their demesne land, which amounted to 840 acres. Less than four months later they sold the manorial lordships, retaining not only the land but the Mote Chancel in Iden church, to Thomas Owens of Rye, esquire, for £683.[157]

Thomas Owens (c1707-1769) was a barrister of the Inner Temple, with offices in Red Lion Square. He was probably a member of the Owens family of Camarthenshire, although the details of his relationship to its known members, which included many lawyers, remains obscure.[158] Thomas Owens was called to the bar in June 1754, and in 1763 was nominated as reader by Clifford's Inn. The notice of his death in *The Gentleman's Magazine* refers to him as 'of the King's Bench', and he was almost certainly the Thomas Owens, secondary to the master of that court, referred to in the *Annual Register*.[159] Thomas married Katherine Norton (1707-1796) as his second wife on 30 December 1751. Her father Ralph Norton of Rye (1666-1750), the leader of the Tory faction in the town, had purchased the lordship of the manor of Iden (similarly divorced from its demesne lands) in 1718. The marriage took place at Playden (although it was entered in the Rye register), perhaps on account of the continuing hostility of the vicar of Rye and the Lamb family towards the Nortons.

Thomas and Katherine Owens rebuilt Tower House, the Norton mansion inside the Landgate in Rye; he served as a county magistrate and was chosen as mayor of Rye in 1766. An insight into his character can be gained by a copy of his letter concerning a dispute with the Frewen family over the seizure of heriots for the manor of Mote in 1767: 'I could not stifle my resentment ... I am apt to be too warm where so apparently ill used and did indeed swear if it would cost me £500 I would file a bill in the exchequer against your uncle'.[160] By a codicil to his will he

---

[155] Thomas Bigg is better remembered as the guardian of his nephew Sir William Blackstone: W. Prest, 'Blackstone, Sir William (1723–1780)', *Oxford Dictionary of National Biography* (Oxford, 2004).

[156] CKS U1515 E1; ESRO NOR 12/8.

[157] ESRO ACC 5164; Thomas habitually signed his name *Owen*, although most other documents in which he is mentioned use the form Owens, which was consistently used by his wife.

[158] For details, see the introduction to the list of the archive of the Norton and Owens families, ESRO NOR.

[159] *Alumni Oxonienses: The Members of the University of Oxford, 1715-1886* (London and Oxford, 1888), ed. J. Foster, 3, 1053; *A Calendar of the Inner Temple Records* 5 (ed. R. A. Roberts. London, 1936), 9; *Gentleman's Magazine* 1769, 271; *ex inf.* Professor Sir J. H. Baker.

[160] ESRO DAP box 108; ESRO QJO 1; ESRO RYE 1/18, f. 110; ESRO NOR 15/124 (Thomas Owens to Charles Frewen); a copy is in ESRO DAP box 108.

left the manor of Mote and his residuary estate to Katherine, and Broomham to her sister Elizabeth Weller. He died aged 62 on 12 May 1769 and was buried at Bath Abbey on 16 May. The will, which includes a bequest of a house in Reigate to the attorney-general Charles Yorke, and chambers in Lyons Inn, was proved in the Prerogative Court of Canterbury (PCC) on 27 May 1769.[161]

Thomas Owens had ended his will 'I hope so valuable a woman will not entrust her happiness in the hands of a second husband'. Katherine was true to his word, and lived as a widow for almost thirty years; her will was proved in PCC on 16 February 1797. She left her estate to John Bradbury, a clerk in the Secretary of State's office, who took the name Norton.[162] Bradbury resettled his estate in 1805. An extensive correspondence with his solicitors survives, from which it is clear that he lived consistently beyond his means, and relied for his income on the disposal of farms from his estate and the sale of land for building. The manors of Iden and Mote were sold for £1000 to Thomas Pix of Woodside in Peasmarsh in 1820, and the mansion in Rye to the tenant George Thompson in 1821.[163] Thomas Pix (1778-1853), whose family had formerly acted as beadles of the manor and stewards of the estates of the Frewen family, was a partner in the Rye Bank and a magistrate. He bought the manor of Ewhurst from Sir Godfrey Webster in 1822, and was prominent in the electoral affairs of Rye. He died at Woodside on 24 June 1853 and his will was proved in PCC on 11 August 1853.[164] His son Thomas Smith Pix died at the age of 96 on 12 January 1900, and bequeathed the estate to his cousin Charles Lewis Lawrence, who in 1891 had been living with his widowed mother in Deptford and working as a clerk.[165] In obedience to the terms of the will, Charles took the additional surname Pix. By 1901 he was at Bulawayo, Rhodesia. In 1913 at Pretoria, unknown to his solicitors, he married Inez Viola Biccard of Middelburg in the Transvaal, a minor. By 1919 he was living at Dogs Hill in Winchelsea, bankrupt, and forced to mortgage elements of his estate to pay his solicitors' charges. Gilbert Plantagenet Mitchell-Innes of Sandrock Hill in Playden bought the Woodside Estate for £18,911 6s 0d on 22 January 1920; included in the sale were the manors of Ewhurst, Iden and Mote.[166]

---

[161] *The Visitation of Shropshire, Taken in the Year 1623, Part 1* (Harleian Society 28 (1889)), ed. G. Grazebrook and J. P. Rylands; for inscriptions in Rye church to Thomas and Katherine Owens see G. S. Butler, 'The vicars of Rye and their patrons; with the mural, slab, and headstone inscriptions in the parish church of St Mary, and the Baptist Chapel, Rye', *SAC* 13 (1861), 280.

[162] The Norton documents in DAP box 108 include the PCC probate of the will of John Bradbury of St Saviour's Southwark, apothecary, 13 Jun 1749, and a commission of Thomas Bradbury as a second lieutenant in the 43rd Marines in 1790, but neither document clarifies John Bradbury's relationship to Thomas Owens or Katherine Norton, although John Bradbury's will is witnessed by a John Norton; L. A. Vidler, who was in touch with a Canon C. H. Norton of Bristol, states that he was a descendant of Ralph Norton's sister.

[163] ESRO DAP box 108.

[164] *VCH Sx* 9 266; ESRO BAT 1004-8; *Sussex Express* 2 July 1853 4A; TNA PRO PROB 11/2177, f. 208.

[165] *Sussex Express* 13 January 1900 5A, 20 January 1900 4E; TNA PRO RG 12/502, f. 104v.

[166] ESRO GBN 20/2; ACC 5164.

The printed particulars, in which the manors appear as Lot 45, demonstrate that the three lordships were still going concerns. Ewhurst consisted of eleven copyhold and twenty-eight freehold tenements producing an income from quitrents of £3 17s 10½d, the five copyhold and eleven freehold tenements of the manor of Iden yielded 17s 10¾d, and the manor of Mote's twenty-six tenements, all freehold, paid quitrents amounting to £3 0s 7d. No courts had been held since 1915, and the vendor reserved the right to hold a court before completion of the sale.[167]

In 1921 Mitchell-Innes sold the manors to Charles Joseph James Bolton Clark of Hooks Hall, Romford, Essex, who died on 2 August 1932. By his will of 29 June 1921, in which he described himself as 'Lord of the Manors of Ewhurst, Iden and Mote in the County of Sussex', he left the three lordships to his nephew John Percival Bolton Clark. Before his death in 1978 J. P. B. Clark told his son that he had sold his lordships, but extensive enquiries by the East Sussex Record Office in the 1980s failed to locate the purchaser.

THE HISTORY OF THE ARCHIVE, ITS FORMATION AND CUSTODY

The early manorial records remained of crucial administrative importance in the seventeenth century. Following the example of his predecessor Sir John Scott, Nathaniel Powell annotated the account rolls with points of interest and potential profit, and intervened actively in the compilation of a survey in 1673. Indeed it is almost certain that we owe the survival of the records to the interest shown in them by Powell, the upwardly-mobile lord, the antiquarian leanings of his steward Richard Kilburne and the determination and pride of their bailiff Thomas Russell.

When in 1524 he partitioned his estates by a clause in his will, Sir William Scott had ordered that the relevant 'evidences, court rolls and writings' of the manors and land should be delivered to his sons John and Edward Scott.[168] Thereafter, custody of the records would have been maintained by the lawyers employed by the lords to act as their manorial stewards. Unless estates were significantly dispersed, a single steward usually acted for all the manors owned by one individual, irrespective of the counties in which the lordships lay. The steward would usually be chosen for the convenience of his practice to the owner's seat; in the case of the Catholic Scott family, lords until 1646, religious considerations seem also to have played a part in the choice of a lawyer. The following table lists the men who can be identified as stewards of the manor of Mote; biographical summaries are contained in the notes.

---

[167] ESRO VID 6/65/12.
[168] TNA PRO PROB 11/21, f. 229v.

Date	Steward	Source
<1551-1551	Mr [John] Wybarne[169]	NOR 15/1
1551+	John Sharpe[170]	NOR 15/1
1587-1589	Vincent Engham, esq[171]	NOR 15/1
1589-1595	Gabriel Morelande[172]	NOR 15/1
1596	Francis More, gent	NOR 15/1
1597-1620	William Cobbes, gent[173]	NOR 15/1
1624-1626+	Anthony Tuttesham, gent[174]	NOR 15/1

[169] The last membrane of ESRO NOR 15/1 is endorsed 'received from Mr Wybarne'. The note applies to two sheets of paper, containing courts for 1551. The distinctive hand in which they are written is that of John Wybarne, as can be seen by comparison with ESRO ASH 206, a court book of the manor of Burghurst in Burwash of which Wybarne was lord. The family was seated at Pembury in Kent from before 1475 (ESRO RYE 137/20), but had interests in Sussex. William Wybarne of Bayham became mortgagee of Boarzell in Ticehurst in 1537, and, with his son John Wybarne, purchased the manor of Burghurst from Anthony Rous in 1538; both these interests had descended to John Wybarne of Hawkwell in Pembury by 1569 (ESRO DUN 1/54; AMS 6779/1/18; DUN 50/4/1; TNA PRO C1/1379/18; C4/Eliz/D5/55). His will of 1590, in which he bequeathed to his friends rings 'after the manner of the serjeant's ring', was proved in PCC on 20 November 1591 (TNA PRO PROB 11/78, f. 261).

[170] Son of Richard Sharpe of Northiam and Alice, daughter of Nicholas Tufton of Northiam; steward of Battle Abbey, c1535; a JP by 1555 until his death on 8 April 1583; on 12 December 1558, with Richard Sackville, James Gage and John Ashburnham, he became a feoffee of Sir John Guldeford, perhaps suggesting Catholic leanings; he married Alice Odiarne of Wittersham with whom he had six sons and seven daughters; in 1567 he lived at Silverden in Northiam, a tenement of the manor of Robertsbridge, but also held land of Mote; in 1575 he was one of the men commissioned by the Lord Warden to examine the constitution of Rye; steward of the manor of Playden, 1582; buried at Northiam, where a brass inscription survives, on 9 April 1583; his will of 1 April 1583 proved in PCC on 4 June 1583 (*The Visitation of the County of Sussex* (Harleian Society 53 (1905)), ed. W. B. Bannerman, 135; TNA PRO C1/857/10; *Calendar of State Papers, Mary I*, 160, *Calendar of Assize Records, Sussex Indictments, Elizabeth*; *A Calender of Post Mortem Inquisitions, 1 to 25 Elizabeth* (SRS 3 (1904)), ed. L. F. Salzmann, 27; *Surveys of the Manors of Robertsbridge, Sussex and Michelmarsh, Hampshire* (SRS 47 (1946)), ed. R. H. D'Elboux, 252; ESRO RYE 47/9/26; AMS 4888; PAR 431/1/1/1; C. E. D. Davidson-Houston, 'Sussex Monumental Brasses, part IV', *SAC* 79 (1938), 79; TNA PRO PROB 11/65, f. 30.

[171] Principal of Staple Inn, an inn of chancery, in 1585 (C. W. Brooks, *The admission registers of Barnard's Inn* (1995), 161, quoting BL Lansdowne MS 47 f.120), and probably identical with the Vincent Ingham of Charing who was made overseer of the will of William Scott of Mote, 23 January 1584 (TNA PRO PROB 11/69, f. 166); in 1557 a Vincent Engham was appointed bailiff to Yarmouth by the Cinque Ports (EKAC NR/CPc/17); of Great Chart, gent, in 1563 when he was jointly bound in connection with a lease of property in Canterbury (CCA DCC BB/77/76), and in 1599 when he released property in Orlestone (CCA U101/II/F/1).

[172] Of Wye in Kent, gent., at his death in 1610. The accounts of the administrators of his estate show that he was buried in the chancel of Wye church; his goods, valued at £58 7s 4d, included books worth £1 6s 8d housed on 33 shelves. He had collected quitrents for John Carey, Lord Hunsdon, (CKS PRC 10/49/196, 2/22/35).

[173] Tenant of Catsfield Place in 1602 (ESRO RAF 25/41); his wife, of Catsfield, presented for recusancy in 1605 and he and Margaret Cobbes in 1607 (*Calendar of Assize Records, Sussex Indictments, James I*); the very catholic will of William Cobbes of Sellindge in Kent and Holborn was proved in PCC on 8 September 1620 (TNA PRO PROB 11/136, f. 176v.).

[174] Probably the man of that name buried at Battle, as 'Mr Anthony Tutsome', on 6 January 1635 (ESRO PAR 236/1/1/1); franchise coroner of the hundred of Gostrow, 1628 (*Sussex Coroners'*

Date	Steward	Source
<1638-1646	Thomas Houghton, gent[175]	NOR 15/1, 5
1648-1673+	Richard Kilburne, esq[176]	NOR 15/2-3
<1685-1685+	Joseph Newington[177]	SAU 1199
<1703-1712	Jeffrey Gilbert[178]	AMS 5691/1/1
1714-1723+	Thomas Frewen[179]	AMS 5691/1/1

Inquests 1603-1688 (London, 1998), ed. R. F. Hunnisett, xxxv); he and his father were of Northiam in 1619 (ESRO FRE 7012; DUN 28/6, 9); of Battle, gent in 1633 (ESRO SAM 30); an Anthony son of Thomas Tutsham gent was baptized at Warbleton, 9 May 1563 (ESRO PAR 501 1/1/1) and was steward of the manor of St Bartholomew's Hospital, Rye in 1618 (L. A. Vidler, 'St Bartholomew's Hospital at Rye', *SAC* 83 (1943), 94); Anthony Tuttesham the younger witnessed a Rye deed in 1626 (ESRO AMS 2327) and both father and son witnessed a Northiam will in 1618; the will of Anthony Tuttesham of Battle, gent, was proved in PCC on 10 February 1635 (TNA PRO PROB 11/167).

[175] Of Middle House in Mayfield (c1594-1669), son of William Houghton of Crebor in Tavistock, Devon and Elizabeth Comber of Shermanbury; principal of Clifford's Inn; in Sussex by 1619, perhaps as clerk to Thomas Aynscombe of Mayfield (ESRO GLY 1671; SAS/WH 313; first witnessed deeds with Nathaniel Powell, with whom he was to be closely associated, in 1623 (ESRO DUN 26/12; AMS 6086/34); in 1624 at Isfield he married as his first wife Mary, daughter of Thomas Aynscombe, whose ancestors had built Middle House, and to whose practice he seems to have succeeded; in 1640 he acted as one of the trustees for the payment of the debts of William Scott and Thomas Scott, and in 1646 assigned the property to Nathaniel Powell; died 30 July 1669 age 75; will proved in PCC on 13 August 1669; Monumental Inscription at Mayfield Church (ESRO DUN 23/1; AMS 3777; SAU 1300, 1301; AMS 4656, 5699; NOR 12/2, 17/4; TNA PRO PROB 11/330, f. 306).

[176] Of Fowlers in Hawkhurst and Staple Inn (1605–1678), lawyer and topographer, see J. Whyman, 'Kilburne, Richard (1605–1678)', *Oxford Dictionary of National Biography* (Oxford, 2004), which under-estimates his involvement in Sussex; steward of Nathaniel Powell's manors of Bodiam, Broomham in Catsfield, Ewhurst and Mote, and of Thomas Gilbert of Eastbourne's manor of Iden; town clerk of Faversham (ESRO FRE 4350, 4365, 4366, 4368, 4384, 4437, 4446, 4450, 4480), attorney of the Cinque Ports in the courts of Common Pleas and Exchequer, 1666-1674 (*The Black and White Book of the Cinque Ports*, ed. K.M.E. Murray, 525, 536); will proved in PCC on 2 January 1679 (TNA PRO PROB 11/359, f. 46).

[177] Of Battle, attorney, son of Thomas Newington, briefly owner of Batemans in Burwash under the will of his aunt Alice Newington, 1687 (ESRO PBT 3/2/28); in 1694 his niece Frances Newington, then under age, was admitted to a Battle manor copyhold by her attorney Sir Nathaniel Powell, whose grandson Sir Christopher Powell, said to be her first cousin, she married in 1728 (ESRO BAT 19-20, Burke *Extinct and Dormant Baronetcies*, 423).

[178] Of Kent and the Inner Temple, judge and legal writer (1674-1726), see M. Macnair, 'Gilbert, Sir Jeffray (1674–1726)', *Oxford Dictionary of National Biography* (Oxford, 2004); he maintained a local practice, in about 1711 acting as referee between Rye Corporation and John Bold in a dispute concerning property in Rye (ESRO DAP 84/3/2) and giving an opinion to the parish officers of Mayfield in a settlement case (ESRO AMS 5588/2/3); his will of 1726 contains a bequest of all his law manuscripts 'under special trust that none should be printed' (TNA PRO PROB 11/612, f. 10).

[179] Of Church House, Northiam, attorney (1691-1767), the son of Thomas Frewen (1666-1731) and Sarah Stevens, he was baptized at Northiam on 29 January 1691. He was married at Northiam on 10 July 1722 to Sarah Bishopp, the daughter of the late Peter Bishopp of Newenden, gent. He acted as steward to his family's Brickwall estate, and was described by Selina Turner, in a letter to Laton Frewen, as 'our valuable relation the worthy lawyer' (ESRO FRE 1388); his will was proved in PCC

Date	Steward	Source
<1762-1765+	Edward Southouse[180]	NOR 15/128
<1791-1793+	Jeremiah Curteis[181]	DAP 1, 107/5-6

Table 4
Stewards of the Manor of Mote

The firm established at Rye by Jeremiah Curteis, under its various styles, continued to act as stewards of the successive lords of Mote until beyond 1893, but by 1901 the business had been acquired by Stileman and Neate of Southampton Street, Bloomsbury, who were still acting in 1919.[182]

Late in the 1950s, Mr Clark brought the court books of the three manors of Ewhurst, Iden and Mote into the Sussex Archaeological Society's museum at Barbican House, Lewes. The curator, N. E. S. Norris, passed a note of the interview to Ken Dickens, the curator of deeds, but although Mr Clark had indicated that he 'might sell for a consideration', the contact was not followed up. Only a few abstracts of title, deeds and indexes to the missing court books remained in the hands of J. P. B. Clark's son, who deposited them in November 1988.[183]

It seems clear that Mr Clark or his father had acquired the current working archive of the manorial stewards – there are no court books or rentals in their deposit at Lewes. The documents edited here, part of a larger accumulation discovered at Lloyds Bank in Rye before 1952, had clearly been separated on account of their antiquarian interest from the main body of documents at some point after 1768, the date of the latest paper in the group. They were acquired from the bank by the Rye historian Leopold Amon Vidler, who in 1952 deposited them with the Sussex Archaeological Society. The Society's curator of deeds listed the papers as HC 175-271, and it paid for the account rolls to be professionally conserved.[184] In June 1982, the papers were transferred, along with the rest of the Society's archival holdings, to East Sussex Record Office, which in 1995 completed a new list of them under the mnemonic reference NOR, representing the Norton family which had held the lordship at the date of the latest document.

---

on 21 February 1767 (TNA PRO PROB 11/925, f. 391); he acted as steward of Bodiam manor, and almost certainly of Mote (BL Add MS 66694).

[180] An attorney in Maidstone in 1768 (ESRO FRE 5939); acting for the estate in 1765 (CKS U1515 E1); in 1768 he still retained the 'Late Lady Powell's court rolls of the said manor of Mote': ESRO NOR 15/128.

[181] Of Rye and Tenterden, attorney (1735-1806), town clerk of Rye 1756-1800, and steward of the Frewen estate, 1759-1799. His son Edward Jeremiah Curteis (1762-1835) of Church House, Northiam, and Windmill Hill Place, Wartling, sat as MP for Sussex 1820-1830. His daughter Anne Katherine Elwood (1796-1873) of Clayton Priory was a noted traveller and writer.

[182] ESRO SAS/DE 305, GBN 20/2, VID 6/65/12.

[183] ESRO ACC 5164.

[184] NOR 15/117 bears an address-label to SAS from N Palmer, 188 Gipsy Road, Bexley Heath in Kent.

The offices of the firm which had acted as manorial stewards since the end of the eighteenth century occupy the same premises as Lloyds Bank, and it was assumed in 1995 that the documents found there had strayed from one part of the building to the other. It now seems more likely that a member of the Pix family, who were both lords of the manor of Mote and partners in the Rye Bank, were responsible for separating the medieval documents from the working archive of the stewards.[185] It was a fortunate move – apart from a few scraps, the substantive archive of the manor's administration is still missing.

THE DIPLOMATIC OF THE DOCUMENTS

The accounts

The rental of 1478 and most of the membranes of the court roll are written on parchment; the accounts, in anticipation of the practice established on many manors towards the end of the fifteenth century, are on paper, as is the survey of 1673. The individual sheets of paper on which the accounts are written measure between 11½ and 12 inches wide, and between 17 or 17½ long; on occasions and for no apparent reason, sheets have been cut to unequal lengths.

The following table analyses the watermarks of the seventy-six sheets of paper of which the accounts consist according to the descriptions in Briquet, *Les Filigranes* (Table 5).[186]

Reference and membrane	Watermark type	Briquet number	Briquet date	document date
NOR 15/103				1464-65
1-2	crown	resembles 4645	1459-69	
3	crown	very close to 4758	1463	
NOR 15/104				1465-66
1	blank			
2	cart	resembles 3545 and 3534	1458 1460	
3	blank			
4	blank			
5	cow's head	resembles 15068	1462	
6	grapes	resembles 13056	1460	
7	ring	resembles 689	1457	

---

[185] There is however little to suggest that Thomas Smith Pix (1807-1900) had antiquarian interests; described in his obituary as 'a staunch and uncompromising Tory of the old school', his chief recreational activity appears to have been cricket: *Sussex Express* 20 January 1900 4E.
[186] C.-M. Briquet, *Les Filigranes* (revised edition ed. A. Stevenson, Amsterdam, 1968).

Reference and membrane	Watermark type	Briquet number	Briquet date	document date
NOR 15/105				1466-67
1	grapes	resembles 13056	1460	
2	*blank*			
3	*blank*			
4	ring	resembles 689	1457	
5	cow's head	resembles 15067	1467	
6	ring	resembles 689, but smaller than version on m4	1457	
NOR 15/106				1467-68
1-7	ring	resembles 689	1457	
NOR 15/107				1470-71
1-6	cow's head	resembles 15068	1462	
NOR 15/108				1471-72
1-2	lamb and flag	26	1467	
NOR 15/109				1472-73
1-5	cow's head *not in Briquet*			
NOR 15/110				1474-75
1	cow's head	resembles 15064	1454-65	
2	balance	version of 2449	1473	
3	cow's head	resembles 14339	1470	
4	balance	version of 2449	1473	
5-6	cow's head	14326	1472	
NOR 15/111				1475-1476
1	cow's head	resembles 14195	1469	
2	armorial three fleur-de-lys	1801	1472	
NOR 15/112				1476-1477
1-5	armorial fleur-de-lys	resembles 1557	1476	
NOR 15/113				1476-1477
1-2	armorial fleur-de-lys	resembles 1557	1476	
NOR 15/114				1477-1478
1-3	fleur-de-lys	7208	1479	
4	pot	12477	1476	
5	fleur-de-lys	7208	1479	
6	Pot	12477	1476	

Reference and membrane	Watermark type	Briquet number	Briquet date	document date
7	[fleur-de-lys	7208	1479]	
NOR 15/115				1477-1478
1-2	shell	4509	1477	
NOR 15/116				1478-1479
1-4	dog	3624	1476	
NOR 15/117				1479-1480
1-6	dog	3624	1476	
NOR 15/118				1479-1480
1-2	dog	3624	1476	
NOR 15/119				1480-1481
1-2	letter P	8573	1478	
NOR 15/120				1480-1481
1	orb; *not in Briquet*			
NOR 15/121				1481-1484
1	letter Y	resembles 9183	1472	

Table 5
Analysis of the watermarks of the paper of the Mote account rolls, 1464-1484

Of the five references in the accounts to the purchase of paper, only one locates the source: an unspecified amount bought at Appledore in 1468. The table suggests that, before Scott took up residence at Calais in 1471, paper was indeed purchased in England, and that the available stocks were relatively old. Once in Calais, nearer the centre of paper manufacture, Scott seems to have bought new stock and sent it to Mote immediately – the accounts for years after 1471 are almost all written on paper which was less than three years old.

The audited accounts are presented in conventional form, by which the accountant is charged with the year's income, which is then discharged by expenditure, with any resulting debit balance mitigated by allowances. Trial sums and totals were initially calculated using dot-notation, with the final figures entered only at the end of the accounting process, possibly at audit.[187] The accounting year begins nominally at Michaelmas – 29 September – although the underlying reality was considerably different, as will be discussed below. The accounts can be divided into those produced before 1471 by the steward William Harlakenden, which are very detailed and complex in their organization, and those written by his successors, which are more conventional in arrangement but lack the wealth of information. Harlakenden was the only accountant during his

---

[187] For dot-notation, see C. T. Martin, *The Record Interpreter* (2nd edn, London, 1910) xii-xiii, and C. Johnson and H. Jenkinson, *English Court Hand* (Oxford, 1915) 1, 75.

tenure of the office of steward, and he accounts as the receiver of Sir John Scott. Between the end of his last account in 1468 and 1476, the terms receiver, bailiff, and bailiff and rent-collector are all employed, and the precise relationship between their duties is obscured by the lack of rolls for several years.[188] From the accounting-year 1476-77, two parallel accounts were submitted, the first by an officer initially described as accountant and subsequently merely as servant, the second by a rent-collector.[189]

Harlakenden's accounts between 1464 and 1468 incorporate separate records of expenditure by John German, who was resident at Mote, as well as by Harlakenden himself, who had a wider oversight of the Scott estates and visited Mote irregularly. The need to accommodate parallel and contemporary records of expenditure in a single manorial account is but one example of Sir John Scott's determination to preserve traditional forms in the face of a reality in which financial information was being recorded by more modern methods. As well as the records of German's separate disbursements, the accounts make frequent reference to 'the lady's paper' and 'the accountant's paper', both of which recorded expenditure week by week. Both household expenses and a detailed record of building-works were kept in 'books of particulars', which were examined by the auditors to check the grossed-up totals, the only figures which appear in the accounts. These books also appear to have been maintained on a weekly basis. The overwhelming tendency of the accounts to be closed at weekends, as demonstrated by Table 6, reflects the extent to which they were based on other, weekly-based, records. There is also evidence that these records were kept in English, and the sums of money represented in less traditional ways: as well as his frequent use of vernacular words for obscure objects, occasionally the clerk began to write an English word, which he hastily corrected to the Latin equivalent, and sometimes corrected an initial *£3* to *60 shillings*, the conventional representation of such sums.

A close examination of the second surviving roll, for 1466, illustrates the difficulty which its compiler encountered in bringing into traditional form financial information which had been recorded in a different way. The expenditure presented by Harlakanden and German occurred not only in different years from those covered by the manorial accounts, but each of their records begins at a different date. The account roll, ostensibly covering the period from 29 September 1465 to the same date in 1466, records expenditure by John German from December 1465 until the same time in 1466, while payments by William Harlakenden begin in June 1465 and last for one year. Further difficulty is caused by the tendency of the accounts to run on past the date of their nominal closure, sometimes into the spring of the following year. This pattern is shown by Table 6, which demonstrates that in most years the period covered by an

---

[188] That accounts are missing can be established by the amounts of the arrears, which are carried forward from one year's account to the next.

[189] The arrears of the bailiff's account of 1476 were transferred to the first rent-collector's account: ESRO NOR 15/111, 113.

individual account was considerably more than a year, but that when an account was closed at an exceptionally late date, and some of the slippage recovered the following year, the timespan of the second account could be considerably less than twelve months.

.

NOR 15/	Year	Date of closure
107	1470-71	before 1 November 1471
108	1471-72	Monday 7 December 1472
	1473-74	Thursday 8 December 1474 (recited in ESRO NOR 15/110)
110	1474-75	Saturday 11 November 1475
111	1475-76	Saturday 8 December 1476
112	1476-77	Sunday 1 March 1478
114	1477-78	Saturday 22 May 1479
116	1478-79	Saturday 15 January 1480
117	1479-80	Friday 12 January 1481

Table 6

Dates of the closure of the Mote accounts, 1470-1480

This phenomenon was at its most marked at the end of the 1470s, when the account for 1477-78 covered a period of sixty-four weeks and that for the following year only thirty-two. The reason for this practice is not easy to establish, and since formal manorial accounts from the 1470s on lay estates are scarce, its prevalence is difficult to determine. It may be the result of the difficulty in assembling all the personnel required to close the accounts, or may echo the rhythm of the building works at Mote, the management of which occupies the greater part of the accounts. The building season began in the early spring and continued to October or November.[190] As a result of these practices, many of the dates within the accounts, unless a regnal year is included, are ambiguous, especially since financial information from a variety of sources, each presumably written in chronological order, have been coalesced into a single section in the account. In the edition, years have been added in square brackets only in cases of certainty; otherwise the record has been left to speak for itself. In the case of dates expressed in relation to moveable feasts, alternative dates have been provided in the footnotes.

Sir John Scott regularly intervened in the accounts, both in the rolls themselves and in the books which lay behind them, adding first-person notes on several of the rolls, which also mention his comments in the subsidiary papers (Illus. 2).

---

[190]   Hamilton Thompson, 'The building accounts of Kirby Muxloe Castle, 1480-1484', 201; Salzman, *Building in England*, 58-59.

The court rolls

The Norton archive at East Sussex Record Office includes three court rolls of the manor of Mote, covering the period 1442 to 1668; the first, for 1442-1551, is edited here. Along with the other manorial documents in the archive, these rolls must have been separated from the current administrative papers of the manor in the nineteenth century. The loss of these latter documents prevents proof of the hypothesis that the entries for the more recent courts at least were subsequently copied up into paper books in line with contemporary practice.

Although it is likely that many bundles of early court rolls are the product of a process of selection and arrangement undertaken by subsequent stewards, it is rare that the evidence is so clear as that presented by the manorial rolls of Mote. Richard Kilburne, who acted as steward of several manors on the Sussex side of the border, employed a standard technique for organising the information contained in the rolls in his care.[191] He would initially gather together the available court rolls, and paginate them in order to facilitate reference to individual entries. Using these page-numbers, Kilburne then produced analytical surveys, tracing the history of each manorial tenement as far into the past as the information extended, and drawing upon rentals, deeds and other available documents. The same surveys also contained sections demonstrating the application of manorial customs and other useful precedents, all using the page-numbers as references. This practice, and its usefulness, is illustrated by his survey of Nathaniel Powell's manor of Bodiam, which tantalizingly refers to entries from court rolls beginning in 1393, almost all of which are lost.[192]

Kilburne's survey of Bodiam is dated 1645, and his work on Mote was completed in 1648. The methodology for these surveys was clearly Kilburne's: he had undertaken a similar exercise on the records of Thomas Foster's manor of Iden in 1643.[193] He paginated the first nineteen membranes of the Mote rolls, covering 1442 to 1551, as 1-38, and formed them into a bundle endorsed AAAAAA;[194] that roll is edited here as the second element of the published text. Two further bundles, consisting of membranes numbered 39-70 (covering 1560-1646, BBBBBB) and 71-82 (covering 1648-1668), were created at the same time.[195]

---

[191] For Kilburne, see pp. lvi, and lxiii above.

[192] ESRO AMS 6692/1/2. The few Bodiam court rolls which survive from before the eighteenth century carry the remains of this system of numeration: HEH BA 900-903 (microfilm ESRO XA 3/22) contains rolls for 1645-1650 numbered 81-83, and BL Add Rolls 66690-95 (microfilm ESRO XA 15/1) include court rolls 1607-1626 and 1645 (membranes 1-14 and 77-80). The roll for 1645 (BL Add Roll 66691) is wrapped in a fragment of the same Pelham marriage settlement which was also used to protect the Mote court rolls for 1648-1668, ESRO NOR 15/3. For the court rolls of Broomham, numbered in the same way, see ESRO ASH 75.

[193] ESRO NOR 13/76.

[194] ESRO NOR 15/1.

[195] ESRO NOR 15/2-3; the membranes of the roll for 1560-1646 were originally foliated 1-16; the numbers 17 and 18 were written on the first two membranes of that for 1648-1668.

The third roll is written entirely in the hand of Thomas Russell, and the second in the various hands of the stewards or their clerks. Compared with them, the earliest roll is somewhat anomalous. Of its nineteen membranes, thirteen are of paper, and have the appearance of drafts; included are four courts for the manor of River. Three membranes are copies made in about 1640 of courts which survive elsewhere in the archive, as does the record of two courts of 1493 which was never, for unknown reasons, incorporated into the scheme.[196] It seems clear that Kilburne found the early court rolls in disarray, and methodized them into a semblance of order. The records of only two courts survive between 1444 and 1481, a gap which can possibly be attributed to the creation of the rental of 1478, for which the missing rolls would have been a major source; it seems that they were separated from the body of the archive and subsequently lost.

The rental of 1478

The rental edited here consists of six parchment membranes, each measuring 11 inches wide and roughly two feet five inches long, sewn together to produce a roll 13 feet 7 inches long. It is written in a fine engrossing hand of the 1470s, with tendencies towards Secretary letter-forms, and is probably the work of a professional scrivener. It was subsequently used by the stewards of the manor in the compilation of later surveys and rentals, as is shown by a number of marginal updates; the latest steward to use the rental was Richard Kilburne, whose characteristic annotations, in red ink, can also be seen in the analytical survey which he compiled in 1646.[197]

In the accounting year 1472-73, John Bookland, a lawyer based in Battle, was paid to compile a new rental, but the roll edited here is not that document, and does not seem to be in Bookland's hand.[198] Bookland's rental was written on paper, and was referred to as 'the new paper rental' in the account rolls as late as 1481. It can probably be identified with ESRO NOR 15/12, or perhaps a lost exemplar for it, which is a long paper roll containing a roughly written and heavily annotated rental. These annotations consist partly of corrections and augmentations, and partly of the names of new tenants of properties which had changed hands by inheritance or purchase since it was originally compiled. By and large, its text in its final form is close to that of NOR 15/13, the document printed here.

Both versions of the rental contain a reference to a stock-deed of a piece of land in Iden dated 20 July 1473. At the end of the paper roll appears a note for a manor court held on 6 May 1480, giving a terminal date for its currency. The parchment rental continues with six entries, 104-109, which are not included in the paper rental. They are written in the same hand as the rest of the parchment

---

[196] ESRO NOR 15/4.
[197] ESRO NOR 15/62.
[198] Bookland probably wrote ESRO ACC 7006/16, a stock-deed of a Mote tenement dated 5 April 1479; a calendar appears as Appendix 1 number 8.

rental, and although they appear to be contemporary may be an addition made soon after the roll had been completed. Two of the six repeat entries which appear earlier in the roll, and two are cast in the form of entries from an undated court roll. The last entry refers to 'Crouchland' in Northiam, held by Thomas John by a rent of seven shillings, a tenure created only on 5 April 1479.[199] On that basis the paper rental, NOR 15/12, can be dated between 1473 and 1479, and NOR 15/13 to shortly before 1480.

More precise dating, based on the updates to the text of NOR 15/12, is impeded by the lack of any records of courts held between 1468 and 1480, probably separated from the main body of rolls in order to assist in the compilation of the rental of 1478 and subsequently misplaced. The tenement held by Edward Hore [51] was probably that which he received from his father's feoffees on 2 October 1477 and which, as *a tenement called The Sore,* he leased to William Tufton on 20 February 1482.[200] The paper rental originally listed 'the heirs of William Blount' as the tenant of 'High Barhams' in Northiam [52]. Blount had been killed at the battle of Barnet on 14 April 1471 and his widow Margaret, the daughter and co-heir of Sir Thomas Etchingham, married John Elrington, the treasurer of the king's household; his tenure, in her right, is annotated above the entry. A further annotation to the same entry on the paper rental inserts *miles,* a rank which is incorporated in the equivalent entry on the parchment rental. Elrington was knighted on 17 January 1478.[201] Both rentals list William Tracy, the master of the Hospital of St Bartholomew at Playden, as tenant of ten acres of land in that parish [88]. Tracy was dead by 3 July 1478, when he was replaced as master by John More.[202] Therefore, if the knowledge of those responsible for compiling the document was up to date, and they compiled it accurately, the rental published here can be attributed to a date between January and July 1478, and the six entries at the end must be additions made within a year of its completion.

The survey of 1673

In the two years after the acquisition of the lordship of Mote by Nathaniel Powell in 1646, the manorial records were extensively used by his steward Richard Kilburne to compile a new analytical survey, a process which he undertook for Powell's other manors of Bodiam, Ewhurst and Broomham in Catsfield at about the same time.[203] The initiative was probably not Powell's – Kilburne had already

---

[199] ESRO ACC 7006/16.

[200] CKS U455 T123/13-14.

[201] *Complete Peerage,* 9, 336-39; Wedgwood, *History of Parliament,* 297-99; both rentals spell the surname *Elderton.*

[202] *VCH Sx* 2 105; *CPR 1476-1485* 105; More was the clerk of the king's closet, and the privy seal writ for his appointment is dated 3 July 1478: TNA PRO C 81/866/820.

[203] ESRO NOR 15/62-63; for Kilburne's analytical surveys of the manors of Bodiam (compiled in 1645 from court rolls dating back to 1393, now lost), see ESRO AMS 6692/1/2; for his survey of

compiled a similar survey of the manor of Iden for its lord Thomas Foster of Eastbourne.[204] Those surveys were relatively rough working documents, but soon after 1670 a decision was taken to produce formal surveys of all Powell's manors. Unlike the survey of 1648, the new project would have an additional element – maps – to be drawn by the bailiff Thomas Russell of Ewhurst.

Thomas Russell (1626-1686) was born in Framfield into a family of yeomen who had owned Uptons Mill since at least 1515. His father Edward Russell, whose probate inventory amounted to £243 8s 2d, was buried at Framfield as 'Edward Russell a Mell' in 1653.[205] Russell was in Ewhurst by 1652, having possibly been recruited by Nathaniel Powell as parish clerk; it was he who wrote the memorandum, signed by Powell, of the appointment of Thomas Sayers as parish register on 20 November 1653.[206] In July 1655 Russell married Susan Pooke, daughter of Thomas Pooke of Sandhurst (d1657), who may have had links with the Puritan community in that parish; their seven children were baptized between 1656 and 1672. Susan died in July 1676 and on 23 April 1678 Thomas married Benetta Evernden of Sedlescombe.[207] As well as his work for Powell, Russell also acted as clerk to Peter Farnden's ironworks at Conster in Brede, wrote deeds, made surveys of land for other local clients, and was still collecting rents in the closing months of his life. Russell was active in the land-market, acquiring twenty acres in Ewhurst from his Pooke cousins and an 84-acre farm in Mayfield from Sir Nathaniel Powell, and his will reveals that he had over £1000 invested in mortgages.[208] Although not a trained lawyer, Russell clearly had an amateur's respect for legal forms. His will of 1683 was dated by regnal year as well as by year of grace, and the document itself was indented – one part was to be left with his wife, the other 'among my writings for my executors'. Although on 2 February 1683 Russell declared himself 'in perfect health and of sound memory', he subsequently became senile. Writing to his son Thomas Russell (1657-1688), the town clerk of Dover, in February 1687, his cousin Richard Seamer of Northiam asked to be sent ten guineas for the three years' rents which Russell's father had collected from Seamer's tenant in Sedlescombe, and which he had omitted from his accounts. He could establish the amount from the receipts 'though some of them (being writ after he had lost

---

the manor of Ewhurst, c1648, see ESRO AMS 4441; for his survey of Broomham in Catsfield, 1645, see ESRO AMS 6692/1/2.
[204] ESRO NOR 13/75-79 of c1643; for the Foster family, see W. Budgen, *Old Eastbourne* (London, 1912), 245-6.
[205] ESRO PAR 343/1/1/1; ADA 137, ff. 51-52; for the deeds of the mill, see ESRO SAS/C 721-56, SAS/LM 192-230.
[206] ESRO PAR 324/1/1/1, f. 47v.; PAR 324/33.
[207] ESRO PAR 324/1/1/1; TNA PRO PROB 11/265, f. 278 (Thomas Pooke); TNA PRO PROB 11/363, f. 313v. (George Pooke, citizen and girdler of London); the Russells received bequests in both wills; ESRO PAR 481/1/1/1.
[208] ESRO DUN 47; DUN 46/6; ACC 2806/1/9/15; AMS 6400/1; AMS 5742/5; AMS 5691/2/36; CHR 4/2/9; TNA PRO PROB 11/383, f. 293.

his memory) are not very perfect'. Russell was buried at Ewhurst on 17 May 1686 and his will was proved at London on 10 June.[209]

Russell's accounts as Sir Nathaniel Powell's bailiff survive from 1662-63, but it is clear from the opening balance that they do not represent the beginning of his service. Between 1671 and 1674 he had a central role in the surveys of Powell's manors of Bodiam (1671), Mote and Ewhurst (1673) and Broomham (1674); the steward Richard Kilburne undertook the documentary work, and Thomas Russell surveyed the manorial tenements, compiled the maps based on his fieldwork and wrote up the courts of survey on the manorial rolls. Although the finished Mote survey seems to have been engrossed by a professional scrivener, the Ewhurst survey is written in Russell's unmistakable hand.[210] Were it not for the survival of Russell's notes and draft maps, the written surveys and maps would give the clear impression of a manor with settled boundaries and tenures; but the subsidiary documents tell a different story. Work on the survey was under way in July 1673, when Powell wrote to the Battle attorney John Purfield to enquire after the boundaries of the manor of Iden Rectory, of which he was steward; in August several tenants signed forms of acknowledgement of tenure.[211] Russell's draft maps, of which eight survive, make clear both his frustration in attempting to make the written descriptions of Mote's tenements match what he found in the field, and Powell's determination to claim as much land as possible for his lordship.[212] The rental of 1478 had included ten acres of land in Playden [88], but Russell was unable to make the bounds or the acreage match the holdings of the current tenant, and the entry was eventually omitted from his survey, as was a piece belonging to John Webb, the incumbent of Burwash. Russell's attempts to put forward the claims of other lords were met with firmness by Powell: 'this must stand ... this must be plotted'; 'I do absolutely deny it, and do therefore desire to see Mr Foster's rentals as well former as late, as you have done mine'. But however peremptory were Powell's comments, Russell was not afraid to contradict him – 'you claim the said lands of

---

[209] ESRO AMS 5691/2/36; PAR 324/1/1/1; TNA PRO PROB 11/383, f. 293; for Thomas Russell the younger, baptized at Ewhurst on 3 January 1658, who died in 1688, unmarried and without a valid will, leaving his brother Edward Russell as his heir, see TNA PRO PROB 6/64, ff. 7, 64 and 71v., PROB 5/664 and PROB 20/2247.

[210] For Thomas Russell's five maps of the manor of Bodiam dated 1671, based on courts of survey held in April and September 1671 (for which see BL Add Roll 66693, microfilm at ESRO XA 15/1), see ESRO AMS 5691/3 and 5692/6; for the notes and draft maps for the survey of the manor of Mote in 1673, see ESRO NOR 15/64-93, and for Russell's map of the tenements in Iden and Playden only, see ESRO AMS 4856; for a copy made in about 1766 of his map of the tenements in Peasmarsh, see ESRO NOR 15/96; for Russell's survey of the manor of Ewhurst, [1673], see ESRO AMS 4440; for his map of the tenements of the same manor in the parish of Ewhurst, 1673, see ESRO AMS 4856, and for copies made for Sir Whistler Webster, owner of Ewhurst but not of Mote, c1755, see ESRO AMS 4442-43; for an unfinished map of 1673, not in Russell's hand, of the manor of Ewhurst's tenements in Northiam, see AMS 3500; for Russell's survey of the manor of Broomham, 1674, see ESRO NOR 16/6, and for his map, drawn in the same year, see ESRO ASH 4378.

[211] ESRO NOR 15/74-78.

[212] The draft maps are ESRO NOR 15/79-86.

Dallet to hold of you; you are wrong therein' and to let his impatience show: 'where Short Crouch is I cannot hear nor understand; I believe it's a name clear dead, and rot and forgot.... I have spent the best part of three days to hunt out and admeasure 25 acres of land and when I admeasured it I was forced to carry two people with me to carry the chain'. Eventually Russell submitted a list of 'queries I desire an answer to before I can perfect my plots', and enjoined Powell to be careful with the maps: 'I have delivered you seven paper plots; pray lose them not for if you do I shall be at a loss'. Finally Russell drafted the survey in individual booklets for each parish; Powell made minor alterations, and the text was engrossed. Unfortunately only one of the maps, showing the tenements of the manors of Ewhurst and Mote in Iden and Playden, survives.

A close comparison of the survey of 1673 with the other manorial documents, and particularly with the deeds which created the tenures which it recorded, reveals that Sir Nathaniel Powell was guilty of sharp practice. In the case of one small tenement, John Pashley had stinted future heriots and fines to four pence certain by a deed of 1455, and in 1467 Sir John Scott had freed a house and twelve acres in Northiam from all manorial liabilities other than the quitrent.[213] Despite his possession of the counterparts of these deeds, and the correct recording of the tenures by the rental of 1478, Powell's survey of 1673 states that all the tenements of the manor of Mote were held by fealty, suit of court, heriot and relief, as well as quitrent. The lack of court rolls prevents us from knowing whether the tenants, in whose hands many of the deeds still remained, ever challenged Powell's assertion of manorial rights which had been sold by his predecessors.

Stock-deeds and manorial tenure at Mote

The documents embodying such sales, and those redefining manorial tenures in general, were termed 'stock-deeds'.[214] Although the phrase was liberally used by Sir Nathaniel Powell and his steward Richard Kilburne in the compilation of the surveys of 1648 and 1673, which are frequently annotated 'I have seen the stock-deed', it was not their personal coinage, and can be found as early as the beginning of the sixteenth century.[215] Although it usually referred to more ancient documents, it could equally be applied to contemporary transactions – a deed of 1645 converting two heriots due to the manor of Broomham Parkgate in Catsfield into money-payments is endorsed *Stock Deed*.[216]

The nature of the feudal relationship between lord and tenant was more flexible than is often supposed, and adjustments of its terms could take place for a variety of reasons at any time. Lords in need of ready cash would be tempted to raise it, to the detriment of their successors, by selling various aspects of their

---

[213] CKS U455 T122/7, T119/26.

[214] Deriving from *OED*, sv *stock* n¹ sense 3, although the usage *stock-deed* is not included.

[215] See Appendix 1, no. 2.

[216] ESRO SAU 267, calendared as Appendix 1, no. 12.

feudal entitlements to their tenants. Outright enfranchisement – the complete ending of manorial tenure – was almost unknown until the eighteenth century, and common only when encouraged by statute, a process which began in 1841.[217] More usual was the conversion of tenure in villeinage or by copy of court roll into customary freehold, but retaining the right to quitrents and manorial services, or the mitigation of those services, for example by converting the lord's right to take the tenant's best beast as a heriot into the payment of a fixed monetary sum. In this process, known as stinting, a practically infinite range of options was possible; they ultimately depended on the relative financial position of the lord and his tenant or tenants, and it must be remembered that, by the eighteenth century, some manorial tenants were the social superiors of the lords of whom they held their land. Sometimes a lord would offer terms to all his tenants, a means by which considerable sums could be raised relatively quickly. That was the technique adopted by John Gage of Firle, who on 20 November 1580 executed at least nine deeds converting copyhold tenements held of his manor of Maresfield into freeholds. As well as pocketing £170 from the transactions, he retained the right to take unlimited heriots and reliefs.[218] Sir Henry Neville of Billingbear in Berkshire was more ambitious: in 1591 he embarked on a conversion of over sixty copyhold tenements of his Sussex manor of Mayfield into freeholds.[219] The deeds produced by such exercises occasionally recited underlying disputes between lords and their copyhold tenants, although such assertions may have been no more than common form.[220]

We are dependent for our knowledge of these transactions upon the deeds which gave effect to them, be it the grant itself, which generally descended with the tenement, or its counterpart which passed with the lordship. In the case of the manor of Mote we are fortunate that several of its tenements were purchased by the Tufton family, latterly earls of Thanet, and the deeds remain in their archive, and that Nathaniel Powell had at least eleven counterparts in his possession in 1648. Appendix 1 presents transcripts or calendars of twelve documents derived from this process, not all of them relating to the manor of Mote, ranging in date from c1280 to 1645.

In the beginning, the function of stock-deeds was to convert unfree tenements, held by villein tenure and uncertain labour-services, into customary freehold. Two examples are printed in Appendix 1. By the first, a deed of the early 1280s, John Moyne, the lord of the manor of Wilting in Hollington, freed the tenure of Wilsham (now Wilsons Farm) in Ashburnham, to Robert de Wilsham, whose father Robert had held it of John's father in villeinage. The

---

[217]   Copyhold Act, 4 & 5 Vict. c.35; the word first occurs in this sense in 1818: *OED*, sv *enfranchise* v. I 3.
[218]   ESRO SAS/G6/31/31-38.
[219]   ESRO ACC 1244.
[220]   For example in the ten deeds executed by Sir Richard Sackville, Earl of Dorset, and his brother Edward freeing tenements held of the manor of Berwick on 1 June 1618, an exercise which grossed over £340: ESRO SAS/G23/3-4, G29/3, G40/56, G41/10-11, 53, BH/P/1/3/2-3, 1/12/1.

quitrent was set at fourteen shillings a year for all services, but Robert was required to attend John's court four times a year, and he and future owners remained liable for heriots, reliefs, wardships, marriages, and two reasonable aids to make their lord's eldest son a knight and to marry his eldest daughter.[221] The second, written in about 1300, is a very similar grant by John de Monceux, lord of Herstmonceux, to Hamo de Fareham. His messuage and land was henceforth to be held by a quitrent of twelve shillings for all services, but nevertheless the lord retained the right to the wardship and marriage of the heir, reliefs, heriots, escheats, suit of court every three weeks and reasonable aids for making his eldest son a knight and marrying his eldest daughter, which were fixed at a shilling each. Like the Wilting deed, the grant also forbade sales to religious houses or Jews.[222] The tenure established by these deeds may seem onerous, but perhaps Robert and Hamo were grateful to be freed from villeinage or unable to pay for more generous terms. By the middle of the sixteenth century, stock-deeds embodying such harsh services were not only an embarrassment, but positively dangerous to the current holders of the property. At least one Sussex landowner felt the need to keep his a secret: the Wilting deed of the 1280s, which freed the tenement but on terms far from beneficial to the tenants, is endorsed in a sixteenth-century hand: *keep this deed very closely, for this is a deed that do show that the lands that is in Ashburnham is held in knight service and ward and marriage; and let it be your trusty friend that sees this deed.*[223]

If such grants were at one end of the spectrum, at the other lay charters which reserved only suit of court and a nominal quitrent of a penny, retained in order to preserve the tenure in the event of an escheat or forfeiture. These were often beneficial grants between gentry families, such as the deed of 1533 by which Sir John Gage of Firle remitted all but a penny from the quitrent of an already freehold tenement of his manor of Hosiers to his cousin John Bolney, who paid £9 for the privilege.[224] The value of a freehold tenement could also be enhanced in other ways: in 1645, William Bishop of Sedlescombe, gentleman, extinguished two heriots to which a small part of his Great Sanders estate was subject by the payment of an unspecified sum of money.[225]

In general, the later the stock-deed, the more generous were its terms, reflecting the increased wealth, independence and indeed ubiquity across the social scale of the holders of unfree manorial tenements, and the loosening and growing unenforceability of feudal ties. Within that pattern, there seems to have been a relaxation of tenures in the fourteenth century, followed by a tendency, by the second half of the fifteenth century, to retain feudal rights. Surviving stock-deeds for tenements of the manor of Mote illustrate this trend, but also display a remarkable inconsistency of terms, even in grants made on the same day. In 1337 John de

---

[221] TNA PRO C146/6965, calendared as Appendix 1, no. 1.
[222] ESRO SAS/P459, calendared as Appendix 1, no. 2.
[223] TNA PRO C146/6965.
[224] ESRO SAS/G 4/32, calendared as Appendix 1 no. 11.
[225] ESRO SAU 267, calendared as Appendix 1 no. 12.

Pashley, engaged in a bitter legal struggle against his stepmother, granted to a Rye merchant a tenement in Peasmarsh which had previously been held by John's villein, reserving only a quitrent of 1s 3d and suit of court; no doubt a sizeable consideration also changed hands.[226] In 1375 Robert Pashley was prepared to release all the services due to him from a tenement in Northiam, retaining only one suit of court a year and a quitrent of 1s 6d.[227] In two grants executed on 17 April 1455, his great-grandson John Pashley reserved a quitrent of four pence, two suits of court and fixed heriots and reliefs of four pence each in a grant to Thomas Harley of Northiam, and yet drove a far harder bargain with the powerful William Tufton, whose Tufton Place in Northiam remained subject to a four-shilling quitrent, heriots and reliefs at will and quarterly suits of court.[228] Sir John Scott also varied the terms on which he was prepared to stint his feudal entitlements: in 1466 John Langport of Sundridge in Kent was relieved of all services, including suit, in return for a quitrent of four shillings, yet in 1479 Thomas John remained liable to seven shillings' quitrent, suit whenever a court was summoned, and a heriot.[229] Finally in 1487 Sir John's son William Scott granted *The Vellex* in Northiam, reserving a penny in lieu of all services.[230] Such disparities can only reflect the amount of money, rarely stated, which tenants were prepared to pay for the freedom of their holdings from seigneurial control. Tenants would often seek to combine the freeing of their holdings with a family settlement. Robert Pashley's charter of 1375 entailed a tenement in Northiam on the issue of the grantees, and in 1398 he made a much more complicated grant, with a triple remainder, to James Bennet of Wittersham and his wife Joan. The stimulus for such grants must have come from the tenants, and lords had little to lose in making them, if the price was right: the deed of 1398 includes a reversionary clause to Pashley and his heirs.[231]

Although early stock-deeds make the former unfree tenure of the holding clear, their later equivalents are usually vague. In a charter of 1479 and in a draft for another of 1481, Sir John Scott refers to the property to be granted as 'a field of my land'. This could imply a former copyhold tenement or a piece of waste, but in all probability indicates an enclosed area of demesne land.

The rental of 1478 reveals that by that date, the manor of Mote consisted entirely of customary freeholds; there were no copyhold tenements. That was also the case in 1442, when all the property transfers enrolled in the earliest surviving court roll relate to freehold tenures. In this respect, Mote is far from unique among the manors of eastern Sussex: in the Rape of Hastings, the lordships of Burghurst, Dallington, Etchingham, Glottenham, Haselden, Mountfield, Socknersh, Warbleton, Wilting and Woodknowle were either exclusively or

---

[226] Harvard Law School Library, Charters 178, calendared as Appendix 1 no. 3.

[227] CKS U455 T124/4, calendared as Appendix 1 no. 4.

[228] CKS U455 T121/4, T122/7, calendared as Appendix 1 nos 5 and 6.

[229] CKS U455 T119/26, ESRO ACC 7006/16, calendared as Appendix 1 nos 7 and 8.

[230] ESRO ACC 7006/17, calendared as Appendix 1 no. 9.

[231] CKS U455 T124/4, calendared as Appendix 1 no. 4; ESRO NOR 15/58, the petition of the heir in tail.

overwhelmingly freehold in their tenure. The situation could have come about in a number of ways. However improbable, it is possible that some manors, particularly ones of recent creation, never included villein tenants, perhaps because all the tenements had been granted out of a sizeable demesne. Some manors were created by an aggressive policy of purchase, by which widely-dispersed property was acquired by a single individual and administered as a manor. Burghurst in Burwash, assembled by Herbert de Burghurst at the beginning of the thirteenth century, is the prime example, with tenements in ten parishes stretching from Ticehurst to Hailsham.[232] Although Edmund de Pashley is a good candidate for a similar campaign a century later, the manor of Mote is largely confined to the parishes surrounding its demesne, and its tenements closely interlock with those of the manor of Ewhurst, from which it may have been partitioned at a date before records survive.

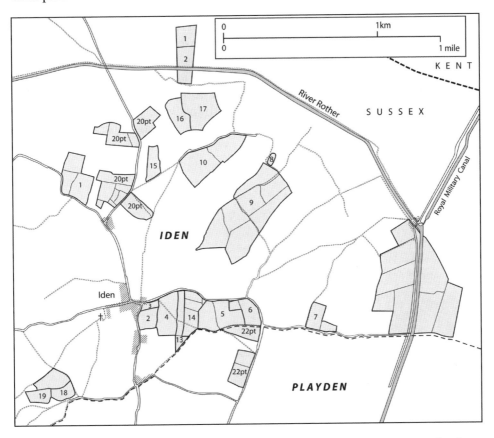

Illus. 8   The tenements in Iden and Playden parishes (based on the work of David and Barbara Martin).

---

[232] M. F. Gardiner, *Medieval Settlement and Society in the Eastern Sussex Weald before 1420* (unpublished PhD thesis, University of London, 1995), 172-74; *Sussex Manors, Advowsons etc Recorded in the Feet of Fines: vol. 1 (SRS 19 (1914)),* ed. E. H. W. Dunkin, 81.

It is more likely that such exclusively freehold tenures were brought about by stinting, the process of partial enfranchisement to which stock-deeds gave effect. What most such manors have in common is their possession by powerful families or by corporations: Etchingham, Glottenham and Mountfield were owned by the Etchingham family, and the manor of Haselden was little more than a vehicle for administering the endowments of Hastings Priory, which were almost exclusively freehold. Such lords were more likely to be bold and innovative in their policies, and a wholesale stinting of the former copyhold tenements of such manors, including Mote, cannot be ruled out. Villein services on Wealden manors were minimal, settlement was dispersed and as we have seen early stock-deeds tended to effect little other than a change of tenure – the lord's right to heriots and reliefs, wardships and marriages was preserved. From the Wealden peasant's point of view, the most important aspect of altered tenure was probably not personal freedom, which he probably already enjoyed, but a change in custom from partible inheritance, common in north-eastern Sussex, to primogeniture.[233] This can have been of little consequence to lords, especially if they were able to preserve the most valuable parts of their feudal income, and it seems that the more powerful had the confidence to make the change comprehensively rather than piecemeal. In the 1560s, the owner of the manor of Burghurst knew that his predecessors had each 'made certain of the copyholders freeholders'. That lord was John Wybarne, who was also the steward of the manor of Mote.[234]

---

[233] On the extent of partible inheritance in north-east Sussex, see Gardiner, *ibid.*, 200-02; the later practice of surrender to the use of the tenant's will, common in Sussex by the seventeenth century, achieved the same end at less expense.

[234] ESRO ASH 206 f. 45v.; for John Wybarne, see Table 3.

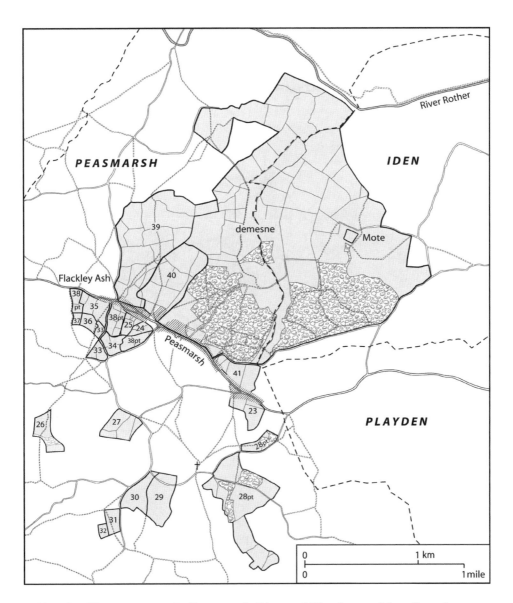

Illus. 9   The tenements in Peasmarsh, Iden and Playden parishes (based on the work of David and Barbara Martin).

Manor of Mote

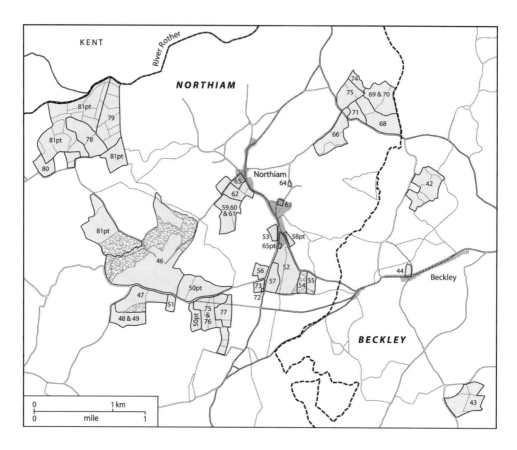

Illus. 10   The tenements in Ewhurst, Northiam and Beckley parishes (based on the work of David and Barbara Martin).

EDITORIAL CONVENTIONS

The four documents presented here have been edited in accordance with the principles set out by R. F. Hunnisett in 1977.[235] Within those rules, the individual format of each document have required slightly differing treatment.

All four documents are presented here in English, although all but the last – the survey of 1673 – were written in Latin. The translation has been fairly literal, largely to avoid over-interpretion of the original text. English words appearing in an otherwise Latin original have been placed between inverted commas, and unusual or aberrant Latin forms are given, in italics and round brackets, after the translation of the word in question.

In the text, surnames appear exactly as they occur in the documents, but forenames appear in their most common modern spellings. Identifiable place-names have been presented in their modern forms. Other than in the 1673 rental, unidentifiable place-names are presented in inverted commas. For the purposes of the index and the introduction, the name-forms of unidentified places used by the 1673 rental have been preferred. These have been rendered in italics in the introduction, and within inverted commas in the index. For the persons index, the forms recorded in Richard McKinley, *The surnames of Sussex* (Leopard's head Press, 1988) and P. H. Reaney, *A dictionary of English surnames* (Routledge, 1976), have been preferred. Although they appear in the text, the surname-prefixes a, at, atte and de have been excluded from the index.

All four documents employ Roman numerals, which have been rendered in Arabic. When they are deployed to represent sums of money, the expression used in this edition follows the practice current when pounds, shillings and pence ceased to be used in 1971, rather than medieval convention, which presented sums up to two shillings in pence, and sums up to five pounds in shillings.

Dates, expressed by the documents using a combination of religious festivals, days, months and regnal years, have all been presented in modern usage, with the calendar year deemed to begin on 1 January. Any ambiguities in the expression of dates have been dealt with in footnotes.

The text presents the documents in their final form, with altered or deleted matter, most frequently sums of money, appearing in footnotes. Sums in dot-notation, entered as a preliminary to the completion of the accounts, have been ignored.

Each entry in the original court rolls, rental and survey occupies a new paragraph, and that layout has been reproduced in the printed text. The individual entries in the accounts appear as running text, the only subdivisions being between the different heads of income or expenditure. This edition presents each entry on a new line, omitting the words *Paid* and *From* from all but the first entry in each section.

---

[235] Hunnisett, *Editing Records for Publication.*

LIST OF ABBREVIATIONS

AC	*Archaeologia Cantiana*
BL	British Library
Black and White Books	*A Calendar of the Black and White Books of the Cinque Ports 1432-1955* (Kent Records; Historic Manuscripts Commission, JP5 (London, 1966)), ed. F. Hull
Cal Inq Misc	*Calendar of Inquisitions Miscellaneous (Chancery) preserved in the Public Record Office* (London, 1916-69)
CCA	Canterbury Cathedral Archives
CCR	*Calendar of Close Rolls preserved in the Public Record Office* (London, 1892-1963)
CFR	*Calendar of Fine Rolls preserved in the Public Record Office* (London, 1911-63)
CIPM	*Calendar of Inquisitions* Post Mortem *and other Analogous Documents* (London and Woodbridge, 1904-)
CKS	Centre for Kentish Studies, Maidstone
Complete Peerage	G. E. C[ockayne], *The Complete Peerage of England, Scotland, Ireland, Great Britain and the United Kingdom, Extant, Extinct, or Dormant* (London, 1910-59), revised and much enlarged by G. H. White
CPR	*Calendar of Patent Rolls preserved in the Public Record Office* (London, 1891-)
EKAC	East Kent Archives Centre, Dover
ESRO	East Sussex Record Office, Lewes
HEH	Henry E. Huntington Library, San Marino, California
HOP	Work in progress by the History of Parliament Trust for 1422-1509 volume; S. T. Bindoff (ed.), *The House of Commons 1509-1558* (London, 1982); P. W. Hasler (ed.), *The House of Commons 1558-1603* (London, 1981)
ODNB	*Oxford Dictionary of National Biography* (Oxford, 2004), ed. H. C. G. Matthew and Brian Harrison
OED	*Oxford English Dictionary* (second edn, Oxford, 1989)
PCC	Prerogative Court of Canterbury
SAC	*Sussex Archaeological Collections*
SRS	*Sussex Record Society*
TNA PRO	The National Archives, Kew
VCH Kt	*Victoria County History of Kent* (London, 1908-)
VCH Sx	*Victoria County History of Sussex* (London, 1905-)
WSRO	West Sussex Record Office, Chichester

BIBLIOGRAPHY OF MAIN WORKS CITED

A Calendar of the Black and White Books of the Cinque Ports 1432-1955 (Kent Records; Historic Manuscripts Commission, JP5 (London, 1966)), ed. F. Hull.

Household Accounts from Medieval England (Records of Social and Economic History, new series XVII, XVIII. Oxford, 1993), ed. C. M. Woolgar.

The Logge Register of Prerogative Court of Canterbury Wills, 1479 to 1486 (Knaphill, 2008) ed. L. Boatwright, M. Habberjam and P. Hammond.

Oxford Dictionary of National Biography (Oxford, 2004), ed. H. C. G. Matthew and Brian Harrison.

Britnell, R. H. 'The Pastons and their Norfolk', *Agricultural History Review* 36 (1988), 132-44.

Du Boulay, F. R. H. *The Lordship of Canterbury: An Essay on Medieval Society* (London, 1966).

Campbell, B. M. S. *English Seigniorial Agriculture 1250-1450* (Cambridge, 2000).

Carpenter, C. *Locality and Polity: A Study of Warwickshire Landed Society, 1401-1499* (Cambridge, 1992).

Dyer, C. C. *Everyday Life in Medieval England* (London, 1994).

Dyer, C. C. *An Age of Transition?: Economy and Society in England in the Later Middle Ages* (Oxford, 2005).

Fleming, P. W. 'Household servants of the Yorkist and early Tudor gentry', in D Williams (ed), *Early Tudor England: Proceedings of the 1987 Harlaxton Symposium* (1989, Woodbridge), 19-36.

Mate, M. E. 'Pastoral farming on south-east England in the fifteenth century', *Economic History Review* second series, 40 (1987), 523-36.

Rawcliffe, C. *The Staffords, Earls of Stafford and Dukes of Buckingham 1394-1521* (Cambridge, 1978).

Richmond, C. *John Hopton. A Fifteenth Century Suffolk Gentleman* (Cambridge, 1981).

Salzman, L. F. *Building in England Down to 1540: A Documentary History* (Oxford, 1952).

Scott, J. R. 'Receipts and expenditure of Sir John Scott, in the reign of Edward IV', *AC* 10 (1876), 250-58.

Wedgwood, J. C. *History of Parliament: Biographies of the Members of the Commons House, 1439-1509* (London, 1936).

Woolgar, C. M. *The Great Household in Late Medieval England* (New Haven, 1999).

ACCOUNTS 1464-1484

Mote manor: the account of William Harlakynden, receiver of Sir John Scott, knight, from 29 September 1464 to 29 September 1465

[ESRO NOR 15/103[1]]

Arrears	*[blank]*

Fixed rents

For the rent of various tenants in the parish of Iden, as appears by the rental	£3 6s 10½d
For the rent of various tenants in the parish of Peasmarsh belonging to the manor	£3 9s 0d
For the rent of various tenants in the parish of Northiam	£3 0s 3½d
For the rent of various tenants in the parish of Beckley	£1 2s 4d
For the rent of various tenants in the parish of Ewhurst	12s 5d[2]
Sum	£11 10s 11d

Hen rents

From one hen from the rent of Robert Gogeler from land called Horsepen at the term of Christmas, sold for	3d

Farm of the demesne lands

The farm of the manor, let to John Mayne this year	£13

Profits of court

The profits of courts held there this year, as appears by the rolls of the same, examined upon this account	7s 0d

Sum total of receipts	£24 18s 2d
Of which	

<Surplus allowed

He accounts for a surplus from his account of the previous year, as appears in the foot [of the account] there £11 16s 0d	
Sum	£11 16s 0d>

---

[1] Attached to this membrane is an extract of the court rolls of 10 June [1606] and 15 March [1618] concerning a freehold tenement consisting of seven acres of woodland called 'Walland' in Iden, quitrent 6d. It dates almost certainly from the compilation of the survey of the manor in 1673 [ESRO NOR 15/64-92].

[2] Followed by a deleted entry, *Fixed rents in Brenzett, by the hand of William Elys £1 15s 9d.*

Rents resolute

And[3] paid the bailiff of the sheriff of the county of Sussex for the sheriff's tourn this year	8d
To the same sheriff for 'blancheferme'	5d
Rent resolute to Lord Dacre for 'Blakelond' in the value of two pounds of pepper, that is to say for 1460-1462, not allowed before	2s 8d
Sum	3s 9d

Allowances of rent

Allowed John Roberd for land called Thornsdale in Iden, charged above in the heading 'Fixed rents' within the sum of £3 6s 10½d, because it cannot be levied[4]	2s 11d
The heirs of Richard atte Wode for land called 'Cotenham' in Iden	1s 8d
John Parrok for his lands in Iden	1d
The manor of the hospital of Rye in Iden	3s 0d
John Asshmynton in Iden, because it is in the lord's hands and let to farm with the demesne lands	1s 6d
William Potyn for 'Sherishothe' in Peasmarsh, charged above within the sum of £3 9s 0d, because it is in the lord's hands and nothing can be levied	2s 6d
Thomas Keriell, knight, for the manor of Kitchenour	1s 3d
Simon Watell for land called 'Brounland' in Peasmarsh	1s 0d
Thomas Foghell for various lands which he holds in Peasmarsh	4d
William Hulles for land formerly Peter Churche in Northiam, because it is in the lord's hands and let to farm with the demesne lands	3d
John Holstok for 'Denyslond' in Northiam	1s 0d
William Bate for lands which lately belonged to Peter Churche in Northiam, because it still cannot be levied	6d
John Benett for 'Le Crabbe' and other parcels of land in Northiam	2s 2½d
John Twisen [*recte* Twysden] and Maud Majour for land called 'Blithelond' and other parcels of land in Northiam	1s 6d
William Lucas, both for land purchased from Robert Edward and land purchased of John Holman called 'Okworthes' in Northiam	6d
Simon Moys for his lands in Northiam	2s 6d
William Hoore of Northiam because John Holman paid his rent within the sum of his own rent, which is charged above in the heading 'Fixed rents'	3d
William Belknapp for 'Piperslond' in Beckley	4s 0d
Margaret Strode for her lands in Beckley	½d
William Tukton for lands formerly John Hochon in Beckley	5d

---

[3] Altered from *he accounts* as a result of the insertion above.
[4] This sentence is repeated at the end of most of the following entries.

William Oxenbrigge for 'Mottislond' formerly Stephen Hekton   2s 6d
William Belknapp for land formerly Stephen Hekton called
'Hektons'   6s 8d
Richard Fenys, knight, Lord Dacre, for 50 acres in Padgham [in]
the manor of Ewhurst   10s 7d
Richard Sote for 'Brekex', charged above in Iden, because it is
allowed to him by his charter   3d
Agnes Kychenore, charged above in Iden   4d
John Dalot for two acres of land by the garden <of John
Watirman>, charged above in Iden   6d
Heirs of [*blank*] Parker late of Hastings for a parcel of land by
Hastings in Hollington called 'Jamysdown'   2s 0d
Sum   £2 10s 3d

Repairs to the manor <by John German; £8 9s 5d>[5]
Paid for five days' carriage of 5000 bricks from Knock House to
The Mote   5s 0d
Hauling timber from the great wood for a day in harvest   1s 0d
Hauling and carriage of wood from the marlpits to the workplace
for 9½ days   6s 4d
Five days' carriage of 'latthis' and sand from Knock House to the
manor of Mote   3s 4d
Two days' hauling wood from various places to 'le sawstage'   1s 4d
Clearing the ground where the new stable is built   1s 0d
To various men for the 'regginge' of the barn there   1s 6d
For their board for nine days   1s 3d
One day's carriage of lime from Knock House to the manor   8d
John Asshmynton for thatching the barn for 2½ days   10d
A boy serving him in the work for 2½ days   2½d
A barrel of 'beere' bought for the consumption of Sir John Scott
and other gentlemen, being at The Mote during Lent, that is the
week before Palm Sunday [7 April 1465], with 4d paid for bread
and 7d for herrings   1s 11d
A barrel of 'beere' bought for various men of Rye when the
distraint was taken upon Thomas Oxebrigge in his lands called
'Holbrokes', with 2d for bread bought for them   1s 2d
Butter bought for them   1d
The board of John Duke, his sons and three men being at The
Mote in 1465-66 trimming timber in Sir John Cheyne's wood for
eight weeks, at 10d a man a week   £1
The board of three men working in the manor for five days   2s 1½d
The board of two sons of John Duke, working there for five weeks
at 10d a week each   8s 4d

---

[5] Added in the margin and linked by a bracket to the first half of the *repairs* section of the account.

The two sons of John Duke, in part-payment of their wages on the eve of Whitsun [1 June 1465]	9s 0d
The board of John Duke, carpenter, eight days	1s 0d
The board of John Mason, working at The Mote for 25 weeks	£1 1s 5d
John Mason for his wages on the eve of Whitsun [1 June 1465]	6s 8d
The board of John Pounde, 'lymebrenner', for four weeks and one day burning lime	3s 5½d
The board of John Page, 'plumber', working at The Mote for eight weeks	6s 8d
The board of Henry Horsekeeper, the lord's servant, serving John Mason for seven weeks	5s 10d
The board of John Hogelot, labourer, hired for two days to help loading timber	3d
The board of John Spayn and two labourers, digging stones for five days	2s 1½d
The board of John Gate and John Preston, labourers, loading timber for one week	1s 8d
The board of John Adam and Richard Sander, collecting timber for ten days, between them	2s 10d
The board of Richard Parocke, carrier, carrying timber for ten days	1s 5d
The board of John Mayne for ten days doing the same	1s 5d
The board of William Baylle, labourer, doing the same	1s 5d
The board of John Mayne of Wittersham for three days	5d
The board of Thomas Cornere for three days	5d
The board of John Oxenbrigge, labourer, for three days doing the same	5d
Richard Parock for carrying stones from 'Hopeshell' to the manor for two days	2s 0d
His board for two days	3½d
Richard Parock for the carriage of 20 cartloads of stones from Knock House to the manor at 5d a load	8s 4d
Richard Parocke for the carriage of timber from Sir John Cheyne's wood to the manor, for 9½ days at 10d a day	7s 11d
William Bailly for the same for 8½ days	7s 1d
John Oxenbrigge for the same for three days	2s 6d
The board of John Gardinere, dauber, daubing on the stable and kitchen for three weeks	2s 6d
To him for his wages	3s 4d
700 four-penny nails bought for the carpenter	2s 4d
Nails bought for the plumber	6d
Tallow bought for the plumber	1d
Thomas Profite for hewing and chopping wood for 'le lymebrenner' for one day, that is to say for his wages	4½d
The board of Thomas Yevenett, attending upon the distraint taken in 'Holebrokes'	1s 0d

Hewing firewood for 'le lymebrenner' for two days and bringing it in	6d
William Makemett, labourer, hired for a day to hew wood for 'le lymebrenner'	4d
Cutting broom for one day	3½d
The carriage of lime from the pit for one day	4d
Two carts hired for a day to carry stones from 'Hopeshell' to the manor	1s 8d
Getting 400 laths at Wittersham	4d
The board of two carriers, carrying stones for two days	3½d
Bringing in firewood to 'le lymepett' for one day	4d
The board of John Duke and his son, to each of them for working for four days on trimming timber, and for its carriage	1s 0d
The board of John Mason with John German for four weeks and two days before 25 December 1465	3s 7d

Repairs to the manor <by William Harlakynden £11 0s 3½d >[6]

The widow of John Netter of Cranbrook for stones bought from her for the chimneys and doors of the manor of Mote by William Harlakynden	3s 0d
The carriage of those stones from Cranbrook to Newenden Bridge	1s 8d
Expenses of John Mason [going] from Appledore to Hastings to look for stone-digging places for the works, and viewing quarries in various places for three days	1s 0d
John Gibbes on 4 July for the board of John Mason and Thomas Mason, being at Fairlight five days trimming stone	1s 6d
Expenses of Thomas Mason, [going] from Fairlight to The Mote	4d
A rope 23 'fadom' long, delivered to John Mason to The Mote	4s 0d
A rope 50 'fadom' long delivered to the plumber there	4s 2d
Four ropes bought to load timber and sent to the manor of Mote	4s 0d
Richard Cornewell for carrying five ropes and other stuff (*stuffer'*) from Woodchurch to the manor of Mote, including 2d for his ferry	6d
Expenses of John and Thomas Mason at Cranbrook for trimming stones and for hauling them from the pit for three days	1s 4d
John Spayne, John Gate and Stephen Adam, labourers, each of them for five days in July digging stones at The Mote at 3d a day each	3s 9d
John Gate and John Preston, labourers, each for six days carting timber, with 2d for their ferry	2s 2d
John Mayne the younger for carrying timber to the manor of Mote for three days	2s 2d
Thomas Corner for carriage of timber to The Mote for four days	3s 4d

---

[6] Added as above, linked to the second half of this section of the account.

John Pounde, 'lymebrenner', being at The Mote for 25 days burning two kilns of lime	8s 0d
Robert Van hired for six days with a 'tugge' to carry timber from Leigh to the manor of Mote	6s 0d
John Duke and his two sons for hewing and trimming timber at the manor of Mote for [blank] weeks	£3 13s 0d
John Mason, mason, for his wages for working at Mote for [blank] weeks, not including the board allowed above to John German	£2 19s 8d
Thomas Mason for his wages working there in the said work for [blank] weeks at 4d a day	£1 11s 4d
Thomas atte Hale, labourer, hired for two weeks to serve the masons at 2d a day	2s 0d
For his ferry	½d
Richard Yonge, labourer, hired for four days to serve the masons	8d
John Freman, labourer, hired for five days to serve the masons	10d
John Goodgrome, labourer, for four weeks labouring at serving the masons	4s 0d
William Orgar, smith, for nails and hinges (*charnall'*) bought from him for 'le Baywyndowe' at The Mote	1s 10d[7]
Paid by the hand of John Mayne for a boat hired to carry [stone][8] from Maytham to John Mayne's gut (*gutter'*)	1s 0d
To a man hired to take charge of the said stone in its carriage as far as the gut	2d
For a boat hired by John Mayne to carry lead from the manor to Appledore	8d
Paid John Mayne for the carriage of sixteen cartloads of sand to the manor	8s 0d
The carriage of wood to 'le lymepett'	6d
John Mayne for the carriage of 30 cartloads of chalk from Knock House to the manor	12s 6d
Sum	£20 12s 6½d

Foreign expenses of the lord

Expenses of my master from Appledore towards The Mote on 8 April 1464[9]	3s 4d
Victuals bought at Appledore and consumed at The Mote on 8 April 1464,[10] with 1s 0d paid for the expenses of William Harlakynden at Appledore that night	2s 11½d
Expenses of John Kendale and William Harlakynden at Rye on	

---

[7] The bracket indicating William Harlakynden's expenditure ends with this entry. The remainder of the section is written in a smaller hand to fit within the sheet of paper.

[8] Written *unam* for *petram*, in error.

[9] Or 1465 if *dicto anno quarto* is to be interpreted as 4-5E4.

[10] Or 1465 if *dicto anno quarto* is to be interpreted as 4-5E4.

Tuesday after St Cross [8 May 1464][11] with 2s 6d paid by John Kendale for the expenses of Sir John Scott's horses	4s 8d
Expenses of Sir John Scott, by the hand of John Mayne	4s 0d
Paid John Mayne for two barrels of 'biere' bought for the lord's household	2s 0d
Sum	16s 11½d

Expenses of the accountant

Expenses of William Harlakynden at The Mote on Tuesday after Midsummer [25 June 1465][12]	6d
His expenses at The Mote to talk with Babilon Graundford and various other persons to prevent Thomas Oxebrigge carrying hay out of 'Holemede' and taking a distraint, with William Harlakynden's expenses at Rye and Wittersham for the same reason for two days	2s 3½d
His expenses towards The Mote on 19 July	4½d
His expenses towards The Mote on 8 August to supervise the lord's workmen there	5d
His expenses going to The Mote for the same reason on 17 August	3½d
His expenses towards The Mote on 31 August surveying the manor and supervising the workmen	3d
His expenses towards The Mote on the vigil of the nativity of the blessed Mary [7 September] for the same reason	3d
His expenses towards The Mote on 11 October and thence to Rye, and staying there overnight to transact various business of the lord	9d
His expenses at The Mote on 6 November and at Rye with John Treygo to enquire for evidences of 'Holebroke', and to speak with Thomas Watell about various business of my master	11½d
His expenses at The Mote on 21 and 22 November, being there to hold the court there	10d
His expenses at The Mote on 18 January to supervise the lord's workmen there	5½d
His expenses at The Mote on 8 May for the same reason	4d
His expenses at The Mote on 31 May to hold a court there and have discussions (*communicandum*) with the tenants there	1s 6d
Expenses of John Hale, servant of the said accountant, going to The Mote on various occasions to transact various business and supervise the workmen as appears in various parcels	2s 5½d
Sum	11s 8d

---

[11] Or 7 May 1465 if 5E4 is to be understood.
[12] Or 26 June 1464 if 4E4 is to be understood.

Foreign payments
Paid to John Lewkenore at Brabourne on Friday after St Michael
[5 October 1464] by the lord's order, as appears by a bill
delivered to William Wright by my master's command   £5
Paid to William Fox by the hand of William Philipp for the
relief of the land of Stephen Sleggys[13]   8s 0d
Money paid to the mourning (*ad luctum*) of Biddenden on [14
September 1464][14] by the lord's command   1s 0d
Paid to John German on 9 April [1465] by the lord's order   4d
Sum   £5 9s 4d

Wages
Wages of John Mayne, collector of rents of the manor of Mote,
by reason of his office this year   6s 8d

Liveries of money[15]
Money paid to the lady at Hall on 24 November 1464[16] to pay
the plumber of The Mote   £1 6s 8d

Sum   £1 6s 8d

Sum of all allowances and payments   £43 13s 10d
And so he has of surplus   £18 15s 8d

---

[13] Altered from *to have a release for the land of* Sleggys.

[14] *In die Sancte Crucis*; alternative dates are the feasts of the Invention (3 May) and Good Friday (30 March 1464 or 12 April 1465); *ad luctum* may refer to a public penance, such as 'creeping to the cross' (which would suggest Good Friday); the entry may be a misreading of an original which read *ludum*, a play (we owe this suggestion to Professor Eamon Duffy), perhaps on the subject of the 'Biddenden Maids'.

[15] The first entry of this section, *Money delivered to Thomas Ovyngton by the hand of William Fox, money received from Thomas Birchele at Brenzett on 26 July 1464* [or 1465 if *dicto anno quarto* (which replaces a deleted *quinto*) is to be interpreted as 4-5E4], *£1 6s 8d*, has been deleted with the annotation *because it is in Orlestone*.

[16] Or 1465 if *dicto anno quarto* (which replaces a deleted *quinto*) is to be interpreted as 4-5E4.

Mote manor: the account of William Harlakynden, receiver of Sir John Scotte, knight, from 29 September 1465 to 29 September 1466

[ESRO NOR 15/104]

Arrears	[*blank*]

Fixed rents

For the rent of various tenants in Iden, as appears by the rental, and by the account of John German, the beadle there	£3 6s 10½d
For the rent of various tenants in Peasmarsh belonging to the manor	£3 9s 0d
For the rent of various tenants in Northiam	£3 0s 3½d
For the rent of various tenants in Beckley	£1 2s 4d
For the rent of various tenants in Ewhurst	12s 5d
Sum	£11 10s 11d

Hen rents

From one hen from the rent of Robert Gogeler from land called Horsepen at the term of Christmas, sold for	3d

Profits of court

The profits of the courts held there this year, as appears by the rolls examined upon this account	6s 6d

Farm of the demesne lands

The farm of the manor of The Mote, let to John Mayne this year	£13

Foreign receipts

Received from my master, Sir John Scott, knight, by the hand of William Brikeman at Hall on 15 February 1467 on [account of] brickmaking (*super factura de Brike*)	£1
Received from my master by the hand of William Brikeman on the same account in the following Lent	£2 6s 8d
Sum	£3 6s 8d

Sum total of receipts

Of which	£28 4s 4d

Surplus allowed

He accounts for a surplus which he had at the foot of his account for the previous year to be acquitted	£18 15s 8d
And paid the bailiff of the sheriff of the county of Sussex for the sheriff's tourn this year	8d

And to the same sheriff for 'le blancheferme'   5d
Sum   1s 1d

Allowances of rent with defaults

John Roberd for land called Thornsdale in Iden, charged above in the heading 'Fixed rents' within the sum of £3 6s 10½d, because it cannot be levied[17]   2s 11d

Heirs of Richard atte Wode for land called 'Cotenham' in Iden   1s 8d

John Parrok for his lands in Iden   1d

The manor of the hospital of Rye in Iden   3s 0d

John Asshmynton in Iden, because it is in the lord's hands and let to farm with the demesne lands   1s 6d

William Potyn for 'Sherishothe' in Peasmarsh, charged above within the sum of £3 9s 0d, because it is in the lord's hands   2s 6d

Thomas Keriell, knight, for the manor of Kitchenour   1s 3d

Simon Watell for land called 'Brounlond' in Peasmarsh   1s 0d

Thomas Foghell for various lands which he holds in Peasmarsh   4d

William Hulles for land formerly Peter Churche in Northiam, because it is in the lord's hands and let to farm with the demesne lands   3d

John Holstok for 'Denysland' in Northiam   1s 0d

William Bate for lands which lately belonged to Peter Churche in Northiam, because it still cannot be levied   6d

John Benett for 'Le Crabbe' and other parcels of land in Northiam   2s 2½d

John Twisden and Maud Majour for land called 'Blithelond' and other parcels of land in Northiam, for the same reason   1s 6d

William Lucas both for land purchased of Robert Edward and land purchased of John Holman called 'Okworthes' in Northiam   6d

Simon Moys for his lands in Northiam   2s 6d

William Hoore of Northiam because John Holman paid his rent within the sum of his own rent which is charged above in the heading 'Fixed rents'   3d

William Belknapp for 'Pipereslond' in Beckley   4s 0d

Margaret Strode for her lands in Beckley   ½d

William Tukton for land formerly John Hochon in Beckley   5d

William Oxenbrigge for 'Mottislond' formerly Stephen Hekton   2s 6d

William Belknapp for land formerly Stephen Hekton called 'Hektons'   6s 6d

Richard Fenys, knight, Lord Dacre, for 50 acres in Padgham [in] the manor of Ewhurst   10s 7d

Richard Sote for 'Brekex' charged above in Iden, because it is allowed to him by his charter   3d

Agnes Kychenore charged above in Iden   4d

---

[17] This sentence is repeated at the end of most of the following entries.

John Dalot for two acres of land by the garden [of John
Waterman] charged above in Iden | 6d

Sum | £2 8s 3d

Repairs to the manor <by John German; £5 3s 11½d>[18]
Paid for the board of John Mason with John German for twelve
weeks from 25 December 1465, working within the manor there | 10s 0d
The board of Thomas Mason, being with the same John for
eleven weeks | 9s 2d
The board of Richard Yonge, labourer, serving the said masons
for four days | 6d
The board of John Freman, serving the said masons for five days | 9d
The board of John Goodgrome, serving the said masons for three
weeks | 2s 6d
The board of John Breggeman, dauber, with his servant for three
days for the ridging (*le reggeyng*) of the stable | 1s 8d
The board of Thomas Mason, mason, working in the manor of
Mote three weeks between Easter and Whitsun [6 April to 25
May 1466] | 2s 6d
The board of John Mason, mason, working on the manor for six
weeks | 5s 0d
The board of John Mason, being with John German for four
weeks between Whitsun and the translation of St Thomas the
Martyr [25 May to 7 July 1466] | 3s 4d
The board of Thomas Mason working within the manor for three
weeks during the same time | 2s 6d
The board of John Goodgrome, labourer, serving the said masons
for eleven weeks | 9s 2d
The board of John Goodgrome for two days on another occasion | 3½d
The board of Thomas Mason and his servant, working within the
manor for seven weeks between St Peter's Chains and All Saints
[1 August to 1 November 1466] | 11s 8d
The board of John Pownde, 'lymebrenner', for three weeks
burning lime | 2s 6d
A labourer hired two days to fell wood for 'le lymebrenner' | 8d
<The board of John Duke and his mates, carpenters, setting
beams in the lord's chamber | 2s 1d
The board of Thomas Profete, dauber, for daubing the lord's
chamber> for two weeks | 1s 8d
The wage of his son, serving him six days | 6d
William Bailly for making a bridge there | 6d <8d>
John Mason and Thomas Mason for their wages on the eve of
Whitsun [24 May 1466] | 9s 0d

---

[18] Added in the margin and linked by a bracket to the first half of the *repairs* section of the account.

Nails bought for the masons and carpenters	1s 2d
John Goodgrome for wages	4s 4d
Thomas Mason for wages on 29 September 1466	10s 0d
Carriage of three cartloads of stone from Fairlight to the manor	5s 0d
Henry Bocher for the easement upon his lands for the passage of their carts	2½d
Food and drink bought for the carriers	9½d
For 150 'dabynglath'	6d
Thomas Profete, dauber, in part-payment of his piecework contract (*conventionis sue ad tascam*)	1s 0d
The same Thomas for 'le reggyng lez corners' of the hall, kitchen, barn, stable and the other buildings of the manor	3s 4d
Two bushels of oats bought for the lord's horses at their arrival there	6d

Repairs to the manor <by William Harlakynden £16 6s 9d>[19]	
Paid to a man hired to guide the carriers of stone from Brede to The Mote	2d
William Gibbes 13 November for carriage of eight cartloads of stone from Fairlight to The Mote	15s 0d
Two iron wedges bought for the masons at Fairlight	6d
William Dobill, smith, for sharpening and mending the masons' tools at The Mote	3s 10d
One spade and a shovel delivered to The Mote	11d
Sieves bought at Hawkhurst, with 1d for the expenses of seeking and fetching them	9d
Thomas Mason and his servant, masons, working at The Mote for 33 days from Easter to Whitsun [6 April to 25 May 1466]	12s 0d
Alan the tiler and his boy, being at The Mote in February laying tiles on the west side of the hall	2s 6d
John Nepsam for the board of Thomas Mason, being at Fairlight for four weeks in August trimming stones	3s 4d
Thomas Mason, mason, for his wages and those of his servant working at The Mote	£1 2s 8d
John Duke and his two sons, each of them for three days working at The Mote upon the chambers of the hall there	3s 0d
The same John and one son working on those chambers for four days in September	2s 8d
John Duke and his two sons working at The Mote in the week before 2 February, making beds, doors, steps, windows, forms and stools	6s 0d
The same John Duke and two sons at The Mote for four days the following week	4s 0d

---

[19] Added as above, linked to the second half of this section of the account.

John Duke and two sons, working at The Mote in the week after 14 February	6s 0d
John Duke and two sons, working there for four days in the last week of February	4s 0d
John Duke and two sons, working at The Mote for two weeks three days in March	15s 0d
John Duke and two sons, working at The Mote for nineteen days between Easter and Whitsun [6 April and 25 May 1466]	19s 0d
Two sawyers sawing 300 feet of board and 'legges'	3s 0d
The same sawyers for sawing 500 feet of board at The Mote	5s 0d
William Brikeman and his mates for their wages for brickmaking on several occasions	£3 3s 4d
John Pownde, 'lymebrenner', for burning lime for eighteen days at The Mote	6s 0d
William Brikeman for 4<½> barrels of beer bought by him at 1s 1d a barrel	4s 4d
William Baylle for ploughing one acre of land at The Mote for 'le brikemen'	1s 0d
Henry Dobill and his mates on 10 April for hedging 78 rods around the field in which 'le brike' is made	6s 6d
Two labourers hired to make a weir between The Mote and the pond	4d
William Hoode, labourer, hired for two days to clear the land (*ad eradicandum*) at the head of the pond, by my master's order	4d
Simon Hykot and John Asshmynton, sawyers, for sawing 500 feet of board on 18 March for the repair of the pound (*punfald'*) at The Mote	5s 0d
Thomas Profite, hired for a week to make pits for placing the gateposts ('gatstokkes') of the pound	1s 0d
Robert Smith for two iron staples and two hasps for the gate of the pound and for ten pounds of ironwork for an oxcart	1s 3d
One pair of 'gojons' and 'hokes' for the gate of the pound	7d
John Bailly for four bucks (*soris*) sent to the manor of Mote in March in my lady's presence	2s 0d
Two iron hooks to hang the storeroom doors	2d
125 four-penny nails	5d
Robert Smyth for a pair of double hinges (*duplici trentcharnell'*) weighing 7½ pounds	1s 0d
A pair of hinges (*charnell'*) weighing 5¼ pounds	9d
Four 'trent rydes' and four hooks weighing three pounds	4½d
One 'trent ryde' and two hooks weighing 2½ pounds	4d
A pair of 'trent rydes' weighing three pounds	4½d
A pair of iron bolts weighing five pounds	7½d
A pair of 'trentrides' and two hooks weighing 7½ pounds, bought for the cellar door	1s 0d

Two 'rydes' and two hooks weighing four pounds	6d
One hundred four-penny nails, bought and delivered to the manor of Mote and a penny of three-penny nails	5d
2000 'prigge' bought and delivered to the manor on 15 February 1466	1s 3d
1000 'prigge' bought by John Duke, carpenter	10d
700 four-penny nails	2s 4d
400 three-penny nails	1s 0d
Robert Smith on 28 February for 'latches, catches' and a pair of 'hokes' for the door, sent to the manor by Philip Churche	1s 10d
150 three-penny nails bought at Wittersham	4½d
A lock bought and sent to the manor	3d
Paid John German to buy laths to repair the manor	1s 0d
Pitch-glue for 'le gabill' at The Mote	1d
John Mayne for carriage of sand from the seashore to the manor for five days	4s 2d
John Mayne carriage of timber from Leigh to the manor for ten days	8s 4d
John Mayne for carriage of wood to the limekiln for one day	8d
John Asshmynton, by John Mayne, for sawing timber, with his board	11s 0d
<William Brikeman on 15 February, for part-payment for brickmaking, by the hand of my master on two occasions	£3 6s 8d>
Sum	£21 10s 8½d

Necessary expenses

One pair of wheels for a wagon and one pair of wheels for 'le oxecourt', bought and delivered to the manor	6s 0d
One pair of wheels for a wagon bought at Rolvenden, with the ferry, and seeking them	3s 6d
Thomas Hodyngfold for one pair of oxen bought from him and delivered to the manor in April	£1 16s 1d
The widow of John Gervays for a mare bought and delivered to the manor in April	18s 1d
One 'gildinge' bought and delivered to the manor for 'le brikemen'	10s 0d
Thomas Engeham for a mare bought from him and delivered to the manor	8s 2d
Richard Nasshe and a boy with him, for driving the oxen and mares from Woodchurch to the manor of Mote in April	5d
Thomas Corner for his labour driving two pairs of oxen and two mares from Small Hythe to the manor on two occasions	3d
Ironwork bought for one 'nebyok' and one 'foryok' and for four links (*lynces*) for the said wagon and for the ox-cart at the manor	1s 6d

Robert Smyth to carry the ironwork from Woodchurch to the manor of Mote	3½d
Two clay pots bought and sent to the lady to the manor of Mote	2d
Half a quire of paper and 'fisshokes'	3d
An empty pipe to make a 'boltingtun'	1s 0d
A half-pipe to make 'wateryngfattes'	5d
The cooper to make the bolting-tun and watering-vats	9d
Wharfage of my master's wine at Rye, and for its carriage to The Mote	4d
John Kendale, my master's servant, on 20 February	5s 0d
Sum	£4 12s 2½d

Expenses of the lord's household

Hugh Shipman of Hythe by the hands of John Kendale, the lord's servant, for the carriage of the household goods of my lord from Hythe to Rye by ship (*per navigium*)	1s 8d
A man hired with a wagon to carry the goods from Rye to The Mote	2d
Money paid to Robert Jay, my master's servant, on 6 March by my master's order	2s 6d
William Bailly for carriage of household goods, one cartload of 'brike', 6½ barrels and a quarter of wheat bought by John Kendale for the consumption of the household	1s 10d
William Bailly for carriage of straw from Leigh to The Mote, firewood to the manor and board from 'le sawstage' to the manor	10d
Two labourers hired for three days to fell wood at The Mote and to prepare it in the last week in April	1s 0d
Four labourers hired for three days to fell and prepare wood at The Mote in the first week in May	2s 0d
Expenses of my master being at The Mote on 7 September and his servants and horses there, as appears in the particulars	3s 11½d
In his expenses at Leigh with Sir John Cheyne [and] at The Mote, considering the construction of the hall, chapel and chamber within the tower of the manor on 16 and 17 September, as appears in the particulars examined upon this account	7s 3d
Expenses of my master and my lady being at The Mote for twelve days from 6 to 17 March, as appears by the particulars examined upon this account	£1 3s 9½d
John Kendale at Mote for two weeks from 21 February to 7 March to provision and prepare everything for the arrival of my master and lady, as appears by the particulars	3s 4d
His expenses waiting at The Mote for the delivery of all the household goods sent there by my master	1s 0d
John Kendale to pay the wife of John Bailly of Rye	2d

Expenses of John German to Winchelsea to discuss my master's 'bere' with the brewer	1½d
Three labourers hired for a day in February to prepare firewood for the master's arrival	9d
Sum	£2 10s 4½d

Accountant's expenses

William Harlakynden being at the manor of Mote on 1 July to supervise the lord's workmen	9½d
His expenses to Fairlight on 2 July to supervise the masons' work and to arrange for their board	1s 3d
His expenses to The Mote on 14 [*blank*] to transact various business and supervise the works	5d
His expenses to The Mote on 23 September to hold a court there	4d
His expenses at The Mote on 14 November	4d
His expenses to The Mote on Monday before the Purification [2 February] and from there to Wittersham and Rye to buy wheat for my master with its ferry homewards	1s 1d
His expenses riding to The Mote on 12 February to supervise the masons, carpenters and other labourers there, that is to say, staying and returning home	11d
His expenses to The Mote on 20 February for the same reason, staying and returning home	7½d
His expenses on Friday and Saturday after St Gregory [12 March] to supervise the lord's workmen there	5½d
His expenses on 5 and 6 May to supervise the lord's workmen there	10½d
Expenses of Henry Heanden going to Brede on 15 September to talk to Robert Oxebregge and other persons about the grant [of a way for] the carriage of my master's stone across their lands	4d
Expenses of John Hale on 14 September from Hastings to Hall to tell the lord that Sir John Cheyne was waiting at Leigh for his arrival	5½d
Expenses of Thomas Mason to go to Fairlight to view the loading of my master's stone	4d
Expenses of John atte Hale, going to The Mote on 5 December to supervise the masons and other labourers there	2½d
Expenses of Philip Church to The Mote on 28 February to take ironwork there	2d
Expenses of John Hale to The Mote on 9 March to carry three pots to my lady there	2d
Expenses of John Hale to go to Biddenden to warn [John] Lillesden pond-maker (*pondour*) to come to my master on 16 March	1d
Expenses of the said John Hale going to The Mote on various	

occasions to supervise the masons and other labourers, as appears
in the particulars   1s 2d
Expenses of Philip Church to The Mote 26 March, transacting
various business there   2½d
Sum   10s 2½d

Wages of the rent-collector
Wages of John Mayne, collector of rent of the manor of Mote
this year   6s 8d

Foreign expenses
Paid the bailiff of the Rape of Hastings, by the hand of John
Maynee, for green wax lost by the lord in the king's courts on
two occasions   15s 4d

Sum of allowances and payments   £51 10s 6d

And so he has of surplus   £23 6s 2d

Mote manor: the account of William Harlakynden, receiver of Sir John Scotte, knight, from 29 September 1466 to 29 September 1467

[ESRO NOR 15/105]

Arrears	[*blank*]

Fixed rents

For the rent of various tenants in Iden, as appears by the rental, and by the account of John German, the beadle and collector of rents there	£3 6s 10½d
For the rent of various tenants in Peasmarsh belonging to the manor	£3 9s 0d
For the rent of various tenants in Northiam	£3 0s 3½d
For the rent of various tenants in Beckley	£1 2s 4d
For the rent of various tenants in Ewhurst	12s 5d
Sum	£11 10s 11d

Hen rents

From one hen from the rent of Robert Gogeler from land called Horsepen at the term of Christmas, sold for	3d

Profits of court

The profits of the courts held there this year, as appears by the rolls	4s 2d

Farm of the demesne lands

The farm of the manor, let to John Mayne this year	£13

Sale of wood

Received from John Mayne for wood sold to him this year, by the manor on its east side	£10

Sum total of receipts [*blank*][20]
Of which

Rents resolute

Paid the bailiff of Thomas Vachan, sheriff of Sussex, for the sheriff's tourn this year	8d
To him for 'le blancheferme'	5d
A rent resolute to Lord Dacre in the value of two pounds of pepper from the rent of land called 'Blakelond' by the hands of John Broun, his collector of rent, both for this year and last	2s 4d
Sum	3s 5d

---

[20] In the left margin is the sum of £34 15s 4d.

Foreign receipts

Received from my master, Sir John Scotte, knight, by the hands of John Cole, the surveyor of the works, for his labour coming from Esher to the manor of Mote to advise on the works of the manor	10s 0d
Received from my master for the costs and expenses of [*blank*] Hunte of Westminster, riding from London to the manor of Mote for advice on the work in 1466-67	£1 0s 4d
Sum	£1 10s 4d
Sum total of receipts	£36 5s 8d
Of which	

Surplus allowed

He accounts for a surplus which he had at the foot of his account for the previous year, to be acquitted	£23 6s 2d

Allowances of rent with defaults

John Roberd for land called Thornsdale in Iden, charged above in the heading 'Fixed rents' within the sum of £3 6s 10½d, because it cannot be levied[21]	2s 11d
Heirs of Richard atte Wode for land called 'Cotenham' in Iden	1s 8d
John Parrok for his lands in Iden[22]	1d
John Asshmynton in Iden, because it is in the lord's hands and let to farm with the demesne lands	1s 6d
William Potyn for 'Sherishothe' in Peasmarsh, charged above within the sum of £3 9s 0d, because it is in the lord's hands and nothing can be levied	2s 6d
Thomas Keryell, knight, for the manor of Kitchenour	1s 3d
Simon Watell for land called 'Brounlond' in Peasmarsh	1s 0d
Thomas Foghell for various lands which he holds in Peasmarsh	4d
William Hulles for land formerly Peter Churche in Northiam, because it is in the lord's hands and let to farm with the demesne lands	3d
John Holstok for 'Denynslond' in Northiam	1s 0d
William Bate for lands which lately belonged to Peter Churche in Northiam, because it still cannot be levied	6d
John Benett for 'Le Crabbe' and other parcels of land in Northiam	2s 2½d
John Twysden and Maud Majour for land called 'Blithelond' and other parcels of land in Northiam	1s 6d
William Lucas both for land purchased of Robert Edward and land purchased of John Holman called 'Okworthes' in Northiam	6d

---

[21] This sentence is repeated at the end of most of the following entries.

[22] Followed by an entry *The manor of the hospital of Rye in Iden 3s 0d*, deleted with the annotation *since it was paid to the lord by the hand of John Greneford.*

Simon Moys for his lands in Northiam	2s 6d
William Hoor of Northiam, because John Holman paid his rent within the sum of his own rent which is charged above in the heading 'Fixed rents'	3d
William Belknapp for 'Piperyslond' in Beckley	4s 0d
William Tukton for land formerly John Hochon in Beckley	5d
William Oxinbregge for 'Mottyslond' formerly Stephen Hekton	2s 6d
William Belknapp for land formerly Stephen Hekton called 'Hektons'	6s 6d
Richard Fenys, knight, Lord Dacre, for 50 acres in Padgham [in] the manor of Ewhurst	10s 7d
Richard Sote for 'Brekex' charged above in Iden, because it is allowed to him by his charter	3d
Agnes Kychenore, charged above in Iden	4d
John Dalot for two acres of land by the garden [of John Watirman], charged above in Iden	6d
Sum	£2 5s 3d

Expenses of the lord's household, with other payments

Carriage of a quarter of wheat from Rye to the mill for the consumption of the household	1d
Carriage of three quarters of wheat from Winchelsea to Rye for the lord's household	6d
A bacon bought for the lord's household at The Mote	3s 4d
Two bushels of salt bought for the household	1s 4d
Ox-meat bought for the household	1s 8d
Poultry bought for the household	5s 0d
Fish bought for the household	4s 5d
Butter bought for the household	1d
Expenses about the loading of a pipe of wine	2d
Wax candles bought for the chapel[23]	1d
Shoeing one of the lord's horses	8d
String (*filum*), soap and lye (*sal alke*)	3½d
Expenses of the accountant carrying wheat	1d
His expenses towards Fairlight on three occasions	6d
'Taynthokys' bought for hanging beds and also for mending an iron 'wegge'	3d
A pair of 'hokys' with a staple bought for a yoke called 'a foryok'	8d
The carriage of four barrels of 'bere' from Rye to The Mote for the household	2d
200 laths, with a penny for their carriage	7d
'Le yaxyng' [fitting an axle] of a wagon	2d
Making a door	2d

---

[23] Followed by *for the household* deleted.

Nails	3d
A hamper (*maunde*) for my lady	2d
Eggs for the household	2d
Money allowed to the accountant as a reward, by my lady's decision	3s 1½d
Carriage of 36 casks of 'chalke' from Knock House to the manor of Mote	16s 6d
Richard Parroke for the carriage of 24 casks from 'Marchauntes Gote' to the manor of Mote	6s 8d
John Boseney for the carriage of six casks of chalk to the manor	1s 8d
John Oxynbrigge for carriage of nine casks of chalk	2s 6d
For the sullage of the chalk	9d
William Bailly for the carriage of a cartload of 'beer' from Rye to The Mote	8d
Sum	£2 12s 8d

Repairs to the manor <by John German; £5 5s 3½d>²⁴
<Of which he was allowed last year £51 10s 0d. Note in all accounts he seeks allowance for certain sums in part-payment to various people. I doubt that it is not included in the totals (*in grossis summis*)>²⁵

Paid for the board of Thomas Mason and his servant, masons, working at The Mote for four weeks before 25 December 1466	6s 8d
The board of Thomas Mason and his servant, working at The Mote for four weeks between 25th December and 2 February	6s 8d
The board of Thomas Mason and his servant, working at the manor for six weeks between 2 February and 29 March	10s 0d
The board of Thomas Mason and his servant for six weeks between 29 March and 2 May 1467	10s 0d
The board of three carpenters, working at The Mote for a week and four days between 25 December and 25 January	4s 2d
The board of three carpenters, working at The Mote for a week and four days in the first week of Lent	4s 2d
The board of two carpenters, working at The Mote for 3½ days in the following week	10d
The board of three carpenters and a labourer, digging pits for the pound for two days in the week before 22 March	9d
The board of three carpenters for two weeks between 29 March and 17 May	5s 0d
The board of John Duke and his two sons for two weeks on another	

---

²⁴ Added in the margin and linked by a bracket to the first third of the *repairs* section of the account.

²⁵ These two comments are written in the margin towards the end of the *repairs* section of the account in a different hand, probably that of Sir John Scott, and in an ink which resembles that in which the totals are written. The first note refers to the expenditure in NOR 15/104 (in fact £51 10s 6d); the meaning of the second is not altogether clear.

occasion working there	5s 0d
The board of a labourer hired for one week to dig sand for 'lez brikemen'	10d
The board of two labourers hired three days to fell wood for three days between 29 March and 17 May	10d
The board of four labourers hired for three days to fell wood for 'lez brikemen'	1s 8d
The board of a tiler and his servant, working on the manor's buildings for one week	1s 4d
The board of Thomas Profite and his servant hired for five days at 'lez regginge' of the buildings	1s 1d
The board of two labourers, hired two days to fell wood against my lady's arrival at the manor	6½d
Thomas Mason, mason, in part-payment for his wages at his journey home at Christmas 1466	10s 0d
Paid to him at Easter 1467 for his wages	5s 0d
The board of John Pownde, 'lymbrenner', being there for three weeks between 29 March and 17 May 1467	2s 6d
Henry Dobyll for clearing (*eradicatione*) the lands by the manor of Mote by contract	13s 4d
Two daubers, hired for two days to daub the small chamber at the entrance on the south side of the tower there, and a cooper for one day to bind vessels	8d
John Pipere, dauber, for making the floor of the hall of the manor, in all things	1s 0d
300 four-penny nails and 100 penny nails bought	1s 3d
Two yokes for wagons	4d
Two daubers hired to daub the small chamber and the kitchen for three days	10d
Thomas Profete, labourer, hired nine days to serve John Mason on 'lez chymeneys' and the kitchen	1s 6d
His board for one [week][26]	10d
The board of John Duke, carpenter, and his two servants, working at The Mote for one week before 4 July 1467	2s 6d
The board of John Mason, working for three days at The Mote	5d
A thatcher hired one day to thatch across the sewer (*cloacam*)	4d
100 'witthis' bought from him for the same	2d
A labourer hired for a day to serve him in the work	2d
The board of the thatcher and his servant for a day	3d
The board of a thatcher, hired to thatch across the timber for a week	10d
His servant to serve him three days, in all things	6d
William Bailly for the carriage of wood to 'le brekemen' for four days	3s 4d

---

[26] Blank in manuscript.

Repairs to the manor <William Harlakenden; £41 10s 2½d>[27]

Paid John Duke and his two sons, working at the manor for 14 days in June 1466	4s 8d
John Duke for each of his two sons for 14 days from 15 June to 8 July	9s 4d
John Duke for 2½ days for his two sons for carpentry	1s 8d
John Duke the younger, by the hand of my wife on 31 October, for hewing timber at The Mote	3s 4d
John Duke, carpenter, and his two sons, hewing timber there for seven <ten> weeks and four days from 8 July to 21 September	£2 6s 0d
John Duke and his two sons for five weeks from 29 September to 23 November	£1 10s 0d
Hamo Coupere, carpenter, working there for 12 days between 1 and 23 November	3s 0d
John Carpenter working there for four days	1s 0d
John Duke and sons, and Hamo Coupere, working there for 17 days from 23 November to 25 December	6s 9d
John Duke working there for five days before 25 December	1s 8d
Paid to John Duke on 28 December for his wages	3s 4d
John Duke and his two sons, working there for two weeks hewing 'bordlogges' and framing the solar in the kitchen (besides 3s 4d paid to him above) before 2 February	6s 8d
John Duke and three others, hewing timber at Robertsbridge	6s 6d
John Duke for his expenses with the others, going to Robertsbridge and back	1s 1d
John Duke and three persons, working there for two weeks in February	6s 6d
Carriage of timber from Robertsbridge to 'le sawstage' for cutting three 'kervys'	1s 4d
Simon Hykot and his mate, sawing 2000 feet of board there	£1
The same Simon and his mate for sawing 3000 [feet of] boards there at another time	£1 10s 0d
200 [sheaves of] reed for covering the timber	2s 0d
John Lynot for covering it	2s 0d
Allowed John Meyne for writing his particulars	4d
Simon Hykot and his mate, sawyers, for sawing 200 [feet of] boards there	2s 0d
John Duke, carpenter, on 25 May for his wages for the week after Trinity [1 to 7 June]	8d
Thomas Bachiler, 'lymebrenner', for burning lime on three occasions	11s 8d <6s 8d>

---

[27] Added in the margin and linked by a bracket to the last two-thirds of the *repairs* section of the account along with other annotations described in note 25 above.

Thomas Bachiler for full payment for 230 quarters of lime before 8
August (besides 12s 0d allowed him by my lady for his board)   15s 0d

Costs of making 'Bryke'[28]
A labourer hired for six days to dig sand for 'le brikmen'   1s 6d
John Austyn, labourer, and his mate, hired for five days in the third
week of October to make faggots for 'le brikmen'   1s 10d
John Austyn and his mate for their ferry   1d
John Meyne for the carriage of 38 cartloads of sand for four days   3s 4d
John Meyne for carriage of wood for two days to 'le lyme oste',
burnt by John Pounde   2s 0d
John Mayne for carriage of two cartloads of straw for 'le brikemen'   1s 4d
Robert Van for 16 cartloads of straw bought from him, with its
carriage from Leigh to the manor of Mote for 'le brikemen'   10s 8d
William Brickman on occasions for making 'brike' this year, as
appears by the particulars examined upon this account   £22 3s 2d
Robert Smyth on 16 May[29] for seven pounds of iron bought from
him for the wagon of the manor   10d
Robert Smyth on 29 May for eight 'platys' and 'broddes' bought
from him for the wagon   11d
<Robert Smyth for a lock bought from him   3½d>
William Dobill for sharpening the masons' tools   11d
William Dobill for seven iron 'boltes', eight iron rings and eight
iron 'gojons' for two 'gynnes' within the manor   2s 4d

Costs of cleaning the pond[30]
Paid William Dyker for making a way outside the pond cleaned
and scoured by John Lillesden   1d
William Hoode working about the cleaning of the pond
of the manor   £1 13s 0d <£2 13s 4d>
John Lillesden for cleaning the pond <by the barn> and for carrying
6950 'hulles' by a 100 of 120, as appears in various particulars   £2 19s 6d
John Lillesden for four days in May, scouring the gut (*gutteram*)
between the pond and the pound, and making 'le mowth' of the
pond, and for making a way from the pond where he carried it out   8d
John Lillesden by the hand of John Mayne for the carriage of 'lez
shorys' [the shoring] of the new pond there   12s 9d
William Austyn hired for 14 days working on the making of 'lez
dammes' there   3s 6d
John Dyne hired for 16 days labouring on the 'dammes'   4s 0d

---

[28] Written in the margin and bracketed against these entries in the body of the *repairs* section of the
account.
[29] Originally written *xvj day*, altered to *xvj die*.
[30] Written in the margin and bracketed against these entries in the body of the *repairs* section of the
account.

John Mayne's servant working in the said work for 15 days	2s 6d
Paid Thomas Mason on 26 March 1467 in full payment for 43 days between 2 February and 29 March 1467 for him and his servant	13s 2d
Sum	£46 15s 6d

Expenses of the household of the lord and lady

Expenses of my master and lady at Oxney Ferry towards the manor of Mote, and returning on 24 and 26 May	1s 11d
Robert Van for the expenses of my lady's horses for two days and nights	1s 4d
The ferrymen at Oxney on 9 July, by the order of my lady	2s 10d
Two oxen bought and delivered to the manor in May	£1 18s 4d
A quarter of wheat by the hand of John Mayne, delivered for the lord's household there	6s 8d
Half a seam of oats by the hand of John Meyne in Lent	2s 0d
A sheep bought from John Mayne delivered to my lady for the household in July	1s 8d
A lamb bought from John Mayne delivered to my lady there in July	10d
Two bullocks delivered to my lady for the household	£1 5s 0d
To my lady for two lambs for the household	2s 0d
One quarter six bushels of wheat delivered to the household	11s 8d
Seventeen bushels of oats, delivered to my lady for the household	4s 3d
Half a wey of cheese, delivered to my lady for the household	3s 4d
Four cartloads of hay, delivered to the lady for the household	8s 0d
John Meyne for the pasture for four oxen for half a year	6s 8d
John Meyne for the pasture for four cows for the same term	6s 0d
John Meyne for the pasture for three mares for the same term	4s 6d
John Meyne for the pasture for three mares of John Lillesden for the same term	4s 6d
Sum	£6 11s 6d

Payment of scots

Thomas atte Hatche, collector of a penny-scot, by the hand of John Mayne for the lands of the manor of Mote	16s 1d

Wages of the collector of rents

In the wages of John Mayne, collector of rents of the manor of Mote	6s 8d

Expenses of the accountant

William Harlakynden, being at The Mote to hold a court there on 15 May 1467	1s 0d
William Harlakynden, being at Rye to talk to the mayor to prevent the discharge of William Brikeman from his pledges: going, staying	

and coming back	1s 1d
William Harlakynden, going to the manor of Mote to supervise the workmen on 8 July	4d
William Harlakynden, going to The Mote for the same reason on 3 October	3d
William Harlakynden, going to The Mote to supervise the brickworkers and carpenters on 17 December: going, staying and coming back	6d
William Harlakynden, riding to Cranbrook to buy stone (including a penny paid to Netter's widow on a contract for 40 cartloads of stone at a shilling a load) on 24 February	10½d
John Hale going to The Mote on various occasions to transact various business and supervise the workmen	6d
John Hale to The Mote on 11 January, to tell John Mayne to fell wood and carry it to 'le brikeost' and to order John German to prepare wood for 'le brikeost', because the 'brikemen' were held up in their work for lack of wood	6½d
Sum	5s 1d

Small expenses

Paid the costs of the steward of the court, being at The Mote on Friday before Whitsun [15 May 1467], by the hand of John German	8d
Four bushels of oats, bought by John German for my lady's horses	1s 0d
William Bailly, for the carriage of beds and barrels from the manor to Rye, by the hand of John German	8d
William Bailly, by the hand of John German, for the carriage of a cartload of straw from Thomas Hatche's house to 'lez brikemen'	4d
A sailor for ferrying my lady's household goods from Rye to Appledore, with the expenses of John German attending upon the said goods	1s 2d
William Bailly for the carriage of two pairs of wheels from Newenden to the manor, that is to say one for a wagon and one for a cart	4d
Sum	4s 2d

Foreign payments

Paid the bailiff of the lord king, by the hand of John German, for green wax lost by the lord in the king's court	13s 4d
John Hamond of Rye, by the hand of John German, for money owed him of old	6s 8d
Alice Maffey, by John German, in part-payment for three quarters of wheat bought for my lady	5s 0d
Sum	£1 5s 0d

Liveries of money
Paid to my lady, by the hand of John German, on 25 October by
the acknowledgement of my lady   £1
Paid to my lady, by the hand of John German, on 31 October
within the manor by the acknowledgement of my lady   8s 0d
Sum   £1 8s 0d

Sum of allowances and payments   £85 19s 6d

And so he has a surplus of   £49 13s 10d

Mote manor: the account of William Harlakynden, receiver of Sir John Scotte, knight, from 29 September 1467 to 29 September 1468

[ESRO NOR 15/106]

Arrears	[*blank*]

Fixed rents

For the rent of various tenants in Iden, as appears by the rental, and by the account of John German, the beadle and collector of rents there £3 6s 10½d

For the rent of various tenants in Peasmarsh belonging to the manor £3 9s 0d

For the rent of various tenants in Northiam £3 0s 3½d

For the rent of various tenants in Beckley £1 2s 4d

For the rent of various tenants in Ewhurst 12s 5d

Sum £11 10s 11d

Hen rents

And for 3d from one hen from the rent of Robert Gogeler from land called Horsepen at the term of Christmas, sold for 3d

Profits of court

The profits of the courts held there this year, as appears by the rolls 5s 6d

Farm of the demesne lands

The farm of the manor of Mote, let to John Mayne this year £13

The farm of a parcel of land, let by the lord to Thomas Profite at 1s 0d, for this and last year 2s 0d

Sum £13 2s 0d

Sale of wood

Wood sold to John Meyne this year £7

Foreign receipts

From Sir John Scotte, knight, by the hand of Dennis Lene, 'brikeleyer', in the week before 12 March 1467[31] 13s 4d

Sir John Scott by the hand of William Mason in the same week 10s 0d

Sir John Scott by the hand of William Mason in the week before [10 April 1468] £1 10s 0d

Sir John Scott at The Mote on 1 May £5

---

[31] *dicto anno vij*, probably a mistake for *viij*, 1468; a later date in *anno vij* is corrected to *anno viij*, and Scott had sent money to Mote by John Adam two days before.

Sir John Scott at The Mote on 30 August	£2
From my lady by the hand of Philip atte Churche	£15
From Vincent Fynche on 22 June 1468	£8 6s 8d
From Sir John Scotte on 16 December 1467 <1468>	£4
From my lady at Hall in August 1468	£5
The issues and profits of the smithy of Mote this year, by the hand of Robert Smyth	4s 10½d
From my master Sir John Scotte on 16 September 1468	£14
From my master Sir John Scotte, by the hand of John Adam, on 10 March 1468 at the time of his journey to The Mote	5s 0d
From my master, by the hand of John Adam at The Mote, for buying ox-meat in 1467-68	£1
From my master upon the cost and expenses of two masons coming from Maidstone to Hall in 1467-68	5s 0d
From my master, by the hands of Henry Prik and his mates, journeying from London to The Mote	6s 8d
From my master, by the hand of the cement maker, at London	2s 0d
My master, by the hand of Peter Brikemason, receiver of money, by the hand of Henry Turner in 1467-68	2s 0d
Sum	£58 5s 6½d

Sum total of receipts	<£90 4s 2½d>[32]
Of which	

<*Surplus allowed*	
He accounts for a surplus which he had at the foot of his account for the previous year, to be acquitted	£49 13s 10d>

Rents resolute

Paid the bailiff of the sheriff of Sussex for the sheriff's tourn	8d
To him for 'le blancheferme'	5d
A rent resolute to Lord Dacre in the value of one pound of pepper, the rent of land called 'Blakelond', by the hand of John Broun, his collector of rents	1s 2d
The churchwarden (*prepositus*) of the church of Iden for 'Romescot'	½d
Sum	2s 3½d

Allowances of rent with defaults

John Roberd for land called Thornsdale in Iden, charged above in the heading 'Fixed rents' within the sum of £3 6s 10½d, because it cannot be levied[33]	2s 11d

---

[32] Replacing *£58 5s 6½d* deleted.
[33] This sentence is repeated at the end of most of the following entries.

Heirs of Richard atte Wode for land called 'Cotenham' in Iden	1s 8d
John Parrok for his lands in Iden	1d
John Asshmynton in Iden, because it is in the lord's hands and let to farm with the demesne lands	1s 6d
William Potyn for 'Shereveshothe' in Peasmarsh, charged above within the sum of £3 9s 0d, because it is in the lord's hands and nothing can be levied	1s 3d
Thomas Keriell, knight, for the manor of Kitchenour	1s 3d
Simon Watell for land called 'Brounlond' in Peasmarsh	1s 0d
Thomas Foughill for various lands which he holds in Peasmarsh	4d
William Hulles for land formerly Peter Churche in Northiam, because it is in the lord's hands and let to farm with the demesne lands	3d
John Holstok for 'Denyslond' in Northiam	1s 0d
William Bate for lands which lately belonged to Peter Churche in Northiam, because it still cannot be levied	6d
John Benett for 'Le Crabbe' and other parcels of land in Northiam	2s 2½d
John Twiseden and Maud Majour for land called 'Blithelond' and other parcels of land in Northiam	1s 6d
William Lucas both for land purchased of Robert Edward and land purchased of John Holman called 'Okworthes' in Northiam	6d
Simon Moys for his lands in Northiam	2s 6d
William Hoore of Northiam because John Holman paid his rent within the sum of his own rent which is charged above in the heading 'Fixed rents'	3d
William Belknapp for 'Piperslond' in Beckley	4s 0d
Margaret Strode for her lands in Beckley	½d
William Tukton for land formerly John Hochon in Beckley	5d
William Oxenbrigge for 'Mottislond' formerly Stephen Hekton	2s 6d
William Belknapp for land formerly Stephen Hekton called 'Hektons'	6s 8d
Richard Fenys, knight, Lord Dacre, for 50 acres in Padgham [in] the manor of Ewhurst	10s 7d
Richard Sote for 'Brekex' charged above in Iden, because it is allowed to him by his charter	3d
Agnes Kychenore, charged above in Iden	4d
John Dalot for two acres of land by the garden [*blank*], charged above in Iden	6d
Sum	£2 2s 9½d

Repairs to the manor - wages of carpenters and sawyers

Paid to John Duke, carpenter, and his two sons, working at the manor for a week in the second week of March	6s 0d
John Duke and three mates in the last week of March and first of April	15s 4d

John Duke and three mates for their wage for a day and a half	1s 11½d
A carpenter working there half a day	2d
John Duke and his two sons between 25 April and 22 May	£1
John Duke, carpenter, and his two sons between 22 May and 5 June	5s 4d
Thomas Carpenter and his son for eight days before 22 July, each of them taking 4d a day without food	5s 4d
John Duke on 21 July for wages	3s 0d
Thomas Carpenter and his son on 12 August, for 13 days between 25 July and 15 August	8s 8d
Thomas Carpenter and his son for 27 days between 15 August and 11 September	9s 0d
John Duke and his two sons between 8 June and 11 September	£3 3s 0d
Thomas Carpenter and his son for 15 days between 11 September and 2 October	10s 0d
John Duke the younger, carpenter, for 15 days between 11 September and 2 October	5s 0d
John Duke and his two sons, carpenters, wages for 11 September to 16 October	£1 0s 10d
Thomas Carpenter and son for 19 days between 2 October and 1 November	12s 8d
Thomas Carpenter and his son 15 days from 30 October to 20 November, for himself at 4d a day and his son at 3d a day	8s 9d
John Duke the younger for [five][34] days	1s 8d
John Duke and his two sons for six weeks and 14½ days from 16 October to 18 December	£1 14s 6d
John German for the board of the carpenters, at the manor for 11½ weeks	£1 10s 2d
John Wardgrove, carpenter, for ten days before 21 September	3s 4d
John Wardegrove, carpenter, for 19 days between 2 October and 1 November	6s 4d
John Wardegrove, carpenter, for 15 days besides his board	3s 9d
Pascal Martyn, joiner, on 8 December for his wages	3s 4d
Pascal Martyn on 15 December for his wages	5s 0d
Pascal Martyn for his expenses going to Faversham to fetch the tools of his craft	1s 0d
Pascal Martyn for 11 days before 29 September	1s 6d
Pascal Martyn in full payment of his quarterage at 25 December	10d
John German for Pascal Martyn's board for 2½ weeks before 25 December	2s 6d
John German for Pascal Martyn's board for six weeks between 10 January and 6 March [1469][35]	6s 0d[36]

---

[34] Blank in manuscript.
[35] There were six weeks between Epiphany and the first Sunday in Lent in 1469 but not in 1468.
[36] Marginated and deleted against the remaining entries: *<allowed in another year>*.

Simon Hykott and John Asshmynton, sawyers, for sawing 1000 feet of boards and timber before 1 May	10s 0d
Peter Colys, labourer, cleaving 'bordlogges' by agreement with him in gross	1s 4d
Simon Hykot and his mate sawing 1000 feet of boards and timber	10s 0d
Simon Hicott and his mate sawing 1000 feet of boards in September	10s 0d
Simon Hicott and his mate on 31 July for sawing boards at Robertsbridge	5s 0d
Simon Hicott and his mate on 21 August sawing boards within the manor	5s 0d
Simon Hicott for sawing 1000 feet of board and timber	10s 0d
Simon Hicott and mate on 11 October sawing 1000 feet of board and timber	10s 0d
Simon Hicott and mate on 16 December sawing 1000 feet of board	10s 0d
John Potyn, carpenter of Wittersham, working in the manor for ten days in the last week of September	3s 4d
Pascal Martyn, joiner, on 19 October for wages	2s 6d
John German for Pascal Martyn's board for three weeks between 20 November and 13 December	2s 9d
John Asshmynton and Simon Hycott, sawyers, on 13 November for sawing 1000 feet of board	10s 0d
Simon Hicot and mate on 12 April, sawing 1000 feet of board	10s 0d
Simon Hicott and mate on 30 September, sawing 1000 feet of board and timber	10s 0d
Simon Hicott and mate on 28 November, sawing 1000 feet of board	10s 0d
John Pippesden for the carriage of nine tons (*tonnell'*) of board from Robertsbridge to the manor	9s 1d
William Austyn, labourer, on 29 June for felling and cutting a great piece of timber and making 'cotilbord' from it	1s 8d
Robert Van for ten 'bordlogges' bought from him for the manor	8s 0d
Robert Van for 80 pieces of timber bought from him in Brabourne, 'Cheffeld' and 'Sabelerslond' for the manor	£1 3s 4d
Sum	£22 16s 9½d

Purchase of stones, with carriage

Paid the widow of John Netter of Cranbrook, by the hand of William Lynche on 21 September, on the purchase of stones from her	13s 4d

The same widow in full payment for 20 loads of untrimmed stone	6s 8d
Richard Chitynden for the carriage of two cartloads from Cranbrook to the manor of Mote on 30 October	3s 0d
John Netter for the carriage of one cartload from Cranbrook to the manor	1s 6d
Robert Bigge for the carriage of two cartloads from Cranbrook to the manor on 29 August	2s 10d
Richard Chitenden for the carriage of two cartloads from Cranbrook to the manor	2s 10d
Adam Bevynden for the carriage of one cartload from Cranbrook to the manor of Mote	1s 6d
John Netter's servant for the carriage of one cartload to the manor of Mote	1s 6d
John Middelton for the carriage of one cartload to the manor of Mote	1s 6d
William Hopper, 'quareman' of Eastbourne, by the hand of William Mason on 15 May in full payment for digging and trimming 350 feet of stones	£1 15s 0d
William Mason and his four men, by the hand of my master, for trimming and hewing of stones at Eastbourne (besides £1 paid in advance by William Harlackynden and besides 10s 0d paid by my master)	£1 10s 0d
<Note that I paid William Mason £1 10s 0d which he repaid William Harlackynden and did not perform the work for it [*deleted*]>[37]	
William Hopper, 'quarryman', for digging and trimming 100 feet at Eastbourne on 3 November	10s 0d
William Rolfe and his mate on 17 August for carrying seven tons (*dol'*) of stones from Eastbourne to John Meyne's fleet	14s 0d
William Rolfe for carriage of the same stones from the quarry to the ship	1s 9d
Four labourers for help in loading the stones	8d
John Meyne's wife for victuals delivered to the sailors carrying the stones and chalk to John Meyne's gut (*gutter'*) on 5 July	8d
William Rolfe and John Monke the same day for carrying 16 tons of hewn stone from Eastbourne to John Meyne's gut by water	£1 12s 0d
Richard Grey, mason, working for ten days at Eastbourne	5s 0d <5s 7d>
William Squyer, being at Eastbourne and Mote in the same work as Richard Grey, for three weeks and ten days	12s 7d
<At Mote he was at my board therefore deduct from wages [*deleted*]>[38]	
Richard Grey working three weeks at the manor of Mote	7s 0d

---

[37] Added in the hand of Sir John Scott.
[38] Added in the hand of Sir John Scott.

John Mason being at Eastbourne for two weeks four days between 25 March and 17 April [1468][39]	9s 10d
William Mason, being at Eastbourne and Mote on the lord's business seeking masons for four weeks between 12 March and 17 April [1468]	16s 0d
<Here William Mason began to work; therefore all the above is disallowed [*deleted*]>[40]	
William Mason on 15 May being at Eastbourne for three weeks between 23 April and 15 May	12s 0d
William Mason and his three mates, by the hands of John Saverey on 1 June, for the hewing and trimming of stones at Eastbourne	£1 10s 0d
William Hopper, 'quarryman', for digging 175 stones at Eastbourne, by the hand of William Mason	17s 6d
William Mason, on 6 July, for the carriage of 16 tons of stones from the quarry of Eastbourne to the ship	4s 0d
Richard Grey, being at Eastbourne for a week for loading and unloading the ship, at his own board	3s 8d
John Meyne for the carriage of 134 cartloads of chalk from his fleet to the manor, and for the carriage of 25 loads of Eastbourne stone from the sea-shore	£2 4s 4d
Thomas Bachiler, by the hand of John German, for carrying chalk into the lord's barn	4d
William Hopper, 'quarryman', by the hand of William Mason on 16 December	10s 0d
John Mason by William Mason at Eastbourne, for three weeks between 23 April and 15 May	11s 0d
Richard Grey working there for three weeks and two days	12s 2d
William Squyer, by the hand of William Mason, working there three weeks	10s 0d
William Mason on 15 May, in full payment of his wages for working at Eastbourne between 25 March and 17 April	11s 0d
Sum	£18 15s 9d

Cost of making 'bryke'

Paid Thomas Brykeman for providing 137,000 of 'bryke' made by William Brikeman by an agreement made with Thomas Brykeman by my master, at 3d a 1000	£1 14s 3d
Thomas Brykeman for making 270,000 of 'bryke' for the construction of the manor, at 1s 10d a 1000	£24 15s 9d
John Meyne for carriage of wood to 'le brykeost' for two days	1s 8d
John Meyne for eight cartloads of straw bought from him, with its carriage to 'le brikeost'	5s 4d

---

[39] This and the next date depend on periods which are possible in 1468 but not in 1469.
[40] Added in the hand of Sir John Scott.

Carriage of a cartload of straw from Iden rectory to 'le brikeost'	6d
John German for a cartload of straw bought from him for 'le brikeost'	1s 0d
Two labourers hired for three days in January 1468 to prepare wood for 'le brikeost'	11d
Three labourers hired for four days to prepare wood at 'le brikeost'	6s 0d
John Oxenbrigge hired for two days in January 1468 to carry wood to 'le brikeost'	2s 6d
Thomas Bachiler, labourer, hired 4½ days to fell wood, prepare it and to load the wagons	9d
Paid James Maplisden for his servant Goler, hired for nine days to fell and prepare wood in the park for 'le brikeost'	1s 6d
Robert Van for one day carrying wood from the park to 'le brikeoste'	10d
Austin Potyn of Peasmarsh on 15 October for felling wood in the park for 'le brikoste'	2d
Ingram Van for two days' carriage of wood from Flackley to 'le brikeost' in the first week of August	1s 8d
Edward Parok for two days to carry wood for the same reason	1s 9d
Robert Simond for the carriage of wood from Flackley to 'le brikeost' for one day	10d
To the servant of Boseney for the carriage of wood for one day for the same reason	10d
John Maffay for the carriage of wood for the same reason for one day	10d
William Dalot for the carriage of wood for one day	10d
John Baker for making [fire]wood for 'le lymekylle'	2s 10d
Thomas Bachiler on 4 June, by the hand of John Hale, for the same reason	1s 11d
John Austyn and his servant, making [fire]wood for 'le brikemakers' in the week before 5 June, with a penny for their ferry	1s 9d
John Austyn and his servant for three days in the last week of May for the same work, with a penny for their ferry	11d
John Yonge for two cartloads of straw bought from him for 'le brikemakers'	1s 7d
John Yonge carrying sand for one day	10d
John Austyn and his servant for 13½ days before 26 May to prepare wood and make faggots for 'le brikeost', with 2d for their ferry on two occasions	4s 10d
John Baker, labourer, hired for a day and a half to prepare wood at Flackley	3d
John Baker for preparing three rods of wood for the same reason	1s 4d

Thomas Bachiler on 20 July by the hand of John Baker, in full
payment for felling and hedging three acres of wood   1s 6d
Robert Van for a parcel of straw bought from him, with its
carriage to 'le brikeoste'   2s 4d
John Meyne for the carriage of brick and sand to the manor for
six days   4s 0d
Sum   £29 2s 0d

Cost of making lime
Paid John Midelton, labourer, hired two days to fell and prepare
wood for 'le lymeoste' in the second week of December   4d
Thomas Bachiler, 'lymebrenner', for 582 quarters of lime burnt
this year on various occasions, taking 14s 0d for a hundred, that is
1⅝d for each quarter   £3 12s 0d
Thomas Bachiler for carriage of the lime into the manor on
various occasions, as appears by the book of particulars   4s 0d
Thomas Profite on 28 October for felling and preparing one acre
two rods and 30 perches of wood for the 'lyme oste' at three
shillings an acre   5s 6d
Sum   £4 1s 10d

Necessary costs
Paid for six 'stopp' (2s 0d), one 'rynge' (1s 0d) and one 'payle'
(2d) bought and delivered to the manor for the masons and for the
stock of the manor   3s 2d
Two 'pykoyses' [pickaxes] bought and delivered to the manor for
the masons   2s 4d
Two iron 'crowes' bought and delivered to the manor   2s 2d
Six 'trayes' bought at Egerton   1s 9d
William Dore and his servant for fetching the 'trayes' from
Egerton to Woodchurch on their backs   3d
Carriage of the 'trayes' from Woodchurch to Appledore   1d
William Dore, smith, for an axe bought from him and delivered to
the manor   7d
Thomas Profite for making 24 hurdles (*clatuum*) for the masons
and making a scaffold from them   2s 0d
William Dore for 15 ells of 'osteclothe' bought from him for the
manor stock   6s 3d
For making it up   5d
Robert Bokelond for 34 fathoms of cord bought from him to tie
'lez scaffold' of the manor   2s 0d
Robert Bokelond for two 'handropes' of 14 fathoms bought from
him for the carpenters   1s 6d
Robert Bokelond for a great 'poley roop' [pulley-rope] of eight
fathoms bought from him   2s 0d

Robert Bokelond on 28 May for a great rope of eight fathoms to haul back timber	2s 6d
Robert Bokelond for 'scaffot lyne' bought and delivered to the manor	2s 0d
An 'estrichebord' bought to make moulds (*patron'*) for windows and chimneys	8d
William Bokeland of Kenardington for 'scaffote lyne' bought from him	5½d
Expenses of John Hale for fetching it	1d
Thomas More for two pairs of wheels, of which one for 'le tugg' to carry timber (1s 6d) and one for the short horse-cart to carry 'brike' (1s 4d), with 2d for their ferry	3s 0d
Henry Ryche, the manor carter, for shoeing his horse	4d
Stephen Coupere for making a 'mashingvat', a 'growt tubbe' and a 'tappetrowh' for the household	6s 8d <8s 4d>
Two panels for two cart-saddles (*sellis carectallis*)	1s 3d
A 'gryndestone' bought from Thomas Harry to sharpen the carpenters' and masons' tools	2s 4d
Shoeing a gelding (*equi 'gillyng'*) called 'Marchall'	3½d
Robert Bokelond on 16 July for a pair of 'repe ropys' and a halter, bought and delivered to Henry Riche at the manor	5d
A 'morter shovill' bought on 20 July for the masons	6d
A 'lyme zeve' bought at Ewhurst Fair for the masons	3d
A 'zeve' bought to clean sand and lime	4½d
Stephen Cowpere for making a 'morter tubbe' and for binding vessels and the wheels of the wagon and the short cart	3s 6d
William Dore, smith, for eight 'shovell' and four 'spadys' bought from him and delivered to the manor	6s 4d
A 'scope' bought at Appledore for throwing sand up out from the pit	2d
Carriage of Pascal Martyn's gear from Faversham to Woodchurch and from Woodchurch to the manor	1s 0d
Two 'shovell trees' bought from Robert Smyth at Warehorne Fair	2½d
Robert Bokelond for two halters delivered to the manor	2d
Two 'trayes' bought for the masons	6d
An iron spike bought for mixing mortar	5d
Sum	£2 19s 7d

Wages of masons

Paid Denis Lene, 'brykeleyer', on 12 April for six weeks at the lord's board (except for three days at his own), including 10d reward	18s 4d
Peter Brickmason for six weeks one day at the lord's board (except three days at his own), including 2d reward	18s 2d
Paul Brikeleyer for six weeks one day at the lord's board (except	

three days at his own), including 2d reward	18s 2d
Denis Lene for six weeks between 25 April and 5 June at his own board	£1 4s 0d
John Danyell for six weeks at his own board	£1 1s 0d
Hugh White, 'brykeleyer', for six weeks at his own board	18s 0d
Peter and Paul, 'brikeleyers', for six weeks each at the lord's board	£1 14s 0d
Peter and Paul, 'brikleyers', for three days in Easter Week	2s 8d
William Mason working at Eastbourne for five weeks in July	£1
Thomas Mason working there for five weeks in July	18s 4d
Richard Grey, mason, working there five weeks	18s 4d
William Squeyr, mason, working with William Mason at Eastbourne for five weeks	16s 8d
Richard Grey working with William Mason at Eastbourne for two days	1s 3d
Denis Lene, 'brikemason', on 21 July for six weeks and three days between 5 June and 24 July	£1 6s 0d
John Danyell and Hugh White, masons, for six weeks three days each, John Danyell at 3s 6d and Hugh White at 3s 0d a week	£2 1s 1d
John Danyell and Hugh White's expenses from London to the manor	1s 8d
Henry Caterall, mason, on 6 July for four weeks from 24 June to 25 July at the lord's board	9s 4d
Peter and Paul, 'brikeleyers', on 6 July for six weeks and two days from 5 June to 24 July, at the lord's board	£1 14s 4d
Henry Caterall, mason, for two weeks and five days from 25 July to 15 August, at the lord's board	6s 9d
Denis Lene, mason, for six weeks from 24 July to 4 September	£1 4s 0d
John Daniell, 'brikeleyer', for five weeks and three days within the same period	19s 3d
Hugh White, mason, for six weeks at the same time	18s 0d
Denis Lene, mason, one week (4s 0d) and Hugh White, his servant for one week (3s 0d)	7s 0d
Peter and Paul, 'brikeleyers', for five weeks and five days each from 24 July to 4 September, at the lord's board	£1 13s 4d
William Mason for three weeks from 15 August to 4 September, at the lord's board	8s 6d
John Mason during the same time, at the lord's board	7s 6d
William Squyer, mason, William Mason's apprentice, for the same time, at the lord's board	6s 6d
Thomas Huntlee, mason, for two weeks from 21 August to 4 September, at the lord's board	5s 0d
William Mason at Eastbourne for three days in the week after 26 June, attending to the loading of stone, at his own board	2s 0d
Henry Caterall, mason, for four weeks from 15 August to 11 September, at the lord's board	10s 0d

The widow of John Netter of Cranbrook for the six days' board of two masons trimming stones in the quarry there	1s 6d
Henry Baker for the dinner and bed of those masons on the first night and for their drink on the way home	6d
Denis Lene, 'brikleyer', on 30 September for three weeks from 11 September to 2 October, at his own board	12s 0d
Denis Lene's servant, Hugh [White], for three weeks at his own board	9s 0d
John Danyell, 'brikeleyer', for two weeks and four days from 10 September to 2 October, at his own board	9s 4d
Peter and Paul, 'brikeleyers', for four weeks each from 4 September to 2 October, at the lord's board	£1 2s 8d
William Mason for four weeks at the lord's board	11s 4d
William Mason for his apprentice's wages at the same time, at the lord's board	8s 8d
John Mason, mason, for three weeks from 8 September to 2 October, at the lord's board	7s 6d
Thomas Huntlee, mason, for four weeks at the lord's board	10s 0d
Richard Grey, mason, from 10 September to 2 October, at the lord's board	5s 0d
Denis Lene, 'brikeleyer', for three weeks and two days from 2 October to 26 October, at his own board	13s 4d
Denis Lene's servant Hugh White for four weeks between 2 and 30 October, at Denis's board	12s 0d
Peter Johnson, 'brikeleyer', for three weeks at his own board	10s 6d
Peter and Paul, 'brikeleyers', for three weeks and five days each from 2 to 30 October, at the lord's board	£1 1s 8d
Thomas Huntlee, mason, for four weeks between 2 and 30 October, at the lord's board	10s 0d
John Mason for four weeks at the same time, at the lord's board	10s 0d
Richard Grey, mason, for four weeks at the same time, at the lord's board	10s 0d
William Mason for four weeks at the lord's board	11s 4d
William Mason for his apprentice for four weeks, at the lord's board	8s 8d
Peter Johnson, 'brikeleyer', for one week, of which two days at his own and the rest at the lord's board	2s 0d
Hugh [White] 'brikeleyer' for one [week]	1s 8d
William Mason on 21 November for one week and five days from 1 to 16 November	5s 4d
John Mason for the second week of November and two days the following week	3s 4d
Richard Grey, mason, for one week five days between 1 and 16 November, at the lord's board	3s 8d

Seven pounds of pitch, 20 pounds of red 'okyr', wax and resin bought for the masons	2s 1½d <2s 6½d>
Half a gallon of oil bought for the masons' use	8d
Two 'zevys' and a 'tray' bought for the masons	8d
Sharpening the masons' tools	1s 4d <3s 4d>
John German for getting the said materials at Rye	4d
John Henfeld for one pound of wax bought and delivered to 'lez brikemen' for their use	8d
Thomas Ryder and William Skynner for a day each, digging the foundations of the larder and 'le withdraght'	6d
John Midelton labouring there for four weeks to the second week of May	3s 4d
William Mason on 16 December for his wages for two weeks and three days, working at Eastbourne with two men, at 4s 0d a week for himself and 3s 0d a week for each of them	£1 5s 0d
<John Cole by the hand of my master, coming from Esher to Mote to advise on the work there	10s 0d
John Hunte of Westminster, coming from London for the same reason, by the hand of my master	£1>
Sum	£38 17s 2½d

Wages of labourers

Paid John Spayn, Richard Reygate and George Shobery, labourers, hired for five days each in the third week of March to pull down the walls (*parietes*) where the janitor's chamber was to be built, at the lord's board	3s 1½d
Robert Van's wife, lodging the labourers at the same time	4d
John Middelton on 27 March, hired to labour for a week in the fourth week of March, at the lord's board	8d
Richard Parrok, labourer, hired for a day to carry timber to 'le sawstage' and firewood into the manor on 4 April	10d
John Middilton, labourer, hired for two weeks to work and serve the masons, at the lord's board	1s 8d
William Yonge, labourer, for three weeks three days to serve the masons, at the lord's board	2s 10d
Thomas Bachiler on 12 April, hired to work and to serve the masons for five weeks, at the lord's board	4s 7d
Thomas Bachiler, to fell and prepare wood for the oven in the kitchen	1s 7d
William Barbour, labourer, to serve the masons for six weeks, at the lord's board except for three days, with 2d reward	4s 8d
John Mighell, 'mortermaker', to labour for six weeks at the lord's board, except for three days at his own, with 2d reward	4s 8d
John Hoore, labourer, for two weeks <and two days> to serve the masons, at the lord's board	1s 8d <2s 0d>

Thomas Profite and his mate, hired to make two pits for the foundations of two chimneys, one at the south end and one at the north end of the tower there, by an agreement made with them	9d
John Mighell, 'mortermaker', to labour for six weeks from 25 April to 5 June serving the masons, at the lord's board	7s 6d
William Yonge <for six weeks> and Richard Morcok for three weeks for working and serving the masons, at the lord's board	7s 6d
William Walys, labourer, and William Johnson for six weeks each serving the masons, at the lord's board	11s 0d
John Midelton, labourer, (four weeks) John Hore (five weeks) serving the masons, at the lord's board	7s 6d
Richard Morcok, labourer, for a week before 5 June serving the masons, at the lord's board	10d
William Walys on 21 July, for wages labouring in the service of the masons for six weeks and 1½ days from 5 June to 25 July, at the lord's board	5s 9d
John Midelton, labourer, serving the masons for two weeks before 20 June, at the lord's board	1s 10d
John Midelton for two weeks from 20 June to 3 July	1s 10d
John Mighell, labourer, serving the masons for six weeks two days from 5 June to 25 July, at the lord's board	7s 11d
William Johnson, labourer, serving the masons for six weeks from 5 June to 25 July, at the lord's board	5s 6d
Richard Morcok, labourer, on 10 July, for serving the masons for five weeks four days, at the lord's board	4s 10d
John Hoore, labourer, for four weeks and four days before 10 July, at the lord's board	3s 8d
Richard Morcok <1s 8d> for two weeks and John Midelton <2s 9d> for three weeks serving the masons, at the lord's board	4s 5d
John Baker, labourer, for two days breaking walls for making the kitchen chimney	4d
Henry Andrew, labourer, for carrying brick to the work for seven weeks, at the lord's board	3s 6d
Hugh Brikeleyer in reward for tiling over the 'withdraght' on the north side of the gate there	4d
John Austyn and his servant at the manor in the first week of August felling wood for 'le brikeoste'	1s 10d
John Bulke, labourer, serving the masons for four weeks, at the lord's board	4s 0d
John Mighell, 'mortermaker', working there for six weeks from 25 July to 4 September, at the lord's board	7s 6d
William Johnson for six weeks at the same time in the same work, at the lord's board	5s 6d
John Hore, labourer, working for five weeks from 6 August to 10 September, at the lord's board	4s 2d

William Walys, labourer, serving the masons there for six weeks
from 25 July to 4 September, at the lord's board   5s 6d

John Hore, labourer, serving the masons for four weeks from 10
July to 6 August, at the lord's board   3s 4d

John Baker, labourer, for the same reason for five weeks five
days from 22 July to 4 September, at the lord's board   4s 10d

John Baker for cutting down weeds (*sarcularum*) within the
manor   2d

Henry Andrew, labourer, for carrying 'brike' to the work, at the
lord's board   3s 6d

Thomas Bachiler, labourer, felling wood for 'le brikeost' in the
first week of August   11d

John Midelton, labourer, serving the masons for seven weeks
from 25 July to 10 September, at the lord's board   6s 5d

Richard Morcok, labourer, working at the said work for six weeks
at the lord's board   5s 0d

Robert Spakman, labourer, for three weeks felling and preparing
wood, at the lord's board   2s 9d

John Goler, the servant of James Maplisden, labourer, labouring
there in various jobs for seven weeks from 7 July to 29 August, at
the lord's board   6s 5d

Lawrence Ednex, labourer, for 40 days carrying 'brike' to the
manor from 7 July to 8 September, at the lord's board   3s 4d

William Johnson, labourer, serving the masons for four weeks
from 3 September to 1 October, at the lord's board   3s 8d

Robert Spakman, labourer, doing various jobs for four weeks, at
the lord's board   3s 8d

William Waleys for three weeks serving the masons from 3 to 24
September, at the lord's board   2s 9d

John Mighell, 'mortermaker', for two weeks from 4 to 16
September, at the lord's board   2s 6d

John Bulke, labourer, serving the masons for three weeks, at the
lord's board   2s 9d

John Clayman, labourer, for three weeks and four days digging
sand for the said work, at the lord's board   3s 4d

Richard Morcok, labourer, serving the masons for two weeks
from 3 to 17 September   1s 8d

Ingram Van carrying wood for four days out of the park to   3s 9d [*recte* 3s 4d]
'le brikost' at 10d a day

Thomas Foughill for carrying wood at the same time, for one day   10d

William Bailly for carrying wood at the same time, for one day   10d

Hugh Sharpe for six days for felling wood within the park   1s 0d

William Tounne, labourer, serving the masons for five weeks
from 25 September to 29 October, at the lord's board   4s 7d

John Bulke, labourer, serving the masons for four weeks from 2 to 30 October, at the lord's board	3s 8d
John Mighell, 'mortermaker', for six weeks to 30 October, at the lord's board	7s 6d
William Waleys, labourer, for three weeks one day serving the masons from 29 September to 1 November, at the lord's board	2s 10d
John Midelton, labourer, serving the masons for four weeks from 29 September to 1 November, at the lord's board	3s 8d
Richard Morcok, labourer, hired for six weeks from 17 September to 30 October, at the lord's board	5s 0d
Robert Spakman, labourer, for nine weeks from 16 September to 20 November, labouring in various jobs on the manor, at the lord's board	6s 7d
John Hore, labourer, for seven weeks from 9 September to 30 October, serving the masons, at the lord's board	5s 10d
James Lucas, labourer, for 3½ days to fell wood in the park for 'le brike' in October	7d
James Maplisden on 6 November for 28 days carrying brick from 8 September to 18 October	2s 4d
Richard Morcok, labourer, for two weeks from 30 October to 12 November, at the lord's board	1s 8d
John Mighell, labourer, working there for two days in November	4d
Hugh Sharpe, labourer, working two days in the said work	4d
John Midelton, labourer, for three weeks serving the masons from 30 October to 20 November, at the lord's board	2s 9d
John Hoore, labourer, for three weeks from 30 October to 20 November, at the lord's board	2s 6d
Richard Morcok, labourer, for three weeks from 12 November to 6 December, at the lord's board	2s 6d
Thomas Bachiler and Hugh Sharpe, labourers, by the hand of John German, helping John Duke carrying timber and board into the lord's barn	4d
John German for the board of Thomas Bachiler's servant Hugh for two days, carrying 'brike' from 'le brike oste' to the manor for the masons	2d
Thomas Bachiler, by the hand of John German, helping John Mighell for five days making mortar, with food included	1s 8d
Thomas Bachiler, labourer, by the hand of John German, for felling wood for charcoal, at piece-work	11s 4d
John German for the board of John Mighell for six weeks from 10 January to 6 March	6s 0d
John German for the board of Richard Morcok for three weeks, helping John Mighell make mortar	3s 0d
John German for the board of Robert Smyth and his boy for a week and a half	2s 6d

John Baker, labourer, helping John German to take distraint on William Belknap's land called 'Pipereslond'	2d
John German for the board of Robert Smyth and his servant for two weeks and five days, working in the manor for the same time	4s 10d
John German for the board of the charcoal-maker in the second week of December	10d
John German for the board of Thomas Bachiler, 'lymebrenner', and his servant for three weeks working in the manor	6s 0d
John German for the board of four carpenters hewing 'bordlogge' at Robertsbridge for one week	4s 0d
John German for the board of a thatcher, thatching over the timber at The Mote for three days	5d
Paid for the ferry of the labourers, coming to and returning from their jobs	2s 11d
The thatcher's servant for his labour and board for three days serving the thatcher, with 2d paid for 100 withies for the same job	8d
Sum £14 11s 4½d <£5 15s 11d>[41]	

Expenses of the household

The expenses of the lord's household at the manor of Mote between 7 and 12 March, as appears by the book of particulars examined upon this account	9s 8d
Paper bought at Appledore, and waiting there overnight	1½d
John Boseney, 'boteman', carrying two quarters of wheat from John Meyne's fleet to Appledore mill by water, and from Appledore to the manor for the household	1s 0d
Richard Parrok, hired with his wagon to carry four barrels of 'biere' and two barrels of white herring from Rye to the manor of Mote	8d
Richard Parrok with his wagon, hired for half a day to carry wood and 'brike' to the manor	6d
Thomas Bachiler, labourer, for his work in the household	1s 0d
Thomas Bachiler for fetching a cade of sprats, one tripod (*tripedem*) and other of the lord's stuff at Oxney Ferry	1d
A boy of Simon Godard as a reward for looking after William [Harlakynden]'s horse at Oxney Ferry during his stay	1d
John Adam in money to pay 'le bierman' at Udimore for the money owed to him on my lady's leaving the manor of Mote before 1 November	2s 6d
John Adam on 27 March for victuals bought for the household	3s 4d
One bushel of peas bought for the household, with a penny for their carriage from Woodchurch to Oxney Ferry	1s 1d
John Adam on 8 April for victuals bought for the household	1s 8d

---

[41] Added in the margin in the hand of Sir John Scott.

The ferrymen of Oxney on 9 April for shipping six bushels of flour and one bushel of peas, and for ferrying John Hale	2d
John Adam for household expenses from 12 March to 15 April, as shown in the book of particulars examined upon this account	14s 8d
John Hale and John Adam at Winchelsea on two occasions to buy fish for the household	2½d
One bushel of onions (3d) and 'beresesyng' bought on two occasions	4½d
Four cows with fours calves bought and sent to the manor of Mote on Friday before 1 May	£2 4s 2d
600 eggs bought and provided for the household and sent to the manor on the same day	2s 6d
Richard Cornewell, labourer, hired to drive the four cows and calves and to carry the eggs to the manor	7d
John Adam for household expenses from 15 April to 2 May, as shown in the book of particulars	9½d
John Adam for household expenses on 22, 23 and 27 April, together with victuals bought and provided, as appears in the book of particulars examined upon this account	£1 9s 2d
John Hale for household expenses on 24 and 25 April, as in the particulars	1s 9½d
John Midelton and John Hale for various business concerning the household	7½d
John Yonge for an ox bought from him for the household	£1 10s 0d
Eight cheeses for the household, with their carriage from Woodchurch to Appledore on 5 May	3s 4d
Household expenses in the first week of May, as appears in the particulars	1s 3d
Victuals bought in the second week of May, as appears in the particulars	1s 10d
Victuals bought in the third week of May, as appears in the particulars	3s 7½d
Victuals bought in the fourth week of May, as appears in the particulars	2s 8½d
Victuals bought in the first week of June, as appears in the particulars	2s 3d
John Hale, sent on various business for the household	7½d
The ferrymen of Oxney for ferrying various necessaries, as appears in the particulars	9d
Parnel Fadry, working in the household for four weeks in various jobs between 25 April and Whitsun	1s 0d
Alice Maffey for three quarters of wheat bought from her by my lady for the household	£1 1s 0d
Victuals for the household in second week of June, as appears by the particulars	2s 4d

Victuals in the third week	11d
John Adam and John Hale, walking and riding on various household business	1s 2½d
Two sieves bought with other necessaries for the household, as appears in the particulars	9d
Expenses of John Midelton, Henry Riche and Richard Morcok, sent by my lady to Appledore to fetch five quarters of malt coming from the manor of Hall	1d
Alice German on 28 June for working in various jobs in the household for six weeks before the last week of June	1s 0d
Victuals bought for the household for the third week of June, as appears in the particulars	2s 6d
Victuals bought for the household in the last week of June	1s 10d
Victuals bought for the household in the first week of July, as appears in the particulars	4s 4d
Victuals bought for the household in the second week of July, as appears in the particulars	2s 8½d
Victuals bought for the household in the third week of July, as appears in the particulars	4s 0d
John Hale, riding to Udimore to fetch seven bushels of 'hoppes' bought from Richard Grove by John Adam for the household, part of five hundred of hops	5s 7½d
John Dykar for cleaning five quarters of wheat at Appledore for the household	5d
Twelve wooden plates and five wooden drinking-bowls bought for the household	7½d
Cheeses bought in the fair of Bethersden for the household	4s 0d
A half-bushel measure and one 'flesshhoke' bought for the household	4d
Alice German on 24 August for working in the household in various jobs for seven weeks from 27 June to Saturday before 24 August	1s 4d
The wife of Thomas Gefferey for four cheeses bought from her for the household	1s 8d
Victuals bought for the household in the last week of July	2s 11d
Victuals bought for the household in the first week of August	2s 7½d
Victuals bought for the household in the second, third and last week of August, as appears by the book of particulars	9s 1d
Victuals bought for the household in the first week of September (my master being there) and in the second week, as appears in the particulars	6s 5d
Victuals bought for the household in the third week of September (my master being there for two days), as appears in the particulars	4s 2d
Victuals bought for the household in the last week of September, as appears in the particulars	7s 7½d

Victuals bought for the household for five days in September and the first two days in October (my master and lady being there for three days), as appears in the particulars — 9s 8d

Expenses of my master being at Reading [Street] on 20 October, as appears in the particulars — 7d

Richard Randislowe for five quarters of malt called 'barlymalt' bought from him and delivered to Appledore for the household — £1 3s 4d

Gabriel Shipman for its carriage from Appledore to the ferry of Oxney — 5d

Victuals bought for the household in first, second, third and last week of October, as appears by the book of particulars — 9s 4½d

Alice Maffey on 15 November, by the hand of John German, in full payment for three seams of oats bought from her for the household — 8s 0d

Victuals for the household in the first week of November, as appears in the book of particulars — 5s 2d

Expenses of the household in the second, third and last week of November, as appears by the book of particulars — 6s 8d

Victuals for the household in the first week of December, as appears by the book of particulars — £1 0s 10d

John German for the milling of 30 quarters of malt for the household — 2s 6d

The wife of John German for working in the household, cleaning clothes and milking the cows for 12 weeks — 2s 0d

John German for two days carrying 18 bushels of wheat to Appledore mill and returning — 5d

John German for going to Rolvenden to buy two pairs of wheels — 4d

Four bushels of oats bought for the lady's capons and the hens of the household — 1s 0d

John Meyne for ten quarters of wheat bought from him for the household — £3 16s 8d

John Meyne for ten seams of oats bought from him and delivered to the household — £2

John Meyne for three bullocks (£2 1s 8d) and one cow (9s 0d) bought from him for the household — £2 10s 8d

John Meyne for eight wagonloads of hay bought from him and delivered to the lord's barn there — 13s 4d

John Meyne for three quarters of wheat bought from him for the household, at 8s 0d for two quarters and 7s 8d for the other — £1 3s 8d

John Spysour of Appledore for storing and delivering eight quarters of wheat for the household — 1s 4d

Five cheeses bought and delivered to the household in October — 1s 8d

Victuals bought by John Adam, the lord's servant, being there on 15 and 16 December, as appears in the particulars — 4s 2½d

Shoeing two geldings ('gillynges') and three mares within the
household   8d <9d>
Thomas Bachiler, labourer, hired for one day on the daubing and
'bemefellyng' of 'le maltchambre', for his share   2d
Ingram Van for the carriage of underwood from 'Prison Grove' to
the manor for firewood for the household in June 1468   4s 2d
John Adam [*entry not completed*]
Sum   £28 0s 6½d <£12 9s 8½d>

Cost of ironwork with the purchase of nails
Paid for 100 four-penny nails and 100 six-penny nails   10d
Two long iron bars, four iron cross-bars (1s 4d) for them for
windows in the janitor's chamber, and for four 'hokys' and two
'catches' (6d) for the same windows, and two 'hokys' (5d) and a
'catche' for the janitor's door   2s 3d
Portage of the ironwork from Woodchurch to the manor of Mote   2d
William Dore on 2 April for 200 four-penny nails bought from
him and sent to the manor   8d
Robert Smyth for 200 four-penny nails (8d), 300 six-penny nails
(1s 6d) and one 'gridyren' (1s 0d) bought from him and sent to
the manor of Mote, with 1d for their portage from Woodchurch to
Appledore   3s 3d
Robert Smyth for 300 four-penny nails and 100 six-penny nails
bought from him on 6 April, and 2d for iron 'hokes'   1s 8d
Two hundred five-penny nails bought for making 'lez scaffotes'   10d
Robert Smyth on 6 May for ironwork weighing 38 pounds   4s 9d
Robert Smyth on 6 May for six bars and 12 'staples' for 'le
gynne' weighing five pounds   10d
Robert Smyth for four 'body plates' for wagons weighing 10
pounds   1s 3d
For 'broddis' (brads) bought from him   2d
Robert Smyth for four iron 'plates' for wagons and for 'le
oxcourt' and for four other 'plates' for the short horse-cart
weighing 9½ pounds   1s 2½d
Two iron rings for 'le gynne' bought from him   6d
Robert Smyth for one 'haps' and two 'staples'   1½d
Robert Smyth on 31 May for 200 six-penny nails sent to the
manor   1s 0d
For 150 five-penny nails sent to the manor   7½d
Ironwork bought from him, weighing 32½ pounds, for two
windows in the upper chamber at the bridge   4s 0d
Robert Smyth for two 'thwart barres' for that ironwork   7d
Robert Smyth for 200 'five-strokenaill' to nail anchors
(*anchoras*) with 1d for John Hale's expenses fetching them   3s 9d
A hundred six-penny nails bought at Small Hythe on 4 June   6d

For making a key for the old lock of the buttery door	2d
Robert Smyth on 25 June for 200 four-penny nails	8d
Robert Smyth for a pair of 'pyncers'	3d
A hundred four-penny nails bought at Small Hythe on 4 July	4d
Two hundred four-penny nails bought at Small Hythe on 11 July	8d
Four hundred five-penny nails bought at Small Hythe on 17 July with 1d for John Hale's expenses fetching them	1s 9d
Robert Smyth for 200 four-penny nails delivered to the manor of Mote on 20 June	8d
William Orgar, smith, for 500 'five-stroke naill' (whereof 300 are six-penny nails and 200 five-penny nails)	2s 4d
Two hundred five-penny nails bought and delivered to the manor on 14 August	10d
A thousand five-penny nails bought on 21 August for the same purpose	4s 2d
Four hundred five-penny nails bought on 28 August	1s 8d
'Hokes' and 'catches' (4½d) weighing four pounds bought at Small Hythe, with a penny for John Hale's expenses fetching them on 31 August and 100 eight-penny nails (8d) for the masons' 'scaffot'	1s 1½d
Six hundred nails (of which 400 six-penny and 200 five-penny nails) bought on 4 September	2s 10d
Twelve 'hokes' and six 'catches' weighing 11 pounds, bought on 4 September	1s 4½d
A hundred 'five-strokenaill' bought on 10 September with 1½d for John Hale's expenses at Small Hythe to make and fetch that ironwork	8½d
Thomas Harry on 17 September for 300 [weight] of iron bought from him and delivered to the manor of Mote	12s 6d
Thomas Harry for two bushels of sea coals bought from him on 10 September	6d
Thomas Gardiner on 21 September for the carriage of four sacks of ashes, one sack of charcoal, an anvil, bellows and other utensils of Robert Smyth from Woodchurch to the sea	6d
Thomas Lynche on 3 October for 500 [weight] of iron bought from him and delivered to the manor of Mote	£1 1s 8d
Two locks bought and delivered to the manor on 3 October	6d
Robert Smyth for his wages for two weeks at the lord's board, working in the manor	5s 0d
Thomas Profite, hired for three days to thatch the masons' lodge and for thatching and 'reggyng' the smithy chimney	8d
William Dobill, smith, for two iron bands weighing eight pounds for the ox-cart	1s 0d
William Dobill for two iron 'stroppes' and two 'swevill' for the wagon	1s 4d

Robert Smyth on 2 November for his wages and his servant for four weeks and three days from 21 September to 1 November	5s 10d
Robert Smyth and his servant for wages for a month from 1 November to 8 December	10s 0d
Five hundred four-penny nails bought by John German 1466-67 for 'le bierding de le maltflore' beyond the kitchen	1s 8d
Richard Heanden for making and burning 34 quarters of charcoal at the manor for the smith in the smithy	5s 8d <5s 10d>
Robert Smyth for his wages and his servant's wages for 13 days before 25 December	5s 5d
Two bushels of sea coals	8d
Robert Smyth for half a sheaf of 'stele'	3½d
For 800 five-penny nails bought at Small Hythe in the first week of August for the same purpose	3s 4d
Expenses of John Hale fetching them	1d
For 100 five-penny nails for 'lez scaffotes' and six 'hokes' (6d) and three 'catches' for the doors and windows above the janitor's chamber	11d
'Hokes' and 'catches' bought at Small Hythe for doors and windows	6d
Sum	£6 6s 8½d <£3 7s 8½d>[42]

Purchase of lead

Paid Thonder of Winchelsea on 21 July by John Netter for 492 pounds of lead	£1 9s 5d
Gabriel Boteman for its carriage from Winchelsea to John Meyne's fleet	5d
James Plommer working there for 12 days before 21 July	8s 0d
James Plommer working there for <five>[43] days from 22 to 30 July at the lord's board	<3s 4d>[44]
Gabriel Boteman for the carriage of 4000 tiles from Appledore to John Meyne's fleet	1s 0d
John Hale's expenses going to Winchelsea to buy the lead	1½d
Sum	£2 2s 3¼d

Payment of marsh scots

Paid John Meyne for three halfpenny-scots and one penny-scot assessed this year on four occasions for the land of the manor of Mote	£2 1s 0d

---

[42] Added in the margin in the hand of Sir John Scott.
[43] Replacing *nine* deleted.
[44] Replacing *6s 0d* deleted.

Payment of a Fifteenth
Paid Roger Wytte and William Gilby, subcollectors of a moiety
of a fifteenth granted to the king in the borough of Wivelridge in
the hundred of Goldspur, for the lord's chattels valued <at £5>, at
<2½d> in the £   <1s 0½d>

Purchase of pasture
Paid John Meyne for the pasture of four oxen   6s 8d
John Meyne for the pasture of four cows   6s 0d
John Meyne for the pasture for two 'gillinges' and four mares   9s 0d
John Meyne for the pasture for two calves   1s 0d
Sum   £2 2s 8d

Accountant's expenses
His expenses at Rye on 7 March to buy victuals for the lord's
household and from there to Hastings to fetch William Mason to
come to the manor of Mote   8d
His expenses at Appledore on the same day for the same reason   3d
John Hale, servant of the lord's receiver, going to the manor of
Mote on 14 and 15 March to provide labourers to demolish the
wall where the janitor's chamber was to be built, to provide for
the carriage of 'brike' to the manor and to pay Robert Symon's
wife for beds for three masons   2½d
John Hale, going to The Mote on 19 March to carry ironwork,
'scopp, trayes' and other necessaries for the masons   2½d
John Hale going to Ashford on 20 and 21 March to certify my
lady of the good governance of the household and all other things
there, with William Yressh's expenses back to Appledore   2d
John Hale to Mote on 26 March to carry 'ropes' and other
necessaries with two horses, with the ferry of Henry Ritchis by
my lady's command   3½d
John Hale to The Mote on 29 March to carry 'trayes' and nails,
with 1s 0d paid to Stephen Cowpere for binding various vessels,
and 2s 6d to John Adam to buy victuals for the household, as
appears in the particulars   4s 2d
The accountant's expenses back from Bexhill, with the expenses
of John Hale to Small Hythe for various business of the lord, with
4d paid to John Wilverynden to prepare firewood for two days   7d
William Harlakynden going home from The Mote on 1 May   1½d
John Hale going to The Mote on 5 May and from there to Small
Hythe to fetch ironwork and other things   5d
John Hale to The Mote and to Small Hythe to fetch various
necessaries on 16 May   2½d
John Hale fetching 'scaffote lyne' from Appledore, and to make
ironwork, with 3d paid for a lock for the storeroom door and 2d

for two iron 'plates' to brace two 'gistes' [joists]	6d
John Hales riding to Sandhurst on 16 June to confer with Vincent Fynche on the lord's business	1½d
John Hale riding to Canterbury on 20 June to confer with my master about certain necessary things and business, and from there to Rochester on 21 June to await his arrival	1s 2½d
John Hale riding to Winchelsea to provide lead for my master	2d
William Harlakynden at Wittersham on my lord's business	4d
John Hale riding to Robertsbridge on 22 July to provide for the carriage of 'bordes' there, and to hand the board over to John Pippesden	5d
John Hale at Ewhurst Fair and at Cranbrook on the same day to provide for carriage for my master's stone	3d
William Harlakynden going to the manor of Mote on 11 August on two occasions	3d
William Harlakynden riding to the manor of Hall on 23 August	3d
William Harlakynden riding to Cranbrook on 24 August to provide carriage for stone there	7d
Henry Henden riding to my master at London on 31 August to get money for my master's workmen and masons	1s 7d
John Hale riding to Winchelsea to provide a tiler	2d
John Hale riding to Hawkhurst on 10 August for the same reason	6d
John Hale, Henry Riche and William Spakman on 26 August at Oxney Ferry to receive my master's lead, with a penny given to the ferryman to help its entry	3d
William Harlakynden to the manor of Mote and back on 16 September	2d
John Hale putting Pascal Martyn on the right way from Mote towards Faversham	1½d
John Hale riding to Udimore on 23 September to fetch three bushels of 'hoppes'	1d
The cost of riding from Woodchurch to the manor of Mote on 27 September and from there to Rye on 28 September to provide beds for my master, and to load a quarter of salt and 15 'weynescot'	3d
John Hale riding to Winchelsea on 6 October to buy bread for the household	1d
John Hale and John Treygoff at Beckley to take the metes and bounds of 'Pipereslond' on 24 October	3d
William Harlakynden at the manor of Mote on 7 December	8½d
William Harlakynden at Mote and at Small Hythe and back on 15 and 17 December	4d
John Hale to Eastbourne for 3½ days in the third week of December to find out about my master's stone, how much had been dug and trimmed and how William Mason was working	8d

William Harlakynden at Battle and Eastbourne to pay the masons | 4½d
Sum | 17s 0d <16s 11d>⁴⁵

Foreign payments

The expenses of Henry Heanden, riding to London in the week
beginning 22 May to confer with my master on various business | 1s 8½d

John Dyer riding to Sandhurst on 17 June to deliver a letter sent
from London by my master to Vincent Fynche | 2d

For 400 'tylelath' at 7d for a hundred and 100 'woghlath' at 2½d
for a hundred, bought on 6 July | 2s 6½d

For 100 'tylelath' bought on another occasion | 7d

Henry Riche and his mate driving animals from Hall to the manor
of Mote, with their ferries | 7d

William Walys to Hastings and Hooe on 12 and 13 August to
warn the masons of their return to the manor of Mote | 6d

John Dyer riding to The Mote on 23 October with a letter from
my master to John Hale | 2d

Carriage of 11 'estrichebord' from William Harlakynden to the
sea to carry them to Mote | 3d

<The costs and expenses of two masons coming from Maidstone
to Hall | 5s 0d

Henry Prike and his mates, by my lord's hand at London, for
travelling to The Mote | 6s 8d

To the mortarmaker by my lord's hand at London | 2s 0d

Peter Brikemason by my lord's hand, receiving the money by the
hand of Henry Turnour | 2s 0d

Sum | £1 2s 1½d

They cannot be allowed here, but should rather be allowed among
the particulars>⁴⁶

Wages of the rent-collector

The wages of the rent-collector of the manor of Mote by reason
of his office | 6s 8d

Thomas Godyng for part of his fee for this year | £1

Sum | £1 6s 8d

*Money delivered: received by John Adam, received by my lady*⁴⁷

To John Adam by the hand of my master Sir John Scott travelling
to the manor of Mote on 10 March 1468 | 5s 0d

To John Adam by my master's hand at The Mote to buy ox-meat | £1

---

[45] Added in the margin in the hand of Sir John Scott.
[46] Added in the hand of Sir John Scott.
[47] Added and deleted, with the annotation *allowed*: *they cannot be allowed here, but should rather be allowed in the particulars.*

To my mistress by my master's hand for buying ox-meat, mutton and malt, sent to Mote in 1467-68	£6 4s 0d
Sum	£7 9s 0d
Sum of allowances and payments	£233 12s 6d
Surplus	£143 8s 3½d[48]

---

[48] Followed by *of which received by his own hands in liquidation of his debt hanging in le unde of his last account of Orlestone £79 18s 8¾d and half a farthing, and he still has a surplus of £63 9s 6½d and half a farthing, deleted with the annotation, in the hand of Sir John Scott, not received here because in next year's account.*

Mote manor: the account of [*blank*], receiver of John Scotte, knight, of his manor of Mote, from 29 September 1470 to 29 September 1471

[ESRO NOR 15/107[49]]

Arrears	[*blank*]

Fixed rents

For the rent of various tenants in Iden, as appears by the rental, and by the account of John German, the beadle and collector of rents there	£3 6s 10½d
For the rent of various tenants in Peasmarsh belonging to the manor	£3 9s 0d
For the rent of various tenants in Northiam	£3 0s 3½d
For the rent of various tenants in Beckley	£1 2s 4d
For the rent of various tenants in Ewhurst	12s 5d
From Babilon Granford for land called 'Spytylland' by Rye	3s 0d
Sum	£11 13s 11d

Hen Rents

One hen from the rent of Robert Gogeler from land called Horsepen at 25 December	3d

Profits of court
None, because no courts were held this year on account of the troubles (*perturbatio mundi*)

Farm of the demesne lands

Received from the farm of the manor let to John Mayne this year	£13
Farm of a piece of land lately let to Thomas Profyte at 1s 0d, nothing this year, because above in 'Fixed rents'	

Sale of wood
None

Foreign receipts <Mote tenth [year]>

From John Meyne, farmer there, by the hand of William Harlakynden on 31 July	£2
John Adam, by the hand of William Harlakynden, for various tools and victuals of the household	18s 0d
Robert Smyth, by the hand of William Harlakynden, from the forge there	4s 0d

---

[49] This is perhaps a draft account, since the totals of the expenditure section are added in the margin in a different hand. It is probably that of Sir John Scott, who has also added a draft balance at the end of the account.

And[50]

Rents resolute

Paid to the bailiff of the sheriff of Sussex for the sheriff's tourn	8d
To him for 'lez blancheferms'	5d
Lord Dacre for the value of one pound of pepper for land called 'Blakelond' by the hand of his rent-collector, John Browne	1s 2d
The churchwarden of the church of Iden for 'Romescott'	½d
Sum	2s 3½d

[The following section, without a heading, represents allowances of rent made for various reasons. At a subsequent date, perhaps in preparation for the following year's account, the body of the entry has been annotated either respited *or* allowed, *and this information, together with the parish in which the land lies, repeated in the margin. These marginalia are not shown here unless they differ from the information in the body of the entry.]*

John Roberd for land called Thornsdale in Iden, because it cannot be levied <respited>	2s 11d
Heirs of Richard atte Wode for land called 'Cotenham' in Iden, because it cannot be levied <respited>	8d
John Parrok for his lands in Iden, because it cannot be levied <respited >	1d
John Asshemynton in Iden, because it is in the lord's hands and let to farm with the demesne lands <allowed>	1s 6d
William Potyn for 'Shireveshoth' in Peasmarsh, because it is in the lord's hands <charged>	1s 3d
Thomas Keryell for the manor of Kitchenour, because it cannot be levied <respited>	1s 3d
Simon Watell for 'Brounlon' in Peasmarsh, because it cannot be levied <received nothing>	1s 0d
Thomas Foughill for various lands which he holds in Peasmarsh, because it cannot be levied <respited>	4d
William Hulles for land formerly Peter Church in Northiam, because it is in the lord's hands and let to farm with the demesne lands <charged>	3d
John Holstok for 'Dynysland' in Northiam, because it cannot be levied <respited>	1s 0d
William Bate for lands late Peter Church in Northiam, because it still cannot be levied <respited>	6d
John Benett for 'Le Crabb' and other parcels in Northiam, because it cannot be levied <charged>	1s 0d <2s 2½d>

---

[50] Followed by a blank space of 15 cm.

John Twisynden and Maud Major for land called 'Blytheland' and other parcels in Northiam, because it cannot be levied \<charged\>	1s 6d
William Lucas for land bought from Robert Edward and from John Holman called 'Okworthes' in Northiam, because it cannot be levied \<charged\>	6d
Simon Moys for his lands in Northiam, because it cannot be levied \<charged\>	2s 6d
William Hoore of Northiam because John Holman paid his rent within his own	4s 0d \<3d\>
William Tukton for land formerly John Hochon in Beckley, because it cannot be levied \<respited\>	5d
William Oxynbregg for 'Motyslond' \<Beckley\> formerly Stephen Hekton, because it cannot be levied \<respited\>	2s 6d
William Belknap for land formerly Stephen Hekton called 'Hektons', because it cannot be levied \<allowed because nothing\>	6s 6d
William Fynys, knight, Lord Dacre, for 50 acres in Padgham [of the] manor of Ewhurst, because it cannot be levied \<respited\>	10s 7d
Richard Sote for 'Brekex' in Iden, because it is allowed him by his charter \<respited\>	3d
Agnes Kechenore in Iden, because it cannot be levied \<respited\>	4d
John Dalet for two acres by the garden [of *blank*][51] in Iden, because it cannot be levied \<respited\>	6d
William Belknap for 'Pipereslond' in Beckley, because it cannot be levied \<respited\>	4s 0d
Sum	£2 2s 9½d

Repairs of the manor \<11th year\>
Labourers

John Heryng, labourer, wages for half a year, by the hand of Henry Turnour	9s 0d
John Mychell, servant of the masons, from mid-Lent to 29 September, by the hand of Henry Turnour	£1 4s 2d
Agnes atte Woode, servant there, by the hand of Henry Turnour	2s 0d
A certain labourer for two days, by the hand of Henry Turnour	4d
Henry atte Helle, labourer, for 2½ days, by the hand of Henry Turnour	6d
Richard Crowche, serving the masons two days, by the hand of Henry Turnour	4d
John Freman, serving the masons nine days, by the hand of Henry Turnour	1s 6d
Thomas Danne, labourer, one week	1s 0d
John Hoore, serving the masons 13 weeks, by the hand of Henry Turnour	13s 0d

---

[51] Previous and subsequent entries read *John Waterman*.

Thomas Neve, labourer, three weeks, by the hand of the lady   3s 0d
Thomas Danne, labourer, by the hand of the lady on various
occasions, as in her paper   15s 8d
Thomas Neve, labourer, by the hand of the lady on various
occasions   5s 0d
John Hoore, labourer, by the hand of the lady on various   3s 10d
occasions
John Myghell, labourer, by the hand of the lady in full payment
from 29 September to 1 November   3s 4d
Thomas Profyt, labourer, by the hand of the lady for daubing,
thatching and other work within the manor   9½d
Two men hewing wood for the chimneys for two days   8d
Stephen Willes and Richard Morekok, labourers, making charcoal
for one week, by the hand of the lady   2s 0d
[*blank*] Watell, labourer, five days by the hand of the lady   10d
                                                                          <£4 6s 11½d>

Masons
John Cornelyus, mason, working for 21 weeks and two days from
1 May to 29 September at 3s 4d a week without board, as in
Henry Turnour's account   £3 11s 0d
John Keche, mason, working for 21 weeks for 2s 6d with board,
as in Henry Turnour's account   £2 12s 11d
Hugh Bryght, mason, for making the corbels in the lady's
chamber, as in Henry Turnour's account   4d
Hugh Bryght, mason, by the hand of the lady as in her paper,
working up to 16 November after the close of the accounts   15s 10d
John Cornelyus, mason, by the hand of the lady within the time of
the account on various occasions for four weeks   13s 4d
John Keche, mason, by the hand of the lady, in full payment until
1 November after the close of the accounts   10s 0d
                                                                          <£8 3s 5d>

Carpenters
To a carpenter for six days, as in Henry Turnour's account   2s 0d
A carpenter for 'lez yaxyng' [attaching axles to] a wagon   2d
Thomas Bolfynche, carpenter, working there on repairs for 48
days, as in the account of Henry Turnour   16s 0d
William Taillour, carpenter, working there on repairs for 35 days   11s 8d
John Knotte, carpenter, for ten days, as in the account of Henry
Turnour   3s 4d
John Pyrvell, carpenter, there for the same time, as in the account
of Henry Turnour   3s 4d
John Welond, carpenter, by Henry Turnour for the same time   3s 4d
William Cokk and William Rolf, carpenters, by Henry Turnour
for six days   4s 0d
John Potyn the elder, carpenter, by Henry Turnour for 11 days   3s 8d

John Duke, carpenter, by Henry Turnour for 3½ days	1s 2d
John Potyn the younger, by Henry Turnour for 16 days	5s 4d
Thomas Bolefynche, carpenter, by the hand of the lady as in her paper, on various occasions	9s 4d
John Duke on various occasions, by the lady	8s 1d
John Taillour, carpenter, on various occasions by the lady	14s 8d
John Potyn, carpenter, by the lady	19s 3½d
	<£5 5s 4½d>

Foreign expenses

A reward by the grace of the lady to John Germeyn, collector of rents, for his expenses in collection for this year only, because of the troubles (*propter inquietudinem mundi*)	6s 8d
A reward to Henry Turnor and his expenses in collecting the farm of Orlestone	16s 11d
	<£1 2s 7d>

Expenses of smiths

To John a Lee, smith, working at the manor on various occasions, by the hand of the lady, as appears in her paper	6s 2d
A man helping him for 13 days	2s 6d
A smith of Winchelsea working there for eight days, as in the lady's paper	1s 6d
A smith making an 'anvyle' for five days, as in the lady's paper	10d
A ton of iron bought from Stephen Curlyng for the ironwork of the manor	
<nothing because John Scott paid it>	<£5 17s 8d>[52]

Expenses of plumbers

To a plumber mending various defects on the tower there for nine days	3s 0d

Expenses of sawyers

Paid by Henry Turnour to various sawyers sawing 2600 feet of boards and timber in the time of the account as in his account, less in all 4d	£1 5s 8d
Paid to various sawyers by the lady for sawing 1000 feet of board	10s 0d
	<£1 15s 8d>

Small expenses, hedging and other things

'Stelyng' of a broadaxe by Henry Turnor for hewing timber in the household	7d[53]
Carriage of four horses at Oxney Ferry with other carriages made there, as in the account of Henry Turnour on various occasions	4s 0d

---

[52] Replacing *£5 6s 8d* deleted.
[53] Followed by an entry *Expenses of Henry Turnour riding to Orlestone to collect the farm as in his account 2s 10d* deleted with the annotation *because in the Orlestone account*.

The making and cleaning of a tunic for Anthony Sellyng | 1s 10d

The carriage of three bushels of salt from the manor of Hall to the manor of Mote by Henry Turnour | 2d

The parish clerk of Iden for his stipend for half a year | 2s 0d

Making a 'nebbeyokke' for a wagon | 2d

Oil bought by Henry Turnour for cleaning the lord's armour | 5d

Expenses of John Heryng by Henry Turnour going on various business | 1s 10d

William Peryman for part of his wages, as in Henry Turnour's account | 6s 8d

John Crawle of Rye for the board of Anthony Sellyng for two days with a pair of hose bought for him, as in Henry Turnour's account | 6d

Paid by Henry Turnour to a cooper for binding vessels on occasions | 1s 8d

William Austyn for digging a ditch between the demesne and William Cheyne for 10½ days by agreement, as in the lady's paper | 5s 8d

Eight locks bought by Henry Turnour for the doors of the manor | 2s 3d

<£1 7s 9d, note eight locks>

Purchase of timber

For 25 oaks bought from Thomas Fowlyn by Henry Turnour as in his account | 6s 8d

Cost of limeburning

Paid by Henry Turnour to Thomas Lymebarner for burning 180 quarters of lime, in full payment as in his account | £1 3s 4d

John Meyne for six days' carriage of unburnt chalk, as appears in his bill delivered to the lady | 5s 0d

John Meyne for the carriage of 32 cartloads of unburnt chalk for 11 days | 9s 6d

<£1 17s 10d>

Household expenses

John Adam, purveyor of the lord's household, from 2 February to 2 June for buying various victuals, as in Henry Turnour's account | £3 6s 8d

John Turnour for two bullocks bought from him by Henry Turnour for the household | £1 8s 0d

A cow bought by Henry Turnour from Thomas Helyer for the household | 9s 6d

Two piglets bought for the household by Henry Turnour | 7d

A quarter of wheat bought from John Meyne for the household | 6s 8d

A quarter of a bullock bought from John Meyne for the household | 5s 0d

Two fat cows bought from John Meyne for the household | 16s 0d

Payment of marsh scots

Paid John Meyne for one marsh scot as appears by the bill
delivered to the lady · 8s 0d

Purchase of pasture and hay

Paid John Meyne for the pasture of four mares for half a year	6s 0d
Hay bought from John Meyne by John Adam	£3 2s 2d
John Meyne for the pasture of four oxen for half a year in the summer	6s 8d
John Meyne for the pasture of four cows for half a year in the summer	6s 0d
Eleven acres of grass bought from John Meyne to make hay	£1 2s 0d

To John Meyne, because John Germeyn was charged with 3s 0d
received from Thomas Profytt for land belonging to the manor, as
appears by the bill delivered to the lady

<£5 5s 10d>

Livery of money

Money delivered to the lord by the hand of John Meyne for the
farm of the demesne lands in the value of [*blank*] oxen delivered
to him, as appears by John Meyne's bill of account · £10

To the lord by the hand of John Meyne, in the value of 12,500
[billets of] firewood delivered to Dover · £1 5s 0d

<£11 5s 0d>

<Outgoings £56 3s 3d, and he has a surplus of £28 7s 2d, of which in liquidation
of his debt from last year £16 12s 10d, surplus £11 14s 4d>[54]

---

[54] Replacing a deleted entry, itself an annotation, *Total outgoings £49 14s 0d, except £21 17s 10d,
he has a surplus of £21 17s 10d, of which paid in liquidation of his debt from last year £16 12s
10d, and so he has surplus £5 5s 0d.*

Mote manor: the account of John German, rent-collector and bailiff of John Scot, knight, from 29 September 1471 to 29 September 1472

[ESRO NOR 15/108]

Arrears

Charged in the foot of the account; but no sum here <query with the last account with the lady>
Rent of the manor of the hospital in Rye   3s 0d

Fixed rents

The rent of various tenants in the parish of Iden	£3 6s 10½d <£2 18s 10½d>
Rent of the master of the hospital of Rye	3s 0d
Rent of tenants in Peasmarsh	£3 9s 0d <£3 9s 10d>
Rent of tenants in Northiam	£3 0s <7½d>
Rent of tenants in Beckley	£1 1s 8d
Rent of tenants in Ewhurst	12s 5d
Rent of John Waterman by Hastings in the right of his wife, daughter and heir of John Parker	2s 0d
Rent of John a Broke of Ninfield	6d
Sum	£10 18s 11d

Farms

William Toughton for land called 'Crowchlond' in Northiam   6s 4d
Of the remainder of the farms of the lands of this manor nothing more by this accountant, because in the account of Henry Fynch, steward

Hen Rents

One hen from the rent of Robert Gogeler from land called Horspen at 25 December   3d

<Profits of court   Nothing, for lack of estreats>

Sum total of the charge   £11 5s 6d

EXPENSES

Rents resolute

Paid to the collector of the tithing of Wivelridge for blanch farm	5d
Lord Dacre for the value of one pound of pepper for land called 'Blakelond', by the hand of Richard Edward his collector	1s 2d
The church of Iden for 'Romscot'	½d
Sum	1s 7½d

Allowances of rents

The rent of John Asshmynton for land called 'Risshetes' in Iden, charged above   1s 6d

Cost of the buildings

Paid for 500 laths bought for the pighouse by the barn, and for the new work in the kitchen and other places in the manor	2s 4d
Prigs and nails for the same	1s 9½d
For 400 [sheaves of] reed for the thatching of the buildings called 'Benettes' in Northiam	5s 0d
Hinges and rides bought for hanging various gates on the lord's land	10d
Sum	9s 11½d

Necessary expenses

Paid for four pairs of traces and four halters bought for the lord's husbandry	1s 0d
One harrow without iron teeth	3d
Two bushels of beans for feeding the boar	8d
One 'taphose'	4d
Carriage hired for 13 quarters of wheat bought at Winchelsea, thence to Rye by water, on two occasions	2s 2d
The servants' expenses about the same	1s 0d
'Turpentyne' with iron nails for the hall windows and elsewhere	1s 0d
<Black leather bought for the same	2d>
Expenses of the accountant and the servants of the manor on various occasions going to Rye, Winchelsea, Appledore, and elsewhere to transact various business, as appears by the accountant's parcels	2s 0½d
Paid at Appledore Ferry for the crossing of the manor servants (*famuli*), and the lord's servants and horses on 20 September	4s 3d
One bushel of sea coal bought at Winchelsea	3d
Pitch bought there	1½d
One pair of hose bought for Simon the kitchen boy	8d
Two pairs of shoes	10d
Sum	14s 9d

Purchase of victuals for the household

Meat, fish, butter and other victuals bought in the market, both for Mistress Isabel Beves and the lord's children and Masters Edward and William Ponyngez, Richard Sakevyle and for the lady and her servants being here at a certain time, and also for the steward of the household, the bailiff and the manor servants and various hired masons, carpenters and other workmen, and of the servants of the lord and of outsiders coming to this manor up to 29 September 1472, and from then to the close of this account on 7 December 1472, as appears weekly by the paper exhibited by the accountant and the steward of the household, and examined by the auditor item by item	£4 13s 6d

One calf <and three lambs> and the geese, capons, piglets and
poultry bought for their consumption as above   £1 0s 6d
Oil bought in Lent for their consumption   1s 6d
Two quarters and one bushel of wheat bought by the accountant
for the household   17s 0d
Six quarters of oats and barley bought by him for malting   11s 8d
Sum   £7 4s 2d

Purchase of stock
Two <one> oxen bought by the accountant from Thomas Fowle
for the stock of the manor   11s 0d
Two bullocks bought from Thomas Watell for the same   18s 0d
Sum   £1 9s 0d

Foreign expenses
Passage at Oxney Ferry for the lady's things when she left The
Mote for Brabourne   6½d
Four oxen taken across Small Hythe Ferry towards Calais by
Patrick Gylle   3½d
<White> wine bought for Anthony Sellyng when he was ill   5d
Two pairs of shoes bought for him and for Isabel Turnour,
servant of Mistress Ponynges   6d
Two pairs of waders (*ocreorum*) called 'waterbotes' for William
Smyth and William Peryman   6s 0d
Reward to <the servants> of John Baile of Rye for carrying the
lord's things sent here from Calais from the ship to his house   5d
Sum   8s 2d

Liveries of money
To the hand of Henry Fynch, steward of the lord's household, on
13 January   10s 0d
To the same Henry on 1 July   10s 0d
To the same Henry on 28 November   10s 8d
To the same Henry on 28 December   3s 4d
To the same Henry on two occasions, as by his paper   £1
Sum   £2 14s 0d

Sum of all expenses and liveries   £13 3s 2d
And so he has a surplus   £2 17s 8d
And he is charged with £7 4s 11d arrears of his last account because he is not
charged above; and so he owes the lord £4 7s 3d; of which is allowed him 2s 0d
for the rent of John Benet for 1469-70; and he still owes £4 5s 3d, which is
charged in his account for next year.

Respited[55]

Respited to the accountant for the rent of Walter Roberd for his
lands called Thornsdale in Iden until he can levy <paid>   2s 11d

And for <part of> the rent of Robert at Wode for his lands called
'Cotenham' in Iden   8d

And for part of the rent of the heirs of John Parrok <Oxenbridge>
in Iden <paid>   1d

And for part of the rent of John Kerioll for the manor of
Kitchenour until it can be levied   1s 3d

And for the rent of Thomas Watell for lands called 'Bromeland'
in Peasmarsh   1s 0d

And for part of the rent of Thomas Fowle for his lands there   4d

And for part of the rent of William Holman for lands called
'Dyneslond' in Northiam   1s 0d

And for part of the rent of Richard Bate for his lands late Peter a
Chirch in Northiam   6d

And for part of the rent of John Benet[56] for 'Le Crabbe'   ½d

And for part of the rent of John Toughton for his lands called
[*blank*] in Beckley   5d

And for part of the rent of William Oxenbregge for lands called
'Mottislond' in Beckley   2s 6d

And for the rent of Lord Dacre for <50 acres> of his land in
Padgham   10s 7d

And for the rent of Richard Sote for land called 'Brekex' in Iden,
because it is not known where it lies   3d

And for part of the rent of John Oxenbridge for land late Agnes
Kechenore in Iden   4d

And for the rent of John Dalet for two acres in Iden which should
be by a garden, but it is not known where it lies   6d

And for the rent of William Belknap for lands called 'Pyperslond'
in Beckley   4s 0d

And for the rent of 'Benettes' for 1470-71   2s 0d

Sum of these allowances £1 8s 4½d;[57] and he still owes £2 16s 10½d

Mote manor: account of the collector of rents and the bailiff there, 1471-72

Grain

Nothing remains, as the manor was in the hands of a farmer last year

---

[55] The following entries are written on the dorse of the roll in the opposite direction from the stock
account.

[56] Replacing *Fissher*, deleted.

[57] Followed by *and so he is in excess £4 4s 0½d* deleted.

Oats
But he answers for 10 quarters of oats bought for seed by Henry Fynch among other things as in the account; sum 10 quarters, and sown on 16 acres of this manor called 'Le Redelond' and 'Presonfeld' and other parcels adjoining at the rate of five bushels an acre, and so it balances

ACCOUNT OF STOCK
He answers for nothing remaining but of the lord's provision and by purchase, for the same reason

Stot mares
Four stot mares of the lord's provision; and four remain

Colts
Four aged 2½ years received as above; and there remain four, of which two are male and two female

Horses and mares
Two horses and three mares for the husbandry (*iconamia*) of this manor received as above

Foals
Five foals born to the mares this year; and there remain five sucking foals, of which three are male and two female

Bulls
One bull received from Brabourne by the lord's provision; and there remains one bull

Oxen
Four <five> oxen received from the lord last year and two by provision sent here to pasture and four by purchase by Henry Fynch, steward of the lord's household; sum 11, of which three sent to the lord at Calais after Whitsun; and there remain eight

Cows
Four received from the lord and six coming from Brabourne received from the lady; sum 10, of which seven slaughtered for this household;[58] and three remain

---

[58] Followed by *before calving* deleted.

Steers

Two received as above and 14 coming from Brabourne from the lady, and six <eight> bought by my lady, 15 bought by Henry Fynch and two bought by John German; sum 41, of which four slaughtered for the household, and nine sent to the lord at Calais; and 28 remain

Heifers

Six bought by the lady, and four by Henry Fynch, and one by John German; sum 11, of which five slaughtered for the household; six remain, of which one strayed

Male and female bullocks

Four bought by Henry Fynche; of which one was slaughtered for the household; and three remain

Calves

Five born to the cows, and two bought by the lady; five were slaughtered for the household; and one remains

Boars

Two boars remain there upon the making of this account on [*blank*] December

Sows

One sow

Pigs

Five pigs

Young pigs

Nine young pigs

Piglets

Eight <six> sucking piglets

Capons

[*blank*]

Cocks and hens

Two cocks and 12 hens

Poultry

[*blank*]

Mote manor: the account of Henry Fynche, receiver of various moneys of John Scot, knight, from 29 September 1472 to 29 September 1473

[ESRO NOR 15/109]

Arrears
He answers for £1 2s 9½d from the arrears of his last account   £1 2s 9½d

Receipts of money of the manor with the farm of lands
Received from John German, collector of rents of this manor, as
appears by the accountant's paper   £2 13s 4d
Nicholas Lynet, for the farm of land called 'Parsonagelond' for
half a year for the term of Easter, and the rest is in the charge of
John German <bailiff of the manor>   11s 8d
John Broun, for the farm of land called 'Blakelond', part of £1
13s 4d, and the rest is in the charge of the bailiff   10s 0d
Robert Smyth, for the farm of one acre at Flackley for this year,
and the rest of the farm is in the charge of the bailiff   4d
Sum   £3 15s 4d

Sales of stock
Five calves sold from the stock of the manor <as in the bailiff's
account>   10s 0d
One stot sold from the stock of the manor   4s 0d
Sum   14s 0d

Sales of reed and the herbage of the meadows
1000 sheaves of reed sold to Babilon Grauntfort at 1s 8d a
thousand [*recte* 100]   16s 8d
1900 [sheaves of] reed at 2s 0d a hundred   £1 8s 0d
Rushes sold in the lord's brooks this year   5d
John Still for the herbage of two acres of meadow   5s 8d
Richard Crowch for the herbage of one acre of meadow   3s 0d
Agistment of the animals of various men agisted there this year,
besides the agistment in the bailiff's account   9s 4d
100 sheaves of reed sold to John Drylond   2s 0d
Sum   £3 14s 8d

Issues of the manor
From three hides from slaughtered stock   4s 8d
One old wagon-wheel sold to Thomas Potyn   6d

William Ham for his board for three weeks	3s 8d[59]
Sum	8s 10d

Sales of wood

Various parcels of wood sold to various people, as appears by the accountant's bills	5s 4d
A parcel of wood sold to Thomas Rider by Henry Turnour in 1471-72, not charged until now	3s 0d
Sum	8s 4d

Foreign receipts

From John at Hale, collector of rents of the manor of Icklesham, as appears by an indented bill dated 12 December 1472	£2 13s 4d
From Clement Rolf without bill	£8
From Lady Agnes Scot on two occasions in April 1473	15s 0d
From the lord on 19 May 1473	£3
From Robert Papeday for the debt of Stephen Curlyng on two occasions this year	£2
From Vincent Fynche	£3 6s 8d
Sum	£19 15s 0d

Sum total of receipts, with the arrears	£29 18s 11½d

EXPENSES

Cost of the buildings

A thatcher hired to place and lay 1950 [sheaves of] reed on the barn of the manor, at his own board	16s 3d
The thatcher for plastering the roof of the barn with clay	2d
A carpenter hired for mending various necessaries in the cowshed and elsewhere	7d
Shingles bought for 'Le Mewe'	11½d
An agreement with John Petyr for preserving mixed lime and sand until etc	5s 2d
For 200 pounds of lead bought for the lodgings (*tabernaculis*)	10s 0d
Sum	£1 13s 1½d

Mowing of reed and corn

John Asshmeston, hired to mow 1000 sheaves of reed	5s 10d
James Oulehale, hired to mow 900 [sheaves of] reed	4s 6d

---

[59] Followed by the entry *Agistment of animals of various men agisted there this year, besides the agistment in the bailiff's account, 5s 11d,* deleted with the annotation *because above.*

Thomas Aas[60] for mowing and binding <750, Thomas Rider 200>
sheaves   5s 1¾d
Mowing, collecting and haymaking of 15 acres of the lord's
meadow, at task   17s 6d
Mowing, collecting and haymaking of seven acres <one rod> of
meadow, at task   8s 5d
Paid William Ham for reaping the lord's corn in harvest, besides
the 3s 0d paid to him by German   1s 0d
Sum   £2 2s 4¾d

Ditching
John Browne for the lord's share of ditching about 30 perches
from 'Le Markedyke' running between the lord's land called
'Blakelond' and the land of John a Broke   10s 0d
Thomas Ryder for ditching on west side of the bridge called
'Parkmedebregge' <to have a way there> for five days   2s 4d
Thomas Ryder and William Austyn for deepening an old ditch
made by them last year, and for making the same ditch at
'Parkmedebregge' towards 'Redeford', as appears by the
accountant's paper   £1 6s 8d
For the lord's share of 35½ perches of new ditching between the
lord's land called 'Stomblebroke' and the land of the manor of
Leigh, beginning at 'Dornetgrove' and going towards 'Le
Redelondz', at 3d a perch, less ½d   8s 10d
Paid John As for his share of hedging and ditching made from 'le
forstall' to 'Parsoneslond', in arrears from last year   9d
Sum   £2 8s 7d

Clearing of land [61]
An agreement made with Stephen Sampson for one acre in 'Le
Calvenlese'   8s 0d
Paid William Ham in part-payment of £1 2s 0d for two acres and
three rods in 'Le Calvelese' <with 3s 8d charged for his board>,
and the rest [paid] by [John] German   8s 5d
Richard Harman in part-payment of 4s 0d for half an acre there,
and the rest not paid because he has not yet done the work   1s 0d
An agreement made by the lord with Stephen Sampson for a
parcel of land in 'Le Calvenlese', as appears by an indented bill
to perform that agreement   £3 6s 8d
Sum   £4 4s 1d

---

[60] Followed by *and others, hired for 1300* deleted.
[61] *Eradicatio et extirpatio.*

Necessary expenses

John Gardener, hired for making the lord's garden beside the old hall within the moat, and for supporting the vines there with pales	5d
Carrying 150 apple trees, bought at Hawkhurst by Vincent Finch, to Newenden	1s 4d
Bringing them to The Mote by water, with the expenses of Thomas Longbregge and Edward Parrok working on them	1s 3d
Planting the trees	3d
Buying leeks and planting them in the lord's garden	4d
Binding wooden vessels, both for the brewhouse and the dairy, and binding the hubs of wagon-wheels, paid by the accountant	3s 2½d
Two pounds of candles bought against midsummer	4d
For altering a brass pot in the kitchen	10d
Castrating pigs	7d
Two whetstones (*cotibus*) bought for sharpening knives	3d
Help hired for making a rick in the summer marsh	3d
Steeling the kitchen chopper	6d
Help hired to carry reed from the marsh to the upland, and for cutting firewood and chopping it	1s 4d
Paid John Maffey the arrears <of an old debt for last year> for carrying chalk and wood to the limekiln within the manor	3s 0d
Help hired for slaughtering animals for the consumption of the household	7d
John Godard, hired to measure various parcels of meadow for mowing	2d
A pair of wheels bought for a wagon	3s 0d
A carpenter hired to fit a wagon with axles	4d
Sharpening and lengthening the ironwork for the ploughs and wagons, and shoeing the horses of the manor	1s 4½d
Henry Symond, hired for threshing a certain parcel of oats from the old stack	5d
Cleaning the latrine in the chamber by the lord's parlour	2d
Sum	19s 11d

Purchases of grain and victuals for the consumption of the household

'Bere' bought for the household, as appears by the accountant's paper	5s 7d
Honey	2d
Three quarters of oats bought by the lady <last year> from Thomas Foulyng for the consumption of this household	6s 0d
Ten quarters of barley bought from Robert a Fanne by the accountant for the same	£2
Paid Robert Symond in part-payment for five quarters of wheat bought by the accountant, and the remainder in the account of the bailiff	10s 0d

Ale and wine bought for John Bokelond upon the making of a rental and engrossing the accounts	8d
Sum	£3 2s 5d

The lord's expenses

A boar bought from Henry Dobill and sent for the lord to Calais	8s 0d
Two bushels of pears (*volemorum*) bought and sent to the lord there	9d
Sum	8s 9d

Stipends of the servants

John Heryng, retained ploughman (*famulus carucarius*), for the Christmas and Midsummer terms this year	10s 0d
John Heryng for his gown by the lady's order	3s 4d
William Amyot, retained ploughman, in part-payment of his stipend, the term of which began at Christmas	11s 8d
Thomas Longebregge for half a year from 29 September to Easter	9s 9d
Henry Symond, retained ploughman, hired for 4½ weeks	3s 5d
Julian Knokke, housemaid, for a year	10s 0d
Joan Hasilden, the other housemaid, for nine months	10s 0d
Agnes atte Wode, servant of this household, up to and for Midsummer	7s 6d
John German, bailiff of husbandry (*ballivus yconamie*) of this manor, for a year ending 29 September 1472, <and the remainder in the account of Marley>	13s 4d
A woman hired for 12 weeks in the summer to <milk the cows and> make cheese	2s 0d
Sum	£4 1s 0d

Foreign expenses

John Heryng, John Adam and others of the lord's servants, for driving various animals from this manor and from Brabourne to Dover, and for transacting business for the lord at Battle, Winchelsea, Appledore and other places, as appears item by item by the accountant's paper, examined upon this account <to 29 September>	7s 3d
Paid by the accountant at Winchelsea for attaching the pledges of Stephen Curlyng at the lord's suit for money which he owes to the lord	8d
Making a plea against them	4d
The accountant's expenses while he was there	8d
Paid at Oxney Ferry for ferrying the lord's servants and their horses, and for carrying across various grains and other things on numerous occasions this year	6s 8d
A lamb bought for Master Edward Ponyngz at Appledore	4d

A meal at Easter for the lady's servants at Iden, by her order	8d
Paid the parish clerk of Iden <for his wages> by the lord's order	3s 0d
Sum	19s 7d

The king's money with marsh scots

Paid John Mayne and John Broke, collectors for the hundred of Goldspur, for the king's assessment on the manor of The Mote, according to a value of £18 a year	£1 16s 0d
John Broke, expenditor of the marsh of Iden, for the lord's land on 5 June 1473	£1 3s 9d
To him for another scot on 7 July 1473	£1 3s 9d
To him in part-payment of a third scot of two pence an acre on 21 August 1473[62]	10s 0d
To him in full payment of the same scot <on 8 September [1473]>	13s 9d
Sum	£5 7s 3d

Livery of money

To Vincent Fynche on 23 January 1474	£4

Sum of all expenses and liveries	£29 7s 1¼d
And so he owes the lord	11s 10½d
Of which, upon:	
Thomas Oxenbregge for reed sold to him last year	9s 0d
William Whitswer for reed sold to him last year	2s 0d
The accountant	10½d
Note the same accountant asks to be allowed his wages by reason of his office for two years	£3 6s 8d

Sheaves of reed

He answers for 1650 sheaves of reed remaining from last year; and for 3900, the issue of the lord's marsh this year <of which 1000 were reaped by the manor servants and the rest at task>[63]; sum <5550>,[64] of which 1950 accounted in thatching upon the barn of the manor, 3000[65] sold in the neighbourhood by the accountant as over, and 600 by the bailiff of husbandry; and it balances

---

[62] Followed by *and the rest by German* deleted.
[63] Replacing the deleted text *besides the issue of the marsh in the same year as in the account of the bailiff of husbandry.*
[64] Replacing *4850* deleted; 5550 expressed in error as 500,550.
[65] Replacing *3950* deleted.

The Mote: account of John German, bailiff and rent-collector of John Scot, knight, from 29 September 1474 to 29 September 1475 [ESRO NOR 15/110]

Arrears

He answers for £9 17s 3¾d, of which 4s 7d upon John
Adam, 2s 0d upon John Waterman, £1 2s 2d upon Vincent
Fynche for his agistment, from the arrears of the
accountant's last account, as shown at the foot of the
previous year's account   Sum £9 17s 3¾d

Fixed rents

From the tenants of Flackley in Peasmarsh as appears by the new rental	£1 11s 4d
Tenants in the vill there	£2 0s 1d
Tenants in Beckley	8s 9d
Tenants in Northiam	£2 18s 9¾d
Tenants in Iden	£2 16s 6½d
From John Chester's rent paid this year, besides 18s 3d which he paid last year	3s 1d
Rent [in Playden][66]	3s 0d
Rent in Ninfield	6d
Rent of tenants in Ewhurst	1s 10d
Lord Dacre's rent	10s 7d
Rent in Hollington	2s 0d
Sum	£10 6s 8¼d

Farms

From John Asshmeston for lands called 'Le Risshet' in Iden containing 1½ acres	1s 2d
John Flecher for a meadow called 'Hammede' in Peasmarsh containing four acres	6s 8d
Thomas Hatche and John German for land [called] 'Perifeld' there containing eight acres	5s 0d
John Brown for land called 'Blaklond' in Beckley containing 30 acres	£1 13s 4d
William at Hill for land called <[blank]> in Northiam containing seven <three> acres	8d
William Towghton for land there called 'Crowchelond' containing 12 acres	7s 0d
Robert Smyth [for one acre in] Peasmarsh	4d
The heirs of Thomas Fowle for three parcels of land there, one called 'Le Welfeld'	8d

---

[66] The document is damaged at this point.

Nicholas Lynet for land called 'Millond' containing 40 acres in
Iden for half a year, and not more because it was in the lord's
hands for the remainder and occupied by his draught animals   [11s 8d]
Sum   £3 6s 6d

Sales of corn and stock
From one bull sold to John Sampson   8s 0d
One ox sold   11s 0d
Half a bushel of beans sold by exchange (*de reperto*)[67]   2d
Two piglets sold   6d
Sum   19s 8d

Summer and winter agistment
From Thomas Park for two oxen for 19 weeks   3s 0d
John Dyne for three bullocks for half a year   3s 4d
John Strete for one bullock for half a year   1s 0d
Richard a Crowche for four bullocks for half a year   3s 4d
James Potyn for four bullocks for the same time   3s 10d
John Coupere for three steers for quarter of a year   1s 6d
John Fletchere for one cow, two heifers and two bullocks for 19
weeks   4s 2d
John Mayne for six heifers for half a year   6s 0d
John Mayne for 23 bullocks for half a year   19s 2d
Edward Parrok for two bullocks for half a year   1s 10d
John Styll for two steers for half a year   2s 0d
John Styll for three bullocks for half a year   [2s] 6d
William Amyot for four oxen for the same time   5s 4d
Thomas Helyer for eight steers for five weeks   5s 0d
Thomas Helyer for two steers going there   1s 2d
Thomas Watell for two steers for 18 weeks   2s 0d
Edith Maffey for one cow and one bullock for a year   4s 0d
Henry Fynche for four bullocks in winter   3s 8d
Henry Fynche for the same four bullocks in summer   4s 0d
Sum   £3 16s 10d

Issues of the manor
From Robert Symond for the herbage of three acres of meadow   6s 6d
John Styll for the herbage of two acres of meadow   4s 4d
Edith Maffey for the herbage of one acre of meadow   2s 0d
John Tolherst for the herbage of one acre of meadow   2s 0d
Babilon Grauntfort for 1000 sheaves of reed sold to him, taken to
Rye by the lord's carriage   £1

---

[67] Alternative meanings are 'from stock' or 'by discovery'.

John Hayne of Rye for 1000 sheaves of reed, taken to Rye by the lord's carriage	£1
John Sutton for 600 sheaves of reed, taken to Rye by the lord's carriage	12s 0d
Thomas Potyn for 150 sheaves of reed, by the lord's carriage	3s 0d
Thomas Sote for 400 sheaves of reed at 1s 8d for a 100, by his own carriage	6s 8d
The keeper of the manor of Thornsdale for 200 sheaves of reed, by his own carriage	3s 4d
Matthew Veter for 700 sheaves of reed at 1s 10d for a hundred, taken to Rye by the lord's carriage	12s 10d
Various dishes of butter sold this year	1s 5d
Five gallons of fat sold by the accountant	2s 6d
Sum	£4 16s 7d

Sales of wood

From a parcel of wood arising from clearance (*eradicatione*) in 'Keryslond', sold to John Berebruere of Rye	£2 13s 4d
John a Wyke for a parcel of wood arising from clearance in the land <called Brekeost Feld>[68]	1s 8d
Sum	£2 15s 0d

Foreign receipts

Received from <William>[69] Hammes for his board when he was on the lord's work, as appears by a tally	£1 0s 6d
From John Reder for his board there for two weeks	2s 0d
Sum	£1 2s 6d

Sum total of receipts, with the arrears	£37 1s 1d

EXPENSES

Resolutes

From which, paid to the church of Iden for 'Romescot' there	½d
The bailiff of the Rape of Hastings for blanch farm	5d
Lord Dacre for the rent resolute of land called 'Blakelond' in the value of one pound of pepper	1s 2d
The vicar of Peasmarsh for the lord's tithes there	5s 0d
The vicar of Peasmarsh, for the lord's sheep being at Flackley this year	4d
The parish clerk for three quarters of the year	3s 0d
Sum	9s 11½d

---

[68] Replacing *aforesaid.*
[69] Replacing *John*, deleted.

Ditching, hedging and land-clearance

Paid John Rider, hired to make six perches of ditch between 'Stumbilbroke' and 'Skerislond', and for setting a hedge on it	1s 6d
The same John Rider hired to make 16 perches of ditch around the wood there on the north, and enclosing it with a hedge above it	2s 8d
John Rider for nine perches of ditching there	9d
John Asshmeston hired to make 60 perches of ditch around land called 'Calvenlese' towards the west, with a hedge above it	10s 0d
William Hammys for making 53 perches of ditch around the same lands towards the east, and enclosing it with a hedge above it	8s 10d
William Hammys for making 49 perches of hedge around the land where the lord's corn is sown this year, on the west side of the lord's new garden	3s 0¾d
Paid John Reder, besides the 6s 8d paid him by Henry Turnor in full payment for the work of clearance in 'Skyreslond'	£2
Thomas Rider hired to make [blank] perches of ditch in 'Calvenlesebrokys'	3s 5d
An agreement made with John Reder to clear a rood of land at 'Brikost'	2s 0d
William Hammys in part-payment of his agreement for clearing land at 'Le Brikeost'	£2
Stephen Sampson in part-payment for his work of clearance	2s 4d
Sum	£4 14s 6¾d

Marsh scots

Three marsh scots of 11s 10d each, of which the last was paid to John Dalet for the lord's land under the level of the marsh	£1 15s 6d

Mowing meadow and reaping reed

John Tolherst, hired to mow 7½ acres of the lord's meadow, spreading the grass and collecting, stooking and stacking the hay, at task	8s 9d
John Sprot and Thomas As, hired to mow there for four days	1s 4d
William Hammes, hired to mow 11 acres of meadow, at the lord's board	3s 2d
Help hired, besides the lord's servants, for making hay and for making ricks in the lord's land, and carriage hired for it	3s 8d
Cleaning, gathering and binding 3350 sheaves of reed	18s 8½d
Mowing and binding 900 sheaves of rough reeds	3s 0d
Sum	£1 18s 8d

Costs of the harvest

Various men and women hired in harvest to reap, gather and bind 16½ acres of oats and 2½ acres of beans by the day (*per dietam*), as appears in a schedule shown by the accountant	14s 3d

Costs of husbandry

Sharpening, lengthening and smithing the ironwork of a plough and a harrow, and mending and working the ironwork of the wagons, with the shoeing of the horses of the manor	3s 4½d
Two new wooden tongues (*linguis*) of harrows bought	2s 0d
A new wagon without wheels bought	5s 3d
Fixing an axle on a wagon	2d
John Sprot and others, hired on various occasions this year to help in husbandry, besides the servants of the manor	4s 7d
Sum	15s 4½d

Expenses of the household

For meat and fish and other victuals bought in the market for the consumption of this household, as appears in the accountant's paper fully examined upon this account, from the day last year's accounts were closed, that is from 8 December 1474, until the day of the closure of this account, namely 20 November 1475, together with the expenses of the auditor during the time he was here	£2 4s 9d
Paid Thomas Potyn, in full payment of four quarters of wheat bought from him last year, as in the account there	11s 0d
Nine quarters of wheat bought for the consumption of the household	£2 17s 8d
One and a half bushels of malted wheat bought for the same	10d
Sum	£5 14s 3d

Necessary expenses

Paid Henry Asshmeston and William Amyot, hired for planting apple-trees sent to this manor by Vincent Fynche in the lord's new garden	1s 2d
Binding various wooden vessels in the manor, and for binding wheel hubs with wooden hoops, and for mending and binding barrels filled with ox-meat, sent to the lord at Calais this year	3s 9d
Half a bushel of hemp seed bought	4d
Making an iron bill bought for husbandry	7d
A 'sedcod'	7½d
Wooden bowls and dishes bought for the household	1s 0½d
A linen cloth bought for wrapping cheese when it is made	7½d
Three nails of tallow bought for making candles	1s 9d
A spade bought for slicing the hay used for animal-fodder	8d
Various items bought for the lord's servants, namely:	
One yard of kersey bought to provide a doublet for Thomas Frauncez	11d
For making the doublet	6d
Two shirts with sleeves bought for him	1s 5d

A pair of hose bought for him	6d
Four pairs of shoes bought for him	2s 0d
Two woollen sleeves bought for him	6d
A pair of gloves bought for him	1d
Two shirts with sleeves bought for John Haymer	2s 0d
Two pairs of shoes bought for him	1s 0d
Making his tunic with a pair of hose bought	1s 1d
Making two gowns of the lord's livery for the same John and Thomas	1s 0d
A pair of shoes bought for the daughter of Margaret Bilbourgh	4d
The offering of Thomas and John by year	4d
Their barber for the year	5d
A foot of leather for cobbling their shoes	1s 0d
Mending a bridle	1d
Shearing four of the lord's ewes	1d
Carriage hired for 3550 sheaves of reed to Rye, of which eight journeys at 6d and the rest at 4d	13s 2d
The collector of the king's fifteenth in [the hundred of] Goldspur this year for the lord's two fifteenths	£1
Sum	£2 16s 11½d

Purchases of corn and stock

One quarter of wheat bought for seed	6s 8d
Two quarters of oats bought for the same	3s 8d
One ox bought from Henry Turnour for the lord's stock	15s 0d
Sum	£1 5s 4d

Stipends

The accounting bailiff	£1
John Heryng, retained ploughman (*famulus carucarius*)	£1
Thomas Frauncez, servant in husbandry, besides his maintenance (*exhibitio*)	5s 0d
Agnes atte Wode, matron of the house	10s 0d
Margaret Bilbourgh, housemaid	13s 4d
A certain Joan, house servant, for one quarter	3s 4d
Joan Pellond, the other house servant, for the same period	4s 0d
Alice at Hope, another house servant, for 22 weeks	7s 4d
John Hammys, in full payment of his stipend, retained to serve in husbandry for 17 weeks, besides the 2s 4d paid to him within the sum of 4s 7d in the title *costs of husbandry*	14s 0d
Sum	£4 17s 0d

The lady's expenses
Various things and victuals bought for the consumption of the lady when she was here in the month of September, as appears by

a bill, besides the stock of the manor as over, namely two quarters
of wheat, two quarters of oats, two oxen, one calf and two ewes
and two lambs   £2 3s 6½d

Foreign expenses
Various expenses of John Heryng and the others going with him,
for driving the lord's animals from The Mote <to Hall and
elsewhere> and driving them back, and for their ferries at Oxney
and Reading [Street] on various occasions during this account,
and for John's expenses for taking the lord's boar to London,
with the expenses of John German collecting the rents of the
manor and transacting other business for the lord's benefit this   13s 3d
year
A clerk hired to write the parcels of the account this year   5d
Twelve pigs, both for the consumption of this household and for
the lord's larder to Calais, of which eight were slaughtered there
within the time of this account   1s 0d
Hiring a boat at Rye twice this year to take bacon and ox-meat in
barrels, and other of the lord's things to Winchelsea to send to
him at Calais   2s 2d
Robert Symond hired for clearing land at 'Brikost' to be
measured by Stephen Sampson   3d
John Adam for catching 12 'phesauns' for the lord   4s 0d
John Adam for slaughtering three oxen and putting them in
barrels for the lord at Calais, and for the boar sent to the lord at   6d
London
John Adam for the board of Agnes atte Wode at the time of her
illness, being with her for a month by order of the lady   2s 8d
Sum   £1 4s 3d

Sum of all expenses and payments   £28 9s 7¾d

And so he owes £8 11s 5¼d, of which allowed to the accountant 8s 7d for the
rent of various tenants because they cannot be levied, namely 6d from Lord
Dacre for land called 'Wallond', 4s 0d from William Bellknap and 4s 1d from
the heirs of Thomas Fowle for land called 'Burdon'; and he still owes £8 2s
10¼d; and he charges himself with 2s 0d for a calf sold upon account, 5s 2d for
two ox-hides and the hides of three bullocks and of a calf and two fleeces sold
by him, and so he owes £8 9s 10¼d; and he owes for 1000 sheaves of reed sold
and carried to Rye last year £1
Of which John Waterman for rent in Hollington for this year and
last   4s 0d
William Chestre for part of his rent this year   3s 10d
[*blank*] of Northiam for his rent there for this year and last   6s 0d

[Mote]: account of the bailiff there on 29 September 1475

[Wheat]

Three quarters two bushels of wheat remained in the granary from last year; no issues of the barn, because there was no sowing; but received six quarters by purchase of William Potyn, one quarter from William Amyot, two quarters from John Mayne <for the consumption of the household>, and one quarter from John a Wyke for seed; sum 13 quarters two bushels, of which one quarter and half a bushel sown on three acres, 12 quarters one bushel for the consumption of the bailiff and the manor servants, and of the lady being here for almost a month and for the consumption of strangers and of the lord's servants, coming to this manor this year and up to the day of the closure of these accounts, namely 11 November, of which two quarters were for the lady's consumption.

Beans

One quarter of beans remained, and was sown on 2½ acres

Oats

<It yields fourfold less two quarters one bushel>
25 quarters and three bushels threshed and winnowed by the servants of the manor, and two quarters four bushels by estimation in sheaves, of the whole issue of the barn of this manor; two quarters bought by the accountant; sum 29 quarters seven bushels, of which eight quarters two bushels were sown upon 16½ acres, two quarters four bushels in sheaves for fattening the oxen, 12 quarters for malting, two quarters <five bushels> for feeding the capons, hens and pheasants, two quarters for the consumption of the lady's horse, two quarters for the consumption of the manor stots at sowing time and of strangers' horses, and four bushels for making flour for the household; and it balances

Malt

Four quarters remained; 12 quarters were malted from oats as above, and 1½ bushels of malted wheat bought; sum 16 quarters 1½ bushels, of which 15 quarters 4½ bushels brewed for the consumption of the bailiff, manor servants, workmen and strangers, with the expenses of the harvest; and there remain in the granary five quarters of malt

ACCOUNT OF STOCK

Stots

A gelding remained, which was lost by disease

Mares

None remained; but three mares were raised from foals as below, and two sent by the lady from the manor of Hall; and five remain

Colts
No males, but three females remained; two males were raised from the young colts as below; sum five, of which three were raised to mares as above; and two males remain

Young colts (pulleoli)
Two males remained; none were raised; two males were raised up with the colts

Foals
None remained; one male was born this year, and no more because the rest of the mares were barren; and one male remains

Bulls
Two bulls remained; one came from the manor of Hall, one was bought by the lord from John Broun; sum four, of which one was sold by the accountant to John Sampson; and three remain

Oxen
Nine remained, of which four were working; 32 were raised from bullocks, 41 bought by the lord from John Broun, 19 sent from Orlestone by Jakson, one bought by the accountant from Henry Turnour, and two were bought by Henry Turnour as in his account; sum 104, of which three were slaughtered for the lord and sent to Calais, two for the consumption of the lady while she was here, 21 sent to the lady at Hall, one died, 24 sent to Jakson to take to Calais, four sent to Calais by John Heryng, and one sold by the accountant; and 48 remain

Cows
Seven remained; seven were raised from heifers, and eight bought by the lord from John Broun on 29 September 1475; and 22 remain

Steers
32 remained; one was raised from the bullocks as below, and six bought by the lord from John Broun; sum 39, of which 32 were raised with the oxen as above; and seven remain

Heifers
Seven remained; two were raised from female bullocks as below; sum nine, of which seven were raised with the cows as above; and two remain

Male and female bullocks
Three remained; 13 were raised from calves as below, eight bought by the lord from John Broun, three came from Hall; sum 28, of which was one raised with the bullocks and two with the heifers as above, one died, one was slaughtered for this household, one, described as a calf, sold <by Henry Turnour as in his account> to John Adam; and 22 remain, of which 20 are male and two female

Calves
Thirteen remained; 16 were born; sum 29, of which 13 were raised with the bullocks, one slaughtered for the household and one for the lady, three sold by Henry Turnour as in his account, one sold on account [*margin*: for 2s 0d]; ten calves remain, of which one is sucking

Hides
One hide of an ox which died of disease, five slaughtered, and the hide of one bullock and two calves slaughtered as above; sum nine, of which four ox-hides were sold by Henry Turnour as in his account, and five sold here by the accountant, of which two were ox-hides

Pigs
Twelve remained; eight were raised from young pigs; sum 20, of which one boar was slaughtered and sent to the lord at London after 1 November 1475, ten slaughtered for this household after the close of last year's account and before the close of this account, namely before the 20 November 1475; nine remain (one boar, three sows and five store-pigs)

Young pigs
Eight remained; eight were raised from piglets, six by exchange (*de reperto*); sum 22, of which one died, eight were raised with the pigs as above and one drowned; and 12 remain

Piglets
Eight remained; 18 were born to the sows; sum 26, of which eight were raised to the young pigs, two sold by the accountant, six for the consumption of this household; and ten remain

Ewes
Three remained; [one by exchange *deleted*]; sum four <three>, of which two were slaughtered after lambing for the consumption of the lady; and two remain

Gimmers
None remained; one was raised from the lambs as below and went for the lady's consumption

Lambs
One remained; four <three> were born to the ewes, and not more because one ewe was barren this year; sum three, of which two were slaughtered for the consumption of the lady; and one female lamb remains

Fleeces
Four remained and still do

Skins
Four from slaughtered [sheep]; two were sold by Henry Turnour and two by the accountant

Reed
3350 sheaves of <plain> reed grown on the demesne lands and 900 sheaves of rough reed; sum 4250 sheaves, of which 3350 sheaves of plain reed and 800 of rough reed were sold; one hundred sheaves of rough reed remain

Accounted[70] with Stephen Sampson the 20 day of December the 15 year of the king [1475]

First paid by me John Scotte upon a covenant of ridding <in 'Calvynlese'> the 12 year of the king	five marks
Item paid by me John Scotte for <ridding of> a shaw in the 'Calvyn lese'	6s 8d
Item paid by [*not finished*]	

Sum £3 13s 4d, of the which he hath ridded the shaw in 'Calvynlese' price 6s 8d; item he hath ridded in 'Calvynlese' 3 acres and half an acre four dayworks, price the acre 10s 0d; Sum 36s 0d; item he hath eared in the said field 14 acres, price the acre 1s 2d; Sum 16s 4d
Sum paid £2 19s 0d; and so he oweth 14s 4d

Item he received of Harry Turnour as appeareth by his account anno quartodecimo	3s 0d
Item he received of John German as appeareth by his account in the 15 year of the king	2s 4d
Item he received of the same a bowl price	8s 0d
Sum	£1 7s 8d

For the which he hath rid in 'Presounesfeld'

---

[70] The following passage added in English in the hand of Sir John Scott.

Mote: account of John German, bailiff, from 29 September 1475 to 29 September 1476 [ESRO NOR 15/111]

Arrears

He answers for the arrears of his last account, with 4s 0d from John Waterman for his rent [in Hollington] in arrears for two years, 3s 10d for part of the rent of <William>[71] Chestre in arrears for 1474-75, and 6s 0d rent placed upon Henry Holstok for two years	£8 9s 10¼d
Received from Babolin Grantford for 1000 sheaves of reed sold to him by the accountant in 1473-74 and charged up to here, as appears by his account	£1
Sum	£9 9s 10¼d

Fixed rents

The rent of the tenants of Flackley in Peasmarsh, as appears in the new paper rental	£1 11s 4d
Tenants in the vill there	£2 0s 1d
Tenant in Beckley	8s 9d
Tenants in Northiam	£2 18s 9¾d
Tenants in Iden	£2 16s 6½d
Part of the rent of William Chestre, not charged beyond 18s 3d charged above in the sum of £2 16s 6½d	3s 10d
Rent in Playden	3s 0d
Rent in Ninfield	6d
Rent of tenants in Ewhurst, besides 10s 7d rent of Lord Dacre there, in arrears for many years	1s 10d
Rent in Hollington	2s 0d
Sum	£10 6s 8¼d

Farms

John German for the farm of the land called 'Perifeld' in Peasmarsh	5s 0d
And the rest of the farms are answered in the account of Henry Turnour	
Sum	5s 0d

Agistment

John Stille for the agistment of three steers in winter	4s 0d
John German for two heifers agisted there for half a year	2s 0d
John German for one bullock for a year and a half	2s 0d
Sum	8s 0d

---

[71] Replacing *John*, deleted.

Issues of the manor

Rushes called 'candelrisshes' sold to various women this year   1s 9d

Sum total of receipts, with the arrears   £20 11s 3½d

Resolutes

Paid to the bailiff of the Rape of Hastings for blanch farm   5d
The vicar of Peasmarsh for the lord's tithes due there this year   5s 0d
The parish clerk of Iden for his wages for Christmas term; and the
rest is in the account of Henry Turnour   1s 0d
Sum   6s 5d

Expenses of the household

Meat and fish and other victuals bought in the market for the
consumption of this household from the close of the other
account, namely from 20 November [1475] to 8 December [1476]
as appears by the bill of the accountant's expenses shown and
fully examined upon this account   £4 3s 11½d
Six quarters of wheat bought from William Potyn for
consumption as above, besides the corn of the manor, as in the
account of Henry Turnour   £2
One bushel of malted wheat called 'hedmalt'   1s 1d
One bushel of oats to make flour for the household   2d
One bushel of coarse salt   5d
A cloak bought for Mistress Isabel Ponyngez for her time here   £1
Milling wheat on various occasions   9d
Sum   £7 6s 4½d

Necessary expenses

Seven pairs of shoes bought for Thomas Frauncez this year   3s 6d
Three shirts with sleeves bought for him   2s 0d
Three pairs of hose <and a cap> bought for him   2s 4d
Making a doublet for him   6d
Making a tunic for him   6d
Four pairs of shoes bought for John Haymer   2s 0d
Two shirts with sleeves bought for John Haymer   1s 11d
Three pairs of hose bought for him   1s 6d
One new doublet bought for him   2s 10½d
Making one new tunic of the lord's cloth for him   6d
Three new pairs of shoes for Joan Bylbery the housemaid   1s 0d
1½ feet of leather bought for cobbling shoes for the servants of
the manor   1s 5½d
Two ironed shovels bought   1s 1d
Wooden dishes bought   1½d
One sieve for dregs (*de pilis*) bought for [*blank*] ale   6d

One sieve bought for winnowing oats	3d
One 'ladefat' bought	4d
One 'shald' bought for cleaning grain	4d
Mending a brass ladle from the kitchen	2d
Binding wooden vessels within the manor	1s 3d
Candles bought against midsummer	4d
Two pounds of wicks bought for the candles	2½d
Paid the rippier (*vectori piscium*) for bringing two salt fish called 'lyngez' from London to Rye	2d
Shingles bought with 'prig' [nails] for mending defects in the barn wall	4d
Iron hinges and rides with iron nails bought for hanging the gate called 'Mersshgate'	1s 9d
Paid John Amyot for enclosing the hayrick with a hedge	1d
Paper bought for the auditor	4d
Sum	£1 7s 4d

Stipends

The accountant's stipend for the year	£1
Joan Pellond, one of the housemaids, for the Christmas term	4s 0d
Edith Maffey, hired for six weeks to winnow grain and perform other works within the manor	2s 0d
Sum	£1 6s 0d

Foreign payments

Paid for bringing various things belonging to Mistress Isabel Ponyngez from Calais to The Mote	2s 6d
One scot assessed upon land called 'Blaklond' to repair the church of Peasmarsh	3s 4d
Sum	5s 10d

Livery of money

Money delivered to the hands of Henry Turnour, the lord's servant, without a bill	£1

The lord's expenses

Various items bought for the consumption of the lord when he was here on two occasions, as appears by bills of expenses, besides the victuals bought for the consumption of the manor household as above	£1 14s 7d

Sum of all expenses and liveries	£13 6s 6½d
And he still owes the lord	£7 4s 9d

And he is discharged for part of the rent of William Chestre charged above in 'Fixed rents' for this year and last, because William's whole rent does not exceed

£1 0s 7d, and the accountant ought to be charged in future at that rate; and [allowed] him 8s 7d unleviable rents, namely 6d from Lord Dacre for land called 'Wallond', 4s 0d from William Belknap, 4s 1d from the heirs of Thomas Fowle for land called 'Burdon'; and allowed him by the lord's order 4s 0d for the agistment of four bullocks of Henry Fynche last year

And he still owes £6 9s 0d, of which is allowed him 2s 9d paid to Robert Smyth for iron work for husbandry, and the shoeing of the manor horses this year

And he still owes £6 6s 3d

He is charged with 1s 0d for the hide of one dead cow as in the account of Henry Turnour, and so he owes £6 7s 3d, of which for the expenses of the lord who was here in December, namely in the purchase of ale, beer, meat and fish, 12s 10½d

And he still owes £5 14s 4½d, of which respited to him 6s 0d for the lands of John Waterman in Hollington for this year and two years past, 9s 0d for the land of Henry Holstok in Northiam for this year and [the] the last [two] at 3s 0d a year

And so he owes to the lord £4 19s 4½d

Allowed him for the offering of two of the servants of the manor 4d, and to the barber for them for a year 6d, and for the expenses of the said accountant going about the manor business 2s 0d, and for making a tunic for Joan Bilborgh 6d; sum 3s 4d

So he owes clear £4 15s 11½d, which is pardoned by the lord except for £1 14s 4d charged in the account of John Maryner for the year 1476-77.

Mote: account of Henry Turnour, accountant, from 29 September 1476 to 29 September 1477 [ESRO NOR 15/112]

Arrears
He answers for the arrears of his last account of the previous
year   £11 14s 10½d

Rent with farms
Received in part of the rent and farms of this manor by the hand
of John Marener, rent-collector there, and not more because the
rest is accounted for by him in his account of this year   £8

Sale of corn
Received from John Donkerkoy for 30 quarters of oats sold to   £4 10s 0d
him

Sales of stock
From Henry Dobill for a mare sold to him   £1
Thomas Bocher of Beckley for four oxen and one barren cow
sold to him   £4 19s 6d
Two heifers sold to him   15s 0d
Two cows and a heifer sold to Thomas Oxonbregge   £1 6s 8d
Two cows and one calf sold to John Sprot   £1 6s 4d
John Sprot for three oxen of the first yoking   £1 18s 0d
John Bocher for one ox and one steer   £1 10s 0d
Thomas Oxonbregge for four calves   9s 4d
John Sprot for one calf   2s 4d
Thomas at Wode of Warehorne for one ox and three steers   £2 13s 4d
Six piglets sold by the accountant   2s 0d
Thirty oxen sold to the lord at Calais   £27
Sum   £43 2s 6d

Farm of oxen
From John Gervays of Ewhurst for the farm of two oxen for half
a year   3s 4d
William Goler for the farm of four oxen for half a year   6s 8d
Stephen Inkpen for the farm of two oxen for a year   6s 8d
Austin Potyn for the farm of two oxen for half a year   3s 4d
Robert Cheseman for the farm of two oxen for half a year   3s 4d
Alan Cresteford for the farm of two oxen for half a year   3s 0d
Henry Dobill for the farm of two oxen for a year   6s 8d
Sum   £1 13s 0d

Agistment and the sale of herbage and reed

From Thomas Hatche for the agistment of one bullock here this year	1s 3d
John Still for the agistment of three steers	4s 0d
Alice German for the agistment of her draught animals for a certain time	1s 4d
John Mayne for his old agistment	6s 0d
John Marener for the agistment of his mare and five bullocks	5s 0d
John Heryng for his agistment	2s 0d
<John Hickot for the agistment of a mare	1s 0d>
William Langport for his five bullocks in summer last year	2s 8d
Margaret Fletcher for one acre of herbage sold to her	2s 6d
Robert Symon for three acres of herbage sold to him	7s 6d
John Maffay and John Still for five acres of herbage sold to them	12s 6d
Alice German for one acre of herbage sold to her	2s 6d
For 7750 sheaves of reed sold by the accountant this year to various people, as appears by name in the accountant's schedule examined upon this account	£7 11s 8d
John Brand for 500 [sheaves of] reed sold to him	10s 0d
Sum	£10 9s 11d

Issues of the manor

For 900 'brykis' sold by the accountant this year	4s 4d
Butter sold piecemeal to various people this year	10s 0d
John Reder for his board for one week	1s 0d
Sum	15s 4d

Sales of wood

Wood sold from the previous year <to William Eston and Henry Bayle>	2s 8d
John Lumbard of Rye for one parcel of wood sold to him at 'Redeforde'	£1 1s 8d
William at Hill and John Bate for wood and the tops of trees sold at Northiam	2s 10d
John Fletcher and John a Wyke for a parcel of wood by 'Cobgate' sold to them this year	10s 0d
Thomas Profete for various parcels of wood at 'Redeford' and elsewhere	10s 0d
John Sprot for one parcel of wood there sold to him	6s 8d
William Sharpe for a certain parcel of wood there sold him	3s 4d
John Eston, Henry Baile, John Goodegrome and Thomas a Watell for one acre of wood at 'Redeford' sold to them in the previous year	£1
Sum	£3 17s 2d

Foreign receipts
Received from Arnulph Barowe on 24 August 1477, as appears in
his account of the manor of Hall in the heading 'Liveries of
Money' £7
From Christopher Gay, the lord's receiver, as appears in his
account of foreign receipts in the heading 'Liveries of Money' for
1476-77 £6
From Christopher Gay as appears in the same account and
heading of 1476-77 £2
Sum £15

Profits of court
Nothing here, but in the account of the collector of rents

Sum of all receipts, with the arrears £99 2s 9½d

Rents resolute
Of which, he accounts for money paid to the rector of Iden for
<all> tithes except the tithes of <grain>, reed and hay, by year by
agreement 6s 8d
The parish clerk for his wages for a year and a quarter at
Christmas 5s 0d
The vicar of Peasmarsh for all tithes owed to him by year 5s 0d
Sum 16s 8d

Cost of the buildings
To John Sherfold and his mate, carpenters, hired to hew 'bord
stokys' for a day 8d
Paid to the plumber of Faversham for mending the roof (*domata*)
of the tower with lead and solder on two occasions, with 31
pounds of solder bought from him for it 12s 0d
A tiler hired to tile on the tower in various places for 2½ days 10d
The hire of carriage, both by water and land, to carry the glass
sent by the lord from Calais to Winchelsea, and from there to The 2s 10d
Mote
Various ironwork bought to fix the glass in the glazed windows,
and to open and close them 7s 0d
John Cornelis, hired to fix iron rides in the stone wall to hang the
glass windows upon, and for mending a chimney in the counting
house for five days 2s 0d
Iron nails and 'prigge' 3s 3d
John Sare, hired to lay 2400 sheaves of reed on the barn and 'le
cartehous' £1 2s 0d
Paid Thomas Profete for plastering part of the roof (*domata*) of
the barn with clay 8d

Two quarters of burnt lime bought	1s 0d
Sum	£2 12s 3d

Cost of the ploughs and wagons

Lengthening and sharpening the ironwork for ploughs and wagons, and for mending and lengthening the teeth of the harrows, together with the iron and steel bought for it, and for shoeing the manor horses	2s 8d
For fixing axles on carts and fitting ploughs with share-beams	7½d
Iron sheaths and nails called 'broddis' bought for the same	6d
Four halters bought	4d
Sum	4s 1½d

Mowing hay and reed, with their carriage

To John Coward, hired for mowing 20 acres in the lord's great meadow	11s 0d
Mowing 6½ acres in 'Redelond Wysh' at task	3s 6d
Help hired to gather and stook the hay at task	2s 0d
Reaping and binding 10,150 sheaves of reed	£2 10s 0d
A man hired to reap and bind 250 sheaves of reed to thatch the barn	1s 4d
Paid for reaping 500 [sheaves] of reed sold to John Brand	2s 6d
Carriage hired to take 4500 sheaves of reed to Rye and Saltcote	15s 0d
Sum	£4 5s 4d

Ditching and hedging

Making 109 perches of hedge on the west side in 'Redeford'	6s 9½d
Making 74 perches of ditch in 'Brekost Feld' and 'Parkmede' with setting hedges on it	9s 3d
Making 50 perches hedge on north side of 'Brekeostfeld'	3s 1½d
Making 60 perches ditch between 'Keryslond' and the lord's great grove, and setting hedges on it	7s 6d
Making 52 perches of ditch and hedge on the east side of 'Kerislond'	6s 6d
Making 160 perches of hedge in the lord's marsh	10s 0d
Sum	£2 3s 2d

Costs of the harvest

Various men and women hired in harvest to reap, gather, bind and stook the lord's corn, besides the help of the manor servants	£1 1s 3d
Gloves bought for the manor servants	6d
Sum	£1 1s 9d

Purchases of corn and stock

Four bushels of wheat bought by the accountant	3s 4d
One quarter <six bushels> of oats bought for seed	6s 5d
Four bushels of beans bought for seed	2s 0d
A mare bought for stock	8s 0d
Six oxen	£5 6s 8d
Nine steers, a cow and two heifers bought from William Dalet	£5 1s 8d
Four steers bought from Thomas Watell and John Sherfold	£1 13s 0d
Nine steers bought from Richard Mayne	£3[72]
Three steers bought from John Sprot and William Goler	£1 7s 6d
Two steers and one heifer bought from William Symond	18s 0d
Three steers bought from John Fletcher	£1 0s 4d
Three steers[73] bought from John Still	£1 4s 0d
Six bullocks bought from Thomas Bocher	£1 2s 0d
Four young pigs	8s 0d
Two geese	5d
A cow bought from William Eston	6s 8d
Sum	£22 7s 10d

Necessary expenses

Paid Thomas Hickett for three old sacks and iron rides and old 'tyghtes' useful for husbandry	4s 4d
A salt-stone bought for the dove-cot	1s 0d
Tanning a horse-hide and making a sack from it	1s 2d
Three ropes bought to carry animal fodder	3d
Dressing (*cavernand'*) a millstone called 'le qwern'	4d
Two hundred wicks bought for candles	3d
Six nails of tallow bought for candles	2s 10d[74]
For binding various wooden vessels in the manor	1s 9d
Philip a Broke, for keeping six steers with him in winter time	10s 0d
A certain smith for curing a horse and a mare from the sickness called the farcy ('le farshon')	8d
Linen cloth bought for wrapping cheese in when it is made	9d
Wooden vessels and dishes	1s 8d
Green candles bought against midsummer	4d
Gelding pigs	2d
Two sieves and scissors	6d
Repairing two sieves and buying two 'tappehosys'	5d
Two quires of paper bought for the auditor	8d
Two pairs of bellows	5d
A bolting-cloth	3½d

---

[72] Originally written *iij* (for £3), but deleted and replaced by *lx s.*

[73] Originally written *bol* (for the English *bullocks*), but deleted and replaced by *bovettis*.

[74] Followed by a deleted entry *A pair of shoes bought for Richard Sprotte 4d.*

Expenses of the accountant on business, going to Rye, Appledore, Calais and elsewhere on various occasions this year	8s 0d
Sum	£1 15s 9½d

Purchase of things for the manor servants
Various things bought for the manor servants being at the lord's maintenance (*exhibitio*), namely:

Two yards of woollen cloth of russet for the tunics of John Haymer and Richard Sprot	2s 4d
Making up the tunics	8d
Woollen sleeves bought for John Haymer	4d
Two pairs of hose bought for him	1s 6d
Three pairs of shoes bought for him	1s 6d
Two pairs of hose bought for Richard Sprott	1s 2d
Four pairs of shoes bought for him	1s 4d
Four pairs of shoes bought for Joan Bilborow	1s 4d
Making her two tunics	10d
Two shirts bought for John Haymer	1s 0d
Shaving John Haymer and Richard Sprot	8d
Two undergarments bought for Joan Bilborow	1s 0d
For altering the sleeves of Richard Sprot's doublet	3d
A pair of hose bought for Joce, the servant of Master William Scotte	1s 3d
A gift to him for points	2d
Two caps bought for Haymer and Sprot	9d
Offerings to the servants at Easter and Christmas	4d
Sum	16s 5d

Purchase of victuals for the consumption of the household

Meat and fish bought in the market for the consumption of this household, from the day when last year's account was closed, namely 8 December 1476, to the end of this account, namely 1 March 1478, as appears weekly by accountant's paper which was examined piecemeal by the auditor upon this account, besides stock as over	<£4 11s 8d>
A quarter (*quartron'*) of salted fish bought for the same	1s 3d
Two cades of herrings	10s 0d
Sum	<£5 2s 11d>[75]

Marsh scots

Paid John Oxonbregge, collector of a scot of a halfpenny an acre for the lord's lands in the marsh	4s 8d

---

[75] Replacing *£4 17s 11d* deleted.

Henry Walter, collector for two scots of a penny an acre, of which the last was on 24 February 1478	18s 8d
Sum	£1 3s 4d
Paid John Oxonbregge, collector of a scot of a halfpenny an acre for the lord's lands in the marsh	4s 8d

Clearing land [76] <b>

Paid Stephen Sampson for clearing in 'Brekeost Feld' for two days	8d
William Hammes and his assistants in part of an agreement to clear the wood on the north side of 'Brekeostefeld'	13s 0d
John Reder for clearing four acres 7½ dayworks between the lord's garden and 'Calvenlese' at 9s 0d an acre	£1 17s 8d
Stephen Sampson, in full payment for clearing ten acres in 'Presonfeld' on the day of the closing of this account, namely 1 March 1478, besides £3 2s 0d allowed in the account of the said Henry [Turnour] for 1475-76	<£1 18s 0d>[77]
Sum	<£4 9s 4d>[78]

Servants' stipends <a>[79]

John Lucas, <retained ploughman>, for the year ending 2 February 1478	£1 1s 4d
John Heryng, retained ploughman, for the year ending 29 September 1477	£1
<For his gown	4s 0d>
John Marener for half a year to Easter 1477	13s 4d
Thomas Rider, servant in husbandry, for half a year ending Easter 1477	16s 8d
Thomas Rider as a reward after that half year	2s 8d
Thomas Hickot, retained ploughman, for the year ending 2 February 1478	£1 12s 0d
Agnes at Wode, the lord's bedeswoman, for a year to 29 September 1477	10s 0d
Agnes at Wode for her wages in arrears from the time of Henry Fynch, late surveyor of this manor, by the lady's order	2s 6d
Margaret Bilbrow, housemaid, for a year to 29 September 1477	13s 4d
Joan Gerard, the other housemaid, to 29 September 1477	16s 0d
For her gown	5s 0d
Sum	£7 16s 10d

---

[76] *Eradicatio et extirpatio*; the <b> following the heading indicates that this section should be read after the section *Servants' stipends*, itself marked <a>.

[77] Replacing *£1 13s 0d* deleted.

[78] Replacing *£4 4s 4d* deleted.

[79] The <a> following the heading indicates that this section should be read before the section *Clearing land*, itself marked <b>.

[*Marginated*] <It is worth £14 1s 6d besides clearing>

Foreign expenses

Paid Margaret Oxonbregge for nursing Christina's son by the
lord's order   £1
Expenses of the lord's son, Master William Scotte, at the time of
taking seisin of the land in the marsh purchased by the lord from
William Cheyne   11½d
John Fletcher going by the lord's order to Walter Robard at
Cranbrook   6d
Thick thread bought for John Marener for making nets for fish,
foxes and rabbits   15s 6d
Ropes and 'cork' bought for the same   11d
Sum   £1 17s 10½d

Expenses at Calais

Money sent to the lord at Calais as in the value of 30 oxen as
above   £27
The expenses of John Heryng and others for driving the oxen,
some of them to Dover and the rest to Smeeth and elsewhere, and
loading a boar, four small bacons and six cheeses on a ship in
The Puddle and transacting other business on behalf of the lord
on various occasions this year   7s 11d
For 198 yards of frieze cloth ('fryse') bought in St Bartholomew's
Fair, London, this year, with 'canvas' and ropes bought for
wrapping and trussing that and other of the lord's cloth inside   £4 6s 8d
Six yards of woollen cloth of russet bought for the lord and lady   £1 18s 4d
Twelve yards of russet bought there   £1 7s 4d
Twelve other yards of russet bought there   £1
Expenses of the accountant undertaking this business, for himself
and his horse for eight days   3s 1½d
Sum   £36 3s 4½d

Sum of all expenses and liveries   £92 17s 0d

And so he owes the lord   £6 5s 9½d
<which is charged in his account for next year>

Mote manor: account [of stock] there on 29 September 1477

Wheat
<It yields tenfold less three bushels, which note>
He answers for ten quarters two bushels of wheat remaining from the issue of the
stack last year to thresh and winnow by the manor servants, and for four bushels

bought by the accountant; <Memorandum that there was sown>[80] upon 15 acres in the field called 'Kerys' before 29 September 1477 five quarters by level measure <of new grain coming from the land called 'Calfenlese'>; and ten quarters six bushels in bread baked for the consumption of household and of the lord; and it balances

Barley
No issues, but he answers for one quarter six bushels bought for seed; and it was sown on three acres; and it balances

Beans
<It yields twofold>
One quarter two bushels from the issue of this year's stack, and four bushels bought for seed; of which six bushels were sown upon two acres, and one quarter for feeding the pigs

Peas
One bushel sent from the lady from Calais; of which half a bushel was consumed by the household and the rest sown

Oats
<It yields sixfold plus one quarter>
62 quarters threshed by the manor servants and three quarters by estimation in sheaves from the whole issue of the barn; sum 65 quarters, of which 12 quarters were sown on 19 acres, 16 quarters in malt as below; two quarters in feed for the poultry and the doves, two quarters four bushels for the consumption of the horses of the manor and of strangers, three quarters for fattening the oxen, four bushels made into flour, and 30 quarters sold in the neighbourhood; and it balances

Mares
One remained; one was bought; sum two, of which one sold to Henry Dobill; and one remains

Stallions
None remained; but one was raised from the colts as below; and one remains

Colts
Three were received from Capel this year; three remain, of which two females, one male

Bulls
One remained and still does

---

[80] Replacing *of which in seed* deleted.

Oxen
30 remained; 24 were raised from the steers, one from the heriot of William
Chestur, six bought by the accountant; sum 61, of which one was sold by the
accountant to John Sprot at the first yoking, one to John Bocher at the first
yoking, four to Thomas Bocher of Beckley, one to Thomas Awode of
Warehorne, butcher, and 30 sold to the lord at Calais; and 22 remain

Steers
24 remained; nine were bought from William Dallot, four from Thomas a Wattell
and John Shorewold, three from John Still, nine from Richard Mayne, five from
John Sprot and William Goler, three from John Fletcher, two from William
Symond and six raised from the bullocks as below; sum 65, of which 24 were
raised up with the oxen, four sold by the accountant of which one to John Bocher
and three to Thomas a Wode; and 37 remain

Cows
14 remained; none were raised up, but one bought from William Dalet <after
calving>, one from William Eston before calving and one from the heriot of John
Sotte; sum 17, of which one barren cow was sold to Thomas Bocher, two after
calving to Thomas Oxonbregge, two before calving to John Sprott and one was
slaughtered after calving for the consumption of the household; and 11 remain

Heifers
None remained; but one was raised up from the female bullocks as below, three
were bought, namely two from William Dalett and one from William Symond;
sum four, of which two were sold to John Bocher and one to Thomas
Oxonbregge; and one remains

Male and female bullocks
Seven remained; ten were raised up from the calves, six bought from Thomas
Bocher; sum 23, of which six were raised up with the steers and one with the
heifers; 16 remain, of which 14 male and two female

Calves
Ten remained; 12 were born to the cows, and not more because two cows were
barren this year; sum 12, of which one died, three were slaughtered for the
consumption of the household, four sold to William Eston and Thomas
Oxonbregge and two to John Sprott; and four remain

Hides
He answers for the hides of one cow and four calves received from slaughter as
above; sum four, which are accounted with the tanner for leather bought from
him to repair the shoes of the lord's servants who are at his maintenance

Pigs
13 remained; four were raised up from the young pigs as below; sum 17, of which 12 were slaughtered for the consumption of the household and a boar and two pigs sold to the lord at Calais; there remain a boar and a sow at mid-Lent

Young pigs
Four remained; six were raised up from the piglets as below, and four bought by the accountant; sum 14, of which four were raised up with the pigs as above; ten remain at mid-Lent

Piglets
Six remained; 25 born to the sows this year; sum 31, of which six raised up with the young pigs as above, 14 slaughtered for the consumption of this household and for strangers coming here, six sold and two died; and three remain

Ewes
Three remained, of which one died before shearing, one was slaughtered after shearing for the lord's consumption; and one remains

Lambs
One was born this year, which was slaughtered for the lord's consumption

Fleeces
Seven remained, and two of the issue of this year; and nine remain

Geese
One gander and one goose bought from the wife of the late John German, the lord's bailiff <and one of her gift>; one gander and two geese remain

Sheaves of reed
10,900 sheaves of reed cut in the lord's marsh this year, of which 2200 sheaves were accounted for in thatching the buildings of the manor and 9300 sold as over; and it balances [*sic*]

Mote manor: the account of John Marener, rent-collector, from 29 September 1476 to 29 September 1477   [ESRO NOR 15/113]

Arrears
He answers for £1 14s 4d, part of arrears of John German the last rent-collector there, pending upon various people and not yet levied, as appears by John German's bill, namely 4s 4d from William Towghton, 1s 10d upon Richard Holman, 1s 8d upon Thomas John, 4s 0d upon Richard Goodwyn, 5s 5d upon John Miller, 1s 6d upon John Corner, 4d upon Parrock of Ewhurst, 1s 0d upon John Gateward, 3s 2d upon Parnel Oxonbregge, 3s 2d upon Thomas

Oxonbregge, 2d upon <Thomas>[81] Edward, 3s 1d upon Thomas Watell, 4d upon
Richard Parrok, 1d upon the lord of Leigh, and 4s 3d upon Robert a Vanne, and
no more because the lord pardoned the rest of John German's arrears at the time
of his death

Sum   £1 14s 4d

Fixed rents
The rent of the tenants of Flackley in Peasmarsh as appears by the
new paper rental   £1 11s 4d
Tenants in the same vill   £2 0s 1d
Tenants in Beckley   8s 9d
Tenants in Northiam   £2 18s 9¾d
Tenants in Iden   £2 16s 6½d
Part of the rent of William Chestre, not charged beyond 18s 3d
charged above in the sum of £2 16s 6½d   3s 10d
Rent in Playden   3s 0d
Rent in Ninfield   6d
Rent in Ewhurst, besides Lord Dacre's rent of 10s 7d in arrears
for many years   1s 10d
Rent in Hollington   2s 0d
Sum   £10 6s 8¼d

Farms
From John Asshmyston for the farm of a piece of land called
'Rysshett'   1s 2d
John a Weke for the land called 'Hammede' in the marsh, four
acres   6s 8d
The heirs of Thomas Foule for three pieces of land at Flackley   8d
William Towghton for land called 'Crowchlond' at Northiam   7s 0d
William Bayly for a parcel of land by his messuage at Flackley   1s 0d
For land called 'Perifeld' this year   5s 0d
John Profete for the farm of a piece of land called 'Frankfe at
Hopehill'   3d
Sum   £1 1s 9d

From <part> of the arrears of various of the lord's tenants at the time of the
death of John German 15s 2d, namely:[82]
William Towghton   4s 4d
Richard Holman   1s 10d
Thomas John   1s 8d
Thomas Watell   5s 1d

---

[81] Replacing *John*, deleted.
[82] This entire section has been deleted, and the margin annotated *nothing*.

The rent of 'Cotnam'	4s 3d

Profits of court

From the profit of one court held 16 September 1476	3s 0d

Sum total of receipts, with the arrears	£13 5s 9¼d

EXPENSES
Wages

The accountant's fee by reason of his office, and for keeping the lord's garden by an agreement made with the lord	£1 13s 4d

Liveries of money

To Henry Turnour, the lord's servant at The Mote, as in his account of this year	£8

Sum of all the allowances	£9 13s 4d
And so he owes the lord	£3 12s 5¼d

Of which sum, the accountant is allowed 2s 6d, part of the rent of the heirs of Thomas Fowle for land called 'Burdons' of which the rent is 4s 1d in the rental and they now hold it for 1s 7d a year during the lord's pleasure, as in the court held at The Mote on 20 January 1478; and 4s 0d from the rent of William Belknappe for 'Piperlond' because it cannot be levied; and 6d from the rent of Lord Dacre for land called 'Wallond', behind for many years for the same reason; and he still owes the lord £3 5s 5¼d, of which <which is charged in his account for next year>

Against

John Waterman for his lands in Hollington, behind for many years	2s 0d
Henry Holstok for his lands called 'Millersfeld' and 'Ferdynges', behind, until it be better known	3s 0d
Richard Goodewyn of the arrears from the time of John German, the collector <paid to the lord at Mote>	4s 0d
John Miller for the same	5s 5d
John Corner for the same	1s 6d
John Parrok for the same	4d
John Gateward for the same	1s 0d
Parnel Oxonbregge for the same	3s 2d
Thomas Oxonbregge for the same	3s 2d
Thomas Edward for the same	2d
Richard Parrok for the same	4d
Lord of Leigh for the same	1d
From the accountant	£2 1s 3¼d
It is worth this year, besides 5s 0d desparate rent of John Waterman <2s 0d> and Henry Halstok <3s 0d>	£10 1s 3¼d

Mote manor: the account of Henry Turnour, accountant, from 29 September 1477 to 29 September 1478 [ESRO NOR 15/114]

Arrears
He answers for £6 5s 9½d from the arrears of his last account — £6 5s 9½d

Fixed rents and farms of land
Nothing here, because they are charged in the account of John Maryner, the collector, this year

Sales of grain

Received from John Twyk for two quarters of wheat sold to him	£1
Cornelius Mason for ten quarters of wheat sold to him	£5
For 17 seams of oats sold to John Donkerkoye	£3 19s 4d
Sum	£9 19s 4d

Sales of stock

Received for two steers sold to John Bocher of Beckley	£1 13s 4d
Two steers sold to Thomas Potyn	£1 13s 4d
Two calves sold to Thomas Potyn	4s 8d
Two oxen of the first yoking sold to John Bocher	£1 14s 0d
Ten steers sold to Thomas Wood of Warehorne	£7 13s 4d
Three cows sold to John Sprotte	£1 10s 0d
One heifer sold to John Sprotte	9s 0d
Three heifers sold to John Sprotte	£1 1s 0d
Four calves sold to John Sprotte	9s 4d
Two cows sold to Thomas Wood of Warehorne	£1
Three calves sold to John Sprott	5s 0d[83]
Two bullocks sold to John Sprotte	10s 0d
Half a slaughtered bull sold to Stephen Sampson	8s 0d

Sales to Calais

The value of eight oxen sent to Calais for the lord's consumption <at Easter year 1478>	£10
The value of twenty oxen likewise	£17
One boar sold to there	13s 4d
Eight oxen at Easter 1479	£10
Sum	£37 13s 4d

Issues of reed with herbage
From John Mafeye for the herbage of two acres of meadow sold to him this year — 7s 0d

---

[83] Followed by *The value of one boar 13s 4d* deleted.

John Adam for 1050 sheaves of reed sold to him	£1 1s 0d
For 150 sheaves of reed sold to John Foule	3s 2d
Joan Goldyng, widow, for 400 sheaves of rough reed	6s 4d
William Sexten for 400 sheaves of rough reed which he cut and carried	2s 7d
George Corner for 750 sheaves of rough reed which he cut in the lord's land and carried	4s 4d
John Mafeye for a parcel of reed sold to him	10d
Thomas Hykotte for the agistment of his horse for 12 weeks	1s 0d
John Heryng for agistment of two bullocks	2s 4d
For 1500 of 'bryke' sold to Robert a Vanne	7s 6d
[Six *deleted*] hides of slaughtered and dead animals sold	6s 4d
Sum	£3 2s 5d

Issues of the dairy

Butter sold this year	3s 10d

Sales of wood

From John Morys of Rye for a parcel of wood sold in land by 'Brykhostfeld'	4s 11d
Thomas Profott for a parcel of wood sold to him	6s 0d
Stephen Ynkpenn for an acre there	12s 0d
One piece of timber sold at Saltcote	1s 8d
Sum	£1 4s 7d

Receipts

From John Maryner, rent-collector of The Mote, as in his account of 1477-78	£8 4s 1d

Foreign receipts

Received from the lord on 23 April 1479	£8 15s 0d
From Christopher Gaye, the lord's servant, in various parcels as in the heading 'liveries of money to the hands of Henry Turnour' in Christopher Gay's accounts of foreign receipts for 1477-78	£34
Sum	£42 15s 0d

Sum of receipts with the arrears	£127 19s 4½d

EXPENSES

Rents resolute

Money paid to rector of Iden for tithes of pasture, calves and other things by agreement	6s 8d
The parish clerk for his wages for a year and a half to Easter 1479	6s 0d

The receiver of the Rape of Hastings for five suits of the sheriff's tourn, in arrears from the time of John Germayn	1s 8d
For blanch farm at 29 September 1478 and Easter 1479	5d
Paid to the churchwardens of Iden for a scot on the lord's land to the use of the church	8s 0d
Sum	£1 2s 0d

Cost of the buildings and mill

For 11 loads of timber bought from Thomas Frebody for the millhouse within the manor	£1 5s 8d
Seven carts hired to carry part of it from Glossams Place to the manor	5s 2d
Seven <nine> oaks bought from Thomas Hatche for the same	4s <11d>
One elm bought from John Edward at Warehorne for the great wheel of the mill	8d
Carriage of the elm <by water to Oxney	10d>[84]
<For its ferry and for shingles and other trees	1s 0d>
The expenses of a carpenter at Oxney Ferry at the same time	5d
Henry Asshemeston, hired to saw 2700 feet of board for the mill	£1 7s 0d
Henry Asshemeston, hired to saw 950 feet of board for the manor	8s 6d
Henry Asshemeston, hired for 9½ days to saw board for the lord's chapel, at his own board	9s 6d
Henry Asshemeston, hired to saw 800 feet of board for the paling of the garden outside the moat	8s 0d
Thomas Profote, hired in gross to plaster the walls of the barn and other places, at the lord's board	2s 0d
Thomas Aleyn eight days, Henry at Hill six days, John Hane six days and Thomas Profote six days, plasterers, at the lord's board, hired to plaster the walls of the mill and to underpin the sill	6s 8d
Hire of a boat to get the millstones sent from Calais from the ship to Rye	3s 4d
Men hired to help with the millstones, with their expenses	1s 0d
A miller sent by the lord to work the millstones	5s 0d
<In dressing (*cavernand'*) the millstones	4s 0d>
John Crowste, hired to balance (*temperand'*) the mill, and to mill there for eight days	1s 4d
For constructing the *marra* of the mill and its shaft, for great hooks and nails, and other ironwork bought from John Twyk <smith> for the works of the mill and for its doors and windows, by tally	11s 10d
For ironwork bought from the same smith for the windows in the tower	5s 0d
Iron nails bought for the same works	5s 4d
A seam of 'prygg' for the same	7s 8d

---

[84] Replacing *with the ferry 10d* deleted.

John Twyk, smith, by another tally for hooks and rides for the
mill, for the ironwork of the windows and of the door of the hall,
and for nails for the chapel

16s 0d

A roofer hired to tile the millhouse for 9½ days

3s 2d

A roofer hired to tile the hawk-house[85]

1s 4d

Plastering its walls

8d

Making a cask (*tonello*) for the mill

2s 8d

An agreement made by the lord with John London, carpenter, for
making *sedilia* and desks with benches in the lord's chapel, in
gross[86]

£2

For 400 <300> stones called 'pavyngtyle' bought for the
pavement of the chapel (besides 100 bought from Robert
Oxenbregge) at 3s 0d a 100

9s 0d

Cornelius Ducheman and his servant, hired for five days to lay
the pavement there

4s 1d

Carpenters from Flanders, sent by the lord to construct the
horsemill: John Veron for 44 days <£1 2s 0d>, Hankyn Mewes
for 48 days <£1 4s 0d>, Robert Romynell for 28 days <11s 8d>,
William Veron for 47½ days (19s 9d)

£3 17s 5d

For iron pulleys with ropes bought from them for the lord's use

12s 0d

Sum

£15 11s 2d

Cost of the ploughs and wagons
Extending and sharpening the ironwork of the ploughs and
wagons, and repairing and lengthening the teeth of the harrows,
with iron and steel bought for the same, with shoeing the manor's
horses

3s 8d

Fixing axles to the wagons, fitting ploughs with share-beams,
repairing and mending them

2s 0½d

Iron plates and nails called 'broddez' bought for the same

6d

Halters, traces and ropes bought during the time of the account

2s 4d

Making a new plough

1s 4d

One 'bendrope' bought

1s 5d

Sum

11s 3½d

Mowing of the meadow <reed and their carriage>
For 38½ acres of meadow mown at task

£1 0s 10d

Help hired to gather and stook the hay

1s 7d

Reaping 1200 sheaves of reed <in March 1478>

6s 0d

Robert Symond and John Mafeye, for carrying 1000 sheaves from
the lord's marsh to Rye

4s 0d

---

[85] From this entry, the remainder of the account is written in a different hand.

[86] This and the following entries marginated *Reparationes capelle* in the hand of Sir Nathaniel Powell.

Reaping 800 sheaves of reed, whether rough or hairy, this year	4s 0d
Reaping 8200 sheaves of plain reed in March 1479, at task	£2 1s 0d[87]
Sum	£4 1s 3½ <£3 17s 5d>

Necessary expenses

Buying a scoop	2d
Dressing (*cavernand'*) a malt-millstone	2d
Gelding pigs	3d
Mending the sickles for reaping grain	7d
Buying a hammer, an iron bill called a 'hegebille' and a pair of iron 'pynsons'	1s 1d
Buying an axe	1s 0d
John Reder, hired to clean pits called 'stewys' in the lord's garden	1s 10d
Help hired to cut firewood	1s 0d
Constructing an iron weighing 34 pounds, bought for the kitchen to hang bowls <in the chimney>	7s 0d
A great spoon of brass bought for the kitchen	1s 4d
Buying wooden dishes and trenchers	6d <11d>
Making and repairing three axes and iron bills with steel	2s 6d
A bolting-cloth (*polentridio*) bought for the bakery	4d
Two knives bought for the kitchen	4d
A sieve bought for the granary	2d
Two men hired by the lord to make a new well within the court of the manor	2s 8d
A cooper hired to bind the 'pipes' for it	2s 0d
One pair of wheels bought for the garden cart	1s 4d
Removing the pound to put the millhouse there	10d
A skiff or boat (*cimba sive batello*) bought at Small Hythe at the lord's order	£1
<And a lock bought for it	6d>
Binding wooden vessels within the manor	2s 8d
Forty pounds of tallow for making candles in winter	3s 0d
William Pellond, hired for pruning and cutting <the tap-roots (*ramis aquaticis*) of the> apple-trees in the lord's garden in winter, and for removing the earth from their roots and replacing it with new earth, working for eight days with the lord's servants	2s 1½d
An agreement made with John Dyker for newly cleaning a fishpond in the orchard in gross, at his own board	6s 0d
Linen cloth bought for the dairy for wrapping cheese when it is made	1s 0d
Three bowls bought for the same	4d
Two small candles bought for the lord's chapel	3½d[88]

---

[87] Followed by *George Corner for reaping and binding 775 sheaves of hairy reed 3s 10½d* all deleted, with the consequent reduction of the sum by the same amount.

[88] Followed by *Binding wooden vessels within the manor 2s 8d* deleted.

A lock bought for the door of Thomas Bellyng's chamber	6d
John Wynterbourn for threshing 32 quarters of wheat	10s 8d
Stephen Ynkpen for his carriage of hay to the stack in the marsh	10d
Paper bought	8d
Sum	£3 14s 1d

Marsh scots

Paid to William Amyott, collector of a scot of a penny an acre, on 8 June	9s 4d
Thomas Jeff for the same on 26 July	9s 4d
John Oxenbregge for the same on 6 December	9s 4d
John Oxenbregge for two pence an acre on 2 February 1479	18s 8d
John Oxenbregge, collector of a scot of a penny an acre, on 25 March 1479	9s 4d
Sum	£2 16s 0d

Ditching and hedging

Edward Bewke for repairing the hedge between 'Brykhostfeld' and the wood	1s 0d
One labourer hired for four days for making a ditch at 'Parkmedbregge'	11d
John Plomtree of Stone for [making] a wall at the end of 'Parkmede' to have a way there, in gross	6s 8d
For digging 40 perches of ditch between 'Melland' and 'Lez Rypez'	10s 0d
For digging 50 perches between the land called 'Gistement' and the mill to the great ditch	8s 4d
Newly making 44 perches of ditch from 'Calvynglez' to the said great ditch	11s 0d
Making 21 perches of ditch by 'Redford' between 'Lez Shetez' and the lord's pasture there	7s 8½d
For making a parcel of ditch between the land of the manor of Leigh and the lord's land called 'Stomblebroke'	1s 6d
For 99 perches of hedge between 'Presynsfeld' and the lord's wood by 'Foxherdes'	6s 2¼d
Sum	£2 13s 3¾d

Costs of the harvest

Various men hired at harvest to reap the lord's corn	5s 11d
Mowing 17½ acres of oats reaped at task, at the lord's keep	5s 10d
Sum	11s 9d

Purchase of corn and stock

In grain bought nothing this year, but paid Simon Briggez for 13 bullocks, two cows and two steers, at 5s 0d a head	£4 5s 0d
John Edward for two cows before calving bought from him	15s 0d
Thomas Ase for two bullocks bought from him	£1 6s 8d
John Gate of Brede for two oxen bought from him	£1 9s 4d
Richard Mayne for four oxen bought him	£3
One gelding bought at Appledore to work in the mill	£1 12s 0d
A horse bought from Thomas Wood of Warehorne for the same	11s 0d
For 13 fowl	1s 1d
One cow bought from Stephen Sampson	5s 4d
Nine bullocks bought from William Sylver	£4 1s 0d
Two oxen bought from John Langle	£1 7s 0d
Sum	£18 13s 5d

Servants' stipends

Thomas Wodhouse, the lord's servant, for a year to 29 September 1478, and from then up to and including Easter 1479, at £1 6s 8d a year	£2
Joan Gerard, now wife of Henry Turnour, for the same time, at 16s 0d a year	£1 4s 0d
John Heryng, retained ploughman, for a year to 29 September 1478, and from then up to and including 25 December 1478, at £1 a year	£1 5s 0d
Agnes Wood for a year and a half to Easter 1479, at 10s 0d a year	15s 0d
Margaret Bilborogh, one of the housemaids, for a year to 29 September and from then up to and including 25 December, at 13s 4d a year	16s 8d
Elizabeth Germyn, the other housemaid, for a year to 25 December 1478, with 6d reward	8s 6d
John Webbe, retained ploughman, for a year to 29 September 1478	11s 0d
And to him for three months to Easter 1479	3s 0d
Thomas Hykott, retained ploughman, for a year to 2 February 1479	£1 13s 4d
John Wynterbourn, servant in husbandry, hired for a month within the time of the account	4s 0d
To him for his stipend for four months	12s 0d
Sum	£9 12s 6d

Purchase of things for the manor servants
Various things bought for the manor servants being at the lord's maintenance (*exhibitio*), namely:

\<Five\>[89] pairs of shoes for John Haymer	\<2s 6d\>
One doublet bought for him and for making for his gown	2s 10d
One shirt bought for him	11d
Woollen cloth for his tunic and for a pair of hose for him bought from John Potyn	2s 3d
A pair of hose bought for George, the lord's servant	1s 4d
Purchase of a doublet and making a gown made for him	3s 4d
Four pairs of shoes bought for him	1s 8d
One doublet for the French groom, and for making a pair of hose and a tunic for him	2s 11d
Four pairs of shoes bought for him	1s 4d
One gown bought for the miller, and its making	2s 3d
Two pairs of shoes bought for him	1s 0d
Cloth bought for a tunic for the lord's servant from Picardy, with one pair of hose for him, together with his shirt	3s 10d
Shoes bought for the French maid and her daughter	1s 0d
Their expenses at Winchelsea on the day of the lord's confessors' and communicants' dinner	6d
[Linen cloth bought for the dairy for wrapping cheese when it is made	1s 0d
Three bowls bought for the same	4d
Two small candles bought for the lord's chapel	3½d
Binding wooden vessels within the manor	2s 8d][90]
One pair of hose bought for Richard Sprot	6d
Sum	£1 8s 2d

Purchase of victuals for the consumption of the household

Various victuals bought in the market, both for the consumption of the household and of the lord, Master William Scott and his servants and those of others, from the close of the last year's account on 1 March 1478 to 1 March 1479, and thence to 22 May 1479, as appears item by item and week by week by the accountant's paper, examined upon this account, besides the manor stock	£16 6s 8½d
Two cades of sprats bought for the same	2s 4d
Four bushels of peas bought for the same	3s 8d[91]
Sum	£16 12s 8½d

Clearing woodland
Paid William Hammez in part-payment of his agreement for five
acres of woodland in the field on the north side of 'Brykhostfeld',

---

[89] Replacing *three* and *four* both deleted; the sum has been increased directly from 1s 6d.
[90] These four entries deleted.
[91] Followed by an entry *Two quarters four bushels of great salt bought for the same 11s 6d*, deleted with the annotation *because among the expenses of the household.*

besides 13s 0d of the same agreement paid him last year, as in
this accountant's account for that year   £1 13s 8d

Liveries to Calais with expenses
Money sent to Calais for the lord in various things, namely in the
value of eight oxen sent from The Mote to Dover on three
occasions <to Easter 1478>[92]   £10
Expenses of John Heryng and others for driving the oxen   4s 9d
Twenty fat bullocks and oxen of the first yoking   £17
The value of two boars, one bought from John Brigez   £1 6s 8d
Slaughtering them at Rye   1s 8d
A boat hired to take the boars to the ship   1s 4d
Expenses of the said 20 bullocks and oxen to Dover   2s 6d
Expenses for getting the things sent by the lady to this manor
from the ship in Rye, Saltcote and other places   1s 10d
To the master of the ship for their carriage   1s 4d
Expenses of John Heryng with other mill-workmen from Calais to
The Mote   1s 7d
The value of eight oxen at Easter 1479   £10
Two bushels of off-cuts of leather from gloves bought for the lady   10d
Sum   £39 2s 6d

Foreign expenses
Medicine bought for Robert Sprott, with the cost of his burial   6s 10d
Paid William Patynden for the lord's livery bought from him by
the yard, in summer 1478   £5 18s 0d
Paid to the farmer of Thornsdale for land in the marsh hired by
the lord to 29 September   8s 0d
Paid to Robert a Vanne for lands hired in the same way to 29
September   12s 0d
Paid to the servant of Robert Brent for leading a horse to The
Mote   1s 0d
Sum   £7 5s 10d

Sum of all expenses and liveries   £125 5s 10¼d
So he owes the lord   £2 13s 6¼d

Mote manor: account [of stock] there on 29 September 1478

Wheat <It yields seven and a half-fold less [four bushels]>[93]

---

[92] Replacing *in the third week of March* deleted.
[93] The margin of the roll is obscured by repair at this point, but the yield can be established from
the previous year's sowing (see NOR 15/112).

37 quarters of wheat threshed at task and winnowed by the servants, of the whole produce of the demesne barns of this manor, of which five quarters seven bushels were sown on 16 acres of land at three bushels an acre of the level measure, 19 quarters five bushels in bread baked for the consumption of the household for a year to 29 September 1478 and from then until 25 December 1478, and 12 quarters sold as over; and it balances

Barley
Six quarters of barley received from the whole stack of last year's sowing; sum six quarters, and malted as below; and it balances

Beans and peas
Nothing this year

Oats <It yields four and a quarter-fold less four bushels>
But he answers for 51 quarters four bushels of oats threshed and winnowed by the manor servants, and two quarters by estimation in sheaves; sum 53 quarters four bushels, of which 15 quarters were sown on [24][94] acres at five bushels an acre, two quarters in sheaves in fattening oxen, two quarters four bushels in feeding geese, capons, poultry and doves, 34 quarters sold as over; sum as above; and it balances

Mare
One mare remains

Horses
One gelding remained; one was raised up from the foals and two bought by the accountant as over; and four remain

Foals
Two female foals remained; one was born to a mare this year; there remain three foals: two female of two years and one male of one year

Bulls
One remained <slaughtered for the use of the household>

Oxen
22 oxen remained; 37 steers were raised up as oxen as below, two oxen bought <at Brede and four from Richard Mayne and two from John Langle>; sum 67, of which one died, one strayed and one was slaughtered for the use of the household, eight sold to Calais at Easter 1478, 20 on 25 November and eight at Easter 1479; there remain 12 oxen <16 are lacking, which are below within the sum of 35 remaining steers>

---

[94] Blank in the manuscript.

Cows
11 cows remained; one was raised up from the calves, two bought from Simon
Briggez <after calving> and two from John Edward and one from Stephen
Sampson; sum 17, of which none died, three were sold to John Sprotte as over
and two to Thomas Wood of Warehorne; there remain 12

Steers
37 steers remained; 14 were raised up from bullocks, 13 bought from Simon
Briggez and two from Thomas Ase and nine from William Silver; sum 75, of
which two died <query>, 37 were raised up with the oxen as above, four sold by
the accountant to John Bocher of Beckley, two to Thomas Potyn, ten to Thomas
Wood of Warehorne and one slaughtered for the household; there remain 35 <19,
of which 16 stand under the heading of oxen as above>

Heifers
One remained; two were raised up from female bullocks, two bought from Simon
Brigez; sum five, of which one was raised up with the cows and four sold to John
Sprott; one heifer of two years remains

Male and female bullocks
16 remained; four were raised up from calves as below; sum 20, of which 14
were raised up with steers and two with the heifers as above, two sold to John
Sprott and one slaughtered for the household; one bull calf remains

Calves
Four remained; 12 were born to the cows this year, and not more as three cows
were barren this year; sum 16, of which two died, four were raised up with the
bullocks as above, two sold to Thomas Potyn as over, seven to John Sprot and
four <one> slaughtered for the household

Hides
There remain the hides of one bull, one ox, one steer and the four calves
slaughtered as above, and of one ox which died as above; sum eight, and they
were sold by the accountant as over; and it balances

Pigs
One boar and one sow remained; ten pigs were raised up from the young pigs as
below; sum 12, of which one boar was slaughtered [to send] to Calais for the
lord and nine for this household; there remain one boar and one sow

Young pigs
Ten young pigs remained; three were raised up from last year's piglets, six were
born this year <and two by exchange>; sum 19 <21>, of which ten were raised
up with the pigs and 11 remain

Piglets
Three piglets remained; 19 were born to the sow this year; sum 22, of which nine were raised up with the young pigs, two died, and six were slaughtered for the household; there remain five piglets

Ewes
One ewe remained, and it died

Fleeces
Nine remained and were delivered to the housekeeper (*matrone domus*) to spin for the use of the lord

Geese
One gander and two geese remained; seven were born; sum ten, of which one died and seven were consumed by the household; and there remain one gander and one goose

Reed
3150 sheaves of reed, the produce of 1477-78, and 8200 the produce to Easter 1479; sum 11,350 sheaves, of which 400 accounted for in thatching the buildings of the manor and 2750 sold to various people as over; and there remain 8200 sheaves of reed

Mote: the account of John Maryner, collector of rents, from 29 September 1477 to 29 September 1478 [ESRO NOR 15/115]

Arrears

He answers for £3 5s 5¼d from the arrears of his last account, with 'leez unde super' as in the foot of his account of the previous year	£3 5s 5¼d

Fixed rents

And from the rent of the tenants of Flackley in Peasmarsh, as appears by the new paper rental	£1 1s 4d
From the tenants in the vill there	£2
From the tenants in Beckley	8s 9d
From the tenants in Northiam	£2 18s 9¾d
From the tenants in Iden	£2 16s 6½d
For part of the rent of William Chestre, not charged beyond 18s 3d charged above in the sum of £2 16s 6½d	3s 10d
Rent in Playden	3s 0d
Rent in Ninfield	6d

Rent of the tenants in Ewhurst <with the rent of William
Tomsett>, besides 10s 7d, the rent of Lord Dacre, in arrears for
many years   <3s 10d>[95]
Rent in Hollington   2s 0d
Sum   £10 8s 8¼d

Farms
John Asshemynton for the farm of lands called 'Le Risshett' (1½
acres), in Iden   1s 2d
John Flecher for a meadow called 'Hammede' (four acres), in
Peasmarsh   6s 8d
Thomas Potyn for land called 'Pyrefeld'   6s 8d
William Toghton for land called 'Crowchlond' (12 acres), in
Northiam   7s 0d
Robert Smyth for one acre in Peasmarsh   4d
The heirs of Thomas Foule for three parcels of land lying
dispersed at Flackley, one called 'Wellfeld'   8d
The farm of land called 'Millond', nothing here as it is in the
lord's hands and occupied by his draught animals this year
John Profote for a small piece of land (one rod) called 'Frankfee
at Hopishille'
<remember 5d next year>   4d
Sum   £1 2s 10d

Sale of rushes
Rushes from the lord's brooks collected by various women this
year   3s 1½d

Profits of court
Received from various tenants to release their suit of court this
year: James a Wood <4d>, William Benett <4d>, John Stille
<4d>, the heirs of Robert Creche <4d>, the heirs of Thomas
Foule <4d>, and 6d from amercements: Thomas Watell <2d>,
Richard Holman <2d>, and Richard Bate <2d>
Sum   2s 2d

Sum total of receipts with the arrears   £15s 2s 3d

[*Rents*] *resolute*
Of which, paid to the bailiff of the Rape of Hastings for the lord's
suit of court for this manor, by the hand of William Tomsette   2s 0d[96]

---

[95] Replacing *1s 10d*, deleted.
[96] Followed by *For blanch farm 5d; to the vicar of Peasmarsh for the lord's tithes* ... deleted.

Expenses for nets

Thread, hemp <and linen> bought from the wife of John Bank for making and repairing the lord's nets	5s 0d
Similar thread bought for the same nets from Joan Cok	1s 3½d
Thin cords bought for a net called 'a tramelnett'	1s 0d
Rope bought for the great net	1s 5d
'Corkys' bought for it	9d
Sum	9s 5½d

Stipends

The accountant's stipend, both for his office as collector of rents, and for making and mending nets, by an agreement made with the lord	£1 13s 4d

Liveries of money

Money delivered to the hand of Henry Turnor, the lord's servant at The Mote, as is shown by his acknowledgement, on various occasions this year	£8 2s 8d
To him by the hand of John Profoote <1s 0d> and 5d for hides bought to cobble the servants' shoes	1s 5d
Sum	£8 4s 1d

Sum of all expenses and payments £10 8s 10½d

and so he owes the lord £4 13s 4½d; of which 2s 6d is allowed him for part of the rent of the heirs of Thomas Fowle for lands called 'Burdons', in the rental at 4s 1d, now held for 1s 7d during the lord's pleasure, as in the court held at The Mote on 20 January 1478; and 4s 0d for the rent of William Belknappe [for land] called 'Pipelond' because it cannot be levied, and 6d from Lord Dacre for 'Wellond', in arrears for many years, for the same reason; sum of these allowances 7s 0d; and he still owes the lord £4 6s 4½d

[Arrears]

John Waterman for his lands in Hollington, in arrears for many years, besides two years in the time of [this] accountant at 2s 0d a year charged upon him	4s 0d
Henry Holstok for his lands called 'Mellerfeld' and 'Ferdyng' at 3s 0d a year, in arrears for the said two years	6s 0d
Richard Goodwyn for his arrears in the time of John German, collector	4s 0d
John Corner for his arrears in the time of the said John German	1s 6d
Parnel Oxonbregge for her arrears in the time of the said John German	3s 2d
Thomas Oxonbregge for his arrears for the same lands for two years in the time of [this] accountant	6s 4d
Richard Parrok for his arrears in the time of the said John German	4d

He now accounts   £3 1s 0½d
[*margin*] It is worth this year besides allowances and respites £11 5s 1d

[*Notes in the hand of Sir John Scott*]
<Memorandum that I believe that whereas he seeks allowance for 2s 0d paid to
the bailiff of the rape for suit of court, it was paid by William Tomsette on top of
his rent
Item he seeks £1 13s 4d for his stipend which is too great an allowance, because
he did not serve for the whole year, because that stipend is not given for
collecting the rents only, but for service in the house, therefore let it be allowed
according to the proportion of his service
Item remember the shilling rent of two acres of land of William Belknap lying by
'les Rypis' and by the lands of John Hatch, for which acres of land in the old
rental John Hatch paid a shilling, as appears in the same rental
Item let there be an enquiry for the rent of a parcel of meadow <of William
Cheyne> lying by a parcel of meadow called 'Cotynham', now of John
Oxsynbregge

£3 1s 0½d; £4 19s 0d>

Mote: the account of Henry Tournour, servant of John Scot, knight, lord of the said manor, from 29 September 1478 to 29 September 1479

[ESRO NOR 15/116]

Arrears

He answers for £2 13s 6d of the arrears of his last account   £2 13s 6d

Fixed rents with farm

Nothing here, because they are charged in the account of John
Marener, the collector of rents, this year

Sales of crops and stock

One ox and one cow sold to Thomas Oxenbrege	£1 12s 0d
One ox sold to John Sprotte	18s 0d
Three oxen of the first yoking sold to Thomas at Wode	£1 12s 0d
Three calves sold to John Sprot	5s 0d
One calf sold to John Sampson	3s 4d
Sum	£4 10s 0d

Sales to Calais

Stock sold to the lord to Calais nothing in this account, because
they are accounted at Easter 1479

Issues of the manor

One parcel of herbage sold to George Corner	2s 8d
Two acres of herbage sold to John White of Wittersham	5s 2d
One acre of herbage sold to John Still	2s 4d
One acre of herbage sold to a man from Saltcote	2s 4d
175 sheaves of reed sold to a man from Stone	3s 5d
100 sheaves of reed sold to John Sampson	1s 10d
3000 sheaves of reed sold to John Wyneburn	£2 15s 0d
1500 sheaves of reed sold to John Henfeld	£1 11s 1d
200 sheaves of reed sold to John Mayhue	4s 8d
150 sheaves of reed sold to John Adam	3s 0d
150 sheaves of reed sold to Thomas Oxenbrege	3s 0d
Two acres of herbage sold to Richard a Crouch	5s 2d
William Hammez for his board with his servant for <clearing there>[97]	13s 8d
A quarter of an ox sold to William Hammez, besides his board	3s 0d
Two barrels of 'bere' sold to William Hammez	2s 2d
250 sheaves of reed sold to Thomas Oxenbrege	5s 6d
Henry Asshmonton, sawyer, for his board	3s 2d

---

[97] Replacing *marling*, deleted.

William Hamme for his board	6s 6d
Sum	<£7 13s 6d>[98]

Issues of the dairy
No sales, because the whole output was consumed by this household

Issues of the mill

Toll of the horsemill from 25 December 1478 until 13 January 1480, besides the toll of Robert a Vanne	£2 10s 0½d

Sales of wood

One parcel of wood at Millhill in Flackley sold to John Donkercoye	<£5 10s 0d>[99]
A parcel of wood there sold to Thomas Watell	£1 16s 8d
A parcel of wood there sold to Robert Lumbard	14s 6d
A parcel of wood there sold to John at Wyke	12s 8d
A parcel of wood there sold to Thomas Profite	4s 4d
<Two acres of> wood sold to Stephen Ynkpenne	£2[100]
A parcel of wood sold to William Sharp	15s 0d
Sum	£11 13s 2d

Receipts

From John Maryner, collector of rents of this manor, as appears in his account of this same year	£4 19s 0d
From him to 25 December 1479	13s 4d
Sum	£5 12s 4d

Foreign receipts

Received from the lord at The Mote	£10
From him there on 30 November 1479	£5
From the lord at Monks Horton on 16 December 1479	£3 6s 8d
From the lord by the hand of Thomas Holme	£2
From Christopher Gay at Hamstreet on 3 May 1479	£6 13s 4d
From him on two occasions at Appledore	£1
From him at Warehorne Fair	£2 13s 4d
From him by the hand of Richard Webbe	£1
From him by the hand of Richard Webbe	£8
Sum	£39 13s 4d

Sum total of receipts, with the arrears	£74 5s 10d

---

[98] Replacing *£7 3s 10d*, deleted.
[99] Altered from *£5 16s 0d*.
[100] Altered from *A parcel of wood … 18s 0d*.

EXPENSES

Payments of tithes and to the church

Of which accounted in money paid to the rector of Iden for the
tithes of the pasture, calves and other \<personal\> things of this
manor by an agreement made with him   6s 8d

The parish clerk for his wages for half a year to 29 September
1479   2s 0d

The vicar of Peasmarsh for tithes there by year   5s 0d

\<Thomas Barbour for wax for the Easter sepulchre   1s 7½d\>

Sum   13s 8d

Costs of the buildings and mill

A carpenter hired to make a door for the store-room   10d

Two carpenters hired to make a door for the hall, and for working
beds (*lettic'*) for 3½ days   2s 4d

John Profite for plastering the walls of the chamber by the
horsemill, for underpinning the sills and for making a floor for
drying malt upon, and for plastering upon the roof (*domate*) of
the said building with earth   3s 0d

900 foot of board for stock and for the old millhouse   9s 0d

2300 'prigge'   1s 10d

The plumber of Faversham hired for his work in laying the lord's
lead and for roofing his own work on the new towers at the gate   £1 2s 0d

John Nowell, thatcher, hired to thatch with reed both on the
millhouse, the adjoining chamber and the barn, laying 3000
sheaves of reed, at his own board   £1 10s 0d

George, a carpenter from Flanders, working in the new horsemill
for 32 days, at the lord's board   10s 8d

John Crowste, hired to dress (*cavernand'*) the millstones of the
mill   1s 4d

Carrying a new wheel made in Kent to Appledore Ferry   6d

John Potyn, carpenter, working on the new millhouse for 45 days
to 13 January 1480, at the lord's board   13s 1½d

William Daly and his mate, working there in the same way for 45
days   13s 1½d

John Ricard, carpenter, working there in the same way for 30
days   8s 8d

John Morescotte working there in the same way for 23 days   6s 10d

Sawing 2100 feet of board and timber for the same work   £1 1s 0d

Richard Bailif of Peasmarsh, in part-payment for timber bought
from him by the lord   £1

A mason hired to place 'tabardes' on the wall of the tower, for
4½ days in all   1s 8d

Sum   £8 5s 11d

Cost of the ploughs and wagons

Extending and mending the ironwork of the ploughs and wagons, sharpening the teeth of the harrows, with iron and steel bought for the same job, together with shoeing the manor horses	4s 8d
Fitting axles to the wagons, and fitting ploughs with share-beams and repairing them	1s 6d
Purchase of 'broddes'	2d
Purchase of ropes and traces	1s 0d
Sum	7s 2d

Mowing of meadows

Mowing 38 acres of meadow in the marsh	£1 0s 7d
George Corner, hired for five days to mow the meadow in the lord's garden	1s 8d
Cutting reed nothing here, because in last year's account	
Help hired to collect hay, besides the work of the manor servants	2s 10d
Sum	£1 5s 1d

Necessary expenses

A winnowing fan bought to clean grain	1s 0d
Wooden bowls, dishes and saucers[101]	1s 8d
Binding wooden containers and making barrels and cups	4s 1½d
Paid Thomas Profote for help in the kitchen at the time the lady was here	1s 0d
Grinding nine quarters of wheat	3s 0d
Help hired for cutting wood and other household works (*operibus hyconomie*)	<2s 11d>[102]
A 'cable' bought for dragging timber	2s 2d
Ropes bought for the stock of the manor	11d
Two pounds of green candles bought	3d
John Symond and others, hired for carrying reed to Rye and for bringing hay from the lord's meadows to the barn in the manor	7s 11d
Hire of a boat to bring the lord's lead from a ship to the town of Rye	2s 2d
Burying the lord's retained ploughman called Pety John at Iden	1s 0½d
A cloth strainer (*cilicium*) bought for the oast for drying malt upon	9s 8d
<Expenses of Richard Seford, carrying sea-fish from Rye to Monks Horton against the churching (*purificatio*) of Mistress Bedyngfeld, and for driving bullocks to The Mote at the same time	2s 0d>
Sum	<£1 19s 10d>[103]

---

[101] Written *scissor'*, presumably the result of a copying error.
[102] Replacing *1s 2d*, deleted.
[103] Replacing *£1 16s 1d*, deleted.

Marsh scots

A scot paid to John Wynborne before 20 July for the lord's land in the marsh	9s 4d
Paid to the parish clerk of Iden after 25 July for another scot for the same lands	9s 4d
To the same parish clerk, collector of a scot payable on 1 November for the same lands	9s 4d
Sum	£1 8s 0d

Ditching and fencing

For <the moiety of 290>[104] perches of great ditch dug between the lord's land called 'Redelond' and the land of William Cheyne, esquire	£1 0s 7½d
For <the moiety of 60>[105] perches of ditch dug between the lord's land called 'Stombilbroke' and the land of the same William Cheyne, esquire	7s 6d
For <the moiety of 12>[106] perches of ditch there	6d
For 24 perches of ditch in the lord's land called 'Stombilbrokez'	8s 0d
And in help [*not finished*]	
Sum	£1 16s 7½d

Costs of the harvest

Various men and women hired in harvest for cutting, gathering and binding the lord's corn, besides the works of the lord's servants	6s 11d
George Corner, hired to reap three acres of barley and 18 acres of oats in gross	8s 2d
Gloves bought for the servants in harvest	6d
Sum	15s 7d

Purchase of corn and stock

Two bushels of barley bought by the accountant from Robert a Vanne for seed	1s 3d
Six oxen bought at Ewhurst Fair	£3 7s 2d
Two oxen and two bullocks bought from John Heryng	£2
One bull, two bullocks and one steer bought from Robert Hony	£1 4s 8d
One cow and one steer bought from William Symond	10s 0d
One cow bought from a man from Saltcote	8s 1d
Two oxen bought from Richard Langley of Brede	£1 8s 8d
Three cows and nine pigs bought at Stone	£1 19s 0d

---

[104] Replacing *145* deleted.
[105] Replacing *30* deleted.
[106] Replacing *6* deleted.

Two cows and five bullocks and one steer bought from Richard
Mayne and John Mayne   £2 13s 8d
Sum   £13 12s 6d

Stipends of the servants
In <full payment> of the stipend of Richard Sefowle, retained
ploughman, for a year to 2 February 1480, besides the 12s 0d
paid him by the lord   14s 8d
John Webbe, retained ploughman, for three quarters of a year to
25 December 1479   9s 0d
Agnes at Wode, the lord's bedeswoman (*oratrix*), for half a year
to 29 September 1479   5s 0d
Elizabeth German for a year to 25 December 1479   10s 0d
The wife of Henry Turnour for half a year to 29 September 1479   8s 0d
Paid Isabel de Cecilia[107] in part-payment of her stipend   3s 4d
<Stephen the brewer>[108] for a quarter to 25 December 1479   10s 0d
William Frend in part-payment of his stipend before 14 January
1480   6s 8d
Sum   £3 6s 8d

Purchase of things for the manor servants
One pair of hose bought for John Frensshe   1s 6d
<Three>[109] pairs of shoes bought for him   <1s 1d>
A belt, purse, knife and points   4d
One pair of hose bought for Simon the farm boy, and a pair of
shoes   1s 2d
One pair of hose bought for Jacomyn, one of the housemaids   6d
Four pairs of shoes bought for her   1s 0d
'Bokeram' bought for her gown, and making it up   3s 4d
One pair of hose and two pairs of shoes bought for Edith   5d
One pair of shoes bought for John Haymer   6d
Half a foot of leather bought for cobbling (*pictand'*) the servants'
shoes   4d
One tunic, with its making, bought for John Frenssh   2s 2d
One pair of shoes for him at 25 December   5d
Two pairs of shoes bought for John Haymer   11d
Sum   13s 3d

Purchases of wine and victuals for consumption by the household
One barrel of red wine   £3 14s 2d

---

[107] *De Cecilia* written after *Fra* deleted, but without interlineations.
[108] Replacing *Richard Bayly*, deleted.
[109] Replacing *Two*, deleted, with a consequent increase in the sum from 8d.

Various victuals bought in the market, both for the consumption
of this household and of the lord <and lady> and of Master
William Scott and his servants, and of strangers, namely from the
close of the accountant's last account, that is from 22 May 1479,
to the day of the closure of this account, which happened on 15
January 1480, as appears week by week and item by item by the
accountant's paper shown and examined upon this account,
besides the stock of the manor   £8 0s 11½d
Four quarters of great salt bought at Winchelsea, with its carriage
to The Mote   14s 5d
Sum   £12 9s 6½d

Clearing[110] *of land and wood*
Paid William Hammez and his brother for clearing oaks in land
called 'le Ripez' to the mill   2s 4d
William Hammez for clearing three acres seven dayworks in the
ponds by the site of the manor   £1 18s 0d
William Hammez, in full payment for five acres by
'Brekeostfeld' cleared by him   3s 7d
Stephen Samson, in part-payment of his marling agreement,
besides 13s 4d received from the lord   £5 13s 4d
In spreading marl on eight acres   10s 8d
Given William Hamme in part-payment of his agreement in
'Stumbilbroke'   11s 0d
Sum   £8 18s 11d

Delivery of things to Calais for the lord
50,000 billets bought from Henry Dobyll for the lord at Calais   £4 11s 8d
100,000 billets bought from John Broke for the same   £10
Paid John Frensshe, a sailor from Folkestone, for taking the lord's
things from Calais to Rye by water   6s 0d
For a closed container for carrying the lord's things which came
from Calais from Small Hythe to The Mote   6d
Sum   £14 18s 2d

Foreign payments
One pair of hose and one pair of shoes bought for Anthony
Sellyng   2s 0d
One pair of hose and three pairs of shoes bought for Mistress
Elizabeth Gernyngham   1s 6d
Sum   3s 6d

---

[110] *Eradicatio.*

Note that the lord paid John Browne of Snargate by Ham[111] Reder
at The Mote   6s 7d

Sum of all expenses and payments   £61 14s 10d
And so he owes the lord £12 11s 0½d, with which he is charged in his account
for next year

Upon [*not completed*]

<Memorandum that the lord paid ...> [*not completed*]

Mote manor: account [of stock] there on 29 September 1479

Wheat <It yields four and a half-fold plus one quarter 2½ bushels>
He answers for 25 quarters four bushels of wheat, the whole issue of the barn of
this manor, threshed and winnowed by the servants of the manor, [except nine
quarters *deleted*]; sum 25 quarters four bushels, of which five quarters three
bushels were sown on 15 acres of land of this manor at three bushels an acre of
the level measure, 20 quarters one bushel in bread baked for the consumption of
the household during the time of this account; sum as above; and it balances

Barley
Two bushels were bought from Robert a Vanne for seed; two quarters <provided
by the lord by>[112] Christopher Gaye for the same; sum two quarters two bushels,
which were sown upon three acres of the land of this manor; and it balances

Oats <It yields two and a half-fold plus one quarter five bushels>
He answers for 37 quarters one bushel of oats, the whole issue of the barn,
<threshed and winnowed as above> this year, two quarters by estimation in
sheaves, [*blank*] <provided by the lord by>[113] Christopher Gaye; of which 11
quarters four bushels were sown on 18 acres of land of this manor at five bushels
an acre plus in total two bushels, two quarters in fattening oxen, one quarter four
bushels in feeding geese, capons, poultry and doves, one quarter four bushels in
fodder for horses, and [*blank*] in malt made for the consumption of the household
during the time of the account

Horses
[Five *deleted*] <four> remained; one gelding came from Robert Brent <and one
was bought by the lord from Robert Philpot>; sum five, and one died; and five
remain

---

[111] Following *Henry* deleted.
[112] Replacing *bought*, deleted.
[113] Replacing *bought*, deleted.

Mares
One remained; two were raised up from the foals as below; sum three, of which one mare after foaling in the lord's gift to John Copyldyke; and two remain

Foals
Three remained; three were born to the mares as above this year; sum six, of which two were raised up with the mares, one in the lord's gift to John Copildyke with the mare; and three male foals remain, of which one is aged 18 months

Bulls
None remained, but one was raised up from the bullocks as below and one was purchased; and two remain

Oxen
12 remained; 35 were raised up from the steers as below, six bought at Ewhurst Fair, two from John Heryng and two from Richard Langle; sum 57, of which one was sold to Thomas Oxenbrege, one to John Sprot, three of the first yoking to Thomas Wode and five slaughtered for the consumption of the household; and 47 remain

Cows
12 remained; one was raised up from the heifers as below, one was bought from William Simond, one bought at Saltcote, three at Stone and two from John Mayne and Richard Mayne; sum 20, of which one was sold before calving to Thomas Oxenbregge; and 19 remain

Steers
35 remained; two were bought from John Heryng, five from Richard Mayne and John Mayne and two from John Honye; sum 44, of which 35 were raised up with the oxen as above; and nine remain

Heifers
One remained; one [was purchased] from Robert Honye, one from William Symond and one from Richard Mayne and John Mayne; sum four, of which one was raised up with the cows as above; and three remain

Male and female bullocks
One bull calf remained; sum one, and it was joined with the bulls as above, and it balances

Calves
None remained, because they were accounted for up to 30 May 1479, but six were born to the cows between 30 May and 29 September 1479; sum six, of which two were slaughtered for the consumption of the household, three sold to John Sprot and one to John Sampson; and it balances

Hides
Five hides of oxen of the first yoking remained, and two from slaughtered calves; sum seven, and they were sold by the accountant; and it balances

Pigs
One boar and one sow remained; one boar and two sows were raised up from the [young] pigs as below, <eight from the young pigs as below and nine were bought at Stone>; sum [five *deleted*] <22>, of which <19> slaughtered for the use <of the household of which> one boar and two sows; one boar and two sows remain

Young pigs
11 remained <five were raised up from the piglets as below>; of which 11 were raised up with the pigs as above; and 15 remain [*sic*]

Piglets
Five piglets remained; [*blank*] were born to the sows this year; of which five were raised up with the young pigs; and four sucking piglets remain

Sheep
None

Geese
One gander and one goose remained, and five were born this year; sum seven, which were slaughtered for the consumption of the household, and it balances

Reed
8200 sheaves of reed remained in the lands of the manor on 15 May 1479, of which 5500 were sold to various people as over and 2700 accounted for in thatching the buildings of this manor; and it balances

Mote: the account of Henry Turnour, servant of Sir John Scott, knight, from 29 September 1479 to 29 September 1480   [ESRO NOR 15/117]

Arrears
He answers for the arrears of his last account of the previous
year, as at its foot   £12 11s 0½d

Rents and farms
From fixed rents nothing, because they are charged in the account
of William Sharp, collector thereof this year
But he answers for 6s 8d from the farm of 'Peryfeld' thus leased
to Thomas Potyn this year; and the rest of the same farm is
charged in William Sharp's account   6s 8d
<And from Leonard [*blank*] for the lord's land at Saltcote, lately
purchased from Thomas Martham, for half a year to 29
September 1479   8s 0d>
Sum   14s 8d

Sales of stock
Received from Thomas Scappe for 16 oxen sold to him   £13 6s 8d
Thomas Knoldam for ten oxen <of the first yoking> sold to him   £5 6s 8d
Sum   £18 13s 4d

Issues of the manor
Received from George Corner for one parcel of herbage in the
marsh sold to him   7s 8d
John Fletcher for one acre of herbage   2s 4d
John Symond for one parcel of herbage   3s 8d
John Wytt for one acre of herbage   2s 4d
William Wever of Wittersham for one acre of herbage   2s 4d
John a Wyke for one parcel of herbage   2s 4d
Ingram a Vanne for one parcel of herbage   1s 4d
Rushes in the lord's brooks sold this year   4s 8d
200 sheaves of reed sold to William Dobyll   3s 8d
300 sheaves of reed sold to John <Potyn>, carpenter, of
Wittersham   5s 4d
400 sheaves sold to John Potyn, tailor   8s 4d
200 sheaves sold to John Wordy of Rye   4s 2d
200 sheaves of reed sold to Thomas Barbour   4s 2d
300 sheaves of reed sold to Robert Pott   6s 3d
200 sheaves sold to John Hobbe   4s 4d
200 sheaves sold to John Eston the younger   4s 2d
200 sheaves sold to the widow of John Ripse   4s 0d
200 sheaves sold to John Eston the elder   4s 0d
200 sheaves sold to the widow of John Aspe   4s 8d

200 sheaves of rushes sold to Thomas Maylarde	4s 8d
200 sheaves of rushes sold to Thomas Pynde	4s 8d
350 sheaves sold to the widow of John Bayly	8s 0d
100 white herrings	1s 4d
William Twyk for one pig sold to him	3s 4d
And for a young pig sold	4d
William Hammes for his board during his work in marling this year	£1 14s 0d
From 23 hides of slaughtered animals, 16 at 1s 4d and seven at 1s 6d	£1 11s 10d
The hide of one steer which died of murrain	1s 0d
Twelve calf skins sold in gross	2s 2d
Sum	£8 12s 1d

Sales of wood, 'bylett' and firewood

Received from John Baudwyn for 10,000 billets sold to him	£1 1s 8d
John Deryk and John Swan for 9000 billets at The Float	£1 1s 0d
Fraryk of Hythe for 1000 billets as above	2s 4d
Richard Swan and Richard Sawnder for 41,000 billets there as above	£4 13s 4d
Thomas Barbour for 5000 billets	10s 10d
Richard Swan for 5000 billets	11s 8d
Henry Swan for 2000 billets	4s 4d
John Deryk for 1500 billets	3s 6d
John Mores for 1000 billets	2s 4d
William Taylour for 1000 billets	2s 4d
William Twyk for 1000 billets	2s 2d
John Fray for 1000 billets	2s 4d
John Adam for 1000 billets	2s 4d
Henry Fletcher for 1000 billets	2s 4d
Henry Fletcher for 1000 billets	2s 3d
Simon Bregges for 1500 billets	3s 3d
John Godewyn for 500 billets	1s 1d
Richard Wyn for 3000 billets	6s 6d
Richard Swan for 1500 billets	3s 6d
Walter Brewer for 1000 billets	2s 6d
Walter Brewer for 1500 billets	3s 11d
Joan Bocher for 1000 billets	2s 0d
Hamo Shepard for 12,000 billets	£1 9s 6d
Fraryk of Hythe for 46,000 billets sold by the lady and delivered by her warrant	£5
William Sharp for wood within 'Cobbe Gate' in the wood there	5s 0d
John a Wyke for one parcel of wood sold to him there	10s 0d
John Lomberd for 500 'faggot leffe' [faggots of brushwood]	2s 1d
Thomas Watell for five wagonloads of 'billet leffe'	3s 4d

John Godegrome for 1000 'faggot leffe'	4s 0d
Richard Hobbys for 500 'faggot leffe'	2s 0d
John Foule of Rye for the same	2s 0d
Richard Wyn for the same	2s 0d
John Fletcher for 400 'faggot leffe'	1s 4d
Richard Crouch for three wagonloads of branches	6d
John Godewyne for 500 'faggot leffe'	2s 0d
For tops (*verticibus*) and branches of trees sold to the said John Godegrome and others	2s 0d
For 100 billets sold by the accountant at The Float	3d
<John Bowyer for 15,000 billets sold at The Float	£2 2 6d
For 500 billets sold there	1s 4d>
Sum	<£20 17s 4d>[114]

Tolls of the mill

Received from Robert a Vanne for mulcture of the lord's horse mill	4s 8d
Toll there	2s 0d
For the same	1s 4d
Received for the same up to the day of the closure of this account, 12 January [1481]	8d
From the toll of the same mill before the 12 January [1481]	1s 2½d
Sum	9s 10½d

Receipts

From John Marener, late collector of the rents of this manor, for his arrears for 1478-79	£1
Received from him for the same	6s 8d
Sum	£1 6s 8d

Foreign receipts

Received from the lord on four occasions	£6 13s 4d
From him as appears by the lord's hand in the accountant's book	6s 8d
From him on 7 October as in the same book, written by the lord's hand	£2
From him for the carpentry work at The Float	£1 6s 8d
From him on 24 December	£1
From the lady	£1 6s 8d
From her by the hand of Richard Seford, with a letter	£3 6s 8d
From her by the hand of William Sharp, collector of the lord's rent	£3
From the rector of Iden	£2
From Mistress Bedyngfeld	£1 3s 4d

---

[114] Replacing *£18 13s 6d*, deleted.

From Christopher Gay at Appledore Fair	£2
Sum	£24 3s 4d

Sum total of receipts, with the arrears	£87 8s 4d

EXPENSES

Of which accounted in money paid to the rector of Iden for the tithes of pasture, calves and other personal things of this manor, by an agreement made with him	6s 8d
The parish clerk for his wages for half a year to 29 September	2s 0d
The bailiff of the Rape of Hastings for blanch farm	5d
<The vicar of Peasmarsh for tithes there this year	5s 0d>
Sum	13s 8d

Cost of the buildings

<Paid to Engill Dowchman, the lord's carpenter, for part of his stipend working within the manor during the time of this account	£1 10s 0d
A thatcher hired to lay 600 sheaves of reed on the manor barn, at his own board	6s 0d>
William Daly, carpenter, hired for 14 days for dividing the high chamber in the south of the tower, for making windows and doors there, and for making screens, doors and windows in the tower and elsewhere	4s 8d
William [Daly] for 25 days and his mate Geoffrey for 28 days hewing timber and making paling within the lower court of the manor, and other works within the manor	15s 4d
Hewing timber[115] for the paling	2s 8d
Timber bought from Henry Fletcher	8d
Ten loads of timber bought from Robert Hony	19s 2d
Sawing 6000 feet, both for paling and for boards for the mill and for stock	£3
William Twyk, smith, for ironwork for the said works	£1
<Thomas Profete, hired for 14 days to plaster the walls in the high chamber of the tower, and of the barn	3s 4d>
Sum	£8 1s 10d

Cost of the mill

Paid to William Croust and John Still for mending millstones	1s 3d
John Sherfold for 11 days, John Potyn for 12 days, John Rycarde for six days, Richard Morestok for 8½ days hired to work on the <new> millhouse, both hewing timber for it and making it, at the lord's board	12s 6d
Richard [Morestok]'s son, helping in the same work for four days	8d

---

[115] Followed by *bought from Richard Bayly* deleted.

John Ricard for 11 days and John Potyn for 14 days working in
the same way | 8s 4d
John Ricard for six days in the same way | 2s 0d
Timber bought from Lawrence Bryce for the same work | 10s 1d
Richard Bayly, in full payment for 15 loads of timber bought
from him last year, besides £1 of it paid to him then | 12s 6d
For felling the wood bought from Lawrence Bryce | 7½d
William Twyk for ironwork, locks and 'boltes', for that building
and for other buildings, [and] for doors and windows in the tower | 16s 8d
1000 shingles | 4s 4d
Sum | £3 8s 11½d

Cost of the ploughs and wagons
Lengthening and repairing the ironwork for the ploughs and
wagons, sharpening and making the teeth of the harrow, with iron
and steel bought for it, and shoeing the manor's horses | 6s 10d
Halters and traces | 8d
One wagon with wheels, bound with iron tyres bought for it | 7s 8d
The cooper for binding the hubs of the wheel with wooden tyres | 3d
A carpenter hired to fix an axle to the wagon and to fit ploughs
with share-beams | 3s 6d
Sum | 18s 11d

Mowing meadow and reed
Mowing 37 acres of the lord's meadow, at task | £1 0s 0½d
Help hired to spread and stook the hay, besides the works of the
manor servants | 1s 0d
Reaping 5700 sheaves of reed in the lord's brooks | £1 8s 6d
Sum | £2 9s 6½d

Marsh scots
Paid to William Sharp, collector, for one marsh scot for the lord's
land there at a penny an acre in April [1480] | 9s 4d
Austin Potyn, collector of a scot of two pence an acre for the
same lands in July [1480] | 18s 8d
The same collector for a penny an acre in October 1480 | 9s 4d
Sum | £1 17s 4d

Making a bridge and a building at The Float in the marsh
Paid Thomas Smyth, carpenter, working for 6½ days on making
a bridge by the lord's Float in the marsh, at the lord's board | 2s 2d
His servant working for the same time | 1s 7½d
William Fletcher helping for one day | 3d
Hewing timber for it | 4d

William Daly, carpenter, hired in the same way working in the same work 12½ days	4s 2d
Geoffrey Carpenter for 14 days and John Elcok for 3½ days, at the lord's board	4s 4½d
Henry Fletcher and John Symond, hired with their wagons to carry timber to the work for one day	1s 8d
Various men hired to remove and dig soil for positioning the bridge	2s 0d
Robert a Broke of Small Hythe by my lord's order, making a gutter at the Float <besides 6s 8d paid by the lord>	13s 4d
Thomas Warner working there for one day	6d[116]
Thomas Warner for 6½ days	3s 3d
Thomas Warner for his two servants working with him there for six days, at the lord's board	4s 0d
John Cheseman, Henry Warner and other labourers hired by the day to dig soil for the gutter, to remove the earth and to make a wall there	8s 0d
John Bocher, in part-payment of his work for a wall to enclose the lord's marsh there	£1 2s 0d
Two men hired to repair and amend the wall at The Float	1s 6d
John Kyngesdown, carpenter, at the lord's order, for his work in making a building at The Float	£1 13s 4d
To him in a reward by the lady's order	6s 8d
Henry Fletcher for hauling timber from the ship to the building for one day	1s 0d
John Blaker for plastering and underpinning the building	6s 0d
3000 'prygge' and 100 iron nails bought for the same work	2s 8d
Richard Sherfold, hired for 14½ days for ditching and widening the 'Le Cryke' at Float, at his own board	4s 10d
Sum	£6 3s 8d

Ditching and hedging

Paid to Edward Bewke and John Cheseman in full payment for 66 perches of ditching between 'Dornett Grove' and 'Stumbilbrokes', besides 8s 0d paid in the previous year	14s 0d
William Hamme for 94 perches of ditching, from the ditch in 'Redeford' to a place called 'Milpond', and enclosing with hedges	19s 7d
William Hamme for 30 [perches] of ditching between 'Parkmede' and 'Brykeostfeld', and enclosing with hedges	5s 7½d
William Hamme for making 63 perches of hedge between 'Foulyslond' and 'Le Millepond'	3s 11¼d
Sum	£2 3s 1¾d

---

[116] Followed by *John Cheseman digging there* deleted.

Costs of the harvest

Help hired in harvest to reap and gather the lord's corn	6d
George Corner for mowing 30 acres	10s 0d
Gloves bought for the servants	8d
Sum	11s 2d

Purchase of corn and stock

One quarter of wheat bought for seed	6s 8d
One quarter of beans bought for the consumption of the household	2s 8d
Two steers and one heifer bought at Robertsbridge Fair	15s 2d
One cow bought there	6s 8d
Four steers bought there	£1 4s 1d
One heifer bought from John Couper of Stone	5s 4d
Two steers <and a cow> bought from George Corner	£1 4s 2d
One steer bought at Ewhurst Fair	9s 0d
Two steers bought there	11s 0d
Three bullocks bought there	11s 4d
Three steers bought from John Yong	£1 8s 0d
One gelding by exchange with John Cote of Ashford	10s 0d
47 sheep (*bidentes*) bought at Seaford	£3 6s 6d
Two boars bought	12s 4d
Sum	£11 12s 11d

Necessary expenses

Threshing 30 quarters six bushels of wheat, at task	11s 9d
Threshing nine quarters of wheat of new grain	3s 0d
Threshing eight quarters of oats	1s 4d
Richard Seford, for his expenses in [driving] animals from Mote to Hall on three occasions	1s 0d
Richard Seford for the ferry of the animals, both from Mote and Hall, with the ferry of sheep at Appledore, together with the ferry <of 20 oxen and their pasture at Small Hythe>	2s 4d
Mending two kitchen pans	4d
Binding various wooden vessels	6s 9d
Gelding pigs	4d
For slitting 25 pigs in their snouts or noses to prevent them from churning up the ground	1s 0d
Stephen Couper for measuring the marled field	4d
John Coward for measuring the lord's mown meadow	4d
Gelding two horses	8d
For carrying four barrels and four cades of herring by water from The Puddle to Rye	1s 2d
William a Grove, for carrying three pipes of salt and one pipe of verjuice from Calais to Udimore, with other of the lord's things brought there	11s 4d

Carriage hired to carry the same things to The Mote, besides the lord's carriage	3s 2d
For carrying four cartloads of malt brought from Sandwich, from Rye to The Mote	2s 8d
For 51 quarters of malt sent from Sandwich by John Alday to Rye	14s 0d
Carriage hired for it, besides the lord's carriage, from Rye to Mote	2s 0d
For [carrying] the lord's things from The Mote to Oxney Ferry, to have with the lady at Hall	10d
Hayne Skypper, for getting the lord's things from Calais to the lord's Float	2s 0d
For carrying timber bought from Robert Hony from Peasmarsh to Mote	2s 10d
Cornelius Mason for putting hooks in the stone wall	1s 0d
Henry Fletcher, hired with his animals to plough for the sowing of oats	1s 4d
A stranger hired to drive the plough	1s 6d
John a Wyke with his servant, for carting hay from the meadow to the stacks in the lord's land	2s 4d
Thomas Hatch for the same	2s 6d
Simon Bregges for grazing one of the lord's foals with him	1s 8d
One axe called a 'flessh axe'	1s 8d
The expenses of John Haymer and others of the lord's servants on business to Hall on various occasions this year	8d
[A pair of hose bought for John Haymer	1s 3d
Two shirts, a pair of hose and a pair of shoes bought for Simon [blank]	3s 1d
Paid the tailor for making his gown	6d][117]
A pair of shoes bought for John Baron	4d
John Fletcher for cutting and clearing trees, briars and thorns on the banks of the moat	10d[118]
Expenses of Henry Turnour and Reynold Dorant, going for the sheep bought at Seaford	2s 8d
Shoeing the lord's horses against the departure of Master William Scott to Trotton on the day of the trental of his mother-in-law	1s 4d
Sum	£4 8s 3d

Making 'la bylett' with carriage	
Paid John Fletcher for making 42,000 billets	£1 1s 0d
Henry Bayly for making 36,000 billets	18s 0d
Nicholas Wygge for making 23,000 billets	11s 6d
Richard Crouch for making 3500 billets	1s 9d
Thomas Bocher with his mate for making 23,000 billets	11s 6d

---

[117] The last three entries are deleted.
[118] Followed by *A pair of 'botewes' bought for the said Simon 1s 0d* deleted.

Wodelond and Sherfold for making 44,000 billets	£1 2s 0d
Henry Bayly for making 3500 billets	1s 9d
Henry Fletcher for carrying 41,500 billets to the lord's Float	£1 4s 2½d
John Godegrome for carrying 8000 billets to there	4s 8d
Simon Bregges [for carrying] 124,000 billets to there	£3 12s 4d
Henry Fletcher with his cart for carrying billets from 'le stak' to the ship at the lord's Float	3s 4d
Edward Parrok for the same for 2½ days	2s 0d
Richard Sherfold of his fee for loading 11,000 billets into the ship	11d
Richard Sherfold for taking 16,000 billets to the ship on another occasion	1s 4d
Sum	£9 16s 3d

Clearing,[119] *with marling*

Paid to workmen for scattering and spreading heaps of marl from [*recte* on] eight acres	10s 8d
An agreement made by the lord with William Hamme for clearing briars, thorns and willows in the lord's meadows in the marsh	8s 0d
Stephen Sampson, in full payment of £10 for marling 16 acres of land in 'Kereslond' (11 acres for ten marks and 13s 4d for each of the remaining five acres)	£3 13s 4d
William Hamme, in part-payment for his work <of clearing> in 'Dornettgrove' besides the 11s 0d paid to him last year	£2 15s 8d
Sum	£7 7s 8d

Purchase of victuals

Various victuals bought by the accountant in the market, from 15 January to 25 March 1480	£1 6s 6d
Two barrels of white herrings bought from Richard Swan in Lent	14s 4d
Sum	£2 0s 10d

Stipends

The stipend of Richard Bayly, in part-payment of his wages, by the lord's order	£1 8s 0d
Agnes atte Wode, the lord's bedeswoman, for three months to 25 December 1479	2s 6d
Elizabeth German for a year to 25 December 1480	12s 0d
Richard Seford for a year to 25 December 1480	£1 10s 0d
Thomas Hykott for three months to 25 December 1479, 1s 8d received from the lord	6s 8d[120]
Richard Sherford for half a year to 29 September 1480	13s 4d[121]

---

[119] *Eradicatio et extirpatio.*
[120] The entry originally read *with 1s 8d received from the lord, 8s 4d*, but the *with* has been deleted, the sum reduced to 6s 8d, and *Nota* added both in the text and margin.
[121] Followed by *William Nowell by the lady's order 3s 4d* deleted.

Simon [*blank*] for a year to 25 December 1480   14s 0d
Reynold Dorant, hired both at haymaking time <subsequently up
to 18 January with 4d for his expenses to Hall   7s 10d>[122]
Sum   £5 14s 4d

Liveries of money
Delivered to the lord's hands by Christopher Gay from the money
from Thomas Knolden for ten oxen of the first yoking sold to
him, with which price Christopher charges himself in his account
of foreign receipts this year 1479-80   £5 6s 8d
To the hands of the <lord>[123] in the value of 46,000 billets by[124]
his order delivered to Fraryk of Hythe   £5
Sum   £10 6s 8d

Sum of all expenses and payments   £77 15s 1¾d

So he owes the lord £9 13s 3¼d, of which is allowed to the accountant 5s 0d for
expenses about the lord's business in buying, selling and other works in various
places, touching his office; so he owes the lord £9 8s 3¼d

Paid Henry Fletcher for 41,000 billets… [*written on the dorse of the account;
unfinished*]

Mote manor: account [of stock] there on 29 September 1480

Wheat <It yields eightfold plus one quarter two bushels>
44 quarters two bushels, the whole issue of the barns of this manor, of which 30
quarters were threshed at task and the rest by the manor servants, and winnowed
by the manor servants; and one quarter bought for seed; sum 45 quarters two
bushels, of which six quarters six bushels were sown on 18 acres of land of this
manor at three bushels an acre by level measure, and 38 quarters four bushels
were consumed by this household; sum as above; and its balances

Barley <It yields fourfold plus six bushels>
Nine quarters six bushels of barley received from the barns of the whole issue,
threshed and winnowed by the manor servants; accounted for in the consumption
of this household; and it balances

---

[122] The insertion follows *and in harvest 4s 0d <5s 2d>*, all deleted.
[123] Replacing *lady*, deleted.
[124] Followed by *her sold to Frary* deleted.

Oats <It yields fourfold plus two quarters five bushels>
48 quarters five bushels of oats received from the barns of the whole issue there, of which eight quarters were threshed at task and the rest by the manor servants, and winnowed by the manor servants; sum 48 quarters five bushels, of which 18 quarters six bushels were sown on 30 acres at six bushels an acre, plus one bushel more, two quarters by estimation in sheaves in feed for oxen, and 28 quarters seven bushels accounted for in the consumption of the household, for malt and for the consumption of horses and poultry; sum as above; and it balances

Horses
Five remained, two died, and three remain

Mares
Two remained, one died before foaling, and one remains

Foals and colts
Three remained and one was born; four males remain of which one is aged 2½ years, two aged 1½ years and one sucking

Bulls
Two remained, one sent to Hall and one remains

Oxen
47 remained; nine were raised up from the bullocks as below and two bought by the lady; sum 58, of which 16 delivered to Hall, 16 sold to Thomas Scappe, ten sold to Thomas Knoldam and six slaughtered for the consumption of the household; and ten remain

Cows
19 cows remained; three were raised up from heifers, two bought by the lady and one bought at Robertsbridge and one bought from George Corner; sum 26, of which six were slaughtered for the consumption of the household, two sent to Hall; sum eight; and 18 remain

Steers
Nine remained; one was bought by the accountant at Ewhurst Fair and two bought by him there, three bought from John Yong by the accountant, two bought at Robertsbridge and four were bought there, and two bought from George Corner, and two bought by the lord and 20 were provided by the lord from John Mayne and 12 came from Hall; sum 57, of which nine were raised up to oxen, two died, nine slaughtered for the consumption of the household and five delivered to Hall; and 33 remain

Heifers
Three remained; one was bought by the accountant at Robertsbridge Fair, one

bought from John Couper of Stone and three bought by the lord from John
Mayne; sum eight, of which two were slaughtered for the consumption of the
household and three raised up with the cows; and three remain

Male and female bullocks
None remained; three were bought by the accountant at Ewhurst Fair and remain,
of which one is male and two female

Calves
None remained; 22 were born, and not more because two of the cows were
barren; one was bought by the lord from John Mayne and one by the accountant
from John Couper; sum 24, of which two died at calving and 12 were slaughtered
for the consumption of the household; and ten remain

Hides
The hides of six oxen, six cow, nine steers, two heifers and 12 calves which were
slaughtered as above; and the hides of two steers which died as above

Pigs
One boar and two sows remained; 15 were raised up from young pigs as below,
two boars were bought by the accountant <and one by exchange>; sum 21, of
which 12[125] (two of them boars) were slaughtered for the consumption of this
household, and one sold to William Twyk; nine remain, of which one is a boar
and three sows

Young pigs
15 remained, 16 were raised up from this year's piglets; sum [*blank*], of which
15 were raised up with the pigs as above; and 11 remain[126]

Sheaves of reed
5500 sheaves of reed received from the lord's brooks this year and 200 received
there; sum 5700 sheaves, of which 2200 sheaves for thatching the new building
at The Float and within the manor, 300 sold to John Potyn, carpenter, 400 to
John Potyn, tailor, 200 to William Dobyll, 200 to John Wardy of Rye, 200 to
Thomas Barbour, 300 to Robert Pott, 200 to John Hobbys, 200 to John Eston the
younger, 200 to John Rypse's widow, 200 to John Eston the elder, 200 to
Richard Apse's widow, 200 to John Maylarde, 200 to Thomas Pynde, 350 to the
wife of the late John Bayly; sum as above; and it balances

'Bylett'
175,000 billets made for stock (*ad stipitem*); of which 1500 consumed by the
lord at Mote, 149,500 sold to various people as over, 500 in the lord's gift to his

---

[125] Replacing *11* deleted; the total has failed to take account of the alteration.
[126] *Recte* 16?

servants Giles and Hanward, 15,500 subsequently sold by the lord and 100 by the accountant; and 7900 remain

Mote: the account of <William>[127] Sharpe, collector of rents, from 29 September 1479 to 29 September 1480   [ESRO NOR 15/118]

Arrears

He answers for the arrears of John Marener, the last rent-collector there, with the allowances   £8 2s 4¾d

Fixed rents

The rent of the tenants of Flackley in Peasmarsh as appears by the new paper rental	£1 11s 4d
The tenants in the vill there	£2 0s 7d
The tenants in Beckley	12s 0d
One hen for the rent of John Brown for <his> messuage called Horspen <by year>	<3d>[128]
The lord's tenants in Northiam	£2 18s 9¾d
The lord's tenants in Iden	£2 16s 6½d
Part of the rent of William Chestre, not charged beyond the 18s 3d charged above in the said sum of £2 16s 6½d	3s 10d
Rent in Playden	3s 0d
Rent in Ninfield	6d
Rent of tenants in Ewhurst, including 2s 0d rent of William Thompsett, besides 10s 7d, the rent of Lord Dacre there, in arrears for many years	3s 10d
Rent in Hollington	2s 0d
From Thomas John for a new rent for land in Northiam called 'Crouchlond', lately purchased from the lord by his charter[129]	7s 0d
Sum	£10 15s 11¼d

<Note there is to be charged next year 9d more for the land called 'Ludwyns' in Beckley>

Farms

From John Asshmynton for the farm of lands called 'Rysshett' (1½ acres) in Iden	1s 2d

From a meadow called 'Hammede' in Peasmarsh (four acres), lately in the hands of John Fletcher, nothing because in the hands of the lord, and occupied with the lord's draught animals; nor received 6s 8d for land called 'Peryfeld' in the hands of Thomas

---

[127] Replacing *John*, deleted.
[128] Altered from *Three hens ... for three years ... 9d* deleted.
[129] For the original charter, see Appendix 1 no. 8.

Potyn, nothing here as in the charge of Henry Tournour

From Lawrence Bryce for one acre in Peasmarsh	4d

From the heirs of Thomas Foule for three parcels of land laying
dispersed at Flackley, of which one is called 'Wellefeld'   8d

From the same heirs for a parcel of brook of the demesne lands
between 'Millond' and 'Hetchislond' (3½ acres), adjoining the
land of the same heirs   1s 4d

From Thomas Prophete for a small parcel of land (one rod) called
'Frankfee at Hopyshill'   5d

From William at Hill for a parcel of land in Northiam   2s 0d

Sum   5s 11d

Profits of court

Profits of three courts, of which the last was held on 13 May   8s 6d
1480

Sum total of receipts, with the arrears   £19 12s 9d

EXPENSES

Of which, paid to the bailiff of the Rape of Hastings for suit of
court for the manor of Mote by the hand of William Tomsett   2s 0d

Stipend

Stipend of the accountant by reason of his office   10s 0d

Liveries of money

Money delivered to the hands of the lady by a bill dated 26 May
1480 in various sums, as in the same bill   £8 18s 11d

Money delivered to the hand of the lord by Henry Walter, the
farmer of Thornsdale, as part of this year's rent   8s 0d

Sum   £9 6s 11d

Sum of all the aforesaid payments £9 18s 11d, and he owes £9 13s 11d; of which
allowed to the accountant 2s 6d for the rent of the heirs of Thomas Fowle for the
land called 'Bordens', the rent of which by the rental is 4s 1d, but he holds the
land <by the demise of John Bokelond> for 1s 7d a year at the lord's pleasure, as
in the court held at Mote on 20 January 1478; and allowed him 4s 0d for the rent
of the land of William Belknap called 'Pyperslond' in Beckley, because it
cannot be levied; and 6d for Lord Dacre's rent for land called 'Wallond' in Iden,
for the same reason; and 2¼d for the rent of Thomas Fyssh' <for land called
'Crabbe'; sum of these allowances 7s 2¼d; and he owes £9 6s 8¾d>

Respited to him: 8s 0d for four years' arrears of the rent of John Waterman in Hollington; 12s 0d for four years' arrears of the rent of Henry Holstok for land called 'Millersfeld' and 'Ferthyng'; 1s 6d for the rent of Thomas Pers in arrears in the time of John German; 8d for the rent of the heirs of Richard Parrok for this year and last; 15s 10d for five years' arrears of the rent of Thomas Oxenbrygge esquire, as in the last account; 10d for the rent of William Strode for land called 'Ludwyns' in Northiam in arrears this year, because distraint cannot be taken there; sum of these respites £1 18s 10d; and he owes £7 7s 10¾d, of which:

John Marener, the last collector and accountant there   £6 9s 8¾d
The accountant   18s 2d

Mote manor: the charge of Henry Turnour, servant of John Scotte, knight, from 29 September 1480 to 29 September 1481   [ESRO NOR 15/119]

Arrears
He is charged with £9 8s 3¼d arrears from the last account of the
previous year, as appears at its foot   £9 8s 3¼d

Fixed rents
Nothing, because it is charged in the account of William Sharp,
collector thereof this year, nor of the farm of 'Peryfeld', without
the farm of the lord's land at Saltcote this year, not received
because in the account of the said William Sharp

Sales of stock
Received the price of six oxen, sold to Edward Brownyng of Snave	£6
Received from the said Edward Brownyng for four northern oxen	£3
Sum	£9

Issues of the manor
Received for 100 sheaves of reed sold to William \<Crowch\>[130] this year	2s 4d
Rushes sold to various people	9s 5½d
Richard Crowche for one acre of pasture there this year	2s 6d
Thomas Profette for a parcel of pasture sold to him this year	3s 0d
John Flegger for a parcel of pasture this year	3s 6d
Voller of Peasmarsh for rent	4s 7½d[131]
Sum	£1 5s 5d

Sales of wood, with 'billet' and firewood
Received from John Bawdwyn of Rye for 20,500 billets	£2 7s 10d
John Ussant for 2500 billets	5s 10d
Henry Swanne of Rye for 2000 billets	4s 8d
Richard Swanne for 6000 billets	14s 0d
Robert a Crowch for 2500 billets	5s 10d
Thomas Barbour for 6000 billets	14s 0d
William Twik for 1000 billets	2s 4d
The vicar of Rye for 1000 billets	2s 4d
John Thomas for 1000 billets	2s 4d
Margaret Maye for 500 billets	1s 2d
William Taylour for 500 billets	1s 2d
William Sharp for a parcel of wood	3s 4d

---

[130] Replacing *Crowforth*, deleted.
[131] The entry is deleted and reinstated, with consequent adjustments to the sum.

John Hobbe of Rye for a parcel of wood	10s 0d
John a Weke for a parcel of wood	15s 0d
Bocherst for a parcel of wood	£1 5s 0d
John Dunkerkoye, brewer, for a parcel of wood	£2 13s 0d
Robert a Crowche for 2500 billets	5s 10d
John Bawdewyn for 500 billets	1s 2d
William Parnell for a parcel of wood	2s 0d
Henry Eston for 2000 faggots	8s 0d
John Adam for 2000 faggots	8s 0d
John Godwyn for one parcel of brushwood	1s 10d
Thomas Hach for 200 faggots	10d
John Flegger for 1000 faggots	3s 4d
Godegrome for faggots	1s 8d
Three thousand billets sold at Float	9s 0d
Thomas Geffe for 2500 old billets from last year	5s 4d
Sum	£12 14s 10d

Tolls
Tolls of the mill this year nothing, because it is occupied by the lord

From William Hamme for his board for 19 weeks	19s 0d

Foreign receipts

Received from the lady on various occasions by her own hands	£9
Received from her by the hands of Richard Bayly	£2
Received from the lord by the hands of Giles Love	£2
Sum	£13

The price of 13 hides of oxen, cows and bullocks sold to James Norley	19s 6d
The price of 12 calf-hides sold to James Norley this year	3s 0d
Sum	£1 2s 6d

<Note that Eme ought to be charged with the skins of sheep and lambs>

Sum total of the charge	£47 10s 0¼d

EXPENSES

Of which, paid to the parish clerk of Iden for his wages for half a year to 29 September 1481	3s 4d
The vicar of Peasmarsh for tithes	5s 0d
To [the bailiff of] the Rape of Hastings for blanch farm and sheriff's fine	5d
Sum	8s 9d

[*Stipends*]

Paid Ingyll, the carpenter, in part-payment of his wages for last year	10s 0d
Edward, the carpenter of Beckley, for hewing a load of timber	1s 4d
Stephen Cowper for making 11 staffs for 'le billes'	3s 4d
Stephen Ase for mowing 2000 [sheaves of] reed	10s 0d
[Richard] Sherfold for <paying>[132] the people who made the walls at Float	£1 6s 8d
James Waller for cutting of 'le creke' at Float	8s 0d
James Waller for remaking a slumped wall in 'le creke'	6s 0d
[James] Warner for making two 'pynnokkes' [culverts]	10d
James Warner and [Richard] Sherfold for digging and underpinning 'le pynnok'	4d
Ingyll the carpenter in full payment of his wages for last year <that is to say on 25 December 1480>	£1
Stephen Sampson in full payment for 'le marlyng' of Kerisland	10s 0d
Stephen Sampson for <spreading>[133] of muck (*crote*) there	2s 8d
William Hamme for 'le redyng' [clearing] of 9¾ acres and four dayworks	£3 4s 4d
Richard Bayly of Peasmarsh for 15,000 billets	£2
Paid Simon <labourer at Mote> in part-payment of his wages	1s 8d
William Nowell <thatcher (*culminator*)> for part-payment of wages	1s 0d
Sum	£10 6s 2d

Mowing hay with other necessities

Paid John Morlen and Lollam for mowing 30 acres of meadow	16s 3d
For four mowers	11d
Wages of eight men in harvest	2s 8d
Wages of three women by the day in harvest	9d
John a Weke for the carriage of hay and timber for four days	3s 4d
Paid <Thomas at> Hach for the carriage of timber for one day	10d
John West, labouring and threshing for seven days	1s 9d
Henry <Lennard> for threshing	6d
John <West> labouring <and threshing wheat> for two days	6d
Richard Mayne for <labouring one day in> making of a 'stakke' <of hay>	3d
Robert Lombard for a plough-share	1s 4d
Robert Smyth, sharpening and repairing the plough irons and other household necessaries	2s 4d
John Smalwod for the sheriff's tourn for three terms	1s 0d

---

[132] Replacing *making*, deleted.
[133] Replacing *le shoeryng*, deleted.

Making a doublet and gown for Anthony Sellyng	1s 2d
Sum	£1 13s 7d

Purchase of wheat and lambs

Paid George Corner for six lambs	6s 0d
Elizabeth Helier for 3½ quarters of wheat	£1 3s 4d
Sum	£1 9s 4d

Costs of making 'billett', with their carriage

Paid various people for making 365,000 billets sold to Rye and remaining in the wood for lack of carriage <as appears by bill>	£9 2s 6d
For the carriage of <100,500>[134] billets from the lord's woods, of which 52,000 to Float and to Rye 43,500	<£3 7s 0d>[135]
Sum	£12 6s 2d

Payments to the lady

Money paid to the lady for the same money by her received from the value of the six oxen sold above	£6
Money paid to the lady by the hand of John Baudwyn for 20,500 billets, whereof the accountant is charged	£2 6s 8d
Money paid to the lady by the hand of Thomas Barbour <for 6000 billets>	14s 0d
Sum	£9 0s 8d

Sum total of allowances £35 8s 0d

And he owes <£12 2s 0¼d>[136], of which he is allowed 5s 0d for firewood sold to John Eston; 5s 4d for firewood sold to Stephen Ynkepenne because it was pardoned by the lord; and so he owes	<£11 11s 8¼d>[137]
Thomas at Wode for oxen sold to him	13s 4d

The accountant of his arrears this year <£10 18s 4¼d which arrearages is assigned to Sir John Scotte>[138]

<And upon Richard Scherfold for 700 old billets, and 4200 billets lost at Float for lack of guarding>

[Stock account]

Wheat

He answers for the remains of the last account nothing; of the produce of this year [*blank*]

---

[134] Replacing *95,500* deleted.
[135] Replacing *£3 3s 8d* deleted.
[136] Replacing *£12 5s 4¼d* deleted.
[137] Replacing *£11 15s 0¼d* deleted.
[138] Replacing *£11 1s 8d* deleted; added in English in the hand of Sir John Scott.

Barley
Of the remains of the last account nothing; but he answers for [*blank*]

Oats
Of the remains nothing; but he answers for [*blank*]

Horses
Three remained

Mares
One mare remained

Foals
Four foals remained

Mote: the account of William Sharp, collector of rents there, from 29 September 1480 to 29 September 1481 [ESRO NOR 15/120]

Arrears
He is charged with the arrears of the last account of the previous
year   £9 6s 8¾d

Fixed rents
The rent of the tenants of Flackley in Peasmarsh, as appears by
the new paper rental   £1 11s 4d
The tenants in the vill of Peasmarsh, as appears by the same rental   £2 0s 7d
The tenants of Beckley   12s 0d
The value of one hen, the rent of John Brown for his messuage
called Horsepen   3d
The rent of the tenants in Northiam, as appears by rental   £2 19s 5¾d
The rent of the lord's tenants in Iden   £3 0s 10½d
Rent in Playden   3s 0d
The rent of Ninfield by the said rental   6d
Rent in Hollington as appears by the same rental   2s 0d
The rent of tenants in Ewhurst, with 2s 0d of the rent of William
Thomsett, besides 10s 7d of the rent of Lord Dacre there, in
arrears for many years   3s 10d
Thomas John for a new rent for land called 'Crowchlond' in
Northiam, lately purchased from the lord by charter   7s 0d
Henry Bayly, for a new rent of a croft or field lately purchased
from the lord by charter   1s 4d

William Wever for part of the tenement of William Blache in Northiam[139]	4d
William Belknap for three acres by 'Pirrifeld' in Peasmarsh	1s 0½d
William Symond for a piece of land in Peasmarsh	3d
Thomas Watyll for 'justesyeld' from his lands called 'Knolle' in Peasmarsh, which were recovered by an examination of the tenants in the court held there on 14 January 1482	4d
Sum	£11 4s 1¾d

[Farms]

John Asshmonton for the farm of land called 'Rysshet' (1½ acres) in Iden	1s 2d
From a meadow called 'Hammede' in Peasmarsh (four acres), late John Flecher <nothing this year because in the lord's hands>[140]	6s 8d
But received by him from Thomas Potyn for the farm of 'Pirrifelde', demised to him this year	6s 8d
Lawrence Bryce for one acre in Peasmarsh	4d
The heirs of Thomas Foule for three parcels of land laying dispersed at Flackley, of which one is called 'Wellefelde'	8d
The same heirs for a parcel of brookland (3½a) of the demesne lands between 'Millond' and 'Hetchislond', adjoining the land of the same heirs	1s 4d
Thomas Profette for one small parcel of land (one rod) called 'Frankfee at Hopishille'	5d
Sum	10s 7d

Perquisites of court

Nothing this year for lack of estreats	
Sum	[blank]

[Sum total of the][141] charge	£21 1s 5½d
[Paid to bailiff of the Rape of Hastings for the lord's] suit of court of the manor of Mote by the hand of William Thompsett	2s 0d
[…]	2s 0d

[Stipend

Paid the stipend of the accountant by reason of his office]	10s 0d

[Liveries of money

…] my said lady	£4 8s 9d
[…] <R Humfrid> … 1 January …	£2 0s 0d

---

[139] Followed by *lately recovered* deleted.

[140] Replacing *thus demised to Thomas Potyn of Wittersham* deleted.

[141] Part of the roll is torn away at this point.

[...] <the lord; note> ... paid to Henry Walter for <four>[142] scots
for   £2 14s 0d
Sum   £9 2s 9d

Sum of all payments   £9 14s 9d

And he owes   £11 6s 8½d
Of which allowed him 1s 4d for amercements imposed upon various of the lord's
tenants because they were pardoned by the lord; 2s 6d for the land called
'Bordons', of which the rent in the rental is 4s 1d, he now holds the land by the
demise of John Bokelonde for 1s 7d during the lord's pleasure, as in a court held
at Mote on 20 January 1478; 4s 0d for the rent of William Belknap called
'Piperslond' in Beckley, because it cannot be levied; 6d for Lord Dacre's rent for
land called 'Wallond' in Iden for the same reason; and he owes £10 18s 4½d.

Respited to him: 10s 0d <8s 0d> for four years' arrears of the rent of John
Waterman in Hollington <before this year>; 9s 0d for three years' arrears of the
rent of Henry Holstok for land called 'Millefeld' and 'Ferthyng' in the time of
John Maryner; 4d for the rent of Thomas Watyll for 'justesyelde' because before
the time of this account he did not know where he could distrain; [4d for the rent
of William Wevere, parcel of the tenement of William Blache in Northiam
deleted]; 1s 0½d for the rent of William Belknap for three acres by 'Pirrifeld';
[1s 2d from John Asshmonton for land called 'Rysshet'; 2s 0d for a parcel of
land within the land of Thomas Foule for the same reason *deleted*]; 3d rent of
William Simon for a piece of land in Peasmarsh for the same reason; 2s 6d rent
of William Belknap for lands late William Oxenbrigge, 'laborer', until William
Belknap can be spoken with; 6d for the rent of 'Raytee' until Reynold Bray can
be spoken with.

Sum of respited £1 1s 7½d; and he owes £9 16s 9d of which:
John Maryner, late collector of rents there, of his arrears   £6 9s 8¾d[143]
Thomas Oxenbrigge of his arrears from the time of John
Germayn and John Maryner, late collectors of rent there   15s 10d
The accountant of his clear arrears of this year   £2 11s 2¼d
Of which:
Paid to Humphrey Egliston 12s 0d; and he still owes £1 19s 2¼d, of which
allowed him 11s 0d paid to the lady in person on 9 February 1482; 13s 0d paid to
the lady last year and not allowed him in the last account, therefore placed here
in the allowances; 1s 6d for the relief of John Osbarn because he showed his
evidences that he ought not to pay relief; 3s 2d for amercements imposed upon
various tenants there in the time of John Maryner, the accountant in 1478-79;

---

[142] Replacing *one* deleted.
[143] Followed by *the accountant of his clear arrears of this year £3 7s 0¼d, consisting of* deleted.

2s 8d for land in Northiam formerly Peter Cherch, charged upon him for this
year and last; and he owes 7s 10¼d
of which, upon [*blank*] Debyll of Hollington for the farm of
James Downe there which lately belonged to John Waterman and
before to William Parker   2s 0d
The accountant for his clear arrears of this year   5s 10¼d

The account of Richard Sherfold of all billets by him received and stallage of the same from Christmas in the 21st year of King Edward the fourth unto the 16th day of May the first year of King Richard the third [25 December 1481 – 16 May 1484][144]   [ESRO NOR 15/121]

First he answereth[145]

First he is charged with 636,500 billets which he hath received at the Float by Henry Turnour within the time of this account

Also he reckoneth for the stallage of 20,000 wood of John Eston by the space of two year	5s 0d
Item for the stallage of Richard Bayliff's by the said space of two year	5s 0d
Item for the stallage of 20,000 of the parson's of Iden by the space of one year	2s 6d
Item for the stallage of 80,000 of Master William Scotte by a year	*[blank]*
Item for the stallage of 24,000 billet for my Mistress Scotte by a year	*[blank]*
Item for the stallage of 30,000 billet for Mistress Ponynges and Mistress Scotte by a year	*[blank]*
Item for the stallage of 4000 billet of John Sutton by a year	6d

Sum of the wood received 636,500 billets

H[enry] Turnour answers:

Whereof delivered to Richard Martham 73,000, price the thousand 2s 8d	£9 14s 8d
Item delivered to Hayne Fissher of Calais 24,000, price the thousand 2s 8d, of the which John Challey had 12,000 and Dame Agnes Scotte received for other 12,000	*[blank]*
Item delivered to William Bondman 17,500 billet which was paid to my master's hands	*[blank]*
Item delivered to Roger Solas in the life of King Edward the fourth 184,000, for the which he paid to my master	*[blank]*

Turnour answers:

Item delivered unto Richard Swan 10,000 billet, and to a man of Hythe 24,000, and to a man of Sandwich 7,000, and to a man of Deal 8,000, price the thousand 2s 8d	£6 10s 8d
Item sold to Margaret Cokkes of Calais 60,000, which she paid to Dame Agnes Scotte	*[blank]*

---

[144] The account is written in English, the phrasing (but not the spelling) of which has been retained.
[145] Followed by *delivered to Richard* deleted.

Tunstall answers:
Item delivered to Sir Richard Tunstall 56,000, price the thousand
2s 4d   £6 10s 8d

Solas answers:
Item delivered to Roger Solas in the month of May the first year
of King Richard [May 1484] 50,000, whereof was 14,000 of
William Scott's wood and 4000 new wood, price the thousand 2s   £5 16s 8d
4d
Item delivered to Johnson of Calais by Richard Sherfold 8000,
price the thousand 2s 8d   £1 1s 4d
Item delivered by the same to John Brigges of Rye 2000, price the
thousand 2s 0d   4s 0d
Item to Piers Batron of Calais 3000, price the thousand 2s 0d, and
to Wisse 500, price 1s 0d   7s 0d
Item sold to Wode of Rye for 600 billet   1s 3d

Turnour answers:
Item[146] sold at sundry times by the said Sherfold <120,000>[147],
price the thousand 2s 0d[148]   £12

Sum total <billet> delivered above 14,000 of William Scotte's
wood and 4000 of new wood   629,600

And so is lost 6400 billet
Also he oweth 700 billet of the old year, price a thousand 2s 4d   1s 7½d
Also there lacked of his last account 4200 billets
Also he is to be charged with the farm of the Float <house and
land> for two years   16s 8d

Sum   18s 3d

Sum total in the charge of Richard Sherfold   £1 11s 3½d

Whereof he asketh to be allowed for bearing (*beryng*) and tailing
(*taylyng*) of 330,000 billet, taking for the thousand 1½d   £2 1s 3d
Also for dyking of 30 rods between Suttons Marsh and mine
upland, for the rod 1d   2s 6d
Item for three locks and keys bought to the house   1s 0d

---

[146] Followed by *he received* deleted.
[147] Replacing *104,000* and *103,000*, both deleted.
[148] Preceded by *2s 8d, 2s 4d* both deleted, and followed by *minus in all 1s 4d* deleted.

Item for making a cove (*cofe*) and a chamber in the cove at the Float	13s 4d
Sum of all allowances	£2 18s 1d
And so he has a surplus	£1 6s 9½d
And for the carriage of wheat from Winchelsea	8d
And for the carriage of salt from the Float to Appledore	1s 0d
[Sum]	£1 8s 5¼d

COURT ROLLS OF THE MANOR OF MOTE, 1442-1551

[ESRO NOR 15/1]

Mote; court held there on Wednesday 4 April 1442

Alan Bryce of Winchelsea admitted in the right of his wife Agnes, daughter and heir of John Bacheler, to six acres at Flackley in Peasmarsh which Agnes inherited on her father's death; the relief is respited to the next court as Agnes is of full age

Default by John Benet of Northiam <2d>, William Oxenbregge <2d>, William Colyn <2d>, Richard Edward <2d>

It is shown by the tenants that Stephen Marchaunt holds three pieces of land called 'Northland' (four acres) by the quitrent of 1s 1d; so distrain him for fealty and relief against the next court.

Joan Kechenhamme comes and offers to make a fine with the lord to respite suit of court until Easter 1443; and the lord, present in court, condones it, because she is blind and unable to see (*absque lumen oculorum suorum*)

William Bate of Northiam came and did fealty to the lord for six acres of land in Northiam, purchased from John Pyerys, lately part of the tenement of John de Gotele

Richard Jamys came and did fealty for a messuage, estimated at a quarter of an acre, which formerly belonged to Peter ate Cherche, purchased from John Pyerys.

John Twysden came and did fealty to the lord for ten acres of land in Northiam purchased from Thomas Wener.

Presented that William Bone and John Bone lately had by the gift and feoffment of William Hope a messuage and four acres of land in Iden to the use of Joan, lately wife of 'the aforesaid William' [Hope] for term of her life, with remainder after her death to Robert Hope, son and heir of William, and his heirs; so distrain William and John Bone for fealty and relief against the next court.

Presented that Richard Cretche of Peasmarsh has purchased a tenement which lately belonged to William Wylmot; so distrain him for fealty and other services against the next court.

Affeerors: Richard Jamys, John Twysden

Mote; court held there on Thursday 5 April 1442

John Parkere of the town of Hastings comes and does fealty to the lord for seven acres of land in High Halton, quitrent 12s 0d, a piece of land (15 acres) called 'The Dewe', quitrent 2s 0d, and a piece of land called 'Smalland' (seven acres), lying within the liberty of Hastings, quitrent [*blank*], purchased from the feoffees of Richard Hunte

Default by William Hall <4d>, John Edward <2d> and William Overay <2d>

It is presented that John Fawkes, dean of Hastings, has purchased 40 acres called 'Groveland', quitrent 5s 0d, from Thomas Norys; the beadle is ordered to distrain John against the next court for fealty and other services

Mote; court held there on Wednesday 7 November 1442

Default by William Toktone <2d>, John ate Broke <2d>, Richard Jamys <2d>, Robert Benet <2d>, William Oxenbregge <2d>, John Chapman <2d> and John Kechenore <2d>

Presented by the tenants that Alan Bryce, in the right of his wife Agnes, holds six acres of land in Peasmarsh, quitrent £1 6s 0d; so distrain him for the quitrent and relief against the next court <again>

At this court we are told that the heirs of John Salerne hold certain lands which used to belong to the master of the hospital of Playden, and they were seized into the lord's hands; and because the beadle has answered nothing to us of the profits, so the tenants are ordered to enquire better against the next court.

Richard atte Crotche comes and does fealty to the lord for a tenement which lately belonged to William Mot.

William Hore comes and does fealty to the lord for four acres of land purchased from the tenement of John Holman by the quitrent of 3d, of which the lord allows to John Holman from his tenement the said 3d

John Parrokke comes and does fealty to the lord for a tenement called 'Vawtes', estimated at four acres

Default by William Tuctone <2d>, John ate Broke <2d>, Richard James <2d>, Robert Benet <2d>, Richard Oxenbregge <2d>

Presented by the tenants that the lord's beadle William Potyn distrained William atte Helle in the lord's fee for arrears of quitrents and services; afterwards came John <Bordere>, bailiff of the Rape of Hastings, and delivered the distraint to the lathe court, and gave him a day to appear at the next court, that is to say [*blank*]; on which the steward wishes to consult until the next court

Presented by the tenants of Iden that Stephen Marchaunt <2d>, Robert Chapman <2d> and John Kechenore <2d> are suitors and have made default

Presented by the tenants of Peasmarsh that William Oxenbregge <2d> is a suitor and has made default

Distrain Thomas Bras and John ate Broke for fealty [and relief *deleted*] for lands purchased from Thomas Vynhawe; distrain John Roser and Richard Foghyll for lands, that is the tenement of Watel, purchased from Thomas Bras and John ate Broke, against the next court

Distrain John Oxenbregge, John Sandere and William Tuctone for fealty for the lands purchased from John Sandere of Northiam, against the next court

Affeered by Richard Cretche, Richard ate Wode

Mote; court held there on Thursday 10 October 1443

Richard Foghyll comes and does fealty to the lord for 100½ acres of land purchased from John Watyll

William Bayly comes and does fealty to the lord for a messuage and an acre of land called 'Rosselys and Lovekenys' which are held of the lord by a quitrent of 7d

The tenants of Northiam present the default of John Holman <2d>, Robert Benet <2d>, Simon Moys <2d> and William Bate <2d>

Distrain John Pyeris <again> for fealty and other services due from the lands formerly John Echene; distrain the abbot of Robertsbridge <again> in his manor of Methersham for 5s 0d quitrent and other services due and accustomed against the next court

The tenants of Iden present the default of John Passhelew <2d> and Robert Chapman <2d>

The tenants of Peasmarsh present the default of Margaret widow of Henry Horne <3d>, Henry Holestok <2d> and Alan Bryce <2d>

Distrain <again> Henry Avanne [to show] how he holds the tenement of 'Covelardys' and what right he has in it

It is presented that Richard Edward died since the last court, after whose death a red steer, worth 5s 0d, was seized as a heriot, concerning which the beadle is ordered to seize better if it can be found; the beadle is ordered to distrain his son and heir John Edward for fealty and relief against the next court

Affeered by John Broke, Richard Fogyll, Richard ate Wode.

Mote; court held there on Wednesday 22 April 1444

The tenants of Iden present the default of Richard ate Wode <2d>, Roger Osebarn <2d> and Robert Chapman <2d>

Ordered to distrain John Edward for the fealty and relief of a toft and a curtilage by the marsh at Brownsmith which are held of the lord by a quitrent of 1s 6d; distrain the tenement of Adam Lodleghe for the quitrent of ½d; distrain

'Carpynysland' for the quitrent of ¼d at Michaelmas; distrain 'la forgeplace' at Brownsmith for the quitrent of [*blank*] against the next court

It is presented that John Edward eloigned (*elongatus est*) a cow which was seized as a heriot after the death of his father Richard Edward, so he is in mercy [*no sum entered*]; also to distrain him to answer to the lord for the trespass against the next court

Ordered as before <again> to distrain John Pyerys for fealty and other services due from the lands which formerly belonged to John Echene; distrain the abbot of Robertsbridge <comes> for 5s 0d quitrent and other services due from his manor of Methersham against the next court

The tenants of Beckley present the default of John Wodelonde <2d>, William Oxenbregge <2d> and Robert Oxynbregge <2d> labourers (*laboreri*)

Ordered <again> to distrain William Oxinbregge for fealty for the lands which he holds of the lord in Beckley

The tenants of Northiam present the default of John Holman <2d>, John Benett <2d>, Robert Benett <2d> and John Holstokke <2d>

The tenants of Peasmarsh present the default of Henry Holstokke <2d> and William Bayly <2d>

Ordered to distrain Richard Skreche for fealty for the lands purchased from William Mot against the next court

Robert Frebody comes and does fealty to the lord for the moiety of a tenement called 'Halstonnestenement' in Northiam, estimated at one acre; ordered to distrain John Frebody for fealty for the other moiety against the next court

Affeered by William Tuctone, William Strode, Richard Foghyll, John Passlew

The Mote; court of John Scott, knight, held there on Friday 30 October 1467

Essoins: none, so proceed to the court

The tenants present that John Cheyny, knight, who held of the lord [*not finished*]

Default of suit of court by William Blounte <2d>, Thomas Oxenbregge <2d>, Walter Robertes <2d>, Katherine Parocke <2d>, Stephen Adam <2d>, Robert Creche <2d>, Thomas at Watyll <2d>, John Nede <2d>, Joan at Hope <2d>, William Lucas <2d>, John Everdyn <2d>, John Myller <2d>, Henry a Forde <2d> and William at Hylle <2d>

[*the whole entry deleted*] The beadle ordered to distrain [Lawrence Schounewater *deleted*] <the tenant of the lands called 'The Fardyngys'> and John Hollestokke against the next court to do fealty to the lord and suit of court and other services withdrawn

The beadle ordered to distrain the tenant of the lands called 'The Fardyngys' and the tenant of the lands called 'Elderton' against the next court to do fealty to the lord and other services withdrawn

John Browne comes and acknowledges that he holds <of the lord> a tenement lying at Horsepen [in Beckley] called [*blank*], paying 5d and a hen, <formerly Robert Goler>

Affeered by Lawrence Bryse and John Oxenbregge

Mote; court held there on Saturday 30 April 1468

Essoins: William Benet by John a Broke

Default of suit of court by Thomas Echingham, kt <+>, William Blunt <2d>, Thomas Oxynbregge <2d>, [William Bayle *deleted*], Robert Creche <2d>, [Lawrence Brice *deleted*], Thomas Watill <2d>, Simon Watill <2d>, John Nedes <2d>, Lawrence Stondwater <2d>, [Thomas Edward <2d> *deleted*, John Brown *deleted*], Joan at Hope <2d>, [John Meyne in the right of his wife *deleted*], John Holstok <2d>, William Lucas <2d>, John Everynden <2d> <and> Henry a Forde <2d>

The beadle ordered to distrain William atte Helle by all his lands to be at the next court to pay the lord a relief and do fealty against the next court

The beadle ordered to distrain the tenant of the lands called 'The Fardinges' and the tenant of the lands called 'Elderton' against the next court to do the lord fealty and other services withheld

William Simon comes to court and does fealty to the lord for the tenements and lands called 'Fesauntes' purchased from William Wendar; and let him have a day until the next court to show the charter

Affeered by John Oxynbregge and John Brown

The tenants present that John Chidcroft holds seven acres of wood called 'Walland', in the old rental called 'Longwallis', which formerly belonged to Lawrence Corvile, and they lie to the lands of John Warner towards the South, to the land of the manor of Mote called 'Walland' by 'Redeford' towards the West, to the lane lying alongside (*per*) the park of Mote towards the North and to the land of Robert Simon towards the East, and owes by year at the four terms of the year 6d

Endorsed [by Sir John Scott]: a rental for the proof of Mr Fynes wood and mine with bounders of the same.

Mote; court held on Saturday 6 May 1480[149]

[Lawrence Brice, Thomas Watell *deleted*], Henry Meteherst, Thomas Sote, [Simon Watell *deleted*], Thomas Potyn with his brother, Thomas Oxenbregge, Richard Holman, William Fissh, Richard James, Richard Godewyn, Thomas Fissh, William Toky, Edward Hore, John Broke, Robert Vanne, John Stille, the tenants of the land late Marchant

Now the court is informed that the son of Thomas Parrok has died, and that John son of the said [John *deleted*] [Thomas], aged seven, is heir; whereupon comes John Pepisden, and shows a charter of 15 April 1469 of lands, messuages etc made to Robert Braborn, John Pepisden, William Toughton and Thomas Toughton to the use of Agnes wife of the said deceased during her life; and [it is ordered *deleted*] to consult with the lord for a heriot

Mote; court held there on 2 May 1481

Essoins: none

There appear at this court Thomas Edward, Thomas Twisden, Richard Holman, William Fissher, <John Broke one> of the feoffees of Richard Bate, Richard James, Richard Godewyn, Thomas Fissher, William Tukton, Edward Hore, William Touke <which William Touke> showed an indented charter of John Scotte, knight, for all services, suits <in court> etc, John Frencham, John a Broke, Lawrence Bryce, Henry Meitehirst, William Dalette, Thomas Profette and Robert Bayliff.

[It appears that Henry *deleted*] Henry Bayliff comes to court and does fealty to the lord for a messuage <let him be distrained for relief> and garden in Flackley [in Peasmarsh].

Distrain [William and R the wife *deleted*] <the land late> John Champ because he does not come to do the lord fealty and pay relief <in land called 'Cropwode' late William Fissher> and William Pertrich for the same cause for the land purchased from John Miller, and William Eston of Rye for 'Houseplace'

Default of suit by William Belknap <2d>, Doctor Brent <2d>, Thomas Oxenbruge <2d>, John Oxenbruge <2d>, Robert de Awne <2d>, Reynold Bray <2d>, Thomas Watell <2d>, Simon Watell <2d>, Thomas Potyn of Wittersham <2d>

Now Henry Bayliff comes and does fealty to the lord for a messuage and garden at Flackley [in Peasmarsh]

The heirs of Thomas Fowle <4d>, the heirs of Robert Creche <4d>, James at Wode <4d>, William [Wode *deleted*] Bennet <4d>, William Lucas <4d>, John

---

[149] This court is entered on NOR 15/12.

Stille <4d>, Ralph Standissh <4d> give fines to the lord to release their suit of court

Sum of this court 3s 10d

Endorsed: let there be a charter by John Scotte, lord of the manor of Mote, to Henry Bayly of Peasmarsh, son of William Bayly of Peasmarsh, concerning a field at Flackley containing three acres <it lies towards the road on the North, to the land of Thomas atte Watyll and the land of Lawrence Bryce East and South, to the land of Lawrence Bryce and the [land *deleted*] <garden> of the said Henry Bayle South and West>

Draft of the grant specified above:

John Scotte, knight, to Henry Bayly of Peasmarsh, son of William Bayly of Peasmarsh, of a croft or> field of his land (three acres) at Flackley (bounds as above), paying 1s 4d to John Scotte as to his manor of Mote, with power of re-entry and distraint for non-payment

River; court held there on 23 April 1482

Essoins: none

John <Sutton> comes and does fealty to the lord <for the lands which he holds of the manor of River> and is admitted tenant

Likewise comes John Osberne and does fealty to the lord <for similar land held in the same way> and is admitted tenant

Likewise comes John Sutton and gives the lord for a fine to have licence to cut 30,000 billets for his hearth <6s 8d>

River; court held there on Monday 11 November 1482

Essoins: none

The tenants there who appear present that John Swotard has alienated his lands <to John Osberne> which he held of the manor of River without the lord's licence <that is to say half an acre of land which is held of the lord in bondage; whereupon comes John Osberne and gives the lord for a fine 6s 8d, and is admitted tenant

John Sutton	<holds 28 acres paying 6s 8d a year>
William Dalette [*deleted*]	<he died and his wife took it>
John Osberne [*deleted*]	<he has alienated to William Parnel>

<Agnes Dalette

William Parnell>

River; court held there on Thursday 15 May 1486

Essoins: [*blank*]

The tenants present the death of William Dalette, who held of the lord as of the manor of River [*blank*] lands in bondage, by which an ox came to the lord as a heriot, of which the lord is possessed; and Agnes Dalette comes and takes the lands from the lord, and is admitted tenant, paying to the lord as anciently accustomed.

They present the death of John Osberne, who held of the lord half an acre of land in bondage, by which a [steer *deleted*] <cow> came to the lord as a heriot

William Parnell came and took from the lord the said half acre which John Osberne lately held in bondage, according to the usage and custom of the manor, paying the lord yearly three grains of pepper; and he gives the lord a fine of 1s 8d to have entry; and is admitted tenant <paid>

Mote; court held there on Monday 14 January 1482

Essoins: none because it is the first court after Michaelmas

Default of suit of court by William Belknap <2d *deleted*>, Thomas Oxenbrigge <2d>, Thomas Twisenden <2d>, William Fissher <2d>, [Henry Holstok <2d>, Richard James <2d> *deleted*], the heirs of Thomas Fissher <2d>, William Partrych <2d>, Edward Hore <2d>, John Frencham <2d>, Reynold Bray <2d> and Doctor Brente <2d>

Richard Bate <4d>, John Stille <4d>, Robert Cretche <4d>, Thomas Foule <4d>, James at Wode <4d> and William Lucas <4d> give fines to the lord to release their suit of court until 29 September 1482

Mote; court held on 22 April 1482

Essoins: [*blank*]

The tenants who appeared present the default of Thomas Twisden <2d>, Richard Holman <2d>, [Thomas Fissher <2d>, Richard James <2d> *deleted*], Richard Godewyn <2d>, William Partrich <2d>, William Tukton <2d>, Edward Hore <2d>, John Oxenbrigge <2d>, William Dalette <2d>, Roger Osberne <2d>, Robert Avan <2d>, [Ralph Standissh <2d> *deleted*] and Austin Potyn <2d>

[Ordered to distrain William Belknap, Thomas Oxbrigge and Reynold Braye to make fealty and pay relief to the lord *deleted*]

Distrain the tenants of the lands of Thomas Oxenbrigge, William Belknap and Reynold Bray to make fealty and pay relief to the lord

Mote; court held there on Monday 11 November 1482

Essoins: none because it is the first court after Michaelmas

The tenants who appeared present the default of [William Belknap <2d> *deleted*], Thomas Oxenbrigge <2d>, Thomas Twisden <2d>, Richard Holman <2d>, Richard Godewyn <2d>, [the heirs of Thomas Fissher <2d> *deleted*], William Partrich <2d>, Edward Hore <2d>, John Oxenbrigge <2d>, Reynold Braye <2d> Doctor Brent <2d> <and [*blank*] Benette <2d>>

Richard Bate <4d>, William Tukton <4d>, John Frencham <4d>, John Stille <4d>, Thomas Foule <4d>, Robert Creche <4d>, William Lucas <4d> and James at Wode <4d> <Doctor Brent <4d>> give fines to the lord to release their suit of court until 29 September 1483

Mote; court held on 3 April 1486

Default of suit of court by [Thomas *deleted*] <Henry> Belknap <2d>, Thomas Oxonbrig, Thomas Twysden <2d>, Richard Holman <2d>, the heirs of Henry Holstoke <2d>, Richard Jamez <2d>, Richard Godewyne <2d>, William Partriche <2d>, Edward Hore <2d>, Lady Elizabeth Elryngton <2d>, Lawrence Bryce <2d>, Richard Hosborne <2d>, Reynold Bray knight <2d> Thomas Wattyll <2d>, the heirs of John Parocke <2d>

The tenants present the death of Henry Medeherst, who held lands called 'Wyblandes'; heriot a pig; so distrain his son and heir John Medeherst for fealty and other services by the next [court]

They say that John a Brooke has died, who held lands called [*blank*]; no heriot, because he showed a charter which excludes the lord; they say that William a Brook is his son and heir, so distrain him for fealty and other services by the next [court]

Ordered to distrain William at Hylle to perform fealty to the lord for the lands late Thomas John by the next [court]

Richard Bate, William Tuckton, John Frencham, the master of the hospital of St Bartholomew, Thomas Foule, the heirs of Robert Creche, William Lucas [and] James at Wood give fines to release suit of court until 29 September 1486

Affeered by John Oxenbregge and Robert a Wane

Mote; court held there in the name of William Scott, esq, Wednesday 21 May 1488[150]

Essoins: none because it is the first court [after Michaelmas]

---

[150] The original enrolment of this court is included in NOR 15/72, from which it was copied into NOR 15/1 in about 1640; the copyist misread *May* as *March*.

The tenants there who appear present that Thomas Tyly owes fealty to the lord for an acre of land at Brownsmith in Beckley, quitrent 4d; whereupon it is ordered [to distrain him]

Next they present the death of Robert Fanne, after whose death fealty and relief became due; whereupon it is ordered [to distrain his heir]

Next they present the death of Thomas Profette, and he died seised, whereupon [it is ordered to distrain his heir]

Next they present that Robert Baisle owes fealty to the lord for all the lands and tenements which he lately had by the gift of Thomas Fowle, for which a relief became due; whereupon it is ordered [to distrain him]

William Broke owes fealty to the lord for all the lands and tenements to which he lately succeeded on the death of his father John Broke, paying 1s 4d quitrent

Next they present the death of Robert Creche, who held by military service a messuage in which he lived and 12 acres of land; his son and heir Richard Creche, aged 25, owes homage and relief, that is to say 2s 6d.[151]

Next that the same Richard [Creche] owes fealty and relief to the lord for all the other lands and tenements to which he lately succeeded on his father's death.

Next they present the death of Henry Meteherst, who held of the lord three acres of land, quitrent 1s 4d; his son and heir John Meteherst owes to the lord fealty and relief of 1s 4d.

Next they present the death of William Bayle, who held of the lord an acre of land, quitrent 6d, on whose death fealty and other services became due to the lord; Thomas Bayle his son and heir owes fealty and relief, so it is ordered [to distrain him]

Next they present that William Partregge owes fealty and relief to the lord for six acres of land lately purchased from John Meller, quitrent 1s 1d; the beadle is ordered to distrain his land <6d> to perform the services; he does not come, so he is in mercy.

Next that John Tuthton owes fealty and relief to the lord for 12 acres of land lately purchased from Edward Horspinde, quitrent 1s 6d, whereupon [it is ordered to distrain him]

Next they present the death of William Thomset, who held of the lord 100 acres of land by military service, after whose death the homage and fealty of his son and heir William Thomset became due to the lord; whereupon the beadle is ordered to distrain by all the lands to the next [court]

Next they present the deaths of Robert Prall, who held three acres of land, John Morefot who held six acres of marsh, Thomas Parok who held 12 acres of land,

---

[151] Altered to *5s 0d* in NOR 15/1.

and Joan Geffe who held three acres of land called 'Kechenfield' by military service, after whose deaths the homages and reliefs of all the lands and tenements became due to the lord from the right and nearest heirs of the tenements; whereupon [is ordered to distrain them]

Richard Holman comes to court and does fealty to the lord and pays relief for a messuage and eight acres of land lately purchased from Richard James and John Lyvet, the feoffees of Lawrence Rysden; and the relief is the whole rent of 3s 10d; he does fealty to the lord and pays relief for four pieces of land with a garden, containing ten acres, lately purchased from Richard James and John Lyvet, the feoffees of Lawrence Risden, of which the relief is 1s 6d.

Thomas Oxenbregge comes to court and gives the lord 4d fine to release suit of court until 29 September 1488, as do Richard Bate, William Tucton, [the lord of Dixter *deleted*], John Frengeham, John Stille, Doctor Brent, Thomas Fowle, the heirs of Robert Creche and James a Wode at 4d each

The tenants who appear present the defaults of Thomas Edward, Thomas Twysden, Henry Holstok, Richard Godewyn, Thomas Fysshe, William Partregge, Edward Hore, the lord of Dixter,[152] John a Brooke, Lawrence Bryce, Henry Meteherst, Robert a Vanne, Reynold Bray, Thomas Profette, Thomas Potyn, Henry Baylyf, Austin Potyn, the heirs of Thomas Parok, [James a Wode *deleted*], each of whom is in mercy.

William Sharpe, beadle there, has strays, the sum of which amounts to 3s 6d; the relict of Sharp ought to be charged with that sum.

Mote; court held there in the name of William Scott, knight, on Monday 4 November 1493[153]

Essoins: none, because it is the first court of this year

To this court comes Joan Profett and does fealty to the lord and pays relief for a tenement and half an acre of land to which she lately succeeded on the death of her husband Thomas Profett

Thomas Cretche does fealty to the lord and pays relief for four acres of land to which he lately succeeded by agreement (*ex assensu*) by the death of his brother Thomas Cretche

The tenants who appear present the death of Richard Jamys, after whose death a heriot and fealty became due to the lord; and the tenants are to enquire whether or not [*unfinished*]

---

[152] Rendered as *Lord Dacre* by NOR 15/1.
[153] The original enrolment of this court is included in NOR 15/4, from which it was copied into NOR 15/1 in about 1640.

The tenants who appear present default by the heirs of Henry Holstok <2d>, Lawrence Brice <2d>, John Oxenbregge <2d>, William Dalet <2d>, Thomas Watille; so they are in mercy

Mote; court held there on Monday 25 November 1493[154]

Essoins: John Meteherst <Simon Watille> by Richard Creche; Richard Usbarn by Henry Crotche

The tenants who appear present default by the heirs of Henry Holstok <2d>, Richard Jamys <2d>, Lawrence Brice <2d>, John Oxenbregge <2d>, William Dalett <2d>, Thomas Watille <2d>; so they are in mercy [the whole entry cancelled]

The tenants who appear present default by the heirs of Henry Holstok <2d>, Richard Jamys <2d>, [Lawrence Brice *deleted*], John Meteherst <2d>, Thomas Watille <2d>, William Aleyn <2d>, Thomas Foulle <2d>; so they are in mercy

To this court comes Thomas Pall and does fealty to the lord and pays relief for a messuage and three acres of land lately purchased [from Thomas Branton and John Corn[er] *deleted*] from the widow of John Parok; and the relief is [*unfinished*]

The tenants present default by the heirs of Henry Holstok, Thomas a Watell, Simon a Watell; so they are in mercy

Mote; court held there on Monday 16th December 1493[155]

Essoins: John Meteherst by Richard Creche; Henry a Croche by Richard Usbarne

Mote; court of William Scott held there on Wednesday 14 May1494

Essoins: [*blank*]

William Parnell does fealty to the lord and pays relief for a messuage and ten acres of land, of which he lately had an estate from Richard Creche; and the relief [and] the rent are 3s 4d

William Parnell pays relief for six acres of land, of which he lately had an estate from Lawrence Bryce; and the relief [and] the rent are 2s 0d

William Parnell pays relief for a messuage with two gardens of three acres of land, of which he lately had an estate from John Wyde, and he from Richard Creche; and the relief [and] the rent are 2s 3d

---

[154] The original enrolment of this court is included in NOR 15/4, from which it was copied into NOR 15/1 in about 1640.

[155] This court is entered on NOR 15/4.

William Parnell [pays relief] for a piece of land called 'Wynderysgrowe', of which he lately had an estate from Lawrence Brice; and the relief [and] the rent are 2d

All the tenants present the death of William Thomsett, who held of the lord a messuage <called Padgham> in which he lived and 100 acres of land adjoining called Padgham by military service; and that his son and heir Thomas Thomset is aged 13 <14> and is seized as a ward

[*margin*] Thomset seized as a ward

The tenants who appear present the defaults of Thomas Oxenbregge esq <2d>, Thomas Tely <2d>, Thomas Twisden <2d>, Richard Holman <2d>, Richard Bate <2d>, William Thogton <2d>, John Thoghton <2d>, John Frengeham <2d>, William Dalate <2d> and the heirs of Thomas Parrok

The beadle is ordered to distrain the land late Henry Holstok, the land late Richard Jamys, the land late Simon Watill, the land late Thomas Foulle and the land late Thomas John to do fealty to the lord, under the penalty of [*blank*] against the next [court]

Mote; court held there on the 15 November 1497

The homage there, sworn, present default by William Tukton <2d>, John Tukton <2d>, William at Hyll <2d>, Agnes Dalet <2d>, John Metteherst <2d>, Thomas Watle <2d> and Richard Creche <2d>

Thomas Twysden <4d>, Richard Holman <4d>, Thomas Frencheham <4d>, the relict of John Stille <4d>, Doctor Brent <4d>, John Frencheham <4d>, William Parnell <4d>, Thomas Parrok <4d>, John Oxenbr' <4d> and Thomas Oxenbrygge <4d> and give the lord fines to release suit of court from 29 September 1497 until 29 September 1498

The homage there, sworn, present that Richard Bate, who held of the lord land called [*blank*], has died seised in demesne as of fee; and they further present that he made a demise of the lands in his name to [*blank*] for a term of years; so there comes to the lord as a heriot an ox valued at 13s 4d, which remains in the custody of Robert Clerk for the lord's stock

John Walter comes and seeks to be admitted to lands called 'Shyreshoth', which formerly belonged to Thomas Potten, Agnes Potten and Richard Potten; he does fealty to the lord and has seisin by the rod

Affeered by Thomas Frencham and Thomas Whyte

Mote; court held there on 19 December 1498

The homage, sworn, present the death of William at Hylle, who held of the lord a messuage with five parcels of land in Northiam; heriot a steer, valued at 10s 0d, which remains for the lord's stock; and as to another piece of land called 'Hellex', containing three acres, no heriot came to the lord because he showed at this court a charter by which the lord ought not to have a heriot; Thomas at Hyll is his next heir and of the full age of 21 years, and he does fealty to the lord and is admitted

John Toughton comes and makes an alienation to William Toughton and Nicholas Toughton of four parcels of land with a garden, containing ten acres, called 'Okworth'; and he [*sic*] is admitted and does fealty to the lord

The homage present the death of Thomas Baylle, who held of the lord a messuage with a garden called 'Hoggettes' in Peasmarsh, and another parcel of land in Peasmarsh called 'Lambys'; no heriot came to the lord because he showed a charter; and furthermore they present that Elizabeth Baylle is his daughter and heir, and is of full age; and she does fealty to the lord, and is admitted

At this court come Thomas Twyseden <4d>, Richard Holman <4d>, Thomas Frencheham <4d>, the relict of John Stille <4d>, Doctor Brent <4d>, John Frencheham <4d>, William Parnell <4d>, Thomas Parrok <4d>, John Oxenbrygge <4d> and Thomas Oxenbr' <4d> and give the lord fines to release suit of court from 29 September 1497 until 29 September 1498

Affeered by Richard Bate and Richard Creche

Mote; court held there on 1 June 1499

Essoins: none

The homage there, sworn, present default of suit of court by the tenants of the land of Edward Belknap <4d>, John Bate <2d>, William Toughton <2d>, Thomas at Hyll <2d>, Thomas Watyll <2d>, John Meteherst <2d>

The court is informed that Joan Broun, daughter and heir of Thomas Pyers, who held of the lord by military service a parcel of land called 'Echynges', has not come to pay relief or do fealty; the beadle is ordered to distrain the tenant of the land against the next [court]

At this court the beadle is ordered to distrain the tenant of the land called 'Wodelondhothes' to do fealty etc

Lawrence Stevyn comes and does fealty to the lord and pays relief for seven acres of land called 'Eldertons'

Thomas Hoore comes and does fealty to the lord and pays relief for 12 acres of land called 'Okford'

Affeered by Nicholas Tughton and Thomas at Hyll

Mote; court held there on 21 October 1499

Essoins: none

At this court come William Parnell <4d>, Doctor Brent <4d>, Thomas Frencham <4d>, Richard Holman <4d>, the heir of John Parrok <4d>, Thomas Twyseden <4d>, John Stylle <4d>, Thomas Oxenbr' <4d> and give the lord fines to release suit of court

The homage there, sworn, present default of suit of court by Thomas at Hyll <2d>, John Walter <2d>, Thomas Potte <2d>, John Metheherst <2d>, Thomas Watyll <2d> and Lawrence Stevyn <2d>

And otherwise they present that all is well

Affeered by Richard Bate <sworn> and Richard Creche <sworn>

Mote; court held there on Monday 21 April 1505

Essoins: none of common suit

The tenants there who appear present the default of Henry Belknap esquire <2d>, John Eldryngton knight <2d>, the tenants of the land of Richard Holman <2d>, the tenants of the land of John Bate <2d>, [Thomas White <car> *deleted*], the tenants of Nicholas Tofton <2d>, [the tenants of the land of Thomas Frencheham *deleted*], John Meteherst <2d>, Thomas Watell <2d>, John Walter <2d>, <the tenant of the land of> Thomas Fowle <2d>

The farmer of Thomas Dygby comes and gives the lord a fine to respite his suit 4d; William Parnell for the same 4d; John Oxynbregge 4d; John Stylle 4d; Doctor Brent 4d

Richard Fray comes and takes by indenture a piece of land containing three acres in Peasmarsh (N: the road; W, S: land of William Parnell), to have and to hold to him and his heirs, paying to William Scott knight a quitrent of 1s 8d, with distraint for non-payment

River; court held there on Monday 21 April 1505

Essoins: none of common suit

The tenants there who appear present default by John Sutton <2d> and William Parnell <2d>; the bailiff ordered to distrain them against the next [court]

Agnes Dalet, relict of William Dalet, comes and shows an indented charter preserving a rent to Sir William Scott, knight, of his manor of River, in these words: grant by William de Godyngge to Robert at Revere of Playden, formerly his villein, of four and a half acres of land with the buildings upon it, in Playden, which Robert inherited; to hold of William, paying every year 2s 1d and two suits of court held at Playden by reasonable summons in the accustomed place, with heriot and relief when they shall happen for all other services, aids and demands, saving the service of the lord king and the earl; warranty by William de Godyngge; 22 August 1329; W: Robert Marchaund of Rye, James Marchaund, John Ambros, Nicholas Paulyn, Thomas Ambroys, Geoffrey Courboyle, Robert Vincent, William de Legh, John de Gleshame, John de Kechenore, John de Oxenbrigge, Geoffrey at Wode, Richard Grove.

Mote; court held there on 23 November 1520

Essoins: [none *deleted*]: Richard Sharfold is essoined by Henry Stylle

Default by Edward Belknap knight, Andrew Windsor knight, the tenants of the land of Thomas Dygby knight, the tenants of the land late Thomas Tylle, the tenants of the land of John a Bate, Thomas Holstok, William Jamys, John Partregge, the tenants of the land of Thomas Frencham, John Dyryk, the tenants of the land of Alexander Dalett, Richard Usbourne, Edward Stephyn, Richard Bokeherst, the heirs of Henry Walter, John Lamport, the relict of Thomas a Weke, Robert Symon, the abbot of Westminster, John Sote, Robert Shepard, Henry Watell, William Symon, Lawrence Gylby, the heirs of Stephen Eston, Thomas Whyte, John Pyper

The heirs of William Hylles come and buy [relief of] suit of this court for one [year] to come; fine 4d paid

Mote; court held there on 13 April 1521

Essoins: none

Richard Sharfold comes and warrants his essoin, as he was essoined at the last court by Richard Stylle

The tenants, sworn, present default by Andrew Windsor knight, the heirs of Thomas Dygby knight, the heirs of Thomas Tylle, the tenants of the land of John Bate, Thomas Holstok, William Jameys, John Partrege, John Metherst <f>, John Dyrryk, Edward Stephyn <infirm>, Alice relict of Thomas a Weke, the abbot of Westminster, John Sote, Henry Watell, William Symon, Lawrence Gylby, the heirs of Stephen Eston, Thomas Whyte, John Pyper; each of them in mercy 2d

They present the death of Henry Stylle, who held of the lord eight acres of land called 'Sedland' in Iden, quitrent 1s 10d, and that he died seised; heriot a steer, valued at [*blank*], which is delivered to the hands of the lord; Thomas Stylle, aged five, is his son and heir; ordered to distrain him by the next [court] for fealty

They present the death of Edward Belknap, knight, who lately held of the lord 24 acres of land at least called 'Pypersland', quitrent 4s 0d; he also held on the day of his death a parcel of land called 'Late William Heghton', quitrent 2s 6d; after whose death the bailiff is ordered to seize his two best animals for heriots, and to distrain Edward's heir or tenant for relief and fealty by the next court

Still distrain Lawrence Gylby to do homage, fealty and other services by the next court

Still distrain John Lamport to do fealty as in the last court

Still distrain the heirs of Thomas Tylle for fealty as in the last court

Mote: court held there on Tuesday 17 September 1527

The tenants say that Edward Beltnap, Andrew Wynsore, the heirs of Thomas Digby, <the tenants of the land of John Batte>, Thomas Holdstok, William Jamys, John Partrigge, the tenants of the land of Thomas Frencham, Alexander Dalet, Richard Usbourne, the tenants of the land of Robert a Van, William Alyn, Henry Walter, Alice widow of Thomas Weke, Richard Sharfold, John Lamporte, the abbot of Westminster, John Soote, John Pyper, the heirs of William Hylles are tenants of this manor and make default; in mercy 2d each

Mote: court held there on Tuesday 29 October 1527

Make search the rolls what kin Herry Cobbe is to Thomas Parrok. Item to make search whether the land of Thomas Parrok came to the same Herry Cobbe by inheritance or by will; and if by will then to know what the will is if ye may.[156]

Essoins: none because the first court of this year

The homage there, sworn, present default by the tenants of the land of Edward Beltenap <2d>, Andrew Wyndsore <2d>, Thomas Tylle <2d>, the tenants of the land of John Bate <2d>, Thomas Holstok <2d>, William Jamys <2d>, John Partrigge <2d>, the tenants of the land of Nicholas Tufton <2d>, the tenants of the land of Thomas Frencheham <2d>, John Meteherst <2d>, Joan Dyryk <2d>, Alexander Dalyat <2d>, Richard Usbourne <2d>, the tenants of the land of Robert a Van <2d>, Henry Walter <2d>, Alice widow of Thomas Wek <2d>, Richard Sharfold <2d>, John Lamport <2d>, the tenants of the land of William Tomesett <2d>, Robert Simon and Joan his wife <2d>, the abbot of Westminster <2d>, John Sotte <2d>, Robert Sheppard <2d>, Henry Watell <2d>, the tenants of the land of Robert Simmond <2d>, Lawrence Gylby <2d>, John Gaston <2d>, Thomas Whyte <2d>, John Piper <2d>, the heirs of William Hyllys <2d>, tenants and suitors of this manor

They present the death of Thomas Holstok, who held of the lord various parcels of land called 'Mylle Fyldes' <and 'Ferdynges'> in Northiam, quitrent 3s 0d; a

---

[156] This entry is written, in English, in the left margin of the roll, against the heading.

heriot became due to the lord; the beadle is ordered to seize the best animal against the next court

Isabel Blechenden comes in the name of the heir of Henry Stelle and gives the lord a fine to release suit of court until 29 September 1528

Mote otherwise Leigh; court held there on Tuesday 9 June 1528

Essoins: [*blank*]

The tenants who appear, namely <Nicholas Toughton, gent>, Lawrence Gylbye, Robert Simon, Thomas Blake, William Symond, Henry Walter, John Meteherst and Robert Rydyall, present the death of Thomas Sharfold, who held of this lordship several parcels called 'Huglates'; heriot a red-gored cow, valued at [*blank*]

They also say that Edward Belknape, Andrew Wynsor, the heirs of Thomas Dygbye and others, as appear in 'le ragman', are tenants and make default, therefore in mercy

William Symond comes in his own name and does fealty to the lord for a piece of land in Peasmarsh, quitrent 3d, which he inherited on the death of his father Robert Simon

Mote; court held there on Thursday 11 September 1539

Essoins: none

Tenants appearing: Thomas Foster, John Dallett, George Fowle, Thomas Tompsett, John Gybbyn, Henry Wattell, Thomas Styll and William Symon, sworn

Who present the names of the tenants who make default as appears by the roll of the next court: Andrew Wynsor knight, Lord Windsor <2d>, William Shelley knight <2d>, Nicholas Deryke <2d>, John Bate <2d>, Richard Broke <2d>, the tenants of the land of Lawrence Ryddall <2d>, William Coke, John Trodys <2d>, John Symon <2d>, Robert Pynde <2d>, Joan Lamporte, widow <2d>, Thomas Holman <2d>, John a Van <2d>, George Syer <2d>, the abbot of Westminster <2d>, John Whyte <2d>, Robert Hollman <2d>, Thomas Partrige <2d>, John Sote <2d>, Henry Sampson <2d>

They further present the death since the last court of Edward Frencheham, who held of the lord in the right of his wife a messuage, garden and 30 acres, quitrent 2s 6d, suit of court, heriot and relief; heriot a cow, valued at 14s 0d, which is seized by the bailiff of the manor

They present that Edward Frencheham also held in the right of his wife three other parcels of land (12 acres), quitrent 1s 4d and the services aforesaid; heriot a mare, valued at 15s 0d, which is seized by the bailiff of the manor

They present the death since the last court of Nicholas Tufton, who held of the lord a tenement called Tufton Place in Northiam containing 100 acres, quitrent 10s 0d, suit of court, heriot and relief; heriot a bullock, valued at 20s 0d, which is seized by the bailiff of the manor

They present that Nicholas Tufton held a messuage and 24 acres called 'Weblonde', quitrent 2s 0d and the services aforesaid; heriot a bullock, valued at £1, which is seized by the bailiff of the manor

They present that Nicholas Tufton held two parcels of land (two acres), formerly Thomas Harle, quitrent 4d and the services aforesaid; heriot a bullock, valued at £1, which is seized by the bailiff of the manor

They present that Nicholas Tufton held seven acres of land called 'Eldertons', quitrent 3s 4d and the services aforesaid; heriot a bullock, valued at £1, which is seized by the bailiff of the manor

They present that Nicholas Tufton held six acres of land called 'Echyn', lying on the denn of Padgham, quitrent 1s 6d and the services aforesaid; heriot a bullock, valued at £1, which is seized by the bailiff of the manor

They present that John Tufton is his son and heir, and owes the lord fealty and relief; the bailiff is ordered to distrain the lands to perform the services against the next court

They present that since the last court Robert Gylby, William Gylby and Thomas Gylby have alienated to Richard Sheperd a messuage and 12 acres, formerly Robert Creche, which are held by the fourth part of a knight's fee and a quitrent of 5s 0d

They present that since the last court Robert Gylby, William Gylby and Thomas Gylby have alienated to Richard Sheperd various parcels of land (eight acres) called 'Cleyton' in Peasmarsh, quitrent 13s 4d

They present that since the last court Anthony Rowse, esquire, has alienated to Thomas Byrchett 3½ acres of land called 'Litle Bawne', quitrent 1s 2d; the bailiff is ordered to distrain Thomas against the next court to perform fealty to the lord

They present that Anthony Rowse, esquire, has alienated to Thomas Foster five acres of land called 'Taylers Lond otherwise Staynes Londe', quitrent 1s 6d; Thomas is given a day at the next court to perform fealty to the lord

They present that since the last court John Dyggeby, esquire, has alienated to Anthony Rowse a parcel of land (30 acres) called 'Hothes', quitrent 3s 2d; the bailiff is ordered to distrain him against the next court to perform fealty to the lord

They present that since the last court John Dyggeby, esquire, has alienated to Anthony Rowse another parcel of land (eight acres) called 'Ludwyns' in Beckley, quitrent 1s 7d

The amercements of this court were affeered by all the tenants who appeared

Mote: court held there 11 October 1541

Tenants appearing: John Symond, John Dalette, Henry Wattell, William Symond, John Mere, sworn

Who present the names of the tenants who make default as appears by the roll of the next court: Andrew Wynsor knight, Lord Windsor, William Shelley knight, Nicholas Deryke, Richard Broke, John Bate, William Coke, the tenants of the land of Lawrence Ryddall, John Trodes, Robert Pende, Joan Lamporte, widow, Thomas Byrchett, Edward Francheham, John Tufton, gent, Thomas Foster, gent, George Fowle, Thomas Tompsett, John Gybbyn, Thomas Stylle, Thomas Holman, John a Van, George Syer, the abbot of Westminster, John Whyte, Robert Hollman, Thomas Partrigge and Richard Sheperd

They present that John Sote, who held a toft of wood containing one acre and more, quitrent 6d, has died since the last court; ordered to seize a heriot; John Sote the younger is his son and heir, aged 11, and in the custody of his mother Magdalen Sote, who comes and requests a day to show her charters to discharge the heriot, which is given to the next court

The amercements of this court were affeered by all the tenants who appeared

Sum of this court [*blank*]

Mote: court held there on Thursday 28 January 1542

Tenants appearing: Thomas Foster, Nicholas Deryke, sworn

Who present that Andrew Wynsor knight, Lord Windsor, William Shelley knight, Richard a Broke, the tenants of the land of Lawrence Ryddall, John Bate, William Coke, John Trodes, Robert Pende, Joan Lamporte, widow, John Symon, John Dalett, Henry Wattell, Thomas Pertregge, William Symon, George Fowle, Thomas Tompset, John Gybben, Thomas Stylle, Thomas Holman, John a Vanne, George Syer, the abbot of Westminster, John Whyte, Robert Holman and John Holman are tenants of this manor and have made default

A further day is given to Magdalen Sote to the next court

The amercements of this court were affeered by all the tenants who appeared

Sum of this court [*blank*]

Mote: court held there on 5 April 1543 [*recte* 1542?]

Tenants appearing: John Dalett, Henry Wattell, William Symon, Nicholas Deryke, Thomas Stylle, sworn

Who present that Andrew Wynsor knight, Lord Windsor, William Shelley knight, Richard a Broke, Thomas Foster, the heirs of Lawrence Ryddall, John Bate, William Coke, John Trodys, Robert Pende in the right of his wife, Joan Lamporte, widow, Thomas Byrchett, Edward Francheham, John Tufton, George Fowle, Thomas Tompsett, John Gybben, Thomas Holman, George Syer, the abbot of Westminster, John Whyte, Robert Holman, Thomas Pertregge, Robert Sheperd, John Symon, John Sheperd and James Sheperd are tenants of this manor and have made default

And otherwise they say that all is well

The amercements of this court were affeered by all the tenants who appeared

Sum of this court [*blank*]

Mote: court held there on Thursday 18 January 1543

Tenants appearing: Thomas Foster, gent, John Dalett, John Shepperd, William Symon, Thomas Croche, sworn

Who present that Andrew Wynsor knight, Lord Windsor, William Shelley knight, Richard Broke, the heirs of Lawrence Ryddall, John Bate, William Coke, John Trodys, Robert Pende in the right of his wife, Joan Lamporte, widow, Thomas Byrchett, Edward Francheham, John Tufton, gent, George Fowle, Thomas Tompsett, John Gybben, Thomas Holman, George Syer, the abbot of Westminster, John Whyte, Robert Holman, Thomas Pertregge, Nicholas Deryke, Henry Wattell and Thomas Stylle are tenants of this manor and have made default

John Sheppard does fealty to the lord for a tenement and adjoining lands (10 acres), late his father William Sheppard (N: road from Rye to London; E: a lane leading from the same road to 'Brodefeld'; S: land of William Symon; W: land of William Symon late Wynders), quitrent 2s 4d, heriot, relief and suit of court; the bailiff ordered to distrain for relief

John Sote, son of John Sote of Playden, deceased, comes and shows his father's will by which he has a toft of wood in Peasmarsh to him and his heirs in tail, and for lack of such issue to his brother John Sote, quitrent [*blank*]

John Sote holds another piece of land (two acres) called 'The Dewe', quitrent [*blank*]

Thomas a Croche acknowledges tenure of this manor of nine acres of land called 'Coteham', which he lately bought from Thomas a Van, quitrent 8s 6d and suit of court, and does fealty

They present that Richard Sheperd, who held a messuage and 12 acres, quitrent 5s 0d, by the service of a fortieth part of a knight's fee, has died since the last court; heriot a grey gelding, seized by the bailiff, valued at [*blank*]

Richard Sheperd held land called 'Clayton' (54 acres in various parcels; N: the road from Goldspur to Peasmarsh church; E: the lane leading to 'Essynham'; S: land of the manor of Marley; W: land of the tenement of 'Grove')

Richard Sheperd held land called 'Lynden' (seven acres; S: road from Goldspur to Peasmarsh church; W: land of the tenement of 'Elderton'; N: land called 'Fowleden'; E: land called 'Le Hoth' held of the manor of Leigh), quitrent 13s 4d; heriot a black ox, seized by the bailiff

Richard Sheperd held land called 'Brodelond' (10 acres; SE: road; W: land of John Tufton, esquire, late the heirs of Robert Creche, called 'Gowges'; S: lane from the road to 'Usshingford')

Richard Sheperd held two parcels of wood (2½ acres) called 'Urent' (S, E: land called 'Highlond'; W: land of William Symon, formerly William Baile), quitrent 1s 10d, suit of court and heriot, namely a black-gored ox, which is seized by the bailiff

Richard Sheperd died seised, and that his heir is his son Robert Sheperd, aged 20

Sum total [*blank*]

Mote: court held there 5 July 1543

Tenants appearing: Thomas Foster, gent, John Dallett, Nicholas Deryke, Thomas Pertregge, Robert Shepperd, sworn

Who present that William Shelley knight, John Bate, Richard a Broke, William Coke, John Trodys, John Symon, Robert Pende, William Lamporte, Thomas Holman, Thomas Croche, John Whyte, Robert Holman, Henry Sampson, George Fowle, Thomas Tomset, John Gybben, Henry Wattell, Thomas Stylle, William Symon, Edward Francheham, John Tufton, gent, Thomas Byrchett, John Sheperd and the tenants of the lands of Lawrence Ryddall, are tenants of this manor and have made default

They present the death since the last court of Andrew Wynsour, Lord Windsor, who held a parcel of land called 'Hothes' (30 acres) in Beckley, quitrent 3s 2d, suit of court, heriot and relief

He also held a parcel of land called 'Ludwyns' (eight acres) in Beckley, quitrent 1s 7d, suit of court, heriot and relief

He also held a parcel of land called 'Hightberyam' (25 acres) in Northiam, quitrent 5s 0d, suit of court, heriot and relief

The bailiff is ordered to seize heriots for the lord; William Wynsor is his son and heir, and of full age, and the bailiff is ordered to distrain him by those lands for relief, and to perform fealty, and for other services due to the lord, against the next court

They present the death since the last court of George Syer, who held a messuage called Horsepen (two acres) in Beckley, quitrent 5d and a hen at Christmas, and suit of court twice a year, as appears by the rental; the bailiff has seized a bay horse for a heriot; Thomas Syer is his son and heir, and of full age; the bailiff should distrain him by those lands for relief, and to perform fealty, and for other services due to the lord, against the next court

Sum total of this court [*blank*]

Mote: court held there on Thursday 5 October 1543

Tenants appearing: John Symon, Henry Wattell, William Symon, John Dallett, Nicholas Deryke, Thomas Croche, sworn

Who present that William Wynsour, knight, Lord Windsor, William Shelley, knight, William Coke, John Trodys, Robert Pynde, Joan Lamporte, widow, Richard a Broke, the tenants of the lands of Lawrence Ryddall, Thomas Holman, John Avanne, Thomas Syer, the abbot of Westminster, John Whyte, Robert Holman, John Sote, Henry Sampson, John Tufton, gent, and George Fowle are tenants of this manor and have made default

They present the death since the last court of Thomas Foster, who held five acres of land called 'Taylours Lande otherwise Staynes Lond' in Iden, quitrent 1s 6d; his sons and heirs are John Foster and Edward Foster, both under eight years old, as appears by a charter shown here in court, by which no heriot is due

Thomas Foster also held lands called 'Goldyng', and three and a half acres of land called 'Vauteslond' in Iden, quitrent 3s 2d, heriot, relief, fealty and suit of court, and that John and Edward are his heirs by charter as above

Thomas Foster also held a piece of land (two acres) late John Marchaunt where there was a dovehouse, and it is called 'Le Wysshe', quitrent 6½d, relief and suit of court once a year; his son and heir is Goddard Foster, who does fealty to the lord here in court and pays the relief, namely half the rent, 3¼d

Goddard Foster comes and shows a charter made by Thomas Foster to a certain Thomas Alman of all his lands and tenements which he lately purchased from Anthony Rowse, esquire, and from Thomas Blake, dated 3 December 1543, discharging the heriot due to the lord for the said lands

Mote: court held there on Thursday 31 January 1544

Tenants appearing: Henry Wattell, John Dallett, Thomas Pertregge, sworn

Who present that William Wynsor, knight, Lord Windsor, William Shelley, knight, Nicholas Deryke, Richard a Broke, John a Bate, William Coke, Thomas Byrchett, Edward Francheham, John Tufton, esquire, John Symon, John Whyte, John Trodes, the tenants of the lands of William Ryddall, Robert Pende, Robert

Sheperde, gent, Joan Lamporte, widow, William Symon, Goddard Foster, Robert Holman, John Mere, George Fowle, Thomas Tompsett, John Gybbon, Thomas Style, Thomas Holman, John a Vanne and George Syer are tenants of this manor and have made default

And further that all is well

Sum of this court [*blank*]

Mote: court held there on Thursday 26 June 1544

Tenants appearing: John Dalett, Thomas Pertrege, Henry Wattell, Nicholas Deryke, Thomas Croche, sworn

Who present that William Wynsor, knight, Lord Windsor, William Shelley, knight, John Tufton, esquire, Robert Sheperde, gent, Nicholas Deryke, Richard a Broke, John a Bate, William Coke, the tenants of the lands of William Ryddall, John Trodys, Robert Pende, William Lamporte, Thomas Byrchett, Edward Francheham, John Symon, William Symon, Goddard Foster, Robert Holman, John Mere, George Fowle, Thomas Tompsett, John Gybbon, Thomas Style, Thomas Holman in the right of his wife, John a Vanne, the heirs of George Syer, the bishop of Westminster and John Whyte are tenants of this manor and have made default

The tenants who appeared were charged to enquire <against the next court> who holds a garden with a building upon it which Thomas Fletcher holds of him [the lord] in demesne (W: the road from Iden Cross to Rye; N: the lands of the lord of The Mote; E, S: the lands of Katherine Perroke)

Mote: court held there on Thursday 6 November 1544

Tenants appearing: John Symon, Goddard Foster, William Symon, Henry Wattell, sworn

Who present that William Wynsor, knight, Lord Windsor, William Shelley, knight, John Tufton, esquire, Robert Sheperde, Thomas Byrchett, Nicholas Deryke, Richard a Broke, John a Bate, William Coke, the tenants of the lands of William Ryddall, John Trode, Robert Pende, William Lamporte, Edward Francheham, John Mere, Robert Holman, George Fowle, Thomas Tompsett, John Gybbon, Thomas Style, Thomas Holman in the right of his wife, John a Vanne, the heirs of George Syer, the bishop of Westminster, John Whyte, John Dallett, Thomas Pertregge and Thomas Croche are tenants of this manor and have made default

They present that since the last court John a Bate, who held certain lands, has alienated them to Thomas Baker

Mote: court held on 29 January 1545

Tenants appearing: John Symon, John Dalett, Nicholas Deryke, sworn

Who present that William Wynsor, knight, Lord Windsor, William Shelle, knight, Thomas Baker, William Coke, the tenants of the lands of William Ryddall, John Trodes, Robert Pende, Thomas Pertregge, Robert Sheperd, John Holman, John Sote, Lord Dacre, William Lamporte, Thomas Byrchette, Edward Francheham, John Tufton, esquire, Henry Wattell, William Symon, Goddard Foster, Robert Holman, James Sheperd, John Walter, Thomas Croche, George Fowle, Thomas Tompsett, John Gybbon, Thomas Stylle, Thomas Holman, Thomas Syer, the bishop of Westminster, John Whyte, Henry Sampson, John Sheperd, James Sutton, John a Broke and [*blank*] Usborne are tenants of this manor and have made default

Mote: court held on 10 April 1545

Tenants appearing: Goddard Foster, Henry Watyle, John Dalett, Nicholas Deryke, sworn

Who present that William Wynsor, knight, Lord Windsor, William Shelley, knight, Thomas Baker, William Coke, the tenants of the lands of William Ryddall, John Trodes, Robert Pende, Thomas Pertregge, Robert Sheperd, John Holman, John Sote, Lord Dacre, William Lamper, Thomas Byrchett, Edward Francheham, John Tufton, esquire, William Symon, Robert Holman, James Sheperd, John Walter, Thomas Croche, George Fowle, Thomas Tomsett, John Gybbon, Thomas Stylle, Thomas Holman, [*blank*] Syer, the bishop of Westminster, John Whyte, Henry Sampson, John Sheperd, James Sutton, John a Broke and [*blank*] Usborne are tenants of this manor and have made default

Mote: court held there on 11 October 1550

Tenants appearing: Robert Shepperd, Goddard Foster, Henry Wattell, Thomas Crouche, John Shepperd and Thomas Stylle, sworn

Who present that John Bate has alienated 26 acres in Northiam, with a barn built upon it, to William Lawles of Rolvenden, who has alienated to Thomas Baker and William Baker, but in what way they know not; and 21 acres lie in Northiam and are held by a quitrent of 4s 0d, and the rest pay 6d

They present the death of John Gybbon of Rye, who held 12 acres called 'Myllerdfeld' in Northiam; the heir is his son Thomas Gybbon; heriot a 'brandyd' ox, delivered to the lord's hands; the relief of 3s 0d is not yet paid

They present the death of Helen Strowde, daughter and heir of Thomas Hylles, seised of lands in Northiam, quitrent 7s 0d; the heir is her son Nicholas Edwards, but it in doubtful whether a heriot be due because her last husband John Strowde survived her, and held the land by the courtesy of England; but because John Strowde is dead, let an arbitrator of the payment of heriot be sought, and the relief which is due has not been paid, although the same Edwards has promised to pay it

They present the default of Lord Windsor, Lord Dacre, John Shelley esquire, John Tufton gent, James Sutton gent, Thomas Byrchett, John a Brooke, William Coke otherwise William a Lye, Robert Pynde, Edward Frencham, John Symon, Robert Hollman and Henry Clarke; each of them in mercy 2d

John Sampson of Peasmarsh came and did fealty for three acres in Peasmarsh called 'Wybblondes'; he has not paid the relief, but it is doubted whether a heriot be due for the same reason as above <he was not tenant by the courtesy of England so no heriot>

Richard Sere came and was admitted to lands called Horsepen in Beckley, which he claims by the last will of his father; because Richard was one of the executors and did not produce the testament, let it be respited to the next court and then to enquire about heriot and relief; the which relief Richard is to pay, but Robert Shepperd is not persuaded (*dissuadabatur*), because he is of the opinion that none should pay relief but he who claims as heir

John Walter of Iden came and did fealty for lands in Iden called 'Le Rysshet otherwise Moreland', and he paid a penny relief, but the heriot is respited to the next court, because Joan Wygsell otherwise Joan Walter, widow, says that she wishes to show a charter of discharge

John Hollman of Northiam came and did fealty for lands in Northiam called [*blank*], quitrent 1s 1d, part of 'Partrygestenement', which he purchased from his father Thomas Hollman

The court is informed that a heriot was seized after the death of William Lampourt for lands in Northiam called 'Bennettes', and that his widow, now wife of Thomas Cheseman, undertook to be responsible for the heriot but has not yet delivered it, so let the heriot be enquired into at the next court, and how Thomas Cheseman holds them, whether in the right of his wife or in the right of William Lamport's heirs, who are still in his custody

John Shepperd of Peasmarsh came and did fealty for lands in Peasmarsh called 'Howlandes otherwise Hotchemans Tenement', but he did not offer relief, and as for the heriot it is presented that John's brother, whose heir he is, had no animal on the day of his death, nor any before; a day is given to John to show the charter of discharge of other lands at Flackley for which he should previously have paid relief

Distrain Thomas Baker and William Baker peremptorily upon the lands in Northiam which they purchased from William Lawles, because they attempted to defraud the lord of the service of the said land, and neither of them has performed suit of court, and William Baker in the face of the court refuses to perform service, and alleges on behalf of his father Thomas Baker that he cannot undertake any journey on account of his age, and that he is so infirm that he cannot make suit and cannot be admitted to make fine as he ought in such a case, in contempt of the court

Edmund Mores came and showed a charter sealed by Edmund Passhelewe, knight, of the land formerly Nicholas Dyryck in Iden called 'Cottenham', by which it appears that the rent is 7s 0d for all service, custom and demand; and he shows another charter for five acres in Iden lying by the land called 'Le Breachez', rent 8d for all service and demand, sealed by Thomas Passhelewe; but concerning the last charter, because it appears by the old rental that there was a certain Thomas Passhelewe who was a tenant of this manor, and not lord of the manor, therefore it is to be doubted whether it be a discharge of the heriot for the lands specified within it, so consult with the lord's counsel

Still distrain William White for fealty as in other rolls; still distrain Robert Pynde for fealty upon land called 'Lovelles'; still distrain John Hollman of Barham as in other court rolls; still distrain John Gibbon for fealty; still distrain the heir of John Sotte for fealty <by the will of his father bearing date 20 May 1541 by which he cannot claim it nor any of his brothers>; still distrain Thomas Partrygge for fealty; still distrain Thomas Byrchett for fealty; still distrain Henry Clarck for fealty; still distrain the heir of [*blank*] Ryddysdale for fealty <some hold the opinion that they cannot be amerced once they have appeared on one occasion and been found to be suitors, because the remedy is solely to distrain>;[157] <none are affeered because they deny that they ought to be amerced>

Mote: court held there on 4 June 1551

Tenants appearing: Goddard Foster, Robert Hollman, William Cocke, John Sampson, Henry Watlye, Thomas Stylde, John Dallett, Nicholas Edwardes, Robert Shepperd

Thomas Gybbon came and did fealty for lands which belonged to his father John Gybbon and his mother Margaret Gybbon, namely for two parts of the land which John Gybbon purchased from Agnes and Joan, the daughters of Hugh Hulstock, and for the third part as son and heir of Hugh's other daughter Margaret; and he pays a relief of 3s 0d, the amount of the yearly rent

John Sampson came and paid a relief of 1s 4d, the amount of the yearly rent, for the lands in Peasmarsh called 'Wybblondes'

Joan Wyggsell, lately wife of Thomas Foster, came and did fealty for lands in Iden assigned to her for the term of her life by Thomas Foster's will; and she has a day at the next court to show the will, and the manner in which the lands are assigned after [her death]; and regarding the heriot and the relief of Goddard Foster, she asserts that she has agreed with the lord

---

[157] This passage is written in French.

It was presented that John Shelley, esq, has died since the last court, so let there be an enquiry at the next court what came to the lord by his death

The tenants say that the tenants of the land of Lord Dacre, Lord Windsor, James Sutton, the tenants of the land of John Shelley, Anthony Pelham, John Tuffton, Edward Frencheham, the tenants of the land of William Lamport, Thomas Baker, Robert Pynde, John Hollan of Barham, John Shepperd, John Walter, Harry Symon, John Symon, Thomas Crowche, Thomas Partrygge, Thomas Byrchett, Harry Clarck, the tenants of the land of George Seer, John a Brooke, the heirs of [blank] Rydsdale, are suitors of this court and have made default

A day is given to Thomas Cheseman to show the charter for the discharge of the heriot and relief which were claimed after the death of William Lamport, and to show his last will

A day is similarly given to Nicholas Edwardes for the lands in Northiam formerly Hylles

A day is similarly given to William Whyte, but regarding the relief he does not believe he ought to pay it, because he claims by the last will of his father, and he was the younger son

A day is given to John Shepperd to pay relief

Distrain the heirs or the tenants of the lands of Nicholas Dyryck for relief; and regarding the heriots, he has shown a deed of discharge for one, as appears in another court [11 October 1550], and regarding the second deed it is still doubted

<Distrain Richard Seer for his relief and heriot which are owed>

Mote: court held there on 25 June 1551

Tenants appearing: Goddard Foster, John Dallett, Nicholas Edwardes, Robert Pynde, Thomas Partrygge, Thomas Cheseman

At this court Goddard Foster showed the last will of his father Thomas Foster, by which it appears that Thomas assigned these lands by the following words:[158] 'I will that immediately after my decease that Joan my wife shall have all my messuage with all the lands belonging to it which I late purchased of Thomas Blake, and also two pieces of land late purchased of Anthony Rous, esquire, lying and adjoining to the same land late purchased of Thomas Blake, the which lands are holden of the manor of Mote, except only one parcel containing by estimation two acres'; and also other lands by these words: 'and also two pieces of land called "The Robbertes" lying together which I late purchased of Anthony Rous, esquire, during her life without impeachment of waste, trusting that she will see the keeping of John and Edward; and after the decease of Joan my wife I will that all my messuages and lands with the appurtenances late purchased of Thomas

---

[158] The will is recited in English.

Black, and also the four pieces of land which I late purchased of Anthony Rous, esquire, with their appurtenances, shall remain to John and Edward my sons and to their heirs'; and for the lands held of this manor Joan did fealty at the last court, as appears by the court rolls.

Nicholas Edwardes came and showed an indented charter of 10 November 1532 by which it appears that John Trowdez and his wife Helen gave to Richard Sharpp, John Hollman, George Syer and Robert Tyler and to the heirs of Richard Sharpp two messuages, four gardens, 30 acres of land, six acres of meadow, 30 acres of pasture, 30 acres of wood, 12 acres of heath [and] 23 acres of marsh to the use of John and Helen for their lives, and after their deaths to remain to Nicholas Edwardes and his heirs under certain conditions there expressed; and because it appears that John Trowdez was a tenant only for the term of his life and not a tenant according to the courtesy of England, Nicholas is discharged from the heriot which was claimed after John's death; and because it appears that Nicholas claims those lands by the said remainder, and not as son and heir of the said Helen, he is discharged of the relief which was claimed for parcel of the said lands which are held of this manor by the yearly rent of 7s 0d.

It was presented that the widow of John Sott had died since the last court; therefore enquire who is the tenant, and that after her death nothing came due, because she was tenant for a term of years only

Thomas Cheseman came and showed an indented charter of 1397-98 by which it appears that Robert Passhele, son and heir of Robert Passhele knight, gave certain lands called 'Le Clenche' in Northiam to James Bennet, paying two shillings a year and two suits of court on 29 September and at Easter for all customs and demands, which charter entailed the land with various remainders with an ultimate remainder in fee simple to Robert Passhele; so concerning the heriot which was claimed after the death of William Lampport, the tenant thereof is now discharged; but the relief is not discharged, because it is incident; and because Thomas Cheseman, who married the widow of William Lampport, occupies the lands and refuses to pay relief or show William's will [and] how he holds the lands, let him be distrained against the next court.

Henry Sampson came and showed an indented charter sealed by William Scott, knight, dated 24 April 1505, concerning 20 acres of land in Flackley, which pays yearly 1s 8d as a rent-charge and not rent service; so he cannot be claimed as a suitor or a tenant of this court.

The tenants present that John Walter of Iden has alienated 17 acres of land in Peasmarsh called 'Shyreshothez', quitrent 2s 6d, to Robert Partrigge, who now comes and does fealty

The tenants present the default of Lord Dacre, Lord Windsor, James Sutton, Anthony Pelham, the heir of John Shelley, John Tuffton, Thomas Byrchett, Edward Frencheham, the tenant of the land of William Lampport, Thomas Baker, John Holman of Barham, John Shepperd, John Walter, Henry Symon, John

Symon, Thomas Crouche, Henry Clarck, the tenant of the land of George Sier, John a Brooke, the heirs of [*blank*] Rydsdale, some of whom are distrained above for fealty and other services

Distrain Richard Seere for the relief of lands at Beckley called Horsepen, but let the heriot be delivered to the lord; distrain John Hollman for the relief of land in Northiam, parcel of 'Partryggestenement', purchased from his father in Calais; distrain John Shepperd for relief and other services from land in Peasmarsh called 'Hoodlandes otherwise Hotchemans' and for lands at Flackley, because he did not come on the day given to him by the last roll

Distrain Thomas Morys for the relief of land called 'Cottenham' which belonged to Nicholas Dyrryck; but concerning the heriots which were delivered, he requests that one should be returned to him, because he showed a charter of discharge for one parcel, for which a heriot was seized, as he says

Distrain Thomas Baker and William Baker upon lands in Northiam for fealty, because they obstinately refuse to do fealty; distrain Thomas Cheseman for relief as appears earlier in this court

[*The last membrane annotated by John Sharpe*] Received from Mr Wybarne.

RENTALS 1478, 1673

Rental of the manor of Mote, 1478[159]   [ESRO NOR 15/13]

Flackley [in Peasmarsh]

1   Thomas Fowle holds on the denn of Flackley lands and
     tenements called 'Denys Kechennores otherwise
     Horneslond' (100 acres) (E: land of the heirs of Robert
     Creche, late William Wynder; S: land of the heirs of Robert
     Creche; W: land of Thomas Oxenbrig'; N: road from Rye
     to London); fealty, relief, heriot and suit of court   3s 4d

2   Thomas Fowle holds other lands and tenements amounting
     in various tenements to 120 acres and more of land, wood,
     meadow and pasture on the denn of Flackley, mixed and
     dispersed both between the lands which he holds of this
     manor and the lands which he holds to farm of the lord, as
     well as mixed between the lands which he holds of the
     manor of Kitchenour; which lands and tenements, except a
     field called 'Fesauntes Felde', lie together and abut SW:
     the road from Rye to London; NW: the road from Flackley
     Ash to Wittersham, and the lands of John Kyriell; N: lands
     of Thomas Hache; SE: lands of the lord of The Mote called
     'Millond'; and of those 120 acres and within those bounds
     are a messuage and 10 acres part of the tenement called
     'Collisland otherwise Berdes', which tenement contains 18
     acres in all, of which the messuage and the land adjoining it
     lie in the corner (*angulariter*) at Flackley Ash (N: road
     from Flackley to Wittersham; E: lands of Thomas Fowle,
     part of his tenement called 'Jolyff', and to the lord's land
     called 'Welfelde'; SW: other land of Thomas Fowle; W:
     the road coming from Rye); the whole rent of the tenement
     is 2s 4d, of which Thomas Fowle pays 1s 2d; the rest of the
     tenement, called 'Bromeland', is in the hands of Thomas
     Watyll as below   1s 2d

3   Furthermore there are other lands and tenements called
     'Jolyff otherwise Brechislond' (15 acres), of which a parcel

---

[159] The rental has been annotated in red ink by Richard Kilburne, the steward of the manor, in the
course of preparing an analysis of the court rolls in 1648. It is headed with a symbol resembling a
hand, used to identify this rental, and lost tenements are marginated *query*. The other annotations,
also presented in angled brackets, are the result of various 16th-century campaigns to identify
tenants; they are not all contemporary.

abuts SE: the private lane (*domestice venelle*) of the lord of
The Mote; W: demesne land of The Mote held by Thomas
Fowle at farm, and other land of Thomas Fowle; SE: land
of Thomas Fowle called 'Bondislond'; SW: land of
Thomas Fowle called 'Berdys'; and other parcels of the
same tenement lie divided, dispersed and mixed with
Thomas's land within those bounds; for which he pays for
all services, except one suit <query>   4s 7d

4   There is there another tenement called 'Bondland otherwise
Wattill' (30 acres), of which the dwelling-house (*mansum*)
is an old messuage, which with its lands abut E: 'Jolyff
otherwise Brechislond'; S: land held by Thomas Fowle of
the manor of Kitchenour; W: demesne land called
'Wellefelde'; N: 'Jolyff otherwise Brechislond'; and the
rest of the tenement lies divided and dispersed between
Thomas's other lands; he owes no suit, relief nor other
service except two suits <query>   6s 8d

5   There is there another tenement of the same Thomas Fowle
called 'Danyelslond' (30 acres) once John Russell, of
which various parcels lie SW: land held by Thomas Fowle
of the manor of Kitchenour; E: demesne land called
'Gistament'; the rest lies dispersed and mixed between his
other lands, and it is difficult to know the metes and
bounds; it does not pay heriot, relief nor other services
except two suits of court[160] <query>   4s 0d

6   Thomas Fowle <query> holds, within the same bounds,
another tenement called 'Kingeswissh' (30 acres; N: a
small stream between those lands and the lands of the
manor of Kitchenour; NE: land of the lord of The Mote
called 'Millond'; and on the other sides it lies to other
lands of Thomas Fowle within the above bounds); it pays
for all services, by charter   1s 6d

7   Thomas Fowle holds one croft (two acres) called
'Fesauntes' (W, N, E: land of Lawrence Brice called
'Flecle', held of the manor of The Mote; S: land of Thomas
Watell called 'Bromelond'); he says that it is part of his
tenement of 'Jolyff', once Norman   [*blank*]

8   Thomas Fowle <query> holds a messuage and garden with
its appurtenances (three acres) late Borden, lying together

---

[160] The paper draft for this rental, ESRO NOR 15/12, adds *by charter*.

at Flackley between the land of his tenement specified
above; and it lies [*blank*]

Memorandum that about 1½ acres of this tenement is to be
found among his other lands, and it was shown by him to
Henry Fynch and John Buklond[161]   4s 1d

9   The heirs of Robert Creche <Richard Shepherd> hold a
     tenement, of which the messuage with its adjoining lands
     (10 acres), late William Wynder, abut N: road from Rye to
     London; E: a lane leading from that road to 'Brodefeld';
     S: land of William Symond late Ralph Sander; W: other
     land of William Wynder; heriot, relief, and suit of court   2s 4d

10   The heirs of Robert Creche hold a parcel of the same
     tenement (one acre) lying below the garden of Thomas
     Fowle and SW alongside (*in longitudine*) the road; and
     pays nothing for that reason[162]   Nothing

11   Lawrence Brice holds there two acres of wood (N, E: his
     land called 'Flekle'; S: road; W: land called 'Bromelond');
     and he says that he owes the lord no rent for it, but that the
     heirs of Robert Creche claim to have it to their tenement   [*blank*]

12   Lawrence Brice <Richard Shepherd> holds there three
     parcels (six acres) called 'Flekle' (E: land of the lord of
     The Mote; S: Lawrence's two acres [of wood: 11]; W: land
     called 'Fesauntes'; N: land of William Bayle); rent 2s 2d,
     of which he denies 2d by charter, and pays 2s 0d   2s 0d

13   William Bayle <Alexander Sheperde gent> holds there a
     messuage with a garden (one acre) in which he now lives
     (N: road from Rye to London; E: the land of the lord of The
     Mote; S: land of Lawrence Brice called 'Flekle'; W: the
     lord's lane leading to the same lands of Lawrence Brice)   6d

14   Robert Smyth <query> holds to farm at Flackley one acre
     of demesne land (E: road; N: lane leading to 'Bromelond';
     S, W: land of Lawrence Brice called Flekle)   4d

15   Thomas Watell <Morley> holds three parcels of land called
     'Bromelond' (eight acres), parcel of the tenement called
     'Berdys'; of which two parcels (six acres) lie together
     (SE: road from 'Norman' to 'Brodefelde'; W: lane from
     'Brodefeld' to Flackley Ash; N: lands of Lawrence Brice

---

[161] Although this memorandum is placed first in the rental, it is clear from the paper draft, ESRO
NOR 15/12, that it applies to entry 8.
[162] The paper draft for this rental, ESRO NOR 15/12, adds *and he says that it is parcel of the same
messuage.*

and Thomas Fowle); the other two acres (E: the same lane;
S: land of William Symond; W, S: land of the heirs of
Robert Creche)   1s 2d

Vill of Peasmarsh

16   The heirs of Robert Creche <Alexander Sheperde gent>
      hold a messuage in which Robert lived with the adjoining
      land (12 acres; NE: road from Peasmarsh to Flackley;
      S: land of Lawrence Brice; W: land of Lawrence Brice and
      of the same heirs); and he holds by the service of a fortieth
      part of a knight's fee   5s 0d

17   The heirs of Robert Creche <Alexander Sheparde gent>
      hold lands called 'Clayton' (54 acres) in various parcels
      (N: road from Goldspur to Peasmarsh church; E: the lane
      leading to 'Essynham'; S: land of the manor of Marley;
      W: land of the tenement of 'Grove'); and they hold land
      called 'Lynden' (seven acres; S: road from Goldspur to
      Peasmarsh church; W: land of the tenement of 'Elderton';
      N: land called 'Fowleden'; E: land called 'Le Hoth' of the
      manor of Leigh)[163]   13s 4d

18   The heirs of Robert Creche <Alexander Sheperde gent>
      hold a messuage with two gardens called 'Hodlond' (three
      acres), late Ingram Vanne (NE: road; S: land of Lory
      Whenham; W: lane from the road to the dwelling-house
      called 'Born') and he pays, with the value of a hen by a
      charter of entail made to John Wigge in 1379/80[164]   2s 3d

19   James at Wode <Tufton; Alexander Sheperde gent> holds
      seven acres called 'Eldertons', lying together in various
      parcels (E: land of Simon Watell, late Richard Wyte the
      elder; S: land of Lory Whenham; W: the lane leading to
      'Elderton'; N: road)   3s 4d

20   Henry Meteherst <Alexander Sampson> holds at 'Le Dewe'
      a parcel of land called 'Wiblond' (three acres) late John

---

[163] The paper draft for this rental, ESRO NOR 15/12, includes these bounds in a footnote to the original entry, which reads: The same heirs hold the lands called 'Clayton and Lynden' <seek the metes and bounds over> (60 acres; W: the street; NE: the lane leading from the street to 'Essynham'; S: the land of John Fynche called 'Suthlond' and the land of William Gilby, late Godesole, called 'Coggeryngheld'; E: land of Lawrence Brice); pays 13s 4d by a charter in fee simple made to John Mot, 12 December 1424.

[164] In 1648 Nathaniel Powell had this charter; he states that the hen was paid in respect of a street leading to the tenement: NOR 15/60 page 52.

Gilby (SE: road; W: land late of John Stephyn; N: land of
Roger Witte)   1s 4d

21 Thomas Sote <Alexander Sheperde gent> holds two acres
called 'Dewe' lying together there (E: lands of Lawrence
Brice; S: land called 'Le Yongen' now Thomas a Parke;
W: lane leading from the road to the land called 'Yonge'; N:
land of John Hony late John Stephyn, held of the dean of [St
Stephen's College], Westminster)   6d

22 Thomas Sote <Alexander Sheperde gent> holds a toft or
wood there (one acre and more; S: road; W, N: land late
John Stephyn; E: land of Henry Meteherst called 'Wiblond')   6d

23 Simon Watell <Alexander Sampson> holds land called
'Knolle' (25 acres; E: lane from the road to the dwelling-
house called 'Le Born'; SE[165]: land of Henry Moteherst late
William Gilby; W: land of Lawrence Brice; N: road), he   10s 0d and
owes heriot and relief by a charter of entail without date   4d for
made to Richard Portesmouth[166]   justiceyield

24 Thomas Watell <Alexander Shepherde gent> holds land
called 'Brodelond' (10 acres; SE: road; W: land of the heirs
of Robert Creche called 'Gowges'; S: lane from the road to
'Usshingford').

He holds two parcels of wood (2½ acres) called 'Urent'
(S, E: land called 'Highlond'; W: land of William Baile[167]),
and he pays heriot, relief with suit of court by a charter of   1s 10d
fee simple of 25 April 1455

25 Thomas Potyn and Austin Potyn <Henry Walter> hold land
called 'Shireshothes' (15 acres) lying by the lord's land
called 'Gistament', and to the land called 'Wilballyngherst'
to the east   2s 6d

26 William Simon <William Simons> holds a piece of land
(S: the road called 'Brodestrete'; E: the lane called
'Cowlarislane' and 'Wynderslane'; N, W: land of William
Simon called 'Bowsettes')   3d

27 Lawrence Brice holds one parcel of land called
'Wyndersgrove' in Peasmarsh, which formerly belonged to
John Wynder and William Wynder (E: land of Lawrence
Brice, late John Cowlard; S: road; W: land of John Watyll

---

[165] Given as SW in NOR 15/12.
[166] In 1648 Nathaniel Powell had the counterpart stock-deed of this tenement: NOR 15/60, page 33.
[167] NOR 15/12 adds *N: the lane leading to Ussyngford.*

called 'Bromelond'; N: land of Lawrence Brice, and
'Fesauntes') 2d

Beckley

28 Thomas Oxenbrigge <Thomas Abington> holds land called
'Le Hothes' (30 acres; N: land of William Belknap called
'Estbexle'; E: land of Thomas Oxenbrigge called
'Ussyngford'; S: road from 'Ussyngford' to the dwelling-
house of Thomas Oxenbrigge; W: another lane leading
from 'Shortcrowch' to the same dwelling-house) 3s 2d

29 John Twisden and others hold to the use of William Strode
and his heirs[168] <Thomas Abington> lands called
'Ludwynes' (eight acres; E, S, W: land of Thomas
Oxenbrigge called 'Hothes'; N: the road from
'Shortcrowch' to the dwelling-house of Thomas
Oxenbrigge)[169] 1s 7d[170]
<10d>

30 William Gowler, feoffee of Robert Gowler <Thomas Davy;
Sere> holds a corner-messuage with the appurtenances
(two acres) called Horsepen in Beckley (S: road; W, N:
land of the heirs of Adam Merden; E: road from the rectory
to Horsepen); and he pays 5d at Easter and Michaelmas and
a hen at Christmas, and two suits of court after that feast, 5d,
by a charter of fee simple of 18 April 1455 a <fat> hen

31 Thomas Edward <Alexander Sampson> holds a corner toft
(half an acre) at Brownsmith (W, N: road; E: land called
'Combe'; S: a lane) 4d

32 William Belknap, esquire <John Shelley> holds land called
'Piperslond' (24 acres; it lies in part E, S, W: land called
'Maidenslond' which are part of the manor of Knelle; and
in part S, W: the land of Richard Brownyng, butcher, which
are part of the manor of Ewhurst; W: land called 'Highlond
Pitte'; N: land of Richard Brownyng, carpenter; N, E: land
called Rogers Wood in the manor of Knelle) 4s 0d

---

[168] NOR 15/12 has *to the use of the heirs of William Strode*.
[169] NOR 15/12 includes at this point a deleted entry *Margeret Strode holds land called 'Hothlond'
(eight acres; N, E, S: land of Thomas Oxenbregge; W: road from Brownsmith to 'Wodelond
Streme'); rent 10d.*
[170] In 1648 Nathaniel Powell had the counterpart stock-deed of this tenement: NOR 15/60, page 82.

Northiam

33   Richard Holman \<John Holman\> holds a messuage, garden
and twenty acres of adjoining land (E: lane from
Quickbourne Cross to land called 'Wolvered'; S: land of
Clement Fippes formerly Robert Ednex; W: land of William
Godewyn and land of Thomas Echyngham, knight; N: land
of Thomas Echyngham, knight)

He also holds two pieces of land (six acres; E: land of
William Belknap, esquire; S: land of Michael White;
W: land of Richard Holman; N: land of Thomas
Echyngham, knight)   5s 6d

34   Richard Holman \<John Holman of Barham\> holds land
called 'Dyneslond' (15 acres; W: road from Newenden to
Quickbourne Cross; N: land of Thomas Echyngham, knight;
E: land of Richard Godewyn; S: lane called 'Berham
Lane'); rent by the rental 4s 0d, but by the charter which is
shown but   3s 0d

35   William Fissh \<Edward Sharpe\> holds a piece of land called
'Cropwodeacr' (W: lane from Northiam church to 'Berham';
N: land of William at Hille; E, S: land of George Perys)   6d

36   Joan Bate \<William Sharpe\> holds certain lands (21 acres;
E: land of Henry Holstok; S: land of George Perys called
Goatley; W: land of William at Hille; N: lane from
Quickbourne Cross to 'Wulvenrede')

She also holds another piece of land (five acres) called
'Berham' (E: land of Richard Holman called 'Sissis'; S: the
said lane from Quickbourne Cross; W: land of Thomas
Fraye; N: land of Thomas Echyngham, knight)   4s 6d

37   Henry Holstok \<Thomas Brigden\> holds two pieces of land
(12 acres) called 'Millerfeld' and 'Ferthynges' (W: land
called 'Lemestrete'; N \<E\>: road from Clench Cross to
Northiam church; E: lane called 'Romestrete'; S: land of the
lord of The Mote called 'Crowchlond')   3s 0d

38   Richard James holds a parcel of land called 'Adamscrofte',
formerly Peter at Chirch (W: road called 'Lemestrete'
leading from Northiam church to Ewhurst; N, E, S: land of
the lord called 'Crowchlond')   3d

39   Richard James \<John Fruen, clerk\> holds a messuage with a
garden and appurtenances (one acre) formerly Peter Chirche

(W: Northiam churchyard; S: land of Robert Oxenbrigge called 'Halton'; E: land of Thomas Echyngham, knight; N: road)[171]   1d

40   Richard Godewyn <the heirs of John Whit hold 'Crowford' and these lands> holds a messuage with a garden and adjoining lands (30 acres), of which certain parts (eight acres) are called 'Heyredez', 'Holerede', 'Collingcroft' and 'Crowford' lying together (N: lane from Beckley to Northiam; E: land of Richard Sander; S: road from Perrymans Cross to Beckley, the land of Thomas Echyngham, knight, the land of Thomas Harle and the land of John Michell; W: road from Newenden to Hastings, and the land of William Benet); he pays, with 3d for the messuage[172] and croft and one parcel of land called 'Benetteslond'

      [*margin*]: note because it is imperfect; note that 8d are the rent of 'Crowford' by a charter of entail made to John   2s 11d
      Gotele and his heirs male in 1400/01[173]

41   William Benette <John Lampard> holds by charter of Robert Passhele, knight, in fee tail[174], a messuage with a garden and five parcels of land (16 acres) called Clench, of which the messuage, garden and four adjoining acres lie S, W: land of Henry Holstok called 'Millersfeld' and 'Ferthynges'; NW: road from Clench Cross to Ewhurst; E: road from <the manor of> Dixter to Northiam church; and the remainder of the land, twelve acres in four parcels lying together lie S: lane called 'Lemestrete'; W: land of William Benette; N: land of Stephen Iham and land late William Dolman; E: land of Thomas Newell and land of William at Hille   2s 0d

42   William Lucas in the right of his wife Alice holds a messuage and three acres adjoining called 'Benetteslond' (E: road: S: land of the heirs of John Benette called 'Pollardys'; W: land of Thomas Echyngham, knight; N: land of the rector of Northiam)

---

[171] NOR 15/12 adds *Memorandum that he gave Peter at Chirche a messuage with other lands of which the rent is 5s 4d by a charter in fee tail of 1399-1400.*
[172] NOR 15/12 adds *in which he lives.*
[173] For the charter of eight acres called 'Croufordes' (E: road leading from Northiam church to Beckley; S: land of John Gotele called 'Holredes', W: land of Henry Sandre called 'Le Bergh', N: land of John Gotele called 'Colynescroft'), quitrent 8d, 19 November 1400, see ESRO FRE 6919.
[174] For the petition of John Bennett, c1460, reciting this charter, dated 3 June 1398, see NOR 15/58; for its production, see the court held on 25 June 1551; in 1648 Nathaniel Powell had the counterpart: NOR 15/60, page 46.

He also holds another parcel of land (three acres) called 'Benetteslond otherwise Gateward' (E: land of William Godewyn; S: land of the heirs of John Benette; W: road; N: land of William Godewyn)

He also holds another parcel of land (two acres) called 'Legatefelde', parcel of Bernetteslond (W: road; N: land of William Langporte; E, S: land of Robert Oxenbrigge)   3s 10d

43   William Lucas in the right of his wife Alice <Frewen and Brigden> holds four parcels of land with a garden (10 acres) called 'Okeworth' (E: land of Edward Hore, land of William Toghton, formerly John Lovell; S: land of Thomas Benette; W: lands which the same Thomas [Benette] holds of the manor of Ewhurst, the land of Edward Hore and the land of Joan a Broke; N: road from 'Malley Crowch' to Beckley)[175]   1s 6d

44   Thomas Fissh <John White> holds land late John Everenden called 'Le Crabbe' (three acres) which were once two parcels, now united (W: land of the rector of Northiam; N: land of John Twisden; E: road from Northiam church to Perrymans Cross; S: land called 'Preshous') and he pays, by charter of fee simple made to Stephen Benette in 1403/04   4¾d

45   Thomas Fissh <the heirs of John White> holds three parcels of land (eight acres) called 'Pollardes' (S: lane called 'Blechislane'; E: road; N: land of William Lucas; W: land of Thomas Echyngham, knight)   2s 0d

46   John Miller[176] <George Bishope> holds a parcel of land containing six acres of scrub (S: land of Thomas Harle; W: land of William Langporte; N: lane called 'Blechislane'; E: road from Northiam church to Perrymans Cross); and it is parcel of the tenement of William Blache   1s 1d

47   William Towghton[177] <Sir John Tufton> holds a tenement called Tufton Place containing about 100 acres of wood, meadow, land and pasture   10s 0d
He also holds in service various lands and tenements which   and other
his tenants hold of him in demesne, of which the total rent is   services[178]

---

[175] In 1648 Nathaniel Powell had the counterpart stock-deed of this tenement: NOR 15/60, page 26.
[176] Inserted in NOR 15/12 over *Hamo Tomset*.
[177] In entries 47-49, NOR 15/12 originally gave *William Towhton the elder and William Towhton the younger*, which was amended to produce the text of NOR 15/13 as edited here.
[178] In 1648 Nathaniel Powell had the counterpart stock-deed of this tenement: NOR 15/60, page 23; the original, granted by John Pashley, esq., on 17 April 1455, survives in the Tufton archive and is calendared as Appendix 1 no. 5; the tenement was formerly held by John Smallfield.

48   William Towghton <Sir John Tufton> holds a messuage
       and 24 acres called 'Weblond', of which the messuage and
       16 acres lie E: the land of William's aforesaid tenement
       [47]; S: road from 'Mable Crosse' to Ewhurst; W: land of
       Parnell Cassyn and the land of George Pers; N: land of
       George Pers and the land of William's aforesaid tenement
       [47]; and eight acres lie in four parcels, with a grove, NE:
       road from 'Mable Crowch' to Ewhurst; E, S: road from
       the said cross to Battle; SW: land of Robert Watte; W:
       land called 'Rede'; N: land of Robert Wat called
       'Homecrofte'   2s 0d

49   William Towghton <Sir John Tufton> holds two parcels
       (two acres), of which one belonged to John Lovell and
       afterwards Thomas Harle (E: land of Edward Hore;
       S, W: land of William Lucas called 'Okeworth'; N: road
       from 'Mable Crowch' to Beckley), and the other parcel
       once belonged to Thomas Harle (E: road from Northiam
       church to Perrymans Cross; S: road from Ewhurst to
       Beckley; W, N: land of Hamo Thomset), for which he
       owes heriot, relief and two suits of court   4d[179]

50   John Jerves[180] <Sir John Tufton> holds a messuage with a
       garden and 12 acres in various parcels called 'Okeworth'
       (E: land called 'Raylond'; S: road from Bodiam to Rye;
       W: land of William Towghton[181] called 'Owlond' and land
       of John Cassyn called 'Chapmans'; N: road called
       'Lotestrete')   4s 0d[182]

51   Edward Hore <Sir John Tufton> holds two parcels of land[183]
       (12 acres) of which one lies E: the tenement of John a Broke;
       S: lands formerly Golet; W: land of the heirs of

---

[179] For the charter of John Pashley, esq, granting this tenement to Thomas Herle of Northiam by a
rent of 4d and two suits of court, 10 April 1455, and a letter of attorney to 'his servant' John
Tregoff of the same date, see CKS U455 T122/7-8; for the deed of purchase by William Tufton the
younger from Thomas Herle of Newenden, 12 October 1471, see CKS U455 T122/9.
[180] Inserted in NOR 15/12 over *William Langport*.
[181] NOR 15/12 has *the elder* deleted.
[182] In 1648 Nathaniel Powell had a counterpart stock-deed of 'Greater and Lesser Ockworths',
granted to Roger Holman at a quitrent of 5s 6d, dated 20 May 1398, which he thought represented
this and the next tenement; it may in fact relate to tenement 33 in this rental: NOR 15/60, page 98.
This quitrent of 4s 0d may be that reserved by a charter of Edmund de Pashley to Alice daughter of
Adam de Dixter, of the messuage and land which Andrew son of Geoffrey de Ocwerse held of him
in villeinage, 3 April 1310: ESRO FRE 6896. On 26 May 1466 Sir John Scott again granted it, at
the same rent of 4s 0d, to John Langport of Sundridge in Kent; it was then described as a tenement
and 12 acres in Northiam (W: road from Rye to Robertsbridge; NW: land of William Toketon; E:
land formerly William Bernette): CKS U455 T119/26.
[183] NOR 15/12 adds *of the tenement of Sore*, which is deleted.

Lawrence Risden called 'Okeworth' and land late Thomas
Harle called 'Lovelles'; N: road from Rye to Bodiam); and
the other parcel called 'Okeworth' lies E, S: land of the heirs
of Lawrence Risden called 'Okeworth'; W: land of Edward
Hore called 'Gretegardyn'; N: road from Rye to Bodiam   1s 6d[184]

52   John Elderton, knight, in the right of his wife Margaret[185]
      <Lawrence Peirs, gent> holds land (25 acres) called
      'Highberham' (SW: road from Newenden to Rye; NW: lane
      leading to the tenement called 'Holmans')   5s 0d

53   John Frengeham and Richard Frengeham[186] <Richard
      Freebody> hold a messuage with a garden and 30 acres
      formerly Simon Mose (E: road from Newenden to Brede;
      W: land of William Towghton[187] late Thomas Harle;
      S, N: land of John a Broke)   2s 6d

54   John a Broke <Francheham> holds three parcels of land (12
      acres; W: land of John Jerves; N: land of John Jerves and
      land called The Mote; E: land of William Partrich and
      others; S: land of Robert Frebody)   1s 4d

55   John Twisden <John Foster> holds four parcels of land (11
      acres) on the corner at Perrymans Cross and dispersed and
      mixed among his own lands there, parcel of the tenement of
      William Blache   1s 7d

56   William Wener holds certain lands, parcel of the tenement
      of William Blache   4d

57   William Hille for land formerly Peter Chirch   8d <now 1d>

Ninfield

58   John a Broke of Ninfield <now Brooke of Winchelsea>
      holds in demesne and service in his own right and in the
      right of his wife, Alice, daughter and heir of William
      Ingram, a messuage and about 60 acres of land, wood and
      pasture (SW: road from The Standard to Hastings; N: road
      from Catsfield to Ninfield; NE: wood called 'Hurstwode';
      SE: land of the tenement of the heirs of John Mavesyn; S:

---

[184] For the charter of Robert de Pashley, kt, granting this tenement to Henry le Hore and his wife
Isabel to hold by a rent of 1s 6d, 24 July 1375, see CKS U455 T124/4, calendared as Appendix 1
no. 4.
[185] Inserted in NOR 15/12 over *The heirs of William Blount.*
[186] Inserted in NOR 15/12 over *Henry a Ford.*
[187] NOR 15/12 deletes *the younger.*

land of William Eston) of which 60 acres, John Webbe
holds of John and Alice in demesne a messuage with the
appurtenances (1½ acres) and John Clerke similarly holds
of them there a messuage containing 1½ acres   6d

Hollington

59   John Waterman in the right of his wife, Joan, daughter and
      heir of John Parker late of Hastings <query>, holds 18
      acres of land and heath called 'James Downe' (E: the
      highway which leads to [*recte* from][188] Crowhurst into the
      road between Battle and Hastings; S: the demesne land of
      John Pownd, late Dalyngrigge; W: land called 'Barnettes
      Downe', now John Bokelond;[189] N: land called 'Serjantis
      Downe', late Robert Adam); and he pays at Easter and
      Michaelmas by a charter of fee tail made to John Parker the
      elder and the heirs of his body, 29 June 1428   2s 0d

Iden

60   William Cheyne holds the manor of Leigh <query>   ½d

61   John Oxenbrigge <<heirs of> Gybon> holds a messuage
      and six acres late John Kechenore (SE: road from Rye to
      'Kentbarre'; W: land of Walter Roberd called
      'Pirrymanfeld' held of the manor of Mote; N: land of the
      dean of [St Stephen's College], Westminster)   3s 0d

62   John Oxenbrigge <query> holds by the same rent three
      parcels (four acres; E: land of Walter Roberd called
      'Bomelond' and the land of Iden church; S: land of Walter
      Roberd called 'Buklond' and the land of Richard
      Dyngelden; W: land of Thomas Potyn; N: road from Iden
      Cross to Thornsdale)

      He also holds by the same rent in service a small parcel of
      land (half an acre) which the heirs of John Boseney hold of
      him in demesne (SW: land called 'Merelande' and
      'Bromefeld'; N: the lane leading to 'Besynewelle';[190]
      E: land of the manor of Leigh)

      He also holds by the same rent in service two acres called
      'Hikkes Acre' which Walter Roberd holds of him in

---

[188] Confirmed by NOR 15/12.
[189] NOR 15/12 has *now Robert Barnett*.
[190] NOR 15/12 has *Bosenywell*.

demesne (E: land called 'Nowlaund'; SE: land called
'Slippyngtye'; N: a small stream; NW: land of the same
[Walter] Robert)   *[blank]*

63   John Oxenbrigge <Foster> holds in demesne a toft and five
      acres in two adjoining parcels called 'Hogles otherwise
      Howletes' (N, E: the street called 'Kyngestrete'; S: land
      late John Parrok; W: land of John Stille)   1s 3d

64   John Oxenbrigge, in the right of his wife Joan <Gibbon's
      heirs, that is Robert Poyns> holds land called 'Cottenham'
      (about seven acres of marsh in two parcels), late Richard at
      Wode lying in 'Hopismerssh' (W, N, E: land of William
      Cheyne, esq; SE: land of Richard Crowch called
      'Hopeslond'; S: land of Richard Parrok)

      [*margin*]: by charter, and if it be more than seven acres, he
      should pay more, and if less, he should pay less[191]   7s 0d

65   John Oxenbrigge <Gibbon, Heiward's wife> holds one acre
      in 'Morislond' late Richard at Wode (S: land called
      'Huntislond'; E: land of John Boseney called 'Estend') for
      which he pays at Michaelmas one suit of court and   1d[192]

66   Richard Fynes, Lord Dacre <Thomas Dallet> <query>
      holds a messuage and about 30 acres of adjoining land
      called 'Reverlond' (W: land of Thomas Passhelew; N: land
      late Richard Dalyngrigge and land of John Dalet; E: land of
      the heirs of Thomas Pope and land of John Dalet; S: road
      called 'Kyngestrete'), and he pays 6s 8d, and a penny for
      scutage when it runs at 13s 4d and if more, more, and if
      less, less, and pays

      [*margin*]: by indenture   6s 8d

67   William Dalette <Thomas Dalet; Fagg> holds a messuage,
      a garden and four acres of land adjoining late William at
      Hoope and once Agatha New (E, S, W: land of Walter
      Robert; N: road from Iden Cross to Boonshill)

      [*margin*]: by indenture   1s 8d

68   The heirs of Thomas Parrok[193] <John Foster> hold a parcel
      of the tenement of 'Golding', that is to say, [a tenement
      cancelled] barn with the appurtenances and 3½ acres called

---

[191] For a recital of this charter, see the roll of the court held on 11 October 1550.
[192] In 1648 Nathaniel Powell had the counterpart stock-deed of this tenement and a tenement called
'The Rysshet', held by a quitrent of 6d: NOR 15/60, page 48.
[193] NOR 15/12 gives *Katherine Parrok*, amended to the reading of NOR 15/13.

'Vauteslond' (E: land of Walter Roberd called 'Malgrove';
N: land of Walter Roberd and land of John Colyn of
Beckley; S: land of Roger Osberne; W: road)   2s 3d

69   Roger Osberne <Thomas Maudsleye, clerk> holds a
     messuage and three acres of land in 'Houndeperystrete'
     (N: land of Katherine Parrok; E: land of Walter Roberd
     called 'Malgrove'; S: land of Roger Osberne called 'Epsys'
     held of the rector of Iden; W: road); and he owes by the old
     rental 1s 8d <[4d] upon John Bochour>, and by the new
     rental but   1s 6d

70   Thomas Passhlew <Gibbon's heirs, that is Robert Poyns>
     holds in demesne a messuage, garden and four parcels of
     land (seven acres; S: road; W: garden and land of the heirs
     of John Parrok, tailor, land of Thomas Eps and land of the
     heirs of John Heyred; NE: land of James Potyn)

     He also holds a piece of land called 'Slitchyng' with a
     parcel of wood (E: land of Lord Dacre; S: land of James
     Potyn; W: lands late the heirs of John Parrok, tailor, called
     'Bornefeld'; N: land called 'Le Breche')

     He also holds in service two parcels of land (five acres)
     which John Oxenbrigge[194] holds of him in demesne (E:
     land of Lord Dacre; S: road; W, N: the tenement of Thomas
     Passhlew)

     He also holds in the same way two other parcels of land
     (seven acres), formerly part of his tenement, which the
     heirs of John Parrok and John Oxenbrigge hold of him in
     demesne; one is called 'Bornefeld' (five acres), now John
     Oxenbrigge; the other called 'Peryfelde'[195] (E: land of
     Thomas Passhlew; SW: land formerly John Heyred; N:
     land called 'Le Breche' and land of John Oxenbrigge)

     And he holds in the same way three pieces of land (three
     acres) called 'John Smythlond',[196] which John Oxenbrig
     holds of him in demesne (E: land called 'Le Breche';
     SE: land of the heirs of John Parrok, tailor; SW: land of
     Thomas Eps; NE: land of the heirs of John Boseney)

     He holds as above a piece of land called 'Upperham' (four
     acres) which the heirs of John Boseney hold of him in
     demesne (W: a lane; E: land of John Oxenbrigge called

---

[194] *John Oxenbrigge interlined over James Potyn in NOR 15/12.*
[195] NOR 15/12 adds *now the said heirs [of John Parrok].*
[196] NOR 15/12 has *Jone Smythlond.*

'John Smythlond'; NE: land of the heirs of John Boseney
called 'Lawersham'; S: land of Thomas Eps)

He pays the lord for himself and for his tenants   3s 0d

71   Richard Parrok <John Fagg> holds nine acres of upland
called 'Cotenham' (W: land of William Cheyny and Robert
Symond; S: garden of William Cheyny and the road;
E: land of Richard a Crowch; N: land of John Oxenbrigge)   8s 6d and

[*margin*]: by indenture[197]   suit of court

72   John Stille <John Foster> holds one parcel of land (nine
acres) called 'Sedlond' (N: road; SW: land of Walter
Roberd; E: land of John Oxenbrigge called 'Howlettes')   1s 10d

73   Walter Roberd <query>[198] holds of the land of William
Golde two pieces of land with a garden (seven acres; N:
road from Iden church to Boonshill; E: land of John Stille
called 'Sedlond'; S: lands of Walter Roberd held of the
abbot of Robertsbridge; W: lands of William Dalet[199])   [*blank*]

74   Walter Roberd <Godfrey> holds in service one garden with
a building (*domus*) upon it which Thomas Flecher holds of
him in demesne (W: road from Iden Cross to Rye; N: lands
of the lord of Mote; E, S: lands of Katherine Parrok); and
he owes relief, heriot, suit and the service of the king and
the earl by charter   6s 6d

75   Walter Roberd <John Foster> holds a piece of land late
John Marchant where his dovehouse was, and in the old
rental it is called 'The Wissh' and contains two acres, and
it lies on the south side there (NE: the dwelling-house of
Thornsdale; SW: land of Walter Roberd late Robert Cogger
and once William Bone; NW: land 'of the same Robert'
called 'Posternhilde'); and he owes relief and suit of court
twice a year[200]   6½d

76   Walter Roberd <Peter Godfrey> holds, with a toft, two
acres of land formerly Penherst (E, N, W: lands of Walter
Roberd held of the manor of Ewhurst; S: road from Iden
church to Thornsdale)[201]   2s 4d

---

[197] In 1648 Nathaniel Powell had the counterpart stock-deed of this tenement: NOR 15/60, page 78.
[198] NOR 15/12 annotates this entry *now* [*John* deleted] <*William*> *Chester*.
[199] Inserted over *John ate Hope* in NOR 15/12.
[200] In 1648 Nathaniel Powell had the counterpart stock-deed of this tenement: NOR 15/60, page 72.
[201] In 1648 Nathaniel Powell had the counterpart stock-deed of this tenement: NOR 15/60, page 37.

77   Walter Roberd <Peter Godfrey> holds other lands (five
      acres) lately granted to John Penherst which formerly
      belonged to John Tauke on the north side of the said two
      acres [76]; two suits by charter and he pays   2s 4d

78   Walter Roberd <Peter Godfrey> holds three parcels of land
      (five acres) lying together called 'Buklond' (S, W: lands of
      Richard Dyngleden; N: lands of John Oxenbrigge late John
      Kechenour; E: lands of Walter Roberd and the lands called
      'Chirch Acre'; SE: lands of John Asshmeston)   [*blank*]

79   Walter Roberd <Peter Godfrey> holds a piece of land (1½
      acres) called 'Pirrymansfeld' with an adjoining lane (NW:
      lands of Richard Crowch; N: land of John Oxenbrigge[202]
      called 'Colyers'; SE: lands of John Oxenbrigge; W: a
      garden called 'Wyndsores' now Richard Dyngleden)   3s 0½d

80   Walter Roberd <Gibbon's heirs, that is Robert Poyns> holds
      a meadow lying by 'Lordiswissh' and three crofts (seven
      acres) which John Hogles lately held in the right of his wife
      Joan, daughter and heir of William Bone, and which
      afterwards belonged to William Marchant (NW:
      'Lordiswissh'; N: land 'of the same Robert' called
      'Conghamlyd'; E: the garden of Thornsdale, 'Hikkes Acre'
      and the lands called 'Slepyntye'; SW: lands called
      'Northamslond'); and he owes by the old rental one suit and   3s 1d

81   Walter Roberd <Joseph Birchett; Richard Wily> holds of
      the tenement of 'Golding' 3½ acres of land called
      'Litelbawnelond' once John Bone, lying together in three
      crofts (SW: lands of John Oxenbrigge; N: road from
      Thornsdale to Iden church; NE: lands of Walter Roberd
      called 'Gretebaunlond' held of the manor of Ewhurst;
      SE: lands 'of the same Robert' called 'Le Strake' and to the
      land of Iden church called 'Chirch Acre')

      And Katherine Parrok holds the rest of the same tenement   1s 2d

82   Walter Roberd <Peter Godfrey> holds a tenement (about 1½
      acres) called 'Malegrove' once Maud Heghton
      (W, N: lands of Roger Osberne and lands of the heirs of
      Thomas Parrok[203] called 'Vautes'; E: lands of William
      Dalet;[204] S: lands 'of the same Robert' held of the abbot of
      Robertsbridge)   1s 7d

---

[202] Inserted over *Alice de Kechenour* in NOR 15/12.
[203] Inserted over *Katherine Parrok* in NOR 15/12.
[204] Inserted over *Joan Hope* in NOR 15/12.

83   Walter Roberd <Peter Godfrey> <query> holds a parcel of
land (1½ acres) called 'Lordiswissh' (NW: lands called
'Sutham'; N: lands of Walter Roberd lying by the garden of
Thornsdale; SE: other lands of Walter Roberd late John
Hogles in the right of his wife Joan); and he must find a
lamp burning before the Blessed Mary the Virgin in Iden   <burning
church   lamp>

84   Walter Roberd <Foster> holds five acres of land called
'Taylorslond otherwise Stayneslond and Westwode' which
belonged to John Markham (N: road from Iden church to
Boonshill; E: lands of William Dalet; S: lands of the heirs of
Richard Parrok called 'Vautes'; W: lands of the hospital of
St Bartholomew [Playden]); and he pays by the old rental   1s 6d

85   Walter Roberd <Peter Godfrey> holds a field (three acres)
called 'Reytey' formerly called 'Bekkesfeld' (W: lands of
William Dalet; N: lands of Walter Robert called 'Goldes';
E: the lands of Style)   6d

86   Thomas Profette <John Foster> holds a parcel of land (one
acre; W: road from Iden Cross to 'Houndenpery'; N: lands
of the hospital of St Bartholomew [Playden]; E: land of the
heirs of John Parrok; S: lands of Thomas Flecher); he owes
one suit at the next court after Michaelmas for all services
by the lord's charter of fee tail of 20 July 1473[205]   1s 0d

87   Richard Fynes, Lord Dacre <John Threele> holds seven
acres of wood called 'Wallond', late John Chetecroft, called
'Heggnewalles'[206] in the old rental, which formerly
belonged to Lawrence Corvile (S: lands of John Warner;
W: land of the manor of Mote called 'Wallelond' by 'Le
Redeford'; N: the lane lying alongside the park (*per
parcum*) of The Mote; E: land of Robert Symond)[207]   6d

Playden

88   William Tracy, master of the hospital of St Bartholomew in
Playden <query>, holds three parcels of land (10 acres)
lying together (E: road from Rye to Playden Hill; S: lands of
the same master and his wood there called 'Spittell Grove';
W: lands of the manor of Leasam; N: a lane there by
'Bekyngfeld'); and he pays in the octave of St Andrew   3s 0d

---

[205] In 1648 Nathaniel Powell had the counterpart stock-deed of this tenement: NOR 15/60, page 75.
[206] Inserted over *Longwallys* in NOR 15/12.
[207] In 1648 Nathaniel Powell had the counterpart stock-deed of this tenement: NOR 15/60, page 22.

Ewhurst

89 Thomas Parrok holds a corner messuage there with a
garden and two adjoining crofts called 'Skowston' (N, S:
road; E: land of the lord of Ewhurst)   4d

90 The heirs of Thomas Perys <Tufton> hold six acres called
'Echyn' lying upon the denn of Padgham (heading SW: the
garden of Padgham; N: lands called 'Maynardes'; E: the
marsh there; S: the lane leading to the marsh)   1s 6d

91 William Thomsette and the others below [entries 92 to 102]
hold the fourth part of a knight's fee and pay 2s 0d; and for
these lands they are accustomed to acquit the lord of The
Mote of suit of the county court and suit of the lathe court
against the lord of the Rape of Hastings; they owe fealty,
homage, heriot and relief as appears in a court held at The
Mote on 1 August 1387 and in other courts following, as   2s 0d
also appears in the custumal book   as it is said

92 William Thomsette and the others below <Richard
Ballard> hold the fourth part of a knight's fee, as appears
by the custumal, by fealty, homage and other services, a
tenement and 159 acres, of which William holds the
messuage, in which he lives, and 100 acres lying
roundabout; and they are called Padgham, of which there
are about 40 acres of marsh (W: lands of Lord Dacre of his
manor of Ewhurst; N: the common stream; E: the marsh of
the heirs of Thomas Perys; S: the uplands of William
Thomsette, Joan Geffe and the heirs of Thomas Perys)   [*blank*]

93 The heirs of Thomas Perys <query> hold nine acres of marsh
called 'Le Strake' (W: the marsh of William Thomsette; N:
the stream; E: the lands of William Towghton; S: the uplands
late Thomas Perys called 'Echyng')   [*blank*]

94 William Thomsette <query> holds three acres of land (N:
lands of Thomas Parrok; E: 'Le Mardyke'; S: other lands of
Thomas Parrok; W: 'Le Synderbergh')   [*blank*]

95 William Towghton <query> holds there 20 acres of marsh
(W: marsh of the heirs of Thomas Perys; N: the common
stream; E: 'Le Mardike'; S: the lands of Robert Pralle, John
Thomset[208] and Thomas Parrok)   [*blank*]

96 Robert Pralle <query> holds there three acres of land (W,

---

[208] NOR 15/12 gives *John Morfot.*

N: lands of William Towghton; E: 'Le Mardike'; S: the
lands of John Morfoote)

[*blank*]

97 John Morfoote holds six acres of marsh (W: lands of
Thomas Parrok; butting E: 'Le Mardyke'; N: lands of
Robert Pralle and William Towghton; S: lands of John
Hony)

[*blank*]

98 Thomas Parrok holds six acres of land (E: lands of John
Hony and John Morfoote; S: lands of the heirs of Thomas
Perys; N: lands of the heirs of Thomas Perys and lands of
William Towghton; and to 'Le Synderbergh')

[*blank*]

99 Thomas Parrok holds six acres of land called
'Baddyngborne' (W, N: lands of the manor of Ewhurst;
E: lands of William Thomsette of his tenement of
Padgham; S: the lane leading to the tenement of Padgham)

[*blank*]

100 Joan Geffe holds three acres called 'Kechynfeld' (W: lands
of William Thomsette of his tenement of Padgham; N: the
marsh there; E: the lands called 'Echyn'; W [*recte* S]: lands
held of the manor of Ewhurst)

[*blank*]

101 John Parrok <query> holds two acres of marsh (N: land of
the heirs of Thomas Perys; E: 'Le Mardike'; S: lands of the
tenement of Padgham; W: 'Le Synderbarow')

[*blank*]

102 Thomas Payne, rector of the church of Ewhurst <query>,
holds one acre (N: lands of John Parrok; E, S: lands of the
tenement of Padgham; W: 'Le Synderbarowe')

[*blank*]

103 Richard Fynes, Lord Dacre <Bromefeld> holds 50 acres of
land, once Padyham; he owes fealty, homage, heriot, relief
and other services as appears by the custumal; of which 50
acres the site of the manor of Ewhurst is parcel, as appears
in various accounts of Ewhurst under the heading *Rents
Resolute*; and the lands late Thomas White called
'Rohamme', the lands of Thomas Padyham at
'Synderbarow' and 'Courtfelde', and the tenements of
'Hordynglynde', 'Le Wergh' and 'Cokfisshlond' contribute
to the payment of the said rent, as appears in a court held at
The Mote on Friday, 4 October 1398, and at other courts

10s 7d

104 Thomas Payne, rector of the church of Ewhurst <query>,
holds one acre (N: lands of John Parrok; E, S: lands of the
tenement of Padgham; W: 'Le Synderbarow')

[*blank*]

[Iden]²⁰⁹

105   The court is given to understand that John Parrok of Iden
   holds an acre of land in Iden which formerly belonged to
   the tenement called 'Houseplace' (W, N: lands of Thomas
   Aps; S: road from Iden church to the tenement of John
   Dalette; [E]: lands of John Oxenbrigge late Passhlew)   *[blank]*

Beckley

106   Memorandum of a parcel of land late William Oxenbrigge,
   labourer, and formerly William Pecham called 'Motelond',
   six capons worth   2s 6d

Peasmarsh

107   William Belknap for a croft (three acres) by 'Pirryfelde'
   belonging to Matthew de Knelle and John de Knelle   1s 0½d

Northiam

108   Distrain Hamo Thomsette for six acres of land lying   1s 1d
   between the lands of Thomas Harle and the lands of the   <cancelled
   heirs of William Langporte and the lane called   here because
   'Betchislane' for rent and to show the charter   before [46]>

109   Thomas John holds 'Crowchlond' in Northiam and owes
   suit of court, heriot and [*unfinished*]²¹⁰   7s 0d

---

²⁰⁹ This and the following four entries, although written in the same hand as the rest of the
document, are clearly additional to it. They probably represent additional memoranda which were
not present in ESRO NOR 15/12, the exemplar on which this rental is based.

²¹⁰ For the original stock-deed of 'Crouchlond' (12 acres) in Northiam, of which all but a croft lay
together (N: road; E: land of the heirs of John Holstok called 'Millersfeld'; S: land of William
Hilles called 'Goselond'; W: land of Stephen Hyham), and the croft of 1¼ acres (S: the same road;
W, N: land of Stephen Hyham; E: land of William Hilles called 'Jakkescroft'), 5 April 1479, see
ESRO ACC 7006/16.

Survey of the manor of Mote, [1673]   [ESRO NOR 15/92]

Iden

1   Cottenham; Sir John Fagg, baronet, holds a freehold tenement
     called Cottenham (10 acres; SW: a road; NW: lands of Lady
     Chute; NE: other lands of Sir John Fagg; SE: lands late
     Thomas Godfrey, esquire); fealty, suit of court, heriot and
     relief, quitrent   8s 6d

2   Vautes; Robert Foster, gent, son and heir of Thomas Foster,
     esquire, holds a freehold tenements called Vawtes, being one
     piece of land (three acres; W: road from Iden Cross to Rye;
     S; other land of Robert Foster called Houndprister; E: another
     tenement of Robert Foster called Taylors otherwise Stanies
     Land and Westwood [4]; N: another tenement of Robert
     Foster called The Acre Tenement [3]); fealty, suit of court,
     heriot and relief, quitrent   2s 2d

3   Acre Tenement; Robert Foster, gent, son and heir of Thomas
     Foster, esquire, holds freely a piece of land now called The
     Acre Tenement (1a 2r 21p; W: road from Iden Cross to Rye;
     N: a way from Iden Cross to Boonshill; E: land of Robert
     Foster called Tailors otherwise Staniseland [4]; S: lands of
     Robert Foster called Vawtes [2]); fealty, suit of court, heriot
     and relief, quitrent   1s 0d

4   Taylors otherwise Staniseland and Westwood; Robert Foster,
     gent, son and heir of Thomas Foster, esquire, holds freely a
     tenement called Tailors otherwise Staniesland and Westwood,
     being two parcels of land (eight acres; W: land of Robert
     Foster called The Acre Tenement [3], Vawtes [2] and Hound
     Priester; N: road from Iden Cross to Boonshill; E: tenement of
     John Woodall, clerk, called Cobbs [13], held of the manor;
     S: lands of the heirs of George); fealty, suit of court, heriot
     and relief, quitrent   1s 6d

5   Sedlands; Robert Foster, gent, son and heir of Thomas Foster,
     esquire, holds freely a tenement called Sedlands, being three
     parcels of land (10 acres; N: road from Iden Cross to
     Boonshill; W: lands late Thomas Godfrey, esquire, called
     Golds [14], held of the manor; in part S: lands of Richard
     Briant in Playden [22], held of the manor; in part E: lands of
     [blank] George, and to his tenement called Hogletts otherwise
     Howletts [6]); fealty, suit of court, heriot and relief, quitrent   1s 10d

6   Hogletts otherwise Howletts; Robert Foster, gent, son and
         heir of Thomas Foster, esquire, holds freely a tenement called
         Hogletts otherwise Howletts, being two pieces of land (six
         acres; N, E: road from Iden Cross to Boonshill; S: lands of
         Richard Briant [22], held of the manor; W: lands of Robert
         Foster called Sedlands [5]); fealty, suit of court, heriot and
         relief, quitrent   1s 3d

7   Boonshill; Robert Foster, gent, son and heir of Thomas Foster,
         esquire, holds a tenement called Boonshill, being one messuage,
         one barn, orchard, garden and three pieces of land (four acres; S:
         road from Popes Marsh, held of the manor of Ewhurst; W, N, E:
         other lands of Robert Foster held of the manor of Ewhurst);
         fealty, suit of court, heriot and relief, quitrent   1s 8d

8   Marchants otherwise The Wishe; John Eversfeild, esquire, in
         the right of his wife for term of her life holds freely a
         tenement called Marchantes otherwise The Wishe (now lying
         common to his drowned marshlands in the right of his wife
         and to his Thornsdale messuage [9]) containing 1a 2r 10p, on
         which stands an old pigeon house (NE: the drowned lands;
         SE: lands of Mr William Chapman; SW: Thornsdale
         messuage and forestall; NW: the way leading to the
         messuage); the tenement hath been formerly divided and
         fenced with a great ditch at each side which is now swerved
         with slubb; fealty, suit of court, heriot and relief, quitrent   6½d

9   Thornsdale; John Eversfeild, esquire, in the right of his wife
         for term of her life holds a tenement called Thornsdale being
         a messuage and seven pieces of land (31 acres; NE: his lands
         called Marchants otherwise The Wish [8]; SE: lands of
         William Chapman and Lady Lawrence; S: lands of Alan
         Grible, gent; SW, W: lands of the heirs of Henry Robbins
         called Thornsdale, held of the manor of Ewhurst; fealty, suit
         of court, heriot and relief, quitrent   2s 11d

10   Bawnefeilds; Frances Holman, widow, the daughter of Henry
         Robbins, holds a freehold tenement called Bawnefeilds, being
         three pieces of land (13 acres; N: road from Iden Church to
         Thornsdale; E, S, W: her other lands called Thurndale, held of
         the manor of Ewhurst); fealty, suit of court, heriot and relief,   1s 2d
         quitrent

11   Rishett otherwise Rysshett; Alan Grible, gent, holds a freehold
         tenement called The Rishett otherwise Rysshet, being one piece
         of marshland, now drowned with salt water (three acres; W:
         marshlands of the manor of Leigh; E: marshland of

Thomas Godfrey, esquire, part of Verriers Tenement; S: piece
of marshland of Alan Grible called Morisland [12]); fealty, suit
of court, heriot and relief, quitrent   6d

12   Morisland; Alan Grible, gent, holds a freehold tenement called
     Morisland, being one piece of marshland, now drowned with
     salt water (four acres; W: lands of the manor of Leigh; N: other
     lands of Alan Grible called Rishett [11]; E, S: land called
     Verriers, late Thomas Godfrey, esquire); fealty, suit of court,
     heriot and relief, quitrent   1d

13   Cobbs; John Woodall, clerk, holds a freehold tenement called
     Cobbs, being a messuage and a piece of land (four acres;
     N: road from Iden Cross to Boonshill; E: lands late Thomas
     Godfrey, esquire, called Golds [14]; S: lands of the heirs of
     [*blank*] George; W: lands of Robert Foster, gent, called Taylors
     otherwise Staniesland [4]); fealty, suit of court, heriot and
     relief, quitrent   1s 8d

14   Golds; Thomas Chidwick, esquire, holds freely a piece of land
     (sometime two pieces) called Golds (seven acres; W: lands of
     John Woodall, clerk, called Cobbs Tenement [13]; N: road from
     Iden Cross to Boonshill; E: lands of the heirs of Thomas Foster,
     esquire, called Sedlands [5]; S: lands of the heirs of [*blank*]
     George); fealty, suit of court, heriot and relief, quitrent   6s 6d

15   Thomas Chidwick, esquire, holds another tenement, being a
     piece of land (two acres) sometime Penhursts (N, E: lands
     called Verriers, held of the manor of Ewhurst; W: lands of John
     Robins called Hedgpitts, lands of [*blank*] May in the right of his
     wife called Hopes, held of the manor of Ewhurst); S: road from
     Iden Cross to Thornsdale); fealty, suit of court, heriot and
     relief, quitrent   2s 4d

16   The Five Acres; Thomas Chidwick, esquire, holds another
     tenement called The Five Acres, being one piece of land (five
     acres; E: two pieces of land called Buckland and Perrymans
     Field [17]; S, W: lands called Verriers, held of the manor of
     Ewhurst; N: Verriers, lands of John Robins called Hedgpitts,
     held of the manor of Ewhurst); fealty, suit of court, heriot and
     relief, quitrent   2s 4d

17   Buckland; Thomas Chidwick, esquire, holds another freehold
     tenement called Buckland and Perrymans Field, being two
     pieces of land (eight acres; S, E: Verriers, held of the manor of
     Ewhurst; in part N and in another part N: a tenement of John
     Robins called Old Marsh, held of the manor of Ewhurst); fealty,
     suit of court, heriot and relief, quitrent   3s 0½d

18 Malgrove; Thomas Chidwick, esquire, holds another freehold
    tenement, being a piece of land called Malgrove (two acres;
    N: land of John Woodall, clerk, late Samuel Landesdale, held
    of the manor; E: a lane leading from Iden parsonage house to
    Rye; W: in part to a way leading to a tenement of Robert
    Foster, esquire, called Young Wood (held of the manor of
    Ewhurst), and to lands called Reity [19]); fealty, suit of court,
    heriot and relief, quitrent   1s 7d

19 Reity; Thomas Chidwick, esquire, holds another freehold
    tenement called Reity, being one piece of land (three acres; in
    part E: lands called Malgrove [18]; E, S, N: lands of Robert
    Foster, gent, called Young Wood); fealty, suit of court, heriot
    and relief, quitrent   6d

20 Sleechings, Barnefeild and Smiths; Dame Grissell Laurence
    holds a freehold tenement, being a messuage and several
    pieces of land called Sleechings, Barnefeild and Smiths, of
    which the messuage and three pieces of land (ten acres;
    SE, E: road from Iden Cross to Kent Bridge; N: lands of Sir
    John Fagg; NW: lands late Thomas Godfrey, esquire;
    SW: lands late Thomas Godfrey, and the lands of Mr
    Chapman and of Alan Grible); two pieces of land (10 acres;
    E: road from Iden Cross to Kent Bridge; S, W: lands of Sir
    John Fagg; N: lands of Alan Grible); one piece of land lying
    over against the last two pieces divided by the said road (five
    acres; W: the road; S: the demesnes of Mote; E: lands called
    Verriers and Hedgepitts held of the manor of Ewhurst;
    N: Wittersham Level); one piece of land lying over against
    the messuage divided with a highway (NW: the highway;
    NE, SE: land of the heirs of Henry Robins; S: lands of
    Thomas Ladd); fealty, suit of court, heriot and relief, quitrent   3s 0d

21 Cotenham; Dame Grissell Laurence holds freely two pieces of
    marshland (now covered with salt water) called Cotenham
    (seven acres; E: the lands of Alan Grible; SP: lands of Thomas
    Chidwicke, esquire; W: in part to lands of Thomas Ladd, late
    John Stevens, and to lands called Lye Marshes, held of the
    manor of Ewhurst; N: other lands of Dame Grissell Laurence);
    fealty, suit of court, heriot and relief, quitrent   7s 0d

    Playden

22 Ashfeilds; Richard Briant, gent, holds freely three pieces of
    land called Ashfeilds belonging to his farm called The Aishe
    (one piece lies E: road from Iden Church to Aishe House; S,

W: lands of the heirs of [*blank*] George; N: lands of Robert
Foster called Sedlands and Hogletts [5-6]; the two other
pieces lie E: road from Aishe House to Hawkins Green; S, W:
lands of [*blank*]; N: lands of the heirs of [*blank*] George);
fealty, suit of court, heriot and relief, quitrent   6s 8d

Peasmarsh

23   Eldertons; Edward Sheppard, esquire, holds a freehold
     tenement called Eldertons, being two pieces of land (10 acres;
     N: road from Flackley Ash to Rye; in part E and S and in part
     W: lands of Sir John Tufton, knight and baronet, and to other
     lands of Edward Shepard; in part W: lands of Thomas
     Hummerson); fealty, suit of court, heriot and relief, quitrent   3s 4d

24   Hoggetts otherwise Huggetts; Edward Sheppard, esquire,
     holds a freehold tenement called Hoggetts otherwise
     Huggetts, being two pieces of land (E: road from Flackley
     Ash to Rye; S, W: lands of Richard Shephard called Fleckleys
     [38]; N: Edward Shephard's tenement called Frayes [25]);
     fealty, suit of court, heriot and relief, quitrent   6d

25   Frayes; Edward Sheppard, esquire, holds a freehold tenement
     called Frayes, being two pieces of land (three acres;
     S: Huggetts Tenement [24]; W, N: lands of Richard Shephard
     called Fleckleys [38]; E: road from Flackley Ash to Rye);
     fealty, suit of court, heriot and relief, quitrent   1s 8d

26   Broadlands; Edward Sheppard, esquire, holds a freehold
     tenement called Broadlands, being three pieces of land (six
     acres; E: a lane leading from the premises near the house of
     John Walters called Young Lands, and so to Peasmarsh
     church; S: lands of the heirs of [*blank*] Birchett called
     Bremps; W: woodland of Sir Charles Shelley, baronet; N:
     other lands of Edward Shephard, being copyhold of the Earl
     of Thanet's manor of Vield and Burcester); fealty, suit of
     court, heriot and relief, quitrent   1s 10d

27   Creeches; Edward Sheppard, esquire, holds a freehold
     tenement called Creeches, being a messuage and two pieces
     of land (10 acres; NE: road from Flackley Ash to Peasmarsh
     church; NE, S, W: lands of Edward Shephard); fealty, suit of
     court, heriot and relief, quitrent   5s 0d

28   Claytons; Edward Sheppard, esquire, holds a freehold
     tenement called Claytons and Lynden, of which the lands
     called Claytons, and 15 pieces called Claytons Land, The

Cock and Hill Lands (80 acres; NW: road from Peasmarsh
church to Rye; NE: a lane leading out of that road to Marley
House; SE: the lands of Marley Farm; S, SW: lands of
Tillingham Farm; SW: lands of the heir of Richard Young
called Grove Farm; W: other lands of Edward Shephard);
Lynden is one piece of land (nine acres; S: road from
Peasmarsh church to Rye; NE: the demesne lands of the
manor of Leigh; NW, SW: other lands of Edward Shephard);
fealty, suit of court, heriot and relief, quitrent   13s 4d

29   Knowles; Richard Wood holds a freehold tenement called
     Knowles, late the lands of Alexander Sampson, being six
     pieces of land (25 acres; N: road at Peasmarsh Green; E: lane
     from Peasmarsh Green to the house of the heirs of Richard
     Younge, and the house of Thomas Grible; S: lands belonging
     to Dewhouse; W: other lands of Richard Wood called
     Knowllis, Ricknolds and Horsefeild [30]); fealty, suit of
     court, heriot and relief, quitrent   9s 4d

30   Ricknolds; Richard Wood holds a freehold tenement called
     Ricknolds and Horsefeild, late the lands of Alexander
     Sampson, being four pieces of land (18 acres; NW: Peasmarsh
     Green; E: the tenement called Knowle [29]; SE: lands
     belonging to Dewe House; SW: the lane from Dewe House to
     Peasmarsh Green); fealty, suit of court, heriot and relief,
     quitrent   3s 4d

31   Weblands; Richard Wood holds a freehold tenement called
     Weblands, late the lands of Alexander Sampson, being two
     pieces of land (five acres; E, S; lane from Peasmarsh Green to
     Pelsham house; W, N: in part to lands of Richard Wood
     called Dew Grove [32], and to lands of the heirs of [*blank*]
     Birchett); fealty, suit of court, heriot and relief, quitrent   1s 4d

32   Dew Grove; Richard Wood holds a freehold tenement called
     Dewe Grove, late the lands of Alexander Sampson, being one
     piece of land (1a 3r 28p; S: the lane to Pelsham house;
     W: Pelsham lands; N: lands of [the heirs of] [*blank*] Birchett; E:
     Wiblands [31]); fealty, suit of court, heriot and relief, quitrent   6d

33   Broadstreet; Thomas Hummersom, gent, holds a freehold
     tenement called Broadstreete, being a messuage and three
     pieces of land (seven acres; E: road from Flackley Ash to
     Peasmarsh church; S: lane from the messuage to the Earl of
     Thanet's lands; NW, and N: in part to the lands of John
     Steevens and to the lands of Richard Shephard); fealty, suit of
     court, heriot and relief, quitrent   3d

34 Broomes; Thomas Hummersom, gent, holds a freehold
tenement called Broomes, being a messuage and three pieces
of land (six acres; W: road from Flackley Ash to Peasmarsh
church; S: lane from the messuage to The Cockhouse;
E, N: lands of Richard Shephard); fealty, suit of court, heriot
and relief, quitrent   1s 2d

35 Winders; Richard Shephard holds a freehold tenement called
Winders, being a messuage and two pieces of land (11 acres;
N: the road at Flackley Ash; E: a lane from Flackley Ash to
Peasmarsh church; S: land of Thomas Hummersome, gent,
called Broadstreete [33], and to lands of Richard Shephard
called Winders Grove [36] and Pheasant Field [37]; W: piece
of land of Richard Shephard, part of his tenement called
Fleckleys [38]); fealty, suit of court, heriot and relief, quitrent   2s 4d

36 Winders; Richard Shephard holds a freehold tenement called
Winders Grove, formerly two pieces of land but now only one
piece (four acres; N: Winders Tenement [35]; W: Pheasant
Field [37]; S: lands of John Steevens; E: part of the tenement
of Broadstreete [33]); fealty, suit of court, heriot and relief,
quitrent   2d

37 Pheasant Field; Richard Shephard holds a freehold tenement
called Pheasant Field, being one piece of land (two acres;
E: Winders Grove [36]; S: lands of John Steevens; W: lands of
Mr Guilford; N: a field of Richard Shephard, part of Fleckley
Tenement [38]); fealty, suit of court, heriot and relief, quitrent   2d

38 Fleckleys; Richard Shephard holds a freehold tenement called
Fleckleys, being six pieces of land (21 acres), of which five
pieces lie together (W: lane from Flackley Ash to Peasmarsh
church; S: Mr [Thomas] Hummersom's tenement called
Broomes [34]; SE: a lane from Broomes messuage to The
Cockhouse; E: Edward Shephard, esquire's Huggetts Tenement
[24], and Frayes [25]; N: road from Flackley Ash to Rye); the
other piece (N: road from Flackley Ash to Rye; E: tenement
called Winders [35]; S: Pheasant Field [37]; W: land of Mr
Guilford); fealty, suit of court, heriot and relief, quitrent   2s 4d

39 Fleckley; Thomas Mocok holds a freehold messuage or
tenement and 20 pieces of land called Fleckley (97 acres;
S: the road at Flackley Ash; W: the road from Flackley Ash to
Blackwall; N: in part to the lands of Robert Hewett, esquire,
and to the demesne lands of the manor of Mote; E: Chauntry
Lands; SE: land of Robert Hewett [40], held of the manor);
fealty, suit of court, heriot and relief, quitrent   16s 6d

40   Robert Hewet, esquire, holds a freehold tenement, being a
        messuage and 15 pieces of land (40 acres; SW; the road at
        Flackley Stream; SE, NE: demesne lands of the manor of
        Mote; NW: Fleckley Tenement [39]); fealty, suit of court,
        heriot and relief, quitrent   5s 6d

41   Sherishoth; John Robbins holds a freehold tenement called
        Sherishoth, being a messuage and six pieces of land (16 acres;
        S: road from Flackley Ash to Rye; E: lands of John Tufton,
        knight and baronet; N: Redford Lane, leading between the
        premises and Mote demesnes from Cophouse to Iden church);
        fealty, suit of court, heriot and relief, quitrent   2s 6d

        Beckley

42   Pipers Land; Sir Charles Shelley, baronet, holds a tenement
        called Pipers Land, being five pieces of land (26 acres; SW, S
        and in part SE: lands of the heirs of John Holman, clerk, late
        Burwash, held of the manor of Ewhurst; SE: lands of Sir
        Charles Shelley called Maidenland; NE: Sir Charles Shelley's
        woods called Rigex Wood otherwise Rogers Wood; in part
        NW: other lands of Sir Charles Shelley; NW, SW: lands of
        the heirs of John Holman, formerly Richard Browning, held
        of the manor of Ewhurst; SE, SW: one other piece of land of
        the heirs of John Holman, formerly Richard Browning; NW:
        road from Beckley church to Knelle); fealty, suit of court,
        heriot and relief, quitrent   4s 0d

43   Hothes; Peter Gott, esquire, holds a freehold tenement called
        The Hothes, being five pieces of land (30 acres; W: in part to
        Peter Gott's close belonging to the messuage called
        Gatehouse, and to the road from Gatehouse to Hayes, and so
        to Peasmarsh; S: Peter Gott's woodlands called [blank]; E: in
        part to Peter Gott's woodlands called Brickherst Wood and
        Fox Twist Wood, and to the land of the heirs of Richard
        White, clerk; N: the way from Gatehouse to Rye); fealty, suit
        of court, heriot and relief, quitrent   3s 2d

44   Horsepen; the heirs of Thomas Davy hold a freehold tenement
        called Horsepen, being a messuage and one piece of land (1a
        3r 35p; S: road from Beckley church to Four Oaks; E: a lane
        leading out of that road to Woodgates Green; W, N: lands of   5d
        the same heirs, held of the manor of Peasmarsh); fealty, suit   and
        of court, heriot and relief, quitrent   a fat hen

45   Riddalls; Jeremiah Robinson holds a freehold tenement called
        Riddalls, being one piece of land near Four Oaks

(3r 24p; NW: road from Four Oaks to Hobbes; SW, S, SE: lands of the heirs of Robert Hewet, esquire); fealty, suit of court, heriot and relief, quitrent   4d

Northiam

46   Tufton; Nicholas [Tufton] Earl of Thanet holds freely a messuage called Tufton Place and 14 pieces of arable, pasture and woodland (100 acres; S: road from Mable Cross otherwise Mable Crouch to Perrymans Cross; W: a lane from Mable Cross, near Tufton Place, to Ewhurst; NW: a gill or rivulet dividing the parishes of Ewhurst and Northiam; NE: a rivulet or watercourse called The Mill River; N, E: lands of Thomas Collins, esquire, late William Brigden; E: lands of the Earl of Thanet called Okeworth [50]); fealty, suit of court, heriot and relief, quitrent   10s 0d

47   Weblands; Nicholas [Tufton] Earl of Thanet holds freely three pieces of land called Weblands, whereon anciently there stood a messuage (20 acres; N: road from Perrymans Cross to Mable Crouch; W: road from Mable Crouch to Staple Cross; S: other lands of the Earl of Thanet); fealty, suit of court, heriot and relief, quitrent   2s 0d

48   Loles; Nicholas [Tufton] Earl of Thanet holds a piece of land sometime called Loles, now The Upper Brambly Field (seven acres; N, W: road from Mable Crouch to Staple Cross in part, and to Weblands [47]; S, E: other lands of the Earl of Thanet); fealty, suit of court, heriot and relief, quitrent   1½d

49   Twelve Acres; Nicholas [Tufton] Earl of Thanet holds freely a piece of land formerly called The Twelve Acres, now The Lower Brambly Field (12 acres; N: Loles [48]; W: road from Mable Crouch to Staple Cross; S, E: other lands of the Earl of Thanet); fealty, suit of court, heriot and relief, quitrent   1s 6d

50   Okeworth; Nicholas [Tufton] Earl of Thanet holds freely two messuages and eight pieces of land called Okeworth, now occupied by Robert Turner and [*blank*] Grinsted (20 acres; W: Tufton lands [46]; N, E: lands of Thomas Collins, esquire; S: road from Perrymans Cross to Mable Crouch), and three (formerly two) other pieces of land, sometime the lands of John Jervis, (eight acres; N: road from Perrymans Cross to Mable Crouch; E: lands of William Bishopp gent [75], held of this manor; S: copyhold lands of Cyril [*recte* Cecil] Tufton, esquire; W: lands of Thomas Frewen, clerk, called Ockford,

held of the manor of Ewhurst); fealty, suit of court, heriot and
relief, quitrent   4s 0d

51   Fower Acres; Nicholas [Tufton] Earl of Thanet holds freely
two pieces of land called The Fower Acres, formerly one
parcel, occupied by [*blank*] Grinsted (four acres; N: road from
Perrymans Cross to Mable Crouch; E, S: lands of Thomas
Frewen, clerk, called Ockford, held of the manor of Ewhurst;
W: other lands of the Earl of Thanet, and to his lands called
Weblands [47]); fealty, suit of court, heriot and relief, quitrent   4d

52   Brickwall; Stephen Frewen, esquire, alderman of London,
holds freely a messuage now called Brickwall and seven
pieces of land called Hayreeds, Holereeds and Collins Crofts
(30 acres; NE: road from Northiam church to Beckley;
E: lands of Stephen Frewen held of this manor; S: the way
from Beckley windmill to Perrymans Oak); fealty, suit of
court, heriot and relief, quitrent   1s 10d

53   Preshers; Stephen Frewen, esquire, alderman of London,
holds a piece of land called Preshers (four acres; E: road from
Northiam church to Perrymans Cross; S, W: glebelands of the
rectory of Northiam; N: lands of John Iggulsden in part, and
to the lands of the heirs of John Iden); fealty, suit of court,
heriot and relief, quitrent   2½d

54   Croufords otherwise Croffords; Stephen Frewen, esquire,
alderman of London, holds eight acres of land called
Croufords otherwise Croffords (W: other land of Stephen
Frewen, held of this manor; S: the way from Beckley
windmill to Perrymans Oak; E: lands of Stephen Frewen
called The Fower Acres [55]; N: road from Northiam church
to Beckley); fealty, suit of court, heriot and relief, quitrent   8d

55   Fower Acres; Stephen Frewen, esquire, alderman of London,
holds a piece of land called The Fower Acres (five acres;
W: Croufords [54]; E: other lands of Stephen Frewen; N: road
from Beckley to Northiam church); fealty, suit of court, heriot
and relief, quitrent   5d

56   Pollards; Stephen Frewen, esquire, alderman of London, holds
three pieces of land called Pollards (eight acres; E: road from
Northiam church to Perrymans Cross; S: a whapple lane;
W: lands of William Bishopp called Blatches; N: other lands of
Stephen Frewen); fealty, suit of court, heriot and relief, quitrent   2s 0d

57   Eleaven Acres; Stephen Frewen, esquire, alderman of
London, holds three pieces of land called The Eleven Acres at

Perrymans Cross (11 acres; E: other lands of Stephen Frewen held of this manor; S: road from Beckley windmill to Perrymans Cross; W: road from Perrymans Cross to Northiam church; N: lands of Stephen Frewen held of this manor); fealty, suit of court, heriot and relief, quitrent 1s 7d

58 Holmans Tenement; Stephen Frewen, esquire, alderman of London, holds two pieces of land (six acres) now called Holmans Tenement; one piece of land, 'on which there was sometime standing a toft' (W: road from Perrymans Cross to Northiam church; N, E, S: other lands of Stephen Frewen, held of this manor); the other piece (W, S: road from Northiam church to Beckley, in part; S, E: lands of George Bishopp, gent, in part; N: other lands of Stephen Frewen); fealty, suit of court, heriot and relief, quitrent 5s 6d

59 Crouchlands; Thomas Collins, esquire, holds freely the moiety of four pieces of land called Crouchlands, which on the death of Robert Edwards[211] descended to Elizabeth, one of his daughters (22 acres; W: road leading from Northiam church, sometime called Lymestreete, now called The Furnace Lane; S, W and in part E: other lands of Thomas Collins; E: lands of John Iggulsden, held of the manor of Ewhurst, in part, NE: lands of Thomas Frewen, clerk, called Millers and Fardings [62]); fealty, suit of court, heriot and relief, quitrent 3s 6d

60 Crouchlands; Thomas Collins, esquire, holds another moiety of Crouchlands, which on the death of Robert Edwards descended to Mary, another of his daughters, who with her husband Thomas Brigden made partition of the premises with her sister Elizabeth and her husband Nicholas Tooke, gent;[212] fealty, suit of court, heriot and relief, quitrent 3s 6d

61 Adams Croft; Thomas Collins, esquire, holds a piece of land called Adams Croft (two acres; W: Lymestreete otherwise The Furnace Lane, leading from Northiam church to Ewhurst church; S, N, E: Crouchlands [59-60]; fealty, suit of court, heriot and relief, quitrent 3d

62 Millers; Thomas Frewen, clerk, holds freely a messuage, garden, orchard and four pieces of land called Millers and Fardings (12 acres), of which the messuage, garden and orchard (two acres; NW: a way or lane leading to Crouchlands; SW: lands of John Iggulsden called Copper

---

[211] His death was presented at a court on 20 October 1575: NOR 15/2 page 45.
[212] The partition was made and the quitrent apportioned at a court held on 26 August 1589: NOR 15/2 page 51.

Lands, held of the manor of Ewhurst; SW: tenement late Mr Samuel Frewen, sometime Abel Glidd; NE: road from Northiam church to Clench Green); and the four pieces (SE: the lane leading to Crouchlands; SW: Crouchlands [59-60]; NW: road called Lymestreete, leading from Clench Green to Ewhurst church; in part NE and SE: lands of Theophilus Tilden called Clench [65]; in part NE: road called Lymestreete); fealty, suit of court, heriot and relief, quitrent   3s 0d

63   Thomas Frewen, clerk, holds freely a messuage, barn, garden and orchard (two acres; SW, S: Northiam churchyard and the lands of George Bishop, gent; E, NE: lands of Thomas Piers, baronet, called Halland Field, held of the manor of Ewhurst; NW: other lands of Thomas Frewen called The Vine, held of the manor of Ewhurst); fealty, suit of court, heriot and relief, quitrent   1d

64   Cropwood Acre; Thomas Frewen, clerk, holds freely a piece of land called Cropwood Acre (one acre; S, W: other lands of Thomas Frewen called Ockmans, held of the manor of Ewhurst; N, E: road from Northiam church to Quickbourne Cross); fealty, suit of court, heriot and relief, quitrent   6d

65   Clench; Theophilus Tilden, clerk, holds freely a messuage and six pieces of land called Clench (14 acres); the messuage and two pieces (SE, SW: lands of Thomas Frewen called Millers and Fardings [62]; NWR: road from Clench Green to Ewhurst church; NE: the highway or waste land called Clench Green); the other four pieces (SE: road from Clench Green to Ewhurst church; SW: lands of John Holman, clerk, called Jackharris Crofts, held of the manor of Ewhurst; NW: copyhold lands of John Sharpe, gent, late Nicholas White, gent, NE: lands of John Holman, clerk, late John Harrison); fealty, suit of court, heriot and relief, quitrent   2s 0d

66   Quickbourne; John Sharpe, gent, holds freely a messuage and ten pieces of land called Quickbourne (33 acres); the messuage and two pieces (E: land of John Sharpe called Bakers otherwise Barhams [67]; SW: road called Whitebread Lane, leading from Weekebridge to Quickbourne Cross; NW: Barham Lane, leading from Quickbourne Cross to Barham house); eight pieces (NE: Whitebread Lane; SE: other lands of John Sharpe, and lands of Thomas Piers, baronet; SW: lands called The Churchlands of Northiam; SE: road from Northiam church to Quickbourne Cross); fealty, suit of court, heriot and relief, quitrent   4s 0d

67   Bakers otherwise Barhams; John Sharpe, gent, holds freely
     two pieces of land called Bakers otherwise Barhams (five
     acres; NE: lands of Thomas Piers, baronet, called High
     Barhams [68]; S: road called Whitebread Lane, leading from
     Weekebridge to Quickbourne Cross; SW: other lands of John
     Sharpe called Quickbourne, namely the messuage and
     adjoining lands; N: Barham Lane); fealty, suit of court, heriot
     and relief, quitrent   6d

68   High Barhams; Sir Thomas Piers, baronet, holds freely four
     pieces of land called High Barhams (25 acres; S: road from
     Weekebridge to Quickbourne Cross; E: demesne lands of the
     manor of Knelle; N: Barham Tenement [69]; NW a lane
     called Barham Lane; SW: lands of John Sharpe, gent, held of
     this manor); fealty, suit of court, heriot and relief, quitrent   5s 0d

69   Barham; William Markwicke, gent, holds freely a messuage
     and four pieces of land called Barham (18 acres; S, SW: lands
     of Thomas Piers, baronet, called High Barhams [68]; E: The
     Six Acres [70]; N: lands of Thomas Piers, baronet, called
     Wolvereedes; NW: other lands of William Markwicke);
     fealty, suit of court, heriot and relief, quitrent   4s 6d

70   Six Acres; William Markwicke, gent, holds freely a piece of
     land (formerly two pieces) called The Six Acres (eight acres;
     E: the demesne lands of the manor of Knelle; W: High
     Barhams [68]; N: lands of Thomas Piers, baronet, called
     Wolvereedes); fealty, suit of court, heriot and relief, quitrent   1s 0d

71   Dynesland; William Markwicke, gent, holds freely three
     pieces of land called Dynesland (18 acres; SE: a way or lane
     called Barham Lane; SW: road called Whitebread Lane,
     leading from Quickbourne Cross to Newenden; NW: lands of
     Thomas Piers, baronet; NE: Vanns [74]); fealty, suit of court,
     heriot and relief, quitrent   3s 0d

72   Lunces otherwise Lymnes; Thomas Odiarne, gent, holds freely
     a piece of land called Lunces otherwise Lymnes (one acre three
     roods; N, W: Blatches [73]; S, E: the road at Perrymans Cross);
     fealty, suit of court, heriot and relief, quitrent   2½d

73   Blatches; Joseph Hovenden holds freely a messuage and two
     pieces of land called Blatches (six acres; W, S: Lunces [72];
     E: road from Perrymans Cross to Northiam church; N: a lane;
     W: lands now or late John Scivier); fealty, suit of court, heriot
     and relief, quitrent   1s 1d

74   Vanns; Thomas Avan otherwise Vann holds freely three pieces
     of land called Vanns (five acres; in part NE, SW: Dynesland

[71]; in part NW, NE: lands of Thomas Piers, baronet); fealty,
suit of court, heriot and relief, quitrent   2s 0d

75   Freebodyes Brookes; William Byshopp, gent, holds freely
        four pieces of land, late Richard Purchin, before Richard
        Freebody, sometime John a Brooke (12 acres; S: a gill or
        rivulet dividing this from the copyhold lands of Cecil Tufton,
        esquire; N, E: in part to the lands of Thomas Baker, sometime
        Edward Frencham, and in part to the lands of William
        Byshopp, sometime Edward Frencham [76]; W: lands of the
        Earl of Thanet, sometime John Jarvis [50]); fealty, suit of
        court, heriot and relief, quitrent   1s 4d

76   Frenchams Brookes; William Byshopp, gent, holds freely a
        messuage and six pieces of land (16 acres), sometime the land
        of Edward Frencham; the messuage and four pieces (N: road
        from Maple Crouch to Perrymans Cross; W: lands of the Earl
        of Thanet, sometime John Jervis [50]; S: the gill or rivulet;
        E: lands of Thomas Baker, the other part of the lands
        sometime Edward Frencham [77]); one piece of arable and
        one piece of wood (seven acres; E, S: lands of Thomas Baker
        called Brookes otherwise Carrolls, held of the manor of
        Ewhurst; W: the copyhold lands of Cecil Tufton, esquire;
        N: the gill or rivulet); fealty, suit of court, heriot and relief,
        quitrent 1s 4d, the proportionable part of the rent of 2s 6d
        which Edward Frencham sometime paid for a messuage and
        30 acres called Brookes[213]   1s 4d

77   Frenchams Brookes; Thomas Baker holds freely four pieces
        of land (14 acres; S, W, N: lands of William Bishopp, gent,
        sometime John a Brooke [75], and his other land sometime
        Edward Frencham [76]; N, E: road from Maple Crouch to
        Perrymans Cross, and other lands of Thomas Baker); fealty,
        suit of court, heriot and relief, quitrent 1s 2d, the
        proportionable part of the rent of 2s 6d which Edward
        Frencham sometime paid for a messuage and 30 acres called
        Brookes   1s 2d

        Ewhurst

78   Etchings Upland; Nicholas [Tufton] Earl of Thanet, holds
        freely two pieces of land called Etchings Upland (24 acres;
        NW, W, S: lands of John Tufton, esquire; E: the marshlands

---

[213] The disparity between the rents was regulated by acknowledgements of tenure, signed by
William Bishop and Thomas Baker on 28 August 1673, for which see NOR 15/75-76.

of the Earl of Thanet called Etchinge Marshes [79]); fealty,
suit of court, heriot and relief, quitrent

1s 6d

79   Etchings Marshes; Nicholas [Tufton] Earl of Thanet, holds
ten pieces of land called Etching Marshes (46 acres; SW:
Etching Uplands [78]; NW: marshlands of John Tufton,
esquire, called Padgham Marshes; N: the channel of the River
Rother; in part E: a watercourse called The Mill River, and to
a parcel of marshland called Prawls Marsh; S: lands of John
Tufton called Padgham Lands [81]); fealty, suit of court,
heriot and relief, quitrent

2s 0d

80   Scowers Towne otherwise Scowlstowne; Edward Muddle,
gent, holds freely three pieces of arable land and a little piece
of woodland called Scowers Towne otherwise Scowlstowne
(15 acres; W, S: road from Ewhurst church to Northiam;
E: demesne lands of the manor of Ewhurst called The Lords
Field; E, N: lands of John Tufton, esquire, held of the manor
of Ewhurst; NW, SW: other demesne lands of the manor of
Ewhurst); fealty, suit of court, heriot and relief, quitrent

4d

81   Padgham [Uplands *deleted*]; John Tufton, esquire, holds
freely 12 pieces of land called Padgham [Uplands *deleted*]
<Marshes and 19 pieces of arable land called Padgham
Uplands> and The Wallers (140 acres); Padgham Marshes
and two pieces of arable lie together (W: demesne lands of
the manor of Ewhurst; N: the River Rother; E: Etchinge
Marshes and Etchinge Uplands [78-79]; S: lands of John
Tufton called Cauties, lately demesne lands of the manor of
Ewhurst); nine other pieces (NW: lands of the Earl of Thanet;
E: a rivulet or watercourse called The Mill River; S: lands of
the Earl of Thanet; W: the Earl of Thanet's lands called Little
Padgham, held of the manor of Ewhurst); the remaining five
pieces called Wallers (E: road from Ewhurst to Northiam; S: a
gill or rivulet dividing Northiam and Ewhurst parishes; W, N:
lands of Thomas Piers, baronet, called Sempstead, held of the
manor of Bodiam); fealty, suit of court, heriot and relief,
quitrent

2s 0d

Appendix 1

STOCK-DEEDS OF MOTE AND OTHER MANORS, c1280-1645

No. 1   Grant for a rent and services, consideration 40 shillings; c1280[214]

John Moyn to Robert de Wylesham

> all the land with its appurtenances in Wilsham in Ashburnham,
> in buildings, gardens, woods, meadows, waters, ways, feedings,
> pastures and all the other easements belonging to it, which
> Robert's father Robert de Wylesham formerly held of John's late
> father John Moyn in villeinage

with freedom of alienation except to religious houses and Jews; to hold
freely of Robert by an annual rent of 14 shillings (3s 6d at Easter,
Midsummer, Michaelmas and Christmas) for all services, customs and
exactions, saving the foreign service of the king and the count as much
as belongs to the land; and saving four suits of court every year to John's
court at Wilting [in Hollington] at the first court after the same quarter-
days, at reasonable summons; and saving to John heriots, reliefs,
wardships, marriages, and two reasonable aids to make his eldest son a
knight and to marry his eldest daughter; warranty clause

Witnesses: Simon de Sancto Leodegario, Simon de Somery, Henry de
Peneherst, John Pechard, Simon de Chelewesham, Alan Bothel, Ralph
ate Beche, Ellis de Thersseleghe, Alan de Wylesham, John Nyweman,
John de Brikedenne, William de Rode, Reynold de Frankewelle

Endorsed, c1560: keep this deed very closely, for this is a deed that do
show that the lands that is in Ashburnham is held in knight service and
ward and marriage; and let it be your trusty friend that see this deed

[TNA C146/6965]

---

[214] John Moyne son of John Moyne, knight, sold the manor of Wilting to William de Stowe in
1285, except for the reversion of the third share held for life by his mother; in 1291 the younger
John Moyne's widow sued Baldwin de Stowe for her dower (*VCH Sx* 9, 84); John Moyne and
Simon de Sumery were the first two witnesses to a stock-deed of a former villein tenement of the
manor of Pebsham in Bexhill, dated 12 October 1278: HEH BA 43.1304.

No. 2   Grant for a rent and services; c1300[215]

John de Manceus to Hamo de Farham

> a messuage with all its appurtenances in Herstmonceux which
> Hamo formerly held of John in villeinage

with freedom of alienation except to religious houses and Jews; to hold
freely of John by an annual rent of 12 shillings (four shillings
Michaelmas, the Purification and Whitsun) for all services, customs and
temporal demands, saving to John wardships, marriages, reliefs, heriots,
escheats, suit of court every three weeks and saving reasonable aids of a
shilling to make his eldest son a knight and to marry his eldest daughter,
and saving the foreign service belonging to the messuage; warranty
clause

Witnesses: Simon de Sancto Leodegario, Alan Bothel, Herbert atte
Berghe, William de Chelwesham, John Russel, John atte Beche, William
atte Forde, John atte Berghe, John de Batelesford, John *clericus*, John
atte Gumsele, John de Stonacr'

Endorsed, c1500: The stock-deed of Fareham that Loterworth hath part
and Robert Lande part

[ESRO SAS/P459]

No. 3   Grant for a rent in lieu of services, 10 Feb 1337

John de Passele to John Paulyn of Rye and to his heirs in tail

> land (7½ acres) at 'Esswitynham' in Peasmarsh which formerly
> belonged to Passele's villein Robert Gerveys (heading E: the
> land of Leasam [in Rye]; W: the land of Peter de Essewitenham;
> S: the land of John ..dlif of 'Esswitenham'; N: the land of
> Leasam)

to hold of Passele by an annual rent of 1s 3d for all services, customs and
demands, except suit of his court twice a year, and the service of the king
and earl which belongs to such a tenement

W: John de Kechenor, John de Glesham, William Joce, Reynold de
Hope, John de Oxcenebregg', John de Kechenham, John the clerk of Rye

---

[215] Three men named John de Monceux were lords of Herstmonceux between 1296 and 1331, but
the hand in which the charter is written suggests a date at the beginning of that timespan.

Armorial seal showing a lion rampant: PASSEZ LE PAN PASSELE

Endorsed: Ms Doc 2,337.2   E/17

[Harvard Law School Library Charters 178]

No. 4   Grant for a rent and suit of court; 24 Jul 1375

Robert de Passhlegh, knight, to Henry le Hore and his wife Isabel and to their heirs in tail

> two crofts of his land called 'Okwertherslond' in Northiam, of which one piece lies N: the road from Ewhurst to Rye; S: the fee of Roger de Asshbornhame [the manor of Ewhurst]; W: the land of Henry le Hore; E: Robert's own fee; the other croft lies E, N: the land of Peter atte Forde; S: the land of John Molette; W: Robert's own fee

to hold of Robert for a yearly rent of 1s 6d at Easter and Michaelmas, one suit of Robert's court at The Mote after Easter by reasonable summons, for all other services, namely heriots, reliefs, wardships, marriages, gifts, aids and all other earthly demands and customs

Witnesses: Robert de Etchynghame, John Gotele, Richard le Hore, Robert Flecher, William atte Wode; at Northiam

[CKS U455 T124/4]

No. 5   Grant for a rent and services; 17 Apr 1455

John Paysshele, esq, son and heir of John Paysshele, knight, to William Tucton of Northiam

> a tenement called Tufton Place (100 acres) in Northiam, which John Smalefylde formerly held

to hold by a yearly rent of ten shillings at Michaelmas and Easter, paying heriot and relief, and four suits of court yearly to his manor of The Mote (at the courts held after Michaelmas, Christmas, Easter and Midsummer), for all other services and secular demands; power of entry and distraint for non-payment after fifteen days

Witnesses: Thomas Alard, William Tomseth, William Athille, William Goodewyn, Robert Beneth, Henry Holstocke, John Tregooff; at his manor called The Mote

[CKS U455 T121/4]

No. 6   Grant for rent and services; 17 Apr 1455

John Paysshele, esq, son and heir of John Paysshele, knight, to Thomas Herly of Northiam

1   a croft lying at Perrymans Cross in Northiam (E: road from
         Northiam to Brede; S: a road; W, N: land of Maud Tomseth)
2   a croft called 'Lovelyscrofte' in Northiam (E: a lane leading to a
         field called 'Ockeworthe'; S, W: land late John Holman; N:
         road)

to hold by a yearly rent of four pence at Easter and Michaelmas, and two suits of court at the two courts held after those terms, heriot of 4d, relief of 4d for all other services and secular demands; power of entry and distraint for non-payment after fifteen days

Witnesses: William Tucton, William Strode, William Bate, John Holman, John Brednex, Stephen Adam, Richard Broke, William Fysshe, John Tregoff; at his manor of The Mote

Counterseal of a barking dog with the legend *passhle*

[CKS U455 T122/7]

No. 7   Grant for a rent in lieu of services; 26 May 1466

John Scott, knight, lord of the manor of The Mote, to John Langport of Sundridge in Kent

         a tenement and 12 acres of land called 'Okkeworth' in Northiam
         (W: the road from Rye to Robertsbridge; NW: the land of
         William Toketon; E: land formerly Thomas Bernette)

paying every year to Sir John Scott 4s 0d at the four terms of the year for homage, wardships, marriages, heriots, reliefs, suits of court and all other secular demands; power of entry and distraint for non-payment after eight days; power of re-entry for non-payment after a quarter of a year

Witnesses: William atte Hille the elder, William Godwyn, William atte Hille the younger, John Broke, W Toughton the younger; at Northiam

Clerk's name in turn-up: Fermory[216]

[CKS U455 T119/26]

No.8   Grant for a rent and services; 5 Apr 1479

John Scott, knight, lord of the manor of Mote, to Thomas John

> his lands and tenements called 'Crouchelond' (12 acres) in Northiam, lying together with the exception of one croft; (certain parcels lie N: the road; E: lands of the heirs of John Holstok called 'Millersfeld'; S: land of William Hilles called 'Goselond'; W: lands of Stephen Hyham; the croft, which contains one acre and one rod, lies S: the same road; W, N: lands of Stephen Hyham; E: lands of William Hilles called 'Jakkescroft')

paying every year to Sir John Scott 7s 0d at Michaelmas and the Annunciation by equal portions, doing suit at his court at Mote whenever it happens to be held, paying heriot according to the custom of the manor; power of entry and distraint for non-payment after the rent-day; power of re-entry for non-payment after a year

Witnesses: John Bokelond, Lawrence Brice, Richard Goodwyn, Thomas Fysshe, William Towghton; at The Mote

[ESRO ACC 7006/16]

No. 9   Grant for a rent in lieu of services; 4 Apr 1487

William Scott, esq, lord of the manor of Mote, to William atte Hyll of Northiam

> a parcel of land and wood called 'The Vellex' (3 acres) in Northiam (W: lands of John Frencham; S: road from Perrymans Cross to Ewhurst church; E: lands of William Toky; N: lands of William atte Hyll)

---

[216] Probably the Thomas Fermory admitted to the Scriveners' Company on 17 June 1434.

to hold of William Scott by a yearly rent of a penny at Michaelmas for all services, customs, heriots, reliefs, suits of court and other demands; power of entry and distraint for non-payment after the rent-day

Witnesses: William Tukton, John Bate, Thomas Frencham; at Northiam

[ESRO ACC 7006/17]

No. 10 Counterpart grant of reduced quitrent for £9; 24 Jan 1533

John Gage, knight, lord of the manor of Hosiers in Firle, to John Bolney of Bolney, esq

> 154 acres of land in Firle,[217] formerly held by John Bolney of John Gage's manor of Hosiers by a yearly quitrent of 11s 0d payable at the feast-days used in the manor, three-weekly suit of court 'and by certain other services'

to be held henceforth by fealty and a yearly quitrent of a penny for all services, exactions and demands; quitclaim by John Gage to John Bolney of 10s 11d of the former quitrent

[ESRO SAS/G 4/32]

No. 11 Grant for a rent and services; 27 Nov 1533

Edward Braye, kt, and his feoffees Richard Sherley, kt, Richard Andrewes, esq, Thomas Sherley, esq, and Edward Elderton, esq, to John Thetchar of Selmeston and his heirs in tail

1   'The Oldeland' (11 acres) (W: alongside a lane called 'Hony Lane')
2   a piece of land (6 acres) formerly divided and separated from the common field of Sherrington (E: alongside JT's land called 'South Horam')
3   'The Krinkk' (1½ acres) (W: alongside the common field of Sherrington)

in which (with other manors, lands and tenements) RS, RA, TS and EE were enfeoffed by EB, Richard Belyngham and Richard Shelley to the use of EB and his wife Lady Beatrice and their heirs male, remainder to EB's right heirs

---

[217] Identified as 'Levetts' by the endorsement.

to hold of the feoffees by an annual rent of 18s 6d and suit of their court of their manor of Sherrington in Selmeston whenever it is held, by reasonable summons, a relief of 18s 6d and a heriot of best beast after every death of a tenant either in fee simple or to uses

Nicholas Mascall and Richard Laci attornies to deliver seisin; given at Sherrington

[ESRO SAS/P461]

No. 12 Grant of a stinted heriot, manor of Broomham [Parkgate] in Catsfield; 16 Apr 1645

Nehemiah Panton of Brightling, gent, and Thomas Collins of Brightling, esq, lords of the manor of Catsfield otherwise Broomham [Parkgate], to William Bisshopp of Sedlescombe, gent

1 three pieces of land (10 acres) in Catsfield (N: William's land called 'Peveland'; S: Catsfield Green; E, W: lands of the heirs of John Christopher, formerly Richard Keate), held as a freehold tenement of the manor by a rent of 2s 1½d, fealty, heriot and suit of court

2 small piece of land called 'Moones' (nine perches long and four perches wide) in Catsfield, held as a freehold tenement of the manor by a rent of 3d, fealty, heriot and suit of court

to be held in future of the manor by William by the existing quitrents but by a heriot certain of 6s 8d for tenement 1 and 1s 0d for tenement 2

Witnesses: Daniel Bassano, Joseph Stace, Jane Bassano, Arnold Edwardes, John Wibare

Endorsed: Stock-deed from Nehemiah Panton and Thomas Collins

[ESRO SAU 267]

Appendix 2

PROSOPOGRAPHY

Beaufitz, Elizabeth at Mote in the accounting-year 1471-72, her name rendered as *Isabel Beves*. Almost certainly Sir John Scott's mother-in-law Elizabeth, widow of William Beaufitz (qv) since 1463. She died in 1488, and made generous bequests to her Scott grandchildren William Scott, Margaret Bedingfield and Elizabeth Poynings.

Beaufitz, William (c1400-1463) of London and Grange, Gillingham in Kent, father-in-law of Sir John Scott. Son of John Beaufitz of Grange and his wife Isabel; MP for Rochester 1425; married Elizabeth, daughter of Thomas Badby of London, fishmonger, and admitted to the Fishmongers' Company, c1430; clerk of the king's cellars by 1440 - after 1458, controller, tunnage and poundage, London, 1442-1447, collector of customs and subsidies, 1447-1452, and of tunnage and poundage, 1451-1457, 1461-1462; active in discounting Exchequer tallies, 1440s; gauger of wines, Bayonne, 1448-1453; deputy to Ralph Butler, Lord Sudeley, chief butler of England (for whom he acted at the Exchequer), by 1458; probably sided with the Yorkist lords in opposition to the Crown; chirographer of the court of Common Pleas, jointly with Henry Unton and Sir John Scott, 1461-1463; dead by May 1463, when administration of his estate was granted by the bishop of London (HOP).

Bedingfield, Margaret (d 1514) daughter of Sir John Scott, second wife of Edmund Bedingfield of Oxburgh Hall, Norfolk (*ODNB, sn* Bedingfield family).

Bookland, John (c1420-1502) a lawyer practising in Battle in the second half of the 15th century. The account for 1472-73 records the purchase of ale and wine for him on the making of a rental and engrossing the accounts: ESRO NOR 15/109; in 1476 he presided at a court, and the tenant of 'Bordons' in Peasmarsh showed the boundaries of the tenement to him at about the same time (NOR 15/13, 118, 121); first witness to a deed granting a tenement at Northiam, 1479 (ACC 7006/16); feoffee, Battle, 1455 (HEH BA 52/1401); owner of house in Battle, 1462 (HEH BA 53/1358); during the 1460s he began to establish an estate at Breadsell in Battle, and recorded the erection of a new barn, hall etc, kitchen and cattle shed between 1465 and 1469 (ESRO RAF 25/16-17); auditor of Richard Fiennes, Lord Dacre, 1464 (AMS 5897/60); steward of the manor of Playden by Rye, 1464 (DAP); feoffee, Heathfield and Hellingly, 1468 (AMS 5872/2); purchases house in Middleborough, Battle, 1470 (HEH BA 53/1402); quitclaims land in Guestling to Battle Abbey, 1474 (HEH BA 53/1353); witness to grant by Sir John Scott, 1479 (ESRO ACC 7006/16); witness to grant to Battle Abbey by Thomas Hoo, 1480 (HEH BA 53/1146); owner of land in Hollington, c1480 (ESRO NOR 15/13); feoffee of 'Rytygh' in Telham, 1483 (LMA ACC 312/228); feoffee of land in Battle, called JB the elder, 1487 (HEH BA 54/903, 1429); grantor of Mispies in Hooe, 1490 (ESRO ASH 4501/134); feoffee of Thomas Pulton granting lands in Kent, 1490 (DYK 566); feoffee 1491 (HEH BA 54/902); called *gentleman* when witness to a Battle deed, 1492 (HEH BA 54/1059); renews rental of the manor of Alciston, 1498/99 (ESRO SAS-G17/37); feoffee of land in Etchingham, 1500 (HEH BA 54/1005); sells messuage in Middleborough, Battle, 1500 (HEH BA 54/1314); abbot and convent of Battle grant land in the borough of Sandlake to their servant JB, 1500 (HEH BA 54/1451); conveyed land at Breadsell, 1501 (ESRO RAF 25/22); grant of land in Kent and Sussex to Vincent Finch and others to use of his will, 1501 (RAF 25/35); JB of Battle's will, 6 August 1501, proved in PCC 3 March 1502 (TNA PROB 11/130).

Cheyney, Sir John   (c1410-1467) lord of the manor of Leigh, which his father William Cheyney (d1441) of Shurland in Sheppey, Kent, had acquired on marriage with Eleanor, daughter of John Salerne, the lord of Leigh who had sat as MP for both Rye and Hastings (HOP). King's serjeant-at-arms by 1445, JP Kent, pardoned for participation in Cade's rebellion; victualler of Calais, and accounted for works at Calais with Gervase Clifton 1453-1457; a Lancastrian. In September 1466 Sir John Scott visited John Cheyney at Leigh, perhaps to discuss the new buildings at Mote; died 20 June 1467 (Wedgwood, *History of Parliament*, 181); in October 1467 the tenants at the Mote manor court made a presentment of his death, which was left unfinished by the steward.

Cheyney, William   (1440-1487) of Shurland in Sheppey, Kent; succeeded his father Sir John Cheyney as lord of Leigh in 1467; in 1477 he sold over 100 acres of marsh in the eastern extremity of Iden to Sir John Scott (TNA C1/405/24). He died 8 May 1487. In 1537 his son Sir Thomas Cheyney (c1482-1558), Lord Warden of the Cinque Ports, exchanged the manor of Leigh with the crown for the former nunnery of Minster in Sheppey (*VCH Sx 9*, 154).

Copledike, John son of John Copledike (c1415-1471), MP for Winchelsea 1450-1451 and for Sandwich, 1461-1462; king's bailiff of Winchelsea from 1456 (Wedgwood, *History of Parliament*, 221-222). He features frequently in other of John Scott's accounts from 1463-66, and may have been in his household as a young man. A commissioner of sewers to enquire into land reclamation in Kent and Sussex, 1477 (*Cal Inq Misc 1422-1485*, 461); of Clement's Inn, 1481, and of Dover (BL MS Harley 5145); probably an attorney or court officer (TNA CP 40/969, m455).

Duke, John (d ?1473) and his two sons, all carpenters, were regularly employed at Mote from the first surviving account for 1464-65 until 1470-71; thereafter the carpenters are rarely referred to by name. He may be identifiable with the John Duke of Rolvenden, whose will of 30 September 1470 and testament of 8 August 1473 were proved at Canterbury on 31 August 1473 (CKS PRC 17/2/195). His first bequest was of 6s 8d to buy and set up a 'new great cross in the place called the rood-loft' of Rolvenden church. John had two adult sons, William and Richard Duke, and a small landed estate in Rolvenden and Benenden. He bequeathed to his son Richard Duke 100 oak-trees of timber called 'howsyngtymber' growing on his brother's land, of which William (to whom his father bequeathed two tan-houses) was to have the bark.

Fiennes, Sir Richard, Lord Dacre in the right of his wife Joan; son of Sir Roger Fiennes, the builder of Herstmonceux Castle; he died in 1483 (*Complete Peerage*).

Finch, Henry (d 1494) Sir John Scott's first cousin: Henry's father William Finch of Netherfield was Isabel Scott's brother. Inherited the manors of Netherfield and Icklesham from his brother, John; lord of the manor of Marley in Peasmarsh. Died in 1494 leaving a widow Alice, two daughters and sons Henry, Philip and Lawrence (*VCH Sx* 9, 107; CKS U455/T108, including a will).

Finch, Vincent — Sir John Scott's first cousin: Vincent Finch's father William Finch of Netherfield was Isabel Scott's brother. Of Battle c1458 (TNA C1/6/137), Gray's Inn in 1466 (HEH BA 5 1938), and Sandhurst in 1468; associated with Sir John Scott as adviser to Lady Ponynges in 1465 (Scott, *Memorials of the Family of Scott*, 116-17); commissioner of array 1472 (*CPR 1467-77*, 351); JP Sussex 1466-1476, and customer of Chichester; in 1472, with Sir John Scott and Robert Worthington, he was granted the office of chirographer of the court of Common Pleas in place of Scott's father-in-law, William Beaufitz (M. Hastings, *The Court of Common Pleas in Fifteenth Century England* (Ithaca, 1947), 281); another Vincent Finch, possibly his son, was of Romney and Sandhurst, and also a lawyer; feoffee of Sir John Scott's children Margaret Bedingfield (qv), 1496, and William Scott, 1504 (Wedgwood, *History of Parliament*, 326); sued as executor of William Harlakenden who had been executor of Robert Horne (TNA C1/135/111).

Gay, Christopher — probably of the Middle Temple in 1479; first son of Thomas Gay of Elmsted, Kent (Harleian Society 74 53); of Elmsted; on 18 January 1486 he appeared at Knole as proctor for Agnes Scott to prove Sir John's will before the prerogative court; collector of tax in Canterbury 1492 (*CFR 1485-1509*, 419); died 1507 (inscription on brass at Elmsted).

German, John — (d c1476) Collector of rents and bailiff of Mote manor, married Alice before 1468.

Grantford, Babylon — (d 1476/7), of Rye and Winchelsea. In the decade from 1441 an esquire of the hall and chamber in the royal household, perhaps as a protégé of Sir Roger Fiennes. In 1444 he married Agnes, the widow of William Finch of Netherfield, and became stepfather to John, Henry and Vincent Finch (qv) and a relative of Sir John Scott, William Finch's nephew (HOP). The target of witchcraft at Icklesham in 1447; active in Rye from 1449, MP Rye, 1459-1463, and the king's bailiff there, 1459-1461 and, jointly with John Grantford, 1466-1474, when John, a yeoman of the crown, succeeded to the office; mayor of Rye 1463-1467, 1475-76; a merchant in Rye, with workshops and warehouses in the market and at the Strand.

Harlakenden, William (d 1481) the executor of Sir John Scott's ally Robert
Horne, who was killed at the battle of Towton in 1461 (TNA
C1/135/111); by his will of 20 April 1481, he requested
burial in the chancel of Woodchurch in Kent, and made very
generous bequests to its fabric and lights, and to the
establishment of masses at Woodchurch for his soul. He left
money for unpaid tithes in Wittersham and Lydd, showing
that his estate extended into those parishes. He appointed his
son Roger the residuary legatee, and left £2 a year for his
grandson Thomas Harlakenden (a future ancient of Gray's
Inn) 'to his exhibition at junior school, and £4 when he goes
over to big school'. William appointed Vincent Finch (qv)
and Robert Wyse as his executors, and Sir John Scott as
overseer. Robert Wyse renounced the executorship, and the
will was proved by Vincent Finch alone on 2 October 1481
(CKS PRC 32/2, f. 533v.).

Lombard, Robert   Mayor of Rye 1476 (*Black and White Books*, 71-72).

Mayne, John   farmer of the demesne of the manor of Mote and rent-
collector between 1464 and 1471, after which date he
frequently supplied livestock to the manor. He owned a
dock, variously referred to as a gut or fleet, from which
stone and other goods were transported to Mote and
Appledore. He was frequently paid to carry building
materials in his carts and wagons, expended money on
behalf of the Scotts and was apparently capable of writing
his own accounts. He served as a tax-collector for the
hundred of Guestling. The John Mayne of Wittersham,
whose will of 19 December 1481 was proved at Canterbury
on 28 February 1482 (CKS PRC 32/2/535), can possibly be
identified with the John Mayne of Wittersham who worked
at Mote for three days in 1464-65.

Netter, John   from the first surviving account in 1464-65 until 1468-69 the
widow of John Netter, and her son John Netter, supplied
stone from their quarry at Cranbrook to the building works at
Mote. In 1467-68 Widow Netter provided lodging for men
working at the quarry, and her son paid Sir John Scott's bill
for the purchase of lead from Thomas Thunder of
Winchelsea. The younger John Netter can probably be
identified with the John Netter of Cranbrook whose will of
20 January was proved at Canterbury on 27 September 1480
(CKS PRC 17/3/325). He had two children under 22 years,
and his mother Alice Netter was still alive. He left lands

called Trenley and Tubslake in Hawkhurst and, appropriately for a quarry-owner whose business damaged the roads, left £3 6s 8d to repair the 'foul ways' between Hartley Cross and Turnden.

Poynings, Sir Edward (1459–1521) of Westenhanger in Kent, son of Sir Robert Poynings (qv); in March 1466 Sir John Scott bought Edward's marriage from his stepfather Sir George Brown of Betchworth, brought him up in his household and married him to his daughter Elizabeth (d1528); appointed overseer of Sir John Scott's will in 1485 (Scott, 'Receipts and expenditure'; *ODNB*, *sn*).

Poynings, Elizabeth (c1460-1528), daughter of Sir John Scott, wife of Sir Edward Poynings (qv); their marriage seems to have broken down by 1487, when she was living at Scots Hall and apparently running the farm; buried at Brabourne in August 1528, brass (*ODNB*, *sn* Sir Edward Poynings).

Poynings, Sir Robert (c1419-1461) of Maidstone, son of Robert, Lord Poynings (1382-1446); MP for Sussex, 1450-1451, Yorkist; killed fighting at the battle of St Albans in 1461 (*ODNB*, *sn* Michael Poynings; Wedgwood, *History of Parliament*, 697). His son Sir Edward Poynings (qv) married Sir John Scott's daughter Elizabeth.

Sackville, Richard (c1460-1524); at Mote in the accounting-year 1471-72. The eldest son of Humphrey Sackville of Buckhurst in Withyham and his wife Katherine Brown, Richard Sackville was born in about 1460 and was therefore a child when at Mote. In about 1480 he married Isabel Digges, one of the daughters of John Digges of Barham in Kent, and a grand-daughter of Sir Gervase Clifton; in 1487 his father put him in possession of his extensive estates. He served as MP for Sussex in 1495 and as sheriff of Sussex and Surrey in 1498 and again in 1517. In 1504 both Sir Edward Poynings and Sir William Scott served with him as feoffees on the purchase of the manor of Milton in Arlington by his brother-in-law James Digges, and at his death Sir William Scott was one of his feoffees (C. J. Phillips, *History of the Sackville Family* (London, 1929) 1, 108-13; Wedgwood, *History of Parliament*, 734).

Scott, Agnes (d 1487) née Beaufitz, daughter of William Beaufitz (qv), wife of Sir John Scott.

Scott, Sir William   (1459-1524) son and heir of Sir John Scott and Agnes
                     Beaufitz, commissioner of array for Sussex and Essex 1484,
                     knighted 1489, justice of the peace 1489-1506, controller of
                     the king's household, sheriff of Kent, marshal of Calais
                     1491, lieutenant of Dover Castle, 1492, steward of Denge
                     Marsh for the abbot of Battle from 1497; of Gray's Inn 1499.
                     Married Sybil, daughter of Sir Thomas Lewknor of Trotton
                     (*ODNB*; *sn* Scott family; TNA C1/1519/71).

Tregoff, John   of Rye, lawyer (c1425-1487), to which he was possibly
                     introduced by Sir John Pashley, whose Cornish estates lay
                     near Tregoff in the parish of St Agnes. Common clerk of
                     Rye by 1446 (CKS U455/T107/1); in 1449 he first attended
                     the Brotherhood of the Cinque Ports as Rye's deputy; his
                     last attendance was in 1483; in 1452 he was appointed by
                     John de Ypres to collect his rents in Rye; in October 1454 he
                     was one of the attorneys appointed to deliver seisin of Mote
                     to John Pashley (*CCR 1454-61*, 44) and in April 1455, at
                     Mote, he wrote a group of charters for Pashley, who
                     described him as his servant when appointing him attorney
                     to deliver seisin (CKS U455/T122-124); between 1455 and
                     1457 he served as bailiff of the rod of the lathe court of
                     Hastings Rape, and also acted as an attorney in the same
                     court; common clerk of Rye, 1461-1474; MP for Rye 1472-
                     1475; churchwarden of Rye 1474; jurat of Rye 1479-1487
                     (Wedgwood, *History of Parliament*, 866; *Black and White
                     Books*, 26-88; ESRO RYE 124/2, 137/14). In 1464-5
                     William Harlakenden consulted him at Rye about evidences;
                     in 1470-71, with John Hale, he took the boundaries of
                     'Pipers Land' at Beckley, in dispute with William Belknapp,
                     lord of the manor of Knelle. His career suggests Yorkist
                     sympathies, and that the break in his service at Rye may
                     have been the result of a Lancastrian resurgence in the town.

Appendix 3

CONCORDANCE OF RENTALS OF 1478 AND 1673

1673	1478	1673	1478	1673	1478
1	71	28	17	55	
2	68	29	23	56	45
3	86	30		57	55
4	84	31	20	58	33
5	72	32	22	59	
6	63	33	26	60	
7		34	15	61	38
8	75	35	9	62	37
9		36	27	63	
10	81	37	7	64	35
11		38	1,12	65	41
12	65	39	1-6	66	
13	67	40	1-6	67	
14	73	41	25	68	52
15	76	42	32	69	
16	77	43	28	70	
17	78-79	44	30	71	
18	82	45	31	72	
19	85	46	47	73	46
20	70	47	48	74	
21	64	48		75	
22	88	49	51	76	54
23	19	50	50	77	
24		51		78	
25		52		79	
26	24	53		80	89
27	16	54		81	91-102

GLOSSARY

The Glossary includes only those English words, the meaning of which is not readily apparent, or which deserve further discussion, and Latin words which have not been translated.

Bierding	Possibly 'bearding' or edging
Bemefellyng	Infill between the beams on the wall, or in a timber building, the wall-plate and the underside of the roof
Bendrope	Binding rope; specifically that use to harness draught animals
Beresesyng	Possibly related to the medieval Latin *bersisa*, meaning barley malt or wort
Beryng	Bearing; recording
Billet	Wood cut and split for fuel
Billet leffe	Billets of brushwood
Blanch farm	Payment or farm to the king in respect of pleas arising from, in this case, the Rape of Hastings
Bokeram	Buckram; fine linen fabric
Boltingtun	Container for sieving out the coarse meal from flour
Botewes	Low boots
Bordlogge	Log from which boards were made
Bord stokys	Board stocks; blocks from which board is cut
Brikemason	Bricklayer
Brodde, broade	Brad nail; thin flat, tapering nail without a pronounced head
Cade	Barrel of fish, often herring, generally containing 720
Charnall	Hinge for door or window
Cofe	Cove; an inner or bed chamber or closet
Cotilbord	Type of wooden board, possibly a dialect word since other occurrences are for Hollingbourne (*AC* 13 (1880), 561) and perhaps for the 'cotbord' purchased for Dover Castle (Salzman, *Building in England*, 243)
Estrichebord	'Eastland' board imported from German or the Baltic
Faggot leffe	Faggots of brushwood
Farshon	Farcy; disease of horses marked by ulcerating swellings, especially on the head and limbs
Flessh axe	Butcher's axe
Foryok	Fore-yoke; element of harness
Fryse	Frieze cloth; coarse woollen cloth
Gillinge	Gillot or mare

Gojon	Gudgeon; the ring on a gate or door which turns on the pintle
Green wax	Lists of forfeitures incurred in the central courts were sent to county sheriffs for collection under the green wax seal of the court of Exchequer
Growt tubbe	Grout tub; tub containing an infusion of malt before or during fermentation
Gutter	Gut; inlet for landing boats, drain for removing water from marshland
Gynne	Gin; winding engine for rope for raising loads
Hedmalt	Meaning not identified
Hulle	Hill; heap, pile
Justesyeld	Payment in respect of property recovered by legal action in the lord's court
Kervys	Curved braces?
Ladefat	Vat for dripping liquids?
Latthis	Laths; strips of wood used in walls to support daub or plaster
Legge	Pole or prop
Marra	*Marra* in classical Latin is a hoe, but in this case it probably is being used for the mill rynd
Mashingvat	Vat containing ground malt and water for preparing the wort for brewing ale or beer
Nebyok	Yoke for attaching a wooden shaft to a cart or wagon
Oste	Kiln, as in 'brikeoste' and 'lymeoste'
Ostecloth	Cloth on which malt or hops are place to dry
Pice	Pick or pickaxe
Pynsons	Pinsons; pincers or forceps
Pipe	Cask for storing liquids or dry goods
Prig	Prignail, sprig; small headless nails
Pykoyse	Pickaxe
Pynnokke	Pinnock, a small bridge over a watercourse; a drain under a road
Regginge, reggeyng	Ridging; the making or covering the ridge of a building
Repe ropys	Ropes to secure reaped crops
Ridding	Clearing land of trees and scrub
Ridging	Plastering over the apex of thatched roofs
Rippier	Carrier of fish to inland markets
Sawstage	Platform on which timber is placed to be sawn
Scaffote lyne	Rope for binding together the timbers of the scaffolding

Scot	Payment by holders of marshland contributing to the maintenance of embankments and ditches
Sedcod	Seedlip; basket for seed used while sowing
Shald	Wooden scoop for winnowing corn
Slubb	Silt, or mud
Stewy	Pond, especially for keeping fish
Stopp	Bucket, see Introduction
Swerve	To block a drainage channel or watercourse with silt or *slubb*
Tabarde	Typically used for a sheet of lead or a stone covering; in this case perhaps referring to coats of arms
Taphose	Strainer placed over a tap-hole to catch solid matter
Tappetrowh	Lead tank fitted with a tap and used for brewing
Taylyng	Tallying; counting up or enumerating
Taynthokys	Tenterhooks; hooks from which anything, but particularly cloth might by hung
Topps	Smaller branches of a tree
Tramelnett	Fishing net designed to hung vertically from floats, often comprising a finer mesh set between two coarser meshes
Traye	Hod for carrying mortar; see Introduction
Trental	Memorial service held thirty days after a death
Trentcharnell'	Hinge
Trent ryde; trentride	Hinge ride
Tugge	Tug; timber wagon
Tyghte	Meaning not identified
Wateryngfattes	Wheeled carts used to water land?
Withdraght	Retiring room
Witthis	Withy; flexible branch, typically of willow, used in building and thatching
Woghlath	Crooked, i.e. second-quality laths
Zeve	Sieve

INDEX OF PERSONS AND PLACES

By Christine Leighton

Place-names have been rendered in their modern form, with the manuscripts' original spelling in brackets. Unidentified places are presented in inverted commas; the forms of such places used by the 1673 rental have been preferred. All places referred to are in Sussex unless otherwise identified by historic county. Surnames are also rendered in their most common modern forms, with those recorded in Richard McKinley, *The surnames of Sussex* (Leopard's Head Press, 1988) and P. H. Reaney, *A dictionary of English surnames* (Routledge, 1976), being preferred. The original spellings to be found in the manuscript are shown in brackets. Although they appear in the text, the surname prefixes a, at, atte and de have been excluded from the index. Names appearing in footnotes are indicated by the page number followed by the letter *n* in italics

L

Lacy (Laci), Richard, attorney, 225/11
Ladd, Thomas, land of, 206/20-21
Lamb, family, lix
'Lambys' [*unidentified*] *see under* Peasmarsh
Lamport (Lampard, Lamper, Lamporte, Lampourt, Lampport),
… (Cheseman), widow of William, 178, 181
Joan, widow, default, 170, 172-76
John, 169, 190/41
default, 168-69
William,
death of, 178, 180-81
default, 176-77
heirs of, 178
tenants of, default, 180-81
will of, 181
Lancaster, house of, xvii-xviii
Lancastrians, attainted, xxviii
Land (Lande), Robert, 220/2
Landesdale *see* Landsdale
Landgate (Land Gate) in Rye,
wall near, xliv
Tower House in, *q.v.*
Landsdale (Landesdale), Samuel, 206/18
Langham, William, prayers for, xxvi
Langley (Langle),
John, goods bought from: livestock, 108, 111
Richard, of Brede, goods bought from:
livestock, 121, 125
Langport (Langporte),
John, of Sundridge, Kent, lxxviii
grant to, 192*n*, 222/7
William, 192*n*
agistment sold to, 90
heirs of, land of, 202/108
land of, 191/42, 191/46
'Late William Heghton' [*unidentified*], 168
Laurence *see* Lawrence
'Lawersham' [*unidentified*], 197/70
Lawless (Lawles), William, of Rolvenden,
land alienated from and to, 177
land purchased from, 178
Lawrence (Laurence),
Lady …, land of, 204/9
Charles Lewis, *later* Charles Lewis Lawrence-
Pix, clerk, cousin of Thomas Smith Pix, lx
widowed mother of, lx
Dame Grissell, 206/20-21
Thomas, feoffee of St Cleres, li*n*
Lawrence-Pix,
Charles Lewis, *formerly* Charles Lewis
Lawrence, bankrupt, lx
Inez Viola (Biccard), minor, wife of Charles
Lewis, lx
Leasam (Levelisham, Levesham) in Rye, lv, 220/3
manor, 199/88
Lee *see* Leigh

'Legatefelde' [*unidentified*] *see under* Northiam
Leigh (Lee, Le Leighe, Liegh, Leighe, Lye, The
Legh, The Leigh) [in Iden], xv, xxx, xliii, 15-16,
227
carriage of goods from: straw, 15, 24; timber, 6,
14
chapel of, xv, xxv, xxv*n*
advowson and patronage of, xvi, xxv
grant of free warren in, xiv
heir of, xv
lord of, 100-101; *see also* Pashley, Sir Edmund
de; Salerne, John
manor, xiv-xv, xvii, li, 70, 107, 174, 186/17,
194/60, 194/62, 204/11, 205/12
demesne land of, 208/28
descent of, xiv, xiv*n*, xv, xv*n*
exchanged for nunnery of Minster Sheppey,
228
lord of, *see* Cheyney, Sir John; Cheyney,
William
purchase of, xiv
manor house,
chaplain at, xv*n*
see also Barons Grange
See also Mote
Leigh (Lee, Legh, Lye),
John, smith, expenses of, 59
William, son of Richard, xv
William, witness, 168
William, otherwise William Cook default, 178
'Lemestrete' [*unidentified*] *see* Furnace Lane *under*
Northiam
Lene *see* Lynn
Lennard, Henry, paid to thresh, 144
Levett (Lyvet), John, land purchased from, 163
Levetts [*unidentified*] *see under* Firle
Lewes, Sussex Archaeological Society's museum in
Barbican House at, lxiv
Lewknor (Lewkenore),
Katherine (Pelham), wife of Sir Thomas, xix
Joan, widow of Sir John, death of, xvii
John, knight, li*n*
payment to, 8
Richard, of Brambletye, knight, uncle of Sir
Thomas, xxiii
Sybil (Scott), daughter of Sir Thomas, of
Trotton, xix, xxiii, li, li*n*, 232
marriage settlement and parentage of, li*n*
Thomas, knight, father-in-law of William Scott,
xix, xxii-xxiii, li
Lillesden, John, pond-maker, 16, 25
paid to clean pond and scour gut, etc., 24
Limeburner (Lymebarner), Thomas, paid to burn
lime, 60
Lincoln, county, Cromwell manors in, xliv
Lincoln Inn Fields, [Midd], lix
'Litelbawnelond' [*unidentified*] *see under* Iden
Lodleghe *see* Ludley

INDEX OF SUBJECTS

By Mark Gardiner and Christopher Whittick

The index lists all references to subjects appearing in the document text. Only matters forming the subjects of substantial discussion in the introduction have been indexed. Subjects appearing in footnotes are indicated by the page number followed by the letter *n* in italics.